COMPLETE RESOURCE BOOK

Searchlights

The all-age resource for
Common Worship
Year C

David Adam

D0493450

kevin
mayhew

First published in 2006 by

KEVIN MAYHEW LTD
Buxhall, Stowmarket, Suffolk, IP14 3BW
E-mail: info@kevinmayhewltd.com
Web: www.kevinmayhew.com

9 8 7 6 5 4 3 2 1

ISBN-10: 1 84417 655 X
ISBN-13: 978 1 88417 655 7
Catalogue No 1500921

Cover design by Angela Selfe
Edited and typeset by Katherine Laidler

Printed in Great Britain

Contents

Introduction

Searchlights is as much about God's search for us as our search for God. God seeks to meet us through his creation, through each other, through our experiences, as well as through Scripture and tradition. *Searchlights* seeks to share in the exciting discovery that God actually looks for us and wants contact with us. God, like the shepherd in the parable, seeks after that which is lost until he finds it (Luke 15:3-7). It is wonderful to discover that if we turn towards God – what the Bible calls repentance – we find he runs almost with an indecent haste to meet us in love and forgiveness (see Luke 15:11-32). In using *Searchlights* we must let this seeking God find us and give himself to us.

Searchlights is also about our probing the darkness and uncertainty of our lives to discover the light and the sureness of God. We are to seek God through the regular reading of the Scriptures, through worship in church, through meeting together and through our day-to-day experiences of life. We may be mature in years and yet a child in our faith. Sometimes a new awareness will come as fresh to us as it would to an infant. Sometimes the lesson for the children may speak stronger than thoughts set out for the adults. If so, let us use that and let it speak to us. The light we search for is the Light of God.

Each Sunday is based on Common Worship and the readings set for the day. Year A will mainly use St Matthew's Gospel, Year B will use St Mark, and Year C will use St Luke. St John's Gospel is used throughout the three years to enrich the season or the passages being used. I have focused mainly on the Gospel readings, trying to draw out various aspects to meet the needs of different stages of life. My overall aim is to show that God seeks each of us and desires to speak to us and through us. The difficult task for all who lead worship is to keep a freshness and a liveliness that can be so easily lost; along with this is a need for the Gospel to relate to our present situation. Remember, God is never boring – by his very nature God cannot be boring; we should not present or preach dullness in his name! Though my overall aim is to come before God and to bring others into the awareness of his presence and love, I have tried to keep these other aims within my sights.

Different age groups need a different approach and things that relate to their experience and ability. Yet I have, as far as possible, kept all groups within the setting of the lectionary readings and season. There are separate lessons for children and young people of each age group to help them grow in the faith. The age-related teaching and worship aim to bring the three groups gradually into the fuller worship of the whole church. On major festivals it is good that the whole church worships together and shares with each other. The aim is not just to give children or adults facts about what we believe but rather to introduce them to the living and loving Lord.

Let all the material be seen as flexible. If you are inspired by a children's lesson or the thought for the week, use that. Let the heart be touched by God; use all your senses in proclaiming his presence and his power.

Draw near to God, and he will draw near to you.
James 4:8

David Adam

How to use this book

What you are to use on the Sunday should be prayed over and pondered from the Monday to the Saturday. Use the set readings for your Bible study and meditation time throughout the week leading to the Sunday. All who are called to teach, preach or lead study groups need to know that their aim is to introduce people to the God whom they know and not to provide a Sunday lecture or lesson. We need to take time to discern what God wants us to say and how we are to do it. Pray, prepare, ponder the words before you seek to present them to others.

Each week is set out as follows:

Aim

It is important to make sure that you focus on what is to be taught. Above all, be sure that your focus is on the Presence and love. You may like to print the aim of the week in any handout or magazine that your church has. If you carry the aim around with you during the week, it often draws other events into focus which you can then relate to others.

Preparation

This is over and above your personal preparation and relates to what the aim is seeking to convey. It also involves seeing that you have the necessary material before the Sunday arrives.

Opening activity

This is an opportunity to show that worship is not just within formal settings and services. It also seeks to attract attention to the issues of the week. The more people who are involved in the activities, the better. Sometimes, if the whole church cannot do the activity, it can be transferred to one of the groups of young people.

Opening prayer

Though this is to focus the mind on the issues of the Sunday, it obviously also helps us to turn our hearts and minds to the ever-present God.

Opening song

This ought to relate to the theme of the day. Sometimes it is good for it to be sung by an individual and for the congregation to sit quietly. If it is a new song, let the musicians play it over two or three times before worship begins.

Readings

It is good to have these printed in the monthly magazine or pew leaflet saying what is to come next week. On the day, if you have a handout, try and include the readings in full. It is important that all who read are audible; if necessary, rehearse the readers. Encourage everyone to read the Scriptures and think about them at home and before coming to church, as this enriches the whole church. Where possible, it is good to use more than one voice for the readings and to include a dramatic presentation. Let there be silences after each reading.

I have used the New Revised Standard Version of the Bible.

As far as the children are concerned, separate and illustrated Bible stories, such as those published by Lion, are a good starting point. Once children can read, the International Children's Bible (New Century Version) is suitable for young readers. There is a helpful dictionary, pictures and maps to go with this version. New Century also produce The Youth Bible for the older ones.

Thought for the day

This is meant to touch the heart and the will as well as the mind. If you are using the thought for the day, do spend a good deal of time with it the week before. This can also be used as preparation for those who are teaching the young people. The thought is meant to lead to some sort of action or reaction.

Question time

The questions are useful for a study group or those who are seeking to teach and preach. Beware of over-analysis and much talk. Make sure you speak to God more than you talk about him.

Illustration

The illustration is meant to go with the thought for the day but can often be used in one of the groups. Find illustrations from your locality that relate to what is going on and which throw a light on the Scripture passages or are enlightened by these passages. Remember, visual aids often speak more directly than words, as does your own way of life.

Intercessions

It is good to start by telling the congregation the response for the prayers and then keep a short silence before the prayers begin. After each section keep a short silence. I have started the intercessions with an act of praise or thanksgiving to God rather than plunging straight in. It helps to give people time to focus their thoughts and their attention on the ever-present God. Sometimes a piece of music playing gently in the background during the intercessions or someone playing a single instrument can create the right feeling. A variety of voices, people, and places around the church for the intercessions are good. Again, make sure they are audible.

Memory verse

For many people learning verses is out of fashion. I find that learning by heart (not just the mind) helps us to store up a treasure we can use in times of dryness or doubt. The verse is used to strengthen our faith and often it is an affirmation of what we believe.

Suggested music

Do not be afraid to use recorded music. Have a variety of instruments and allow children to take part in simple playing. The organ is not always the ideal instrument for setting the scene or leading the people. Remember music is important to people and often helps to set the atmosphere and get into the right frame of mind. Music can be used to set a feeling of calm and to give people a space to express themselves. Involve as many people in the musical presentation as is possible or practical. Remember, young children love making and playing instruments.

The main sources of music I have used are:

Hymns Old and New: One Church, One Faith, One Lord (Kevin Mayhew, 2004)

New Hymns and Worship Songs (Kevin Mayhew, 2000)

The Children's Hymn Book (Kevin Mayhew, 1997)

Kidsource (Kevin Mayhew, 2002)

Celtic Hymn Book (Kevin Mayhew, 2005)

Candles, Lamps and Torches each have their own aims, teaching, activities and songs. The names for these groups imply the receiving of light and the giving out and handing on of light.

CANDLES – 3-5 year olds

This group especially needs to be made to feel at home in church, to be welcomed and accepted. There is need for much play and song and a lot of adult attention. It is good to involve young parents with this group as helpers; they often learn as much as the children. It is important that the feeling given to the children is that they are loved and cared for by God who is ever with them. Parents should be encouraged to see what their child is doing and to pray with them each week.

LAMPS – 6-10 year olds

This is an age range of greatly varying abilities, so it may be necessary to split the group into two and use the teaching and activities according to their ability. This age group is very ready to adventure and stretch themselves. Let what they do help to extend their awareness and vision of each other, of what is around them and of their God. Some at least will enjoy reading out aloud and many will like a little drama; seek to use this potential as much as possible.

TORCHES – 11 plus

This is the group that the church finds hardest to keep. There is a feeling they have heard it all and know it all! Help them to discover that church can be fun and yet at the same time bring before them the depths of life and faith that are to be discovered, adventured and enjoyed. These young people are journeying towards adult life and cannot be treated just as children. Respect their growing pains and their problems: if possible, allow any of them to talk freely to you. It is important to have more than one adult present in our dealings with these young people. An additional helper is always useful. Encourage this group to become part of the church congregation as often as possible. It is best if they have specific tasks that are theirs to do within the main body of the church. Readers, intercessors, musicians and singers, future teachers and priests can come from this group. Remember you are dealing with the Church of today and tomorrow in these young people. Strengthen their faith and support them in their searching.

ADVENT
First Sunday of Advent

Aim
To affirm that whatever happens our God is with us.

Preparation
Prepare the Advent candles. Have a candle for each of the Sundays in Advent and a central candle to represent Christ.

Opening activity
Get someone to enter with a lighted taper and announce:

> God created light out of darkness.
> Jesus is the Light of the World.
> The Spirit of God enlightens us all.

As the first Advent candle is lit, let someone else say the following prayer.

Opening prayer
God, we thank you for our ancestors in the faith, Abraham and Sarah, Isaac and Rebekah, Jacob and Rachel, for all who passed their faith on to us.
You are their God and our God:
you are their Father and our Father.
Help us to know that as you came to them you come to us.
Amen.

Opening song
Be still and know that I am God

Readings
Jeremiah 33:14-16
Psalm 25:1-9
1 Thessalonians 3:9-13
Luke 21:25-36

Thought for the day
Apocalypse now
St Mark wrote his Gospel believing that the world would soon end. St Luke, in his Gospel and in Acts, anticipates that the Church will go through a protracted time of delay (Luke 21:9) and suggests that we cannot know when the end will come. Yet Luke does expect the apocalypse (see Luke 10:1-23, 12:1–13:9, 16:19-31, 17:20-37, 20:27-40).

In 21:5-24 Luke uses the traditional language to tell us of the time when the world as we know it will come to an end. Already some of the events had taken place, like the destruction of the Temple in Jerusalem.

At the climax of the apocalypse the sun, the moon and the stars and other 'powers of heaven' will be shaken – that is, destroyed. There will be distress among the nations and the roaring of waves. The rule of Rome, which is seen as an agency of chaos, must be replaced by God's rule and peace. Underlying the idea of 'the end' is that the power and love of God never fail. Whatever happens to the world or to us, God is with us. God does not leave us.

For some people today the apocalypse came with the storming of the Twin Towers, with the tsunami on the day after Christmas, with the hurricane that overwhelmed New Orleans. But amidst all of this distress God was still present and caring for his people. God comes to us and is with us now.

The fig tree (Luke 21:29-31) is unusual in that its fruit appear before its leaves. By the time the leaves show summer is near and there are fruit on the tree.

Luke 21:34-36 gives advice on how to be ready to face disasters. Do not take to drink, for it is not really an escape. Do not try and insure yourself with money or amass riches against that day, for they will be of no use; rather use your material resources for the benefit of the community.

Turn to God in prayer, for God is your hope and your strength. Remember the world is not permanent but God is. When troubles come, as they will, God will not leave us alone. We belong to eternity and are being prepared to come before God.

Question time
Advent rejoices in the God who has come, will come and is come to us. Can you give examples of each of these comings of God?

How do you show that you believe that God is always with you?

Illustration
Airports can be sad places for it is where we often say farewell to friends and loved ones who are not coming with us. We see them off and then we go to the 'departure lounge' before going to the 'terminal gate'. Don't you find those words a little threatening, if not downright depressing? You are among the departing and have come to the terminal – it sounds awful! What lifts the spirit is what is beyond. You are not stuck there, for you are off to be with a loved one, to a richer and a fuller life, or escaping from the pressures of work. The terminus is not the end but a place where we get off or set off for somewhere better.

St Luke seeks to tell us that when *things* come to an end *we* do not, for our God cares for us and is with us.

Intercessions
Blessed are you, Lord our God,
for you are an ever-present help in our troubles.
You are our strength, our song and our salvation.
We come before you in faith and seek your love.

We give thanks for the Church throughout the world and for all who have kept faith in you.

We remember all who are being persecuted for their faith,
all who are being scorned or rejected
because of their beliefs.
We ask you to give new courage and hope
to those who have lost faith
and all who walk in darkness.

Silence

God, our love and our light,
come to us and lighten our darkness.

We give thanks for the land in which we live
and we ask your blessing upon all who are leaders
in government and in society.
We pray especially today for areas
where law and order seem to have broken down
and where chaos rules.
We ask your blessing upon any who are suffering
from disasters, flood or famine.

Silence

God, our love and our light,
come to us and lighten our darkness.

We praise you for all the love we have received
and we ask you to protect and guide all our loved ones.
Bless our homes and our families with your gift of love.
We pray especially today for any who are suffering
from the breakdown of family life
or from broken or strained relationships.

Silence

God, our love and our light,
come to us and lighten our darkness.

Lord God, giver of life,
we thank you for our well being
and we remember before you all who are ill or suffering,
all who are finding life overwhelming
and all who cannot cope.
We pray especially for those who are lonely
and feel no one cares.

Silence

God, our love and our light,
come to us and lighten our darkness.

God, giver of life,
we thank you for life in all its fullness
and we remember in your presence
friends and loved ones who are departed from us.
We pray especially
for all who have lost their lives this week
in acts of violence or in accidents.
May they rejoice in life eternal.

Silence

Merciful Father,
**accept these prayers
for the sake of your Son,
our Saviour Jesus Christ.
Amen.**

Memory verse

To you, O Lord, I lift up my soul. O my God, in you I trust.
Psalm 25:1

Suggested music

All my hope on God is founded
Come, thou long-expected Jesus
Do not be afraid

CANDLES

Aim

To help the children to understand more of Christmas and to prepare for it.

Teaching

Who has someone coming to stay for Christmas? How do we get ready for them? Sometimes people may call at your house without you knowing they were coming, but it is nice to have visitors. Can you think of anyone who came as a surprise to your home? I would like to tell you of someone who had a surprise visitor to her house.

Mary was only a young girl and she had been left to look after the house. Her parents must have been out doing something else. Perhaps her father was out at work. Mary was alone and she was wondering about Joseph. She loved Joseph and was going to marry him (make sure the children understand and that they can say 'Mary' and 'Joseph'). Soon it would be time for Mary to leave her home and go and live with Joseph. When she heard someone at the door she was very happy because she thought it might be Joseph but it was not. It was someone she did not know and when he said he was a messenger from God – an angel – Mary was afraid. She hid her eyes and did not speak. But the angel said to her, 'Do not be afraid, Mary. God has sent me and God is very pleased with you. He knows that you love him and he wants you to do something really special for him. God wants you to have a baby who will be called Jesus.'

Mary was not really sure what the angel meant or how it was possible for her to have this baby. The angel told Mary that God would make it happen if she would say that she would do what God wanted.

Mary said, 'I will do what God wants.' Suddenly the angel was gone. He had gone back to God and said, 'I have delivered your message and Mary has said, "Yes": she will have the baby Jesus and will look after him.'

The name of the angel is Gabriel and he is a favourite messenger of God.

Activity

We are going to make an angel to put on our tree.

We will also count how many stars are on the sheet and that will tell us how many Sundays there are before Christmas comes. These four Sundays are called Advent Sundays and they tell us about our God coming to us.

Prayer

God, we thank you for the angel Gabriel
and for all the messages you send to us.
Help us to get ready for Jesus and for Christmas Day.
Amen.

Song

Kum ba yah

LAMPS

Aim

To look at the God who comes.

Teaching

Who can tell me what we mean by past, present and future? Tell me something that has happened in the past; now something that is in the present; now something that is in the future. Who knows the words for the past and the future if the word for the present is 'is'? 'Was' is for the past and 'shall be' is for the future. Because our God has always been and always will be, we can say, 'God was, God is, God shall be'. Let us say that together. Now I will tell you about God in the past the present and the future:

Once upon a time, in the past, there was a man called Moses and God asked him to do some very hard things to get his people free. Moses had to take them across a big desert (check they know what a desert is); they had to go through burning hot land where there was no water. Then they had to walk through the sea. Moses was afraid that he was not strong enough but God said to him, 'Do not be afraid because I am with you.' God said he would not leave Moses on his own and this gave Moses strength.

Can you tell me of other people in the past who have known God was with them? (Encourage them to tell Bible stories and other stories.)

God has promised that in the future, whatever happens, he will be with us. Even when there are troubles in the world, even when the way is dark, God promises he will go with us and will care for us.

What is good to know is that God is always with us. He is with us now and we can speak to him. God loves us and wants us to love him.

Activity

Make a Christmas card with Joseph and Mary travelling towards Bethlehem. Look at the maze and help the travellers on their journey.

Prayer

God, you have always been ready to help your people.
You will be with us whatever happens.
Help us to know you are with us now.
Hurrah for the Lord is here:
his Spirit is with us.
Amen.

Song

Learn at least the chorus of 'Do not be afraid'.

TORCHES

Aim

To explore beginnings and endings and the idea of life eternal.

Teaching

King's Cross Station is a terminus. What does that mean for the trains? What does it mean for the passengers? Yes, they collect their luggage and go off somewhere else. Can you tell me of other places where there is a terminus?

For most of life when something ends, another thing begins. The end of school is the beginning of holidays or the beginning of work. The end of the year is the beginning of another year. (Seek other examples.)

When a ship or a plane disappears over the horizon and we say, 'It is gone', someone else is seeing it appear and saying, 'Look at what is arriving'.

God is described as the Alpha and the Omega – that is, the beginning and the end. God is to be found in all beginnings and endings. When things come to an end, God is there and does not leave us. Even when there is great chaos and darkness, though we may not see him, God is always with us.

We should learn to say throughout our lives, in good times and in bad, 'The Lord is here: his Spirit is with us.'

As Christians we do not believe that death is the end but only the beginning of a great adventure. How can we say that?

Activity

Explore the meaning of this prayer of St Augustine and get the group to talk about it.

All shall be Amen and Alleluia.
We shall rest and we shall see,
we shall see and we shall know,
we shall know and we shall love,
we shall love and we shall praise.
Behold our end which is no end.

At the end of the session let five members of the group say loudly a line each and the whole group say slowly and clearly the last line all together. It would be good if they can do this before the whole congregation.

Prayer

Glory be to the Father
and to the Son
and to the Holy Spirit,
as it was in the beginning,
is now
and shall be for ever.
Amen.

Song

Father, we love you

Second Sunday of Advent

Aim

To look at the Benedictus and to rejoice in our saving God.

Preparation

Prepare the Advent candles. Have a candle for each of the Sundays in Advent and a central candle to represent Christ.

Opening activity

Have someone enter with a lighted taper and announce:

> God created light out of darkness.
> Jesus is the Light of the World.
> The Spirit of God enlightens us all.

As two of the Advent candles are lit, let someone else say the following prayer.

Opening prayer

God, we thank you for the prophets
who told us of your love and salvation.
We give thanks for Isaiah and Amos,
Jeremiah and Malachi,
Ezekiel and John the Baptist.
You are their God and our God:
you are their Father and our Father.
Help us to know that as you came to them
you come to us.
Amen.

Opening song

Christ, whose glory fills the skies

Readings

Baruch 5:1-9 or Malachi 3:1-4
Canticle: Benedictus – Luke 1:68-79
Philippians 1:3-11
Luke 3:1-6

Thought for the day

The opening chapter of St Luke's Gospel shows God working through the old priest Zechariah, Elizabeth and John the Baptist. To look at the Canticle set for today's readings and how it came about will help us to understand why John the Baptist suddenly comes on the scene.

Zechariah was a priest belonging to the section of priests of the line of Abijah. Both Elizabeth and Zechariah were descended from the priestly house of Levi. Zechariah was given the honour of a lifetime by being chosen to offer incense at the time the sacrifice was made. There, alone in the Temple, Zechariah meets an angel of God who tells him Elizabeth will have a son who will be the herald for the Messiah. Zechariah is truly lost for words – he cannot speak. He is meant to come out and bless the people but he cannot say anything. They wonder why he is delayed and then realise he has seen a vision.

Though Zechariah cannot speak, his mind is still able to work. During the nine months of his silence he composed the prayer of blessing we know as the Benedictus.

Luke 1:68-79 is sometimes called the Benedictus from the Latin for 'blessing'. It has the feel of the Old Testament and suggests that the story of John and of Jesus continue God's story of mission and redemption. The Benedictus is a typical Jewish prayer of blessing known as a berakah, which begins by blessing God and then tells of his gracious acts in creation and redemption.

The Benedictus begins by saying that the God who has been faithful throughout the history of Israel again comes to his people. This is a God who comes and comes again and again; this is the God who comes to us today as he did yesterday. God comes to us that we may know the glorious liberty of the children of God, not so much a rule-imposing God but a freedom-giving God. Do we know the freedom that God offers to us?

This freedom is offered to us through a 'mighty Saviour' whom God has raised up in the house and lineage of David.

Through the prophets God promised us salvation, whether from the apocalypse or from the hands of our enemies, and death is seen as an enemy. This salvation is through God's mercy that is his loving kindness.

St Luke recalls God's promise made to Abraham and declares we should be free to worship God without fear, holy and righteous in his sight. We are called to live without fear before God for we are to know him as the God of love, to enjoy a relationship with the living God and to reflect his holiness.

The work of John the Baptist is explained in verses 76-79. These words echo the last book in the Old Testament (Malachi 3:1) and so offer a continuity and see John as the one who goes before the king to prepare his way. John will do this by calling people to repent, to turn around and find forgiveness.

The dawn that will destroy the darkness is coming through God's mercy and loving kindness. That dawn is Christ who is the Light of the World, who comes to shine on those who dwell in darkness and in the shadow of death and to guide our feet on to the way of peace.

Question time

Do we spend time preparing others and ourselves for the coming of our God?

How do we make room in our lives and welcome the God who comes?

Illustration

In the time of Jesus, when a king was about to make a journey a messenger was sent out before him. Each area would be told the king was coming. This was so that they could prepare properly. They would fill in any holes in the road and level off any awkward bumps so that the king's journey would be smooth and without hindrance.

The other task of the messenger was to make sure that people prepared themselves properly, and if the king was coming to stay, there would be room for him and that the people would give him attention.

John the Baptist was to prepare the way for Jesus, so that the people would be ready to accept him.

Intercessions

Blessed are you, Lord God of Israel,
for you come to your people and set them free.
Through the light of Christ
you deliver us from darkness and the shadow of death
and guide us into the way of peace.

As we remember John the Baptist and all the prophets,
we give thanks for men and women of vision
through the ages.
We ask you to guide and bless
all preachers of the word and ministers of the sacraments,
all who teach the faith
and all who influence our daily lives.
We pray for all who are struggling
for freedom in their faith
and for those who are imprisoned because of their beliefs.

Silence

Lord, open our eyes to your presence
and our hearts to your coming among us.

We give thanks for those who do research,
all scientists and biologists,
for all responsible for our health and well-being.
We ask your blessing upon all doctors and nurses.
We pray for the World Health Organisation
and for all who strive to free us from disease and illness.

Silence

Lord, open our eyes to your presence
and our hearts to your coming among us.

Lord, help us to know your presence in our homes.
We ask you to protect and guide our loved ones
in to the ways of peace.
We remember before you all who suffer
from oppression or violence in their homes.

Silence

Lord, open our eyes to your presence
and our hearts to your coming among us.

We give thanks for your love and healing power
and ask your blessing upon all who are suffering,
all who long for freedom
and all who are caught up in debt.
We pray for any who have lost their homes
or their work at this time,
especially any who have been separated from loved ones.

Silence

Lord, open our eyes to your presence
and our hearts to your coming among us.

We give thanks
that you have delivered us from the darkness of death
and offered us the light of life eternal.
We rejoice in the fellowship of all your saints
and we pray for friends and loved ones
who are departed from us.

Silence

Merciful Father,
accept these prayers
for the sake of your Son,
our Saviour Jesus Christ.
Amen.

Memory verse

He has raised up a mighty Saviour for us in the house of his servant David.
Luke 1:69

Suggested music

On Jordan's bank the Baptist's cry
Dear Lord and Father of mankind
Bless the Lord, my soul

CANDLES

Aim

To introduce the children to Joseph.

Teaching

Who can remember the name of the angel who came to Mary and told her about her baby? Let us all say, 'The angel Gabriel'.

Mary wanted to tell Joseph what the angel had said to her, especially that she was going to have a baby.

Joseph was working with some wood when Mary came to him. He used to mend things and make things. He liked mending broken tables and chairs; he mended boxes and sometimes ladders. Sometimes when people were going to throw things away, Joseph persuaded them to mend them. He wanted to make some things for his house, ready for when Mary would come and live with him. Do you know what you call someone who works with wood? Let us all say, 'Joseph is a carpenter'.

Joseph listened to Mary when she told him about the angel and about the baby, and he found it all hard to understand. Joseph did not know what to do. After Mary had gone home and Joseph had gone to bed, the angel came to him in a dream. The angel spoke to Joseph and said, 'Joseph, God wants you to love Mary and the baby she will have. God wants you to call the baby Jesus because he will save his people.' After Joseph heard this he woke up and the angel was gone. Joseph loved Mary and looked forward to the baby being born.

Later Joseph told Mary that they would have to get ready to go on a long journey to Bethlehem (get the children to repeat 'Bethlehem'). It was about 76 miles, a very long way. Joseph would walk but he wanted Mary to ride the donkey. He knew Mary would be very tired and soon the baby Jesus would be born. It was a long, long journey. Very late one night they arrived and all the hotels and inns were full. But a friendly innkeeper gave them a stable they could sleep in.

Joseph and Mary said thank you to God that they had arrived safely in Bethlehem.

Activity

Play 'pin the tail on the donkey' as this will help to remind the children what a donkey is.

We will colour Joseph, Mary and the donkey on the sheet. Let us count how many Sundays there are until Christmas.

Prayer

God, we thank you
for the donkey that carried Mary to Bethlehem
and that Jesus was born there in a stable.
Amen.

Song

Little donkey

LAMPS

Aim

To tell the story of Zechariah and the birth of John the Baptist.

Teaching

Who knows the name of the mother and father of John the Baptist? His mother's name was Elizabeth. Do you know anyone with this name? Elizabeth was married to Zechariah. That is a harder name to remember – let us say it together.

Zechariah and Elizabeth had no children. They would have liked to have had a son so that he could follow in the work of his father. Now they were getting old and did not think that they would ever have children.

Zechariah was a priest and often went to the Temple for services. At home he helped in the services of the synagogue (explain). He hoped that one day he might be asked to do something special at the Temple in Jerusalem and he *was* asked. He was asked to offer incense to God as a sign of worship and love. Only one person was allowed to do this for all the people, so he was in that part of the Temple by himself. Zechariah prayed to God that he might do the work properly and with love.

While he was making the offering, which caused a lot of smoke, he was surprised to see someone there in the room with him. He thought he would be on his own. Then he realised this was no ordinary person: this was a messenger from God. Do you know what a messenger from God is called? Yes, it was an angel. Zechariah began to shake with fear. But the angel said, 'Do not be afraid, for your prayer has been heard and your wife Elizabeth will have a son and you will call him John.'

Zechariah was not sure about this and doubted what the angel told him. So the angel said, 'Because you have doubted, you will now be unable to speak until the time when the baby is born.' Suddenly the smoke of the incense moved and the angel was gone. Zechariah wondered if he had dreamt it all. But when he tried to speak he found he could not. He opened his mouth but the sounds would not come out.

People were waiting for him to come out and say a prayer. They wondered why he was so long. When he did come out he could not speak to them; he had to make signs. When he went home Elizabeth was worried about his voice. But he made signs and wrote that his voice would come back.

While he was unable to speak to *people*, Zechariah could still speak to God in prayer. At last, after being silent for nine months, Zechariah held in his arms his own son. When they wanted to know the baby's name, Zechariah had to write it down. He wrote, 'His name is John.' As soon as he did this he was able to speak again and he sang a song to God.

What the angel said to him had come true. He had a little boy and he also had his voice back. The little boy grew up to be John the Baptist.

Activity

See if the children can mime different jobs – a carpenter, a driver, a footballer, a singer, a teacher, a priest. Some may like to mime what a parent does as a job, or jobs done around the house like hoovering, sweeping, washing-up or cooking.

Prayer

God, we thank you for our voices,
that we can speak and shout and sing.
Let us remember every day to speak to you in prayer.
Amen.

Song

Come on and shine

TORCHES

Aim

To look at Zechariah and his song.

Teaching

Today we are going to look at the song of Zechariah. It is called the Benedictus. Zechariah was married to Elizabeth. They were sad because they were getting old and had no children. As a priest, Zechariah was given the opportunity to offer incense in the Temple during the time the sacrifice was offered. This was a great honour and would only happen to him once in his lifetime. There would be no one else in that special part of the Temple, only Zechariah offering to God. While he was in the Temple alone, he had a vision: he saw an angel of God. The angel spoke to him and told him how his wife Elizabeth would have a son. Zechariah could hardly believe this and was lost for words – in fact, he could not speak at all. Meanwhile, the people waited outside for Zechariah to come and give them a blessing. He took a long time and when he came he could not say anything. The people realised he had seen or experienced something special.

For the next nine months Zechariah was unable to speak; all the time his wife was expecting a baby. When the baby was born Zechariah and Elizabeth were very happy. After eight days, when they were to name the child, Zechariah asked for something to write on and then he wrote, 'His name is John'. Almost straightaway Zechariah discovered he could speak again. Zechariah was very excited and he began to praise God. Perhaps he made this song up in his head when he could not speak.

Read Luke 1:68-79.

Let members of the group read a verse each. Tell them the baby would grow up to be John the Baptist. Ask them to decide whether the verse they read is about God the Father, John the Baptist or about Jesus. Encourage the group to explore ideas such as 'mighty saviour', 'saved from our enemies', 'and you, child', 'to prepare his ways' and so on.

Activity

Play 'charades'. Choose well-known TV programmes. Then choose a few stories from the Gospels. If someone cannot act it well, let them try and draw it.

Prayer

Blessed are you, God our Creator,
for you love us and care for us
and you sent your Son to be our Saviour.
Amen.

Song

Oh! Oh! Oh! How good is the Lord

Third Sunday of Advent

Aim

To show that our faith is one of joy and love.

Preparation

Prepare the Advent candles. Have a candle for each of the Sundays in Advent and a central candle to represent Christ.

Opening activity

Have three children enter with a lighted taper and announce a line each:

> God created light out of darkness.
> Jesus is the Light of the World.
> The Spirit of God enlightens us all.

As three of the Advent candles are lit, let someone else say the following prayer.

Opening prayer

God, we thank you for Zechariah and Elizabeth
and for the birth of their son, John the Baptist.
We give thanks that he prepared the way
for the coming of Jesus.
Grant that we who are baptised may be ready
for the coming of our Lord.
You are their God and our God:
you are their Father and our Father.
Help us to know that as you came to them
you come to us.
Amen.

Opening song

Rejoice in the Lord always
(Sing as a round.)

Readings

Zephaniah 3:14-20
Canticle: Isaiah 12:2-6
Philippians 4:4-7
Luke 3:7-18

Thought for the day

John the Baptist came out of the desert like a hell-fire preacher. He came warning people that the way they were going was wrong; they needed to turn around to repent. He warned them that words would not save them – only trying to do what is good. They could not say, 'We are Jews so we shall be saved.' Even with Jesus would come a time of judgement. This is hardly a Gospel: there is not much good news here, though there are plenty of practical warnings about the road we choose and about how our actions make us prepared or unprepared for the coming of Jesus.

In contrast with John the Baptist stands today's reading from the Letter to the Philippians (4:4-7). 'Rejoice in the Lord always.' Rejoice in his love and in his saving power.

Rejoice in his birth and in resurrection. Above all, rejoice in his presence and his love. 'Again I say, rejoice.' As Christians, we need to show the joy of knowing the love and salvation of God. Christians who impose a heavy load on people do God a disservice. St Teresa of Avila rightly prayed, 'Lord, deliver us from sour-faced saints.'

'Let your gentleness be known to everyone.' This does not mean being made a fool of, but it does mean not imposing on others or forcing them to do things. As God deals gently with us, we have to learn to deal with others in the same way.

'The Lord is near' is the message of John the Baptist and of Advent. Do you accept the reality of it? The Lord is not far away from you but close at hand. Prayer is not a long-distance call but talking to a loving God who is close to you and with you. Learn to relax in the presence and in the love and power of God. Do not worry – much of our anxiety stems from feeling alone and without help. You are not alone. The Almighty is with you and cares for you. Speak to him in prayer and supplication; let your requests be made known to God. Remember a thankful heart cannot be a sad heart! Appreciate the world, people and the abiding presence. Then the peace of God – it is his gift – will keep guard of your heart and mind in Christ Jesus. Now *that* is Gospel!

Question time

Do we spend enough time enjoying the presence and the love of God that is offered to us?

What do you think of the statement 'a thankful heart cannot be a sad heart'?

Illustration

There was once a young girl who was always told off at home. Whatever she did, she was criticised (a bit like Cinderella). Nothing could please her parents and they often seemed angry with her. Never did they show their love. The girl felt ugly, she developed asthma and eczema. Later still she went into a psychiatric hospital because she was so depressed and felt useless. It seemed no one could make her better.

One day a hospital orderly noticed that beneath her sad face was a beautiful young woman. When he talked to her she was intelligent and interesting. Soon he formed a relationship with her, bringing her presents and praising the artwork she did. At this she seemed to glow. The orderly got permission to take her out on the odd Saturday. Soon they were deeply in love. Once she knew she was loved she began to smile. Her work was appreciated and soon her eczema and asthma seemed to disappear. There was a new peace and joy in her life. I can tell you she married the orderly and became a good artist. The loving presence of another had transformed her life.

Intercessions

Lord our God, we give you thanks
and rejoice in the great love that you have for us:
we rejoice in your presence and in your peace.

We pray for your whole Church
as it prepares for the Christmas season.
May it encourage people to come before you
in joy and in celebration.
Bless all who preach and all who teach the faith:
may they show the joy of knowing you and your love.
We pray today for all who are burdened with guilt
or with living only by the law.

Silence

God, ever present,
reveal yourself in peace and joy.

We give thanks for places of relaxation and refreshment.
We pray for all who help us
to enjoy life and to live in peace.
We remember in your presence all who are over-worked
or heavily burdened.
We remember all who are deeply in debt
or who feel that they cannot cope with life.
We ask your blessing upon all who are finding life hard
or who are lonely.

Silence

God, ever present,
reveal yourself in peace and joy.

We give thanks for our homes and our loved ones.
Bless our families and our friends
with an awareness of you and your love.
We pray for all who suffer from broken homes
or homes where there is little joy
or where there is violence or abuse.

Silence

God, ever present,
reveal yourself in peace and joy.

We seek your blessing
upon all who are oppressed or depressed,
upon all whose lives are filled with sorrow or pain.
We remember those who are battling
with a long-term illness
and those who feel they are losing mobility or agility.
We remember in your presence
all who are struggling at this time.

Silence

God, ever present,
reveal yourself in peace and joy.

We give thanks for the gift of life and for life eternal.
We pray for loved ones departed
and for all who have entered the joy of your kingdom.

Silence

Merciful Father,
**accept these prayers
for the sake of your Son,
our Saviour Jesus Christ.
Amen.**

Memory verse

The Lord is near. Do not worry about anything, but in
everything, by prayer and supplication, with thanksgiving, let your requests be made known to God.
Philippians 4:5b, 6

Suggested music

Rejoice, the Lord is king
Hark, a herald voice is calling
Make way, make way

CANDLES

Aim

To introduce the children to the shepherds.

Teaching

Do you remember where Joseph and Mary went when
they left home? They went a long way to Bethlehem.
(Let us all say, 'Bethlehem'.) There was no room in the
hotels or inns but a kind innkeeper gave them a stable
where they could rest and sleep.

Not everyone was asleep because some people were
working all through the night. Do you know anyone who
has to work at night? Doctors and nurses sometimes
work at night, some factory workers and bakers also
work at night, and police work at night. I want to tell
you about some brave men who stayed out at night in
the hills overlooking Bethlehem. They were shepherds.
What does a shepherd look after?

They were out on the hills to protect their sheep in
case a wild animal came to try and eat them. Wolves
were often hunting at night and there might even have
been a lion looking for something to eat. Sometimes
wicked men came to steal the sheep. So the shepherds
had to be brave and to keep on the lookout for anything
that was happening. They had to keep their eyes wide
open and listen carefully.

Suddenly they thought they heard a noise like singing.
Maybe it was from the one of the inns down in Bethlehem.
No, the sound was coming from the sky. The sound
they heard was angels singing, 'Glory to God in the
highest and on earth be peace.'

The shepherds were brave men but they were afraid
for none of them had ever seen an angel. So the shepherds
tried to hide their faces with their hands (let us do this).
But the angels said, 'Do not be afraid, we have come
with good news. We will not hurt you. We have come to
tell you that a very special baby will be born this night
in Bethlehem. Jesus is coming and he is coming to your
town tonight.' The shepherds were amazed and while
they were thinking about this baby, the angels started to
sing again, 'Glory to God in the highest and on earth be
peace.' Then suddenly the sky was quiet because the
angels had gone. The shepherds could only see the moon
and the stars.

'Come on,' said one of the shepherds, 'let us go down
into Bethlehem and see if we can find this little baby
that the angels told us about.'

Activity

Get the children to act out the story. You may like to
provide tea-towel headdresses for the shepherds and
tinsel circles for the angels to wear. You could get them
to do it twice with the shepherds being angels and the
angels being shepherds.

We have some shepherds to colour in and get ready for going to Bethlehem.

Prayer

God, we thank you
for the angels and the shepherds.
May we also show our love for Jesus.
Amen.

Song

While shepherds watched

LAMPS

Aim

To begin the Christmas story with the journey to Bethlehem.

Teaching

Who has ever gone on a long walk? What is the longest distance you think you have ever walked? You may have been on a walking holiday and camped out each night.

Before the days of cars the fastest people could travel would be on a horse. A donkey was often used but it did not go so fast. Most people walked to wherever they were going.

I want you to imagine how long it would take you to walk to . . . (give an example of a well-known place about 80 miles from home). What would you need for the journey? You would certainly need some food. You may need to have a tent or some money to stay in a hotel. You might like to take a first-aid kit. Let us pretend we are setting off. We have a pack on our back and a stick in our hand. We will go around the room marching and singing, 'We are marching in the light of God'. Let us first stand still and practise singing.

Now that we have marched around the room, I will tell you of a journey. (If possible, show a map of the Holy Land.) We are going to go from Nazareth to Bethlehem. Can someone come and show me where Nazareth is and where Bethlehem is? It is not far on a map – our fingers could walk it very quickly. But it is as far as (name a place) is from here.

Now this was the journey that Joseph was getting ready to go on. He had put some food on the donkey and some water. He put a blanket on the donkey for Mary and a small rolled-up tent on the back. Joseph would walk all the way. After they left Nazareth they would go down by the hills of Samaria, travelling near the river Jordan. They would then pass by the edge of Jerusalem. There were lots of people on the road: many were walking, some were on donkeys, camels or horses. The road was very busy and at night there were many tents and campfires. Because Mary was soon going to have her baby she was very tired.

Not long after Jerusalem, Joseph and Mary had only six miles to go but Mary was very slow. She was frightened that the baby might be born on the journey. Joseph looked after her very carefully until at last they reached Bethlehem. As they entered the city it was getting quite dark. The shepherds had already lit fires on the hillsides. Joseph said a big thank-you to God for they had arrived safely.

Activity

March around the room to the music 'We are marching'. When the music is turned down, the last one to stop is out, as is anyone who stops marching when the music is playing.

Prayer

God, we thank you that wherever we go
you are there.
You never leave us
and are always ready to help us and hear us.
Amen.

Song

We are marching in the light of God

TORCHES

Aim

To encourage the young people to get inspiration from the Advent candles.

Teaching

When the days are getting dark, what do you do to see well? Yes, you put on a light. There is an old saying: 'It is better to light one small candle than to complain against the darkness.'

Advent comes at the darkest time of the year. During the Advent season is the shortest day – the time when darkness seems to triumph over light. This is one of the reasons we choose to light candles and, as the darkness increases, we light even more candles.

How many Sundays are there in Advent? There are always four. That does not mean that it is a full four weeks from the first Sunday in Advent until Christmas. There are only three weeks and a day from the first Sunday of Advent to the fourth. Christmas can be the next day or a whole week after. As the Sundays go by, we light more candles until four are lit and then five when it comes to Christmas.

So today we light three candles.

We light the first when we give thanks for all who have gone before us in the faith, from Abraham up to the present day. I will say, 'God, I thank you for Abraham and Sarah.' Then in turn I want you to say, 'God, I thank you for . . .' and add the name of someone who was faithful to God.

When the second candle is lit we give thanks for people of vision, especially for the prophets. It is harder to think of people of vision but you could include those who you think have improved our world. I will say, 'God, I thank you for Elijah.' Then in turn I want you to say, 'God, I thank you for . . .' and add the name of a visionary or a prophet.

The third candle is for a single person. Does anyone know who it is for? It is for the last of the prophets. Not the last in the Old Testament but the one who told of Jesus coming into the world. It is for John the Baptist. We should listen as he says, 'Prepare the way of the Lord.'

All of these people have brought more light and hope into our world. And for them we have lit three candles.

Activity

Have a set of Advent candles or use a group of tea lights on a saucer. (Do remind the young people to be careful with the lit candles.) As the first candle is lit, say the prayer below. As the second candle is lit, let the group invent a sentence of invitation for God to come, using the word 'come' and the refrain 'come among us'. At the lighting of the third candle, play the music of 'O come, O come, Emmanuel' and sing the first verse. Try to use this activity as a meditation with gaps of silence between sentences.

Prayer

Lord of light, come:
come among us.
Lord of love, come:
come among us.
Lord of peace, come:
come among us.
Lord of hope, come:
come among us.
Lord of joy, come:
come among us.

Song

Colours of day

Fourth Sunday of Advent

Aim

To look at the song of Mary – the Magnificat.

Preparation

Prepare the Advent candles. Have a candle for each of the Sundays in Advent and a central candle to represent Christ.

Opening activity

Have someone enter with a lighted taper and announce:

> God created light out of darkness.
> Jesus is the Light of the World.
> The Spirit of God enlightens us all.

As four of the Advent candles are lit, let someone else say the following prayer.

Opening prayer

God, we thank you
for the message of the angel Gabriel to Mary.
May we learn the obedience of Mary,
serving you with joy and accepting Jesus into our lives.
You are her God and our God:
you are her Father and our Father.
Help us to know that as you came to Mary
you come to us.
Amen.

Opening song

Magnificat (Chant)

Readings

Micah 5:2-5a
Canticle: Magnificat or Psalm 80:1-8
Hebrews 10:5-10
Luke 1:39-45 (46-55)

Thought for the day

Mary's song is born out of love for God and an awareness of the Scriptures. Mary's song is very like the song of Hannah in 1 Samuel 2:1-10. Both songs sound like psalms. Hannah gives thanks for the promise of a child, as she had been unable to bear children up to that point, and she gives thanks to God for his care of the lowly and the oppressed. Mary gives thanks that through her pregnancy the world will come to know its Saviour. By saying 'Yes' to God, Mary is seen as a model of obedience and trust. Mary's song begins by giving thanks to God for his redemption. The important thing to note is that the God who has acted in this way in the past acts now. Our God is not of the past alone or to be projected into the future; our God is of the now and is with each of us now. The Lord is with you.

Mary rejoices in the presence, in God her Saviour. Like the saints of old, Mary will be called blessed, for God has looked with favour upon her lowliness. Yet Mary has made this possible by saying 'Yes' to God. It is the mighty one who has done great things, and holy is his name. God has the same loving kindness for all who fear him from generation to generation. We need to take time to experience this loving kindness towards us.

God's presence is a revolutionary power: the presence of God changes things. In his power God scatters the proud in the thoughts of their hearts. Things do not happen in our own goodness or power alone but because God loves us. We are not chosen because we are clever or skilful but because God cares for us and loves us. This love cannot be earned, only accepted and responded to.

It is not to the powerful that God submits. God puts an end to the world's worship of might and prestige; God often raises up the humble and the lowly. God cares for all, and those open to his love are raised up, rich or poor, common or royal. In fact, no one is common in God's eyes, for all are precious.

It is a strange experience to discover how happy many poor people are and how miserable are so many with lots of possessions and riches. Jewish belief was sometimes distorted to suggest that the more you gained on earth, the more God loved you. It was suggested that if you are very rich, then God favours you. But this is not so. You are not measured by what you possess. There are many so-called well-off people who are empty. You can even see it in their desire always to fill themselves with something. Those who know God are satisfied and realise their lives are filled with good things.

God acts as a God who keeps covenant: he keeps his promises and remembers to be merciful.

If we would learn the Magnificat and its attitudes to God and the present, our lives would be greatly enriched.

Question time

How often do we seek to say 'Yes' to God?

As God's kingdom comes when we obey the king, are there ways we can help in the coming of the kingdom?

Illustration

Love matters more than riches. This is well illustrated by the story of King Midas. In his greed he accepted the offer that all he touched would turn to gold. Very exciting! He touched plates, leaves, statues and they all turned to gold. He would soon be the richest man in the world. But his food also turned to gold and he began to starve. He touched his daughter and she turned to gold and he lost her warmth and her love. He had sold himself for riches and now he was poor indeed. He had all the gold you could dream about but he was poor within. Fortunately, this condition was reversible. Midas could lose the desire for gold and become loving and happy once more. When asked if he would like this rather than gold his reply was 'Yes'.

Intercessions

God, we thank you for the obedience of Mary
and for all who help to bring in your kingdom
by seeking to do your will.

We give thanks
for your faithful people throughout all ages.
Lord, guide your Church
that it may know your will and serve you faithfully.
We pray for the Church working in areas of poverty,
war or oppression.
May we all strive to reveal your love and your peace.
We ask your blessing on this congregation
as we seek to serve you.

Silence

Lord, guide us:
let your kingdom come among us.

We pray for the time when the kingdoms of this world
will become the kingdom of God.
We look forward to when there will be peace
upon the whole earth.
We pray for the work of all peacemakers,
for the United Nations and all peacekeeping forces.
We ask your blessing upon all who are caught up
in war or terrorism at this time.

Silence

Lord, guide us:
let your kingdom come among us.

We give thanks for the Blessed Virgin Mary,
for welcoming Jesus into her life.
May we know your presence in our homes
and seek to bring in your kingdom through our actions.
We pray for all families
who are going through difficult times
and who are struggling.

Silence

Lord, guide us:
let your kingdom come among us.

We give thanks for all who care for the ill and the suffering.
We ask your blessing
upon the work of doctors and nurses,
upon hospitals and hospices.
We remember all who are ill
or who have been injured in accidents
or through acts of violence.
We pray for them and their loved ones.

Silence

Lord, guide us:
let your kingdom come among us.

We pray for all our loved ones departed from us,
who are now in the fullness of your kingdom.
We rejoice in the fellowship of all your saints,
giving special thanks today for the Blessed Virgin Mary.

Silence

Merciful Father,
**accept these prayers
for the sake of your Son,
our Saviour Jesus Christ.
Amen.**

Memory verse

My soul magnifies the Lord and my spirit rejoices in
God my Saviour.
Luke 1:46, 47

Suggested music

Tell out, my soul
Take my life, and let it be
Like a candle flame
O come, O come, Emmanuel

CANDLES

Aim

To rejoice at the birth of Jesus.

Teaching

Do you remember that last week we heard about shepherds? And what else? Do you remember where the shepherds were? They were in the hills around Bethlehem. (Let us all say 'Bethlehem'.) We know the names of two people who were in Bethlehem and in a stable trying to sleep. Who were they? Joseph and Mary (let us say their names together). They had travelled for a good few days and were now very tired.

Joseph was trying to make Mary comfortable among the hay and straw. He put down a blanket for her to lie on. Nearby the donkey was happily eating hay and you could see its shadow on the wall. The shadow seemed to be eating hay as well. In the corner of the stable a cow and a few hens were sleeping. It was nice and warm and Joseph hoped they too would soon sleep.

Mary could not sleep because she knew that Jesus was going to be born, there in the stable. There among the hay Mary was ready for the baby Jesus to come into the world. Joseph was watching and ready to help her. When Jesus came, Joseph helped to make him nice and tidy and Mary hugged him close to her and said, 'Welcome to our world, Jesus.' (Let us say the same.) Once she had hugged him and kissed him she gave the baby Jesus, who was asleep, to Joseph, and he gently and quietly put him in a manger beside them as it looked like a nice bed. Now Joseph could watch while Mary and Jesus got a little sleep.

Activity

At the start play 'Sleeping tigers'. The children pretend they are tigers asleep in the jungle. Anyone who moves, even twitches, is out. If necessary, an occasional loud noise often causes a reaction!

Get the children to act out the birth of Jesus. Then get them to make a simple Christmas card to take home or a birthday card for Jesus.

Prayer

God, we thank you for the birth of Jesus.
Help us to love him as he loves us.
Amen.

Song

Away in a manger

LAMPS

Aim

To discover how much the children know of the Christmas story.

Teaching

Last week we talked about the journey from Nazareth to Bethlehem. Can you remember how far they travelled? By the end of the week Mary would be very tired. They were travelling very slowly because Mary's baby was due to be born. This meant that by the time they got to Bethlehem the places that put people up were full. An eastern khan (the nearest to a hotel) was really a common place where everybody slept together with little privacy. People did not remove clothes to sleep and they shared a fire or fires on which they cooked their own food. The khan was often very noisy, especially when friends and relatives were meeting there. Do you think Mary would have liked her baby to be born among all those crowds and the noise? I think she was pleased when the innkeeper said she could use the stable. The stable might have been a separate building or a cave in the hillside. What would you find in the stable? Hay, donkeys, cows, hens and maybe a camel. They would spend the night with the animals. They had a blanket but what would Mary and Joseph use to make themselves more comfortable? They would use the straw that the animals also used for bedding. Here Jesus would be born.

Activity

Let us pretend we are making a film of the scene. What do you want to show in the stable? What would Joseph be doing? There is no nurse, or helper for Mary, only Joseph. Do you think he might be a little worried? Once the baby is born, how could we show the joy of Mary and Joseph?

Joseph would help to see that Jesus was clean and wrapped in swaddling bands. (See if the children can explain what these are.) Once Mary is asleep, where does Joseph put Jesus? (Make sure they know what a manger is.) Now let us have a Joseph and Mary and act it out.

Prayer

God, we thank you for our parents,
for all the love and care they show for us,
and we thank you for the love and care
that Mary and Joseph gave to the baby Jesus.
Amen.

Song

See him lying on a bed of straw

TORCHES

Aim

To continue using the Advent candles as inspiration.

Teaching

We are now at the last Sunday in Advent. How many candles do we light? Can anyone remember the people we gave thanks for with the first candle? Ancestors in the faith. Whom did we remember with the second candle? Prophets and visionaries. The third candle was for an individual. Who was that? John the Baptist.

Sometimes the fourth candle is a different colour. It can be rosy pink whilst the other candles are purple for Advent. The first three candles looked back to the Old Testament. This candle looks to the beginning of the New Testament. It is not for Jesus – that is the bigger candle we light on Christmas day. So who is it for? It is for Mary, the mother of Jesus. Because Mary said 'Yes' to God, Jesus could be born in the world. As disobedience separates us from God, to obey brings us closer to him. God never leaves us but we separate ourselves from him through turning away from him. If Mary had said 'No, thank you' to God, then Jesus could not have been born. Though God can do all things, he wants us to work with him, and that is how his kingdom comes on earth.

The candles can be seen to represent faith (of our ancestors), hope through vision (of the prophets), repentance and preparation (as with the message of John the Baptist) and obedience (as that of Mary), but, above all, they tell us of the light that shines in the darkness of our world. Jesus is the Light of the World.

Activity

Divide the young people into four groups and get each group to prepare a sentence or two for the lighting of a single candle. You need to tell them which candle they are to light. Light one for faith and our ancestors, one for prophets and hope, and so on. If possible, have the room in darkness for the candle-lighting. Keep a silence in the darkness.

As a taper is lit, let someone say, 'It is better to light one candle than to complain against the darkness.'

Someone else says, 'Jesus Christ is the Light of the World.' Let each group have the taper in turn and pass it carefully to every member of their group before the last one lights the candle and the sentence or sentences are said. After the last group add the prayer below (you can use different people to say each line).

Prayer

Eternal Light, shine in our hearts.
Eternal Power, deliver us from evil.
Eternal Wisdom, scatter the darkness of our ignorance.
Eternal pity, have mercy upon us.
Grant that we may ever seek your face,
with all our heart and soul and strength;
and in your great mercy
bring us at the last to your holy presence.
Amen.
Alcuin of York 735-804

Song

Lord, the light of your love (*Shine, Jesus, shine*)

CHRISTMAS
Christmas Day

Aim
To celebrate the coming of the Saviour into the world.

Preparation
Invite children to come to church dressed as shepherds or angels. Some can come as Mary and bring a new doll with them and some can come as Joseph. Let them choose. If there is a mother in the congregation with a new baby, encourage her to bring her baby as the baby Jesus.

Opening activity
Let five people have tapers and each say a sentence as they light the Advent candles. The four could come from each corner of the church. Let the Jesus candle be lit by the mother or father of the baby who is brought to church.

Let each say a line as they light a candle:

Rejoice in the Light of Christ,
the Light that scatters the darkness,
the Light that gives hope to the world,
the Light of Christ who is come among us,
the Light who will guide us always.

Opening prayer
Jesus, Light of the World,
shine upon us
and grant this may be for us
a happy and blessed Christmas.
Amen.

Opening song
O come, all ye faithful

Readings
Isaiah 9:2-7
Psalm 96
Titus 2:11-14
Luke 2:1-14 (15-20)

Thought for the day
It is important to capture both the ordinariness and the extraordinariness of the birth of Jesus.

Jesus was born at the time of registration ordered by the Roman emperor Augustus and enforced by Quirinius the Roman governor of Syria, which included Palestine. This registration was to determine how much back-breaking tax could be extorted from the community.

So Joseph had to travel from Galilee and Nazareth down to Bethlehem in Judea. The journey is almost 80 miles. There would be many people on the roads, either sleeping rough or seeking accommodation. The eastern inn would not provide food, only a fire to cook on, fodder for the animals and a shelter. The stable would be a better place for a mother about to give birth. Swaddling clothes was the normal way to wrap up a baby.

Up on the hills overlooking Bethlehem were shepherds. These men were despised by the orthodox people of the day. The shepherds could not keep the ceremonial rules of washing.

Taxes, journeying, stables, shepherds are things we know. But there is another world – or, to put it a better way, the hidden part of our world – breaking in. It is the world of angels, of God, of heaven. If we lose sight of this world, it is like trying to understand a picture by looking at a negative. The two worlds belong together. We have to open our eyes to the God who comes in Jesus and who comes to us. We have to make room for God in our lives and let him be born in us. If we fail to give time to the presence and say we are too busy, we descend to a world that is only a material world and so we have a distorted picture of what the world and life is. At Christmas we are invited to enjoy the reality that God loves the world and is in the world, that God comes to us in what we think is ordinary. The mystery of the Word made flesh is waiting to be revealed to us. Let us be still and give thanks for the birth of Jesus and welcome him into our lives and homes.

Question time
Do we make time to be aware that the world has more to it than what is seen and heard?

How can we make room in our hearts and lives for Jesus?

Illustration
There was a Scottish farmer who refused to believe the Christmas story. Though his wife and children went to church, he refused to and often mocked them. Why should God lower himself to be like us? It is foolish talk.

Once when it was snowing, the family went to church. The farmer noticed that the snow was getting much worse. Suddenly he heard a thump against his window and then another. He went out to see what was happening. There in front of him was a large flock of geese which had got lost in the storm.

The farmer was kind and felt for them. He wanted to help them. He realised that they could shelter in his barn. He got behind them and tried to drive them in, but they only scattered. Then he tried by laying a trail of food to the barn door, but the geese did not take any notice. There was nothing he could do to get them to enter the barn.

About to give up on them he said to himself, 'Why don't they follow me? If I were a goose, I could lead them into the barn. If I looked like one of them, I could save them.'

Suddenly he stopped and thought about what he had said: he could only save them by becoming like them. Suddenly he understood the great love of God for humankind. He fell to his knees in the snow and gave thanks to God for his great love.

Intercessions

Glory be to God in the highest,
to our God who has come among us
and taken upon him our flesh.
God, we give you thanks and praise
for your wonderful gift of yourself.
Help us to know your presence in our lives
and in our homes.

We rejoice with the whole Church
as it celebrates your love for us.
We ask your blessing upon any churches
where there is oppression or persecution at this time.
We pray for all who will preach the word
and celebrate the sacraments
today and throughout this season.
We pray for those who will celebrate
in refugee camps and prisons
or completely on their own.
We remember those who would have liked
to have been with us in our worship.

Silence

Jesus, proclaimed by the angels, born of Mary,
come and abide with us.

We give thanks for the message of the angels
and we pray for peace on earth
and goodwill among all peoples.
We pray for all who are caught up in war or violence
at this time.
We remember the world's poor, the homeless
and any who live in fear or anxiety.
We pray for all who feel neglected or unwanted.

Silence

Jesus, proclaimed by the angels, born of Mary,
come and abide with us.

We give thanks that our Lord
was born into an ordinary family
and lived in an ordinary home.
We ask your blessing
upon all our loved ones and friends this Christmas:
may we know your presence in our joys and celebrations.
We remember all who have to spend this Christmas
away from their homes and loved ones.

Silence

Jesus, proclaimed by the angels, born of Mary,
come and abide with us.

We give thanks that Christ became human
that we might share in the Divine;
that through Christ is our salvation.
We pray for all who are ill or unable to enjoy life.
We remember those who are fearful for their future
or who are unable to cope with the present.
Lord, may they know your love and care for them.

Silence

Jesus, proclaimed by the angels, born of Mary,
come and abide with us.

We give thanks that you came to earth
to lift us into heaven.
You took upon you our life
that life could be eternal.
We remember loved ones who have died this year
and those with whom we have spent Christmases past.
Lord, grant to them the gift of life and joy eternal.

Silence

Merciful Father,
accept these prayers
for the sake of your Son,
our Saviour Jesus Christ.
Amen.

Memory verse

To you is born this day in the city of David a Saviour,
who is the Messiah, the Lord.
Luke 2:11

Suggested music

Child in the manger
Cloth for the cradle
Ding dong, merrily on high
Infant holy, infant lowly
Joy to the world
Once in royal David's city
Silent night
The Virgin Mary had a baby boy
What child is this
While shepherds watched

(Of course, any carols that would fit the service or are
well known by the congregation could be used.)

CANDLES, LAMPS and TORCHES

There are special occasions when it is important for the
whole congregation to worship together and Christmas
is one of them. There are no worksheets for Christmas
Day as there is plenty of activity within the service.
Involve the children and young people as much as
possible. Let them read Christmas poems or prayers.
Involve them with the crib and crib figures if you have
them. Above all, let it be a day for families enjoying
being together in church.

First Sunday of Christmas

Aim

To encourage people not to 'suppose' the presence of Jesus but to seek to know he is with us.

Preparation

The Advent and Christmas candles continue to be lit.

Hide an important object under a pew and then tell the congregation that you have 'lost' something in church and you would be grateful if they could find it.

Opening activity

Light the Advent and Christmas candles. Let people come from the four corners of the church and another down the central aisle. Let each say a line as they light a candle:

Rejoice in the light of Christ,
the Light that scatters the darkness,
the Light that gives hope to the lost,
the Light of Christ who is come among us,
the Light who will guide us always.

Let all the candle lighters then turn to the congregation and say:

The Lord is here:
his Spirit is with us.

Opening prayer

O God, you never leave us,
you are always with us.
Open our eyes to your presence
and our hearts to your love this day and always.
Amen.

Opening song

Once in royal David's city

Readings

1 Samuel 2:18-20, 26
Psalm 148
Colossians 3:12-17
Luke 2:41-52

Thought for the day

This story is the only glimpse we get of Jesus as a boy. Joseph and Mary used to go all the way to Jerusalem every year to celebrate the Passover. When Jesus was 12 it was time for him to go too, for at 12 a Jewish boy became a man. He then became 'a son of the law' and had to take the obligations of the law upon himself. So at 12 Jesus went up to the Passover festival for the first time.

The city would be crowded for the festival. Families and friends travelled there together, the young folk met up with friends and relatives and enjoyed being in each other's company. After the Passover the women usually set off earlier in the day for they would travel more slowly than the men. Later on the men would set off and the two groups would not meet up until the evening. Mary and Joseph supposed that Jesus was in the other's company. Joseph thought he was with Mary's group and Mary thought he was with Joseph and his group. They supposed him to be with one of the groups when in fact they had left him behind. Every mile they travelled took them further away. It was not until the evening when they had searched the camp that they knew he was missing. As they had travelled a day, it took another day to return to Jerusalem. By now Joseph and Mary were distressed and anxious for the safety of Jesus.

When they found him he was in the Temple. At the Passover it was the custom for the Sanhedrin to meet in the Temple to discuss religious and theological matters. And there was Jesus among them. It is wrong to think of Jesus leading this group; rather he was fascinated by them and their words. The Jewish phrase 'hearing and asking questions' is used for any student learning from his teachers.

You can feel the relief and anxiety in Mary's voice as she says, 'Child, why have you treated us like this? Look, your father and I have been searching for you in great anxiety.'

In his reply Jesus gently takes the title of 'father' from Joseph and gives it to God. As a good Jewish son, now that he has come of age, he must be about his Father's business. Here is a pointer to who Jesus really is. Being the Son of the Father does not free him from obedience to his earthly home. The references to growing in strength and in wisdom and in divine and human favour (Greek: charis = grace) are good Jewish qualities as reflected in 1 Samuel 2:21, 26 and Proverbs 3:5.

Question time

Do we too often suppose Jesus to be in the company without our seeking him out?

How can we seek out the presence in our church and community?

Illustration

There are so many ways that people can get lost. There is a lovely story of an absent-minded professor from Edinburgh. He used to travel regularly by train and all the ticket collectors knew him. Once by the gate he was anxiously going through his pockets and after a while the ticket collector asked if he could help. 'I have lost my ticket,' said the professor. 'That's all right, sir, we all know you. You can get on the train.' 'But,' said the professor, 'I need my ticket because I do not know where I am going.'

It is easy to get lost in this world. Do you know where you are going?

Intercessions

Blessed are you, Lord our God,
for in your great love for us
you sent your Son into the world.
Blessed are you, Lord Jesus Christ,
for you are one with us

and through you we have life eternal.
Blessed are you, Holy Spirit of God,
for you come to us and inspire us.

We give thanks for the early days of Jesus at Nazareth,
for his learning and his growing.
We pray that the Church may be ready
to nurture young people in their faith,
so that they may grow in spirit
as well as in mind and body.
We ask your blessing upon Sunday schools, Bible classes,
Confirmation classes and all places of learning
within the Church.
Guide with your Holy Spirit
all who are called to teach the faith
and all who preach the word.

Silence

Lord, ever present,
help us to rejoice in your love and power.

We give thanks for our knowledge and experience
and ask your blessing upon all who have taught us.
We pray for schools, colleges and universities.
We ask your blessing on all who learn through their work.
Lord God, guide all who influence our minds and spirits
through the media, through television and CDs,
through music and through films.

Silence

Lord, ever present,
help us to rejoice in your love and power.

We give thanks for the care and protection of our homes,
especially for all who have shared their lives
and their love with us.
We pray for all who come from homes
where there is discouragement
or a lack of love and understanding.
We remember especially
any children who have been taken into care.

Silence

Lord, ever present,
help us to rejoice in your love and power.

We give thanks for the wisdom of doctors and nurses
in their care for all who are ill.
We pray for all who are suffering at this time,
especially any who have been separated from a loved one
or who have lost a child.
We pray for children separated from loved ones
through illness or accidents,
for all refugees and homeless people.

Silence

Lord, ever present,
help us to rejoice in your love and power.

We give thanks for the life of Jesus
and the offering to us of eternal life.
We pray for friends and loved ones
who are departed from us.

Silence

Merciful Father,
**accept these prayers
for the sake of your Son,
our Saviour Jesus Christ.
Amen.**

Memory verse

Let the peace of Christ rule in your hearts, to which indeed you were called in the one body. And be thankful.
Colossians 3:15

Suggested music

Unto us a boy is born
The heavenly child in stature grows
A great and mighty wonder

CANDLES

Aim

To show that Jesus was like any child and could get lost.

Teaching

Every year in the spring time Joseph and Mary went to Jerusalem to pray to God and to learn about God in the Temple. This was a long way to go, so when Jesus was small he could not go. Mary and Joseph used to leave him with some friends and went on their own. But when Jesus was 12 they said he was old enough to go to Jerusalem with them.

Jesus was very excited that he was going to Jerusalem and to God's special church called the Temple. He got up early and helped Joseph to put things on the donkey that they would need. (Let the children guess at what would go on the donkey.) Jesus would play with his friends and relations who were travelling the same road. It was fun going to Jerusalem. At night Joseph put up a little tent for them to sleep in. As Jesus rolled into a blanket he could hear grown-ups singing and talking to each other around campfires. The journey was great fun but Jesus looked forward to being in the Temple and seeing all the wonderful things.

When they got there Jesus really enjoyed being in the big Temple looking at all sorts of things and listening to the teachers. He did not realise when his mother set off for home. Later in the day Joseph also left for home and thought Jesus was with Mary, so Jesus got left behind.

That night when Joseph caught up to Mary he asked, 'Where is Jesus?' Mary said, 'I thought he was with you.' Now they were worried and visited all the other tents to see if Jesus was with their friends or relatives but he was not there. They had travelled a whole day so it took them another day to get back to Jerusalem. Then they started looking for Jesus and asking people if they had seen him.

At last they found him. Where do you think he was? He was in the Temple listening to the teachers and learning from them. Mary was so glad but she asked Jesus why he had not noticed that they had gone home. He said did she not know where he would be. He was in God's house and doing God's work. Then they all went home to Nazareth and it was there Jesus grew up to be strong and wise.

Activity

The children could act this story of Jesus travelling and being lost, and Mary and Joseph looking for him. You could have the parents go out of the room whilst 'Jesus' hides somewhere.

Prayer

God, we thank you for our homes and family
and for all who love and care for us.
Amen.

Song

Jesus' love is very wonderful

LAMPS

Aim

To show that Jesus could get lost like any 12-year-old.

Teaching

Have you ever been lost? How did it happen? If you wander away from your parents in a strange place or a big shop, it is easy to get lost. How were you found? No doubt your mother got all sorts of people to go and look for you. When a parent loses a child it is a very frightening and sad time. They get very troubled in case something awful has happened to their child. The mother and father will not be happy until the child is found again.

Once Jesus got lost. It happened when he was 12 years old and he went to the big city Jerusalem for the first time since he was a baby. Jesus was now counted as being grown up at 12, so at the Passover Festival (explain) he would go with Mary and Joseph to Jerusalem. They would travel with other people from Nazareth, so Jesus would be with other boys of his own age. No doubt Jesus found it all very exciting. The city would be very busy and the Temple would be full of people. Jesus probably enjoyed every moment. There were men teaching in the Temple and Jesus was really interested in what they were saying. After the festival Jesus did not notice that his parents had set off for home. Mary set off with the other women early in the day. Joseph and the men set off later. Some of the children left with their mothers and some came on later with their fathers. Mary supposed Jesus was with Joseph; Joseph supposed Jesus was with Mary. Only in the evening, when it was getting dark, did they realise he was not with either of them. They visited their friends and relatives in their tents but he was not with any of them. He must have been left behind; they had lost him.

Because they had travelled all day it took another day to get back to Jerusalem and again it was getting to the evening. It was not until the next day, the third day since they lost Jesus, that they found him. You can imagine how Mary had cried and how both Mary and Joseph were anxious to find Jesus. How happy she was when she saw him standing listening to the teachers in the Temple. Mary went over to him and said, 'Child, why have you treated us like this? Look, your father and I have been searching for you in great anxiety.'

Jesus seemed to be surprised that they thought he was lost. Did they not know this was where they should have expected to find him? He said to them, 'Did you not know I must be in my Father's house?' Mary thought these words were a little strange and she would remember them always. Jesus then set off for home with them. There in Nazareth he grew strong and wise loved by God and people.

Activity

Play a game of hide and seek. Send two people out of the room and then choose a 'Jesus' from the rest. When the two return, let everyone else be sitting in a circle or a line. The two have to ask someone, 'Have you seen Jesus?' They can nod and look towards him or shake their heads and close their eyes. When they ask 'Jesus', that person must smile and not nod or shake his head. If they fail to recognise this, they must keep looking. If they do, two more people can be sent out and we can start again.

Prayer

Lord God, you are always with us.
Help us to seek you and to know you;
to know you and to love you.
Amen.

Song

C is for the Christ Child

TORCHES

Aim

To show how Mary and Joseph supposed Jesus travelled homeward with them.

Teaching

Have you ever set off supposing you have all that you need, only to find you have left something behind? (Get examples.) There was once a man who went shopping in a shopping centre and then drove home. Only when he got home did he remember he had left his wife in the shopping centre. He had to drive 15 miles back to where he had been to find his wife waiting and wondering what had happened. You can imagine what she said to him when he told her what he had done!

When Jesus was 12 he was considered an adult. He was no longer a child but a man. That means most people in this group would be counted as adults. For Jesus this meant he would be able to go to the Passover festival in Jerusalem. He would be able to celebrate the time when his people were rescued from the land of Egypt. A lot of people from Nazareth and round about would travel all the way to Jerusalem; friends and families travelled in groups. No doubt Jesus walked with some of his relatives and friends. At night he would enjoy the campfires and sleeping in a tent under the stars.

After they had all been to the festival the group made their way home. Usually the women set off early in the day in a large group with some of the young people. Then later in the day the men and some more of the young people set off to catch up to them.

In the evening when the meal was ready Mary

wondered where Jesus was. She asked Joseph and he said he did not know; he had not seen him all day. Mary had supposed that Jesus was with Joseph and Joseph supposed Jesus had been with Mary. 'Don't worry,' said Joseph, 'Jesus will be with some of his friends or our relatives.' But when Jesus did not turn up, Joseph searched the camp and could not find him. Jesus was not with them; he was not in the company. You can easily imagine how distressed Mary and Joseph became. They would have to go back all the way to Jerusalem, which was a day's journey. This would be the second day without Jesus.

Only on the third day after searching and asking people did they find him. Jesus was in the Temple listening to the teachers. He was enjoying learning about God's people. Mary went up to him and said, 'Child, why have you treated us like this? Look, your father and I have been searching for you in great anxiety.'

Jesus seemed amazed that they did not know where he was. He said to them, 'Did you not know that I must be in my Father's house?' Mary did not understand what Jesus was saying to her but she would always remember it. Jesus went home with them to Nazareth and grew strong and wise, loved by the Father and by people.

Activity

Have two sets of the alphabet on pieces of paper. Spread them face downwards on the floor. Let the group collect the letters so that everyone has a similar number. They are to look at their letters but not show them to anyone. Now without revealing their letters they are to make the word JESUS. They can only use sign language to show they have a letter or not. Because there are two J's, E's and U's it makes the game more complex and calls for a lot of cooperation. This is not a competition: it is the task of the whole group to make the name.

Prayer

Lord Jesus, we thank you for becoming one with us
and sharing our joys and sorrows.
Help us to know you are always with us
and let us not lose our awareness of you
through neglect or busyness.
Amen.

Song

Hallelu, hallelu

Second Sunday of Christmas

Aim
To continue to rejoice in the Word made flesh.

Preparation
We continue to light the Advent and Christmas candles. You might like to have a poster with the words 'The Lord is here' in bold letters.

Opening activity
Light the Advent and Christmas candles. Let people come from the four corners of the church and another down the central aisle. Let each say a line as they light a candle:

Rejoice in the Word made flesh.
Rejoice in the Word who dwells among us.
Rejoice in the Word of Life.
Rejoice in the Word of Truth.
Rejoice in the Word who will guide us always.

Let all the candle lighters then turn to the congregation and say, 'The Lord is here: his Spirit is with us.'

Opening prayer
We give thanks that all that was promised has come true, for our God has come among us.
Father, let us know the Word who lives
and who comes to us,
Jesus Christ our Lord.
Amen.

Opening song
Be still, for the presence of the Lord

Readings
Jeremiah 31:7-14
Psalm 147:12-20
Ephesians 1:3-14
John 1:(1-9) 10-18

Thought for the day
St John's Gospel begins as the book of Genesis begins: that is, 'In the beginning'. John adds to Genesis by presenting Jesus as the 'logos' – the Word – through whom God created the world. Without Jesus the world is seen as a place of chaos and darkness. Jesus brings light and life to the world. This is a light that cannot be overcome, no matter how dark it gets. As he is the light of all people, he is our light. The great message of these opening words of St John is that we are offered light and life through Jesus Christ. Jesus himself will come to us and abide with us, protecting us from darkness and death. This is a wonderful offer.

But Jesus gets poor reception. 'He was in the world, and the world came into being through him; yet the world did not know him. He came to what was his own, and his own people did not accept him.' Time and again Jesus is given a poor reception: he is scorned and rejected, he is ignored and passed by. People are too busy for him. They have no time. There is still no room at the inn or in the heart. So many things crowd out Jesus. What about you? Have you given Jesus a good reception over this Christmas season?

Remember, 'to all who received him, who believed in his name, he gave the power to become children of God.'

Learn the memory verse (John 1:14). You should be able to say, 'The Word became flesh and lived among us, and we have seen his glory.'

Question time
Are our lives ordered in such a way that we have time and space for Jesus?

How can we show each day that 'the Lord is with us'?

Illustration
Some people live in poor reception areas for television or radio. The signal cannot get to them so the picture or the sound is blurred, fuzzy and cannot be enjoyed properly. Many things can cause bad reception. People can live too far from the transmitter. Sometimes it is just that their aerial is pointing the wrong way and it needs to be turned around. Are you sure you are pointing in the right direction? At other times it is something close that destroys reception – a motor without a suppressor, or a lot of leaves on nearby trees that can block the signal. Then again it can be the opposite: there is too much interference because the set is too receptive. All sorts of sounds distort what we need to hear. We need to be able to finely tune to make proper contact. This is as true of prayer as it is of radio waves.

Intercessions
God, we give you thanks for the New Year
and for all the opportunities that you offer us.
Blessed are you, Lord our God,
our Creator and our Redeemer.
Through your great love
your Son has shared in our joy and sorrow
and has delivered us from death.
Blessed are you, Lord God, giver of life and life eternal.

We give you thanks for all preachers of the word,
for translators of the Bible and for Bible publishers.
We pray for all who produce Bible guides,
commentaries and study notes.
We ask you to bless all who read and study the Scriptures.
We pray that we all may know the true and living Word
that is Christ our Lord.
May we know him as present in our lives
and with us always.

Silence

Come, Lord:
be known among us

We pray for all who are involved in giving us information
through the daily news and newspapers,
for all who communicate with us

through the written or spoken word.
We remember all who suffer from deafness
or who are unable to speak.
We pray for all who have difficulty in communicating
and who are often misunderstood.

Silence

Come, Lord:
be known among us.

We give thanks for those who taught us to read and write.
We ask your blessing on our friends and our loved ones.
We pray that in this New Year
we may learn to be sensitive and caring for each other.

Silence

Come, Lord:
be known among us.

We pray for all who are fearful for their future,
those who are awaiting a doctor's diagnosis
or an operation,
for all who are terminally ill.
We remember all who live in areas of war
or natural disaster.
Lord, bless all who work in caring for others
and relieving their anxiety.

Silence

Come, Lord:
be known among us.

We ask your blessing upon our loved ones
who are now departed from us.
May they know newness of life in your kingdom.

Silence

Merciful Father,
accept these prayers
for the sake of your Son,
our Saviour Jesus Christ.
Amen.

Memory verse

The Word became flesh and lived among us, and we
have seen his glory.
John 1:14

Suggested music

Brightest and best
A man there lived in Galilee
God is love, God is love, God is love for us
When our God came to earth

CANDLES

Aim

To show that God loves us and wants us to be happy.

Teaching

Happy New Year, everyone. Let us show we are happy
people by smiling and showing happy faces. (At this
point do the activity of sad and happy faces.) Let the
children enjoy this by showing their saddest and happiest
face.

God is always bothered when someone is sad
because he loves us and wants us to enjoy the life he has
given us. Because there were a lot of sad people in the
world, Jesus was sent so that they would know that
God loves them and wants them to be happy.

Once there was a little boy who was not very happy.
He had a very sad face. When other people looked at
him it made them sad as well. (Make a sad face at someone – and then they have to look sad.) Sad people can
soon make other people look sad. His mother and
father had been away because his mother was poorly.
When his mother got better they came back and the little
boy's sad face changed to a happy one. (Make a happy
face at someone.) Then because they had been away
they gave him a present. It was a kitten and it purred
every time he stroked it. The little boy smiled because
he was very happy. When people saw his smile it made
them smile too. Now let us pass a smile right round the
room.

God sent Jesus so that we could all be happy. God
wants us to enjoy his world and be glad. Let us all smile
because God loves us. If someone asks you today why
you smile, tell them it is because God loves us.

Activity

I want you to watch my face. (Put on a sad face. Move
your hand down from your brow to below your neck;
as you do so, reveal a happy face.) What do you think
has happened to my face? What sort of face was it?
What sort of face did it become? Let us all make sad
faces. Now put your hand over your face and let your
face become happy.

Prayer

God, I thank you for making me happy.
Help me to smile and make others happy too.
Amen.

Song

Thank you, Lord, for this new day

LAMPS

Aim

To explore the idea of the 'Word made flesh'.

Teaching

Get a volunteer to read Genesis 1:1-3 and someone else
to read John 1:1. Write 'God loves us' for someone else
to read. People are able to communicate with each other
through speaking or through writing words. Ask for
examples. If people cannot speak or if someone cannot
hear, we have to use signs or act out what we want.
Could anyone tell me they are hungry without using
words? Could someone show they are tired? How
could you say to someone, 'I love you'?

If we listen to Genesis again and St John again they are both about when the world was made. And one says, 'In the beginning God . . .' What does the other say? The 'Word' is a sort of secret name for Jesus who was there at the very beginning. John says the 'Word was made flesh'. That is hard to work out. Can anyone tell me what you think it means? It tells us that Jesus was born and lived on earth.

Jesus is often called by different names. He is called 'the Word'. What else is he called? He is called the Christ, Saviour, Son of God, Light of the World. Some of these are in a wordsearch for you to find.

God loved the world and cared for everyone. He saw that they needed help and that they needed to know he loved them. So God sent his Son into the world. Jesus came to tell us about God's love not only in words but also by his whole life. All that the Bible had promised, all the words of the prophets, comes true and happens when Jesus is born, lives, dies and rises again for us.

Activity

Have the names of some animals on pieces of paper and ask different children to see if they can mime them or draw them.

There is a wordsearch on the activity sheet.

Prayer

Jesus, we thank you for coming to live on earth
and for showing us God the Father's love.
As you love us, help us to love you.
Amen.

Song

God is love: his the care

TORCHES

Aim

To show that God keeps his promise in the Word made flesh.

Teaching

What did you get for Christmas? Did you get what you hoped for? Was anyone promised a special present?

Sometimes when you are promised something it is exciting to wait for it. (Give an example – I was promised a bike.) But promises are not the thing itself; they only tell us what could be. Promises only make us look forward in hope.

What is a cheque? Show one that says, 'I promise to pay £1,000,000'. If you were given this, wouldn't it be very exciting? But it is not the same as money. Often cheques like this are sent to people but written across them are words like 'Specimen'. (You may be able to show one from some organisation.) This is not a promise that you will win the money but only that you may win if you are lucky. Sometimes such cheques are sent to almost every house. They are not promises but only an invitation – and usually for you to spend your money!

When God makes a promise he always keeps it. For hundreds of years God promised that the Christ would come – that is, the one who would save God's people. God actually sent many people but the real Saviour needed to save us from death. Then at last – in God's time – the promise was fulfilled when Jesus was born. The words became a reality, not just a promise. In his Gospel St John says, 'The Word became flesh.' Not only is God's promise fulfilled in Jesus but because Jesus is God he has come that we might share in his kingdom as he shared in ours.

Activity

Write a promise to God. (You may see this as part of your New Year resolutions.) Write a promise about your daily prayer and when you will do it.

You might like to explore the idea of some of the 'false promises' of advertising. You could then get the children to write a good and honest advertisement about the love of God.

Prayer

God, we thank you for the faithfulness of your word
and for Jesus, the Word made flesh.
May we find in him the way to life eternal.
Amen.

Song

King of kings and Lord of lords

EPIPHANY
The Epiphany

Aim

To show we are all seekers and need to come to the Christ.

Preparation

Have a star on a pole and figures of the three wise men. Have three children dressed as wise men with their gifts and five other children to carry the Advent and Christmas candles.

Opening activity

As the opening hymn is sung, let the star lead the procession, followed by the candle-bearers, then those who are carrying the figures, and lastly the children dressed as wise men.

At the end of the first verse, the star will be placed behind the crib. Then the candles are lit with the appropriate prayers.

Verse two will have the gold-bearing figure placed at the crib and the child dressed as the gold-bearer should come to the crib.

Verse three will have same actions with the incense-bearer and the fourth verse with the bearer of myrrh.

At verse five the children dressed as wise men should kneel before the Christ child at the crib.

During the final chorus let the children stand up and bow to the Christ and then go dancing back to their places.

Opening prayer

O God, who brought wise men to Jesus
by the leading of a star,
bring us to know and to love your Son,
Jesus Christ our Lord.
Amen.

Opening song

We three Kings of Orient are

Readings

Isaiah 60:1-6
Psalm 72:(1-9) 10-15
Ephesians 3:1-12
Matthew 2:1-12

Thought for the day

We do not know where the wise men came from: we only know they came from east of the Holy Land. We do not know whether it was the Near East or the Far East. By tradition they are of different nations: one black, one oriental and one white. The important thing is that they were all Gentiles – they were not Jews. The Epiphany is about Jesus being revealed to the nations of the world. The Magi were the priestly leaders of Persia, now Iran, in the same way as the Levites were for the Holy Land. In leading these Gentiles to Jesus, God makes good the promise to Abraham and Sarah that their descendants would be a light and a blessing to the nations. These men were seekers. They may have been rich, they may have been clever, they may have been men of authority, but, above all, they were seekers. They needed something else in their lives. They needed a living relationship with their God. St Augustine of Hippo reminds us that we are all seekers when he says, 'You have made us for yourself, and our heart is restless until it finds its rest in you.'

In their quest these men searched the heavens and the earth, they spent time and energy, they risked their lives by travelling at night, they refused to be put off but journeyed on. Some must have laughed at them, others must have scorned their search, but they would not be put off.

In a sense they did not know where they were going but they did know whom they were seeking. They went to the wrong place by going to the obvious: they went to Jerusalem and to Herod. Herod's title was 'king of the Jews'. Fortunately, they realised their mistake and later did not tell Herod where Jesus was. From Jerusalem they journeyed on to Bethlehem. At last they were able to offer themselves and their gifts; their search was over and they could return home rejoicing. In them, the beginning of Jesus being revealed to the world had begun.

We need to know our lives cannot be really fulfilled if we do not know our God. We have to seek out his presence and come before him. Like the wise men, we may take a few wrong turnings, we may be laughed at, scorned or put in danger, but we must not be put off until we come before him and know him.

Question time

Why do you think it was important that the Christ should be revealed to the Gentiles?

How can we encourage new seekers in their search for Christ?

Illustration

(This can be said by three different people.)

I bring gold because I am a rich man. I have all sorts of wonderful possessions and I have a good mind. I really am well off. I can buy whatever I want. But there are some things money cannot buy. You cannot buy love or health; you cannot buy peace of mind or eternal life. I offer gold to the One who can give me what money cannot buy.

I bring frankincense, the precious gum of a tree. Incense is used in worship. I am well-off, with a good mind. But it is easy to feel self-sufficient or over-important. I need to look beyond myself, to look at the mysteries and wonders of life. I need to know God to be satisfied. In adoration I offer incense to the One who meets my needs and tells me God is here.

I bring myrrh that relieves pain, for I have tasted many sufferings. I am a clever man but I cannot escape pain or the fear of death. I offer myrrh for all the sorrowful people of the world, for all who are heavily burdened, for all whose labour is hard. I offer myrrh for all who are in pain or distress, to the One who tells us that God cares. God will give us freedom. God will relieve our pain. God will give us life eternal.

Together:
We offer our gifts to God who gives himself to us.

Intercessions

Blessed are you, Lord our God,
who by the leading of a star
brought seekers from other nations
to bow before the Christ child.
As they offered their gifts and their lives,
may we offer ourselves to you in love and adoration,
for you are the giver of life and life eternal.

Lord, as you led the wise men to the Christ,
lead us to know you and your love.
We pray for all who are seekers and pilgrims,
all who search for the meaning of life and for purpose.
We remember all who have lost touch with you
or who have no faith.
We pray for all who are caught up in materialism
or who are self-centred.
We ask that the Church may reach out
to draw others to you.
We seek guidance for all bishops, priests and deacons.
May we all be led to a vision of you and your love.

Silence

Lord, guide us by your light
and bring us to your glory.

We give thanks for people of talent,
for men and women of vision,
for all who improve this world by their lives.
We ask your guidance
upon all who influence the lives of others.
Bless all teachers, writers and those who influence us
through the press and broadcasting.
We ask you to guide all who are leaders
of people or nations.

Silence

Lord, guide us by your light
and bring us to your glory.

We give thanks that Jesus lived in an ordinary home.
We ask your blessing upon our homes and loved ones.
May we know your presence and peace
in our lives and in our work.
We pray today for the lonely
and all who feel neglected or unwanted.
We remember all who suffer from violence or abuse
in their homes.

Silence

Lord, guide us by your light
and bring us to your glory.

Lord, we come with the sorrowing and sad people
of our world,
with all who live in fear or anxiety.
We pray for refugees and homeless people.
We remember all who are in pain or distress at this time.
May they all know that you love them and care for them.
We ask your blessing on all healers
and on relief organisations.

Silence

Lord, guide us by your light
and bring us to your glory.

We give thanks for the promise of eternal life
through the coming of your Son.
We rejoice in the fellowship of all your saints.
May our loved ones departed
know the fullness and joy of your eternal kingdom.

Silence

Merciful Father,
accept these prayers
for the sake of your Son,
our Saviour Jesus Christ.
Amen.

Memory verse

Arise, shine; for your light has come, and the glory of the Lord has risen upon you.
Isaiah 60:1

Suggested music

Earth has many a noble city
O worship the Lord in the beauty of holiness
Songs of thankfulness and praise

CANDLES

Aim

To help the children to share in the seeking for the Christ child.

Teaching

Once there were three very wise men. They were all very clever. One was very rich and had lots of gold. He could buy whatever he wanted. He had servants and a very nice house. If he ordered something, he soon got it. But there was one thing he wanted most of all: he wanted to know that God loved him and cared for him. So that he could do that, God sent a star to guide him and to bring him to Bethlehem and to where Jesus was. (Show the gold crown – see Activity below – and say, 'This is for the first wise man.')

The second wise man often took services in his church. When he did this he made a special offering of a nice smelling smoke to God by burning incense. (You could demonstrate by burning a little incense or a joss stick.) Often looking into the smoke he prayed that he might see God a little clearer. Wouldn't it be lovely if he could stand before God? So that he could do that, God sent a star to guide him and to bring him to Bethlehem and to where Jesus was. (Show the silver crown and say, 'This is for the second wise man.')

The third wise man was very clever. He knew all sorts of interesting things but he was often poorly. He often took a medicine called myrrh to make his pain go away. He often asked God to take his pain away for ever. So that he could do that, God sent a star to guide him and to bring him to Bethlehem and to where Jesus was. (Show the white crown and say, 'This is for the third wise man.')

Because they were following the same star, the wise men came together. They travelled by night (why?) until they came to where Jesus was. They offered him gifts. (Do the children know what they are?) There was gold from the rich man, frankincense from the priest, and myrrh from the man who had been poorly. And all of them bowed down and offered themselves to Jesus.

Activity

Have three cardboard crowns. Colour one gold, a second silver and leave the third white. Play musical crowns. Get the children to stand in a circle and carefully pass the crowns around. When the music stops, whoever has a crown must put it on and walk around the circle. After this is done a few times tell them the next time it happens the people with the crowns will become the three wise people seeking Jesus. You may like to have some curtaining that the wise people can use as cloaks.

Have a star passed around the rest of the group and when the music stops that person will be the star.

Get everyone to sing 'Guide us, guide us, little star' (see below) and let the star wander around the room. Sing it again and let the wise people follow the star. If possible, have a group of crib figures or a picture of the wise men for the star to end up at. Let the wise people bow or kneel before the Christ child. On the third singing let all the group follow the star and come to kneel or stand before the Christ child. Now the prayer can be said.

Prayer

O God, who by a star
led the wise men to Jesus,
help us to come to Jesus and offer him our love.
Amen.

Song

Guide us, guide us, little star,
we have travelled very far.
We have seen your lovely light
as we journey through the night.
Now we come to Christ our King
and our love to him we bring.

(Sing a line at a time to the tune 'Twinkle, twinkle, little star'.)

LAMPS

Aim

To encourage the children to see themselves as seekers who are able to offer themselves to God.

Teaching

Once there were three very clever men. One was very rich, one was a priest and the third, though clever, was often poorly. Each of them wanted to know God better.

The rich man could buy anything he wanted. He could order it or have it made. All around him were beautiful and expensive things. But there are some things money cannot buy. Can you think of any? Health, love, life – and you cannot buy God. The rich man felt a great emptiness in his life and knew he could not fill it with any thing – only God could do that. So he decided he would look for God until he found him. When he found him, the rich man would offer a gift and himself to God.

The next man was a priest and he worked in a church. Every day he offered prayers to God and with them offered frankincense (incense). Does anyone know what it is? It is the gum from a tree. When it is burnt it produces smoke and a nice smell. (If possible, give a demonstration using incense or a joss stick.) The smoke as it swirled was an offering to God and it was a sign that we believe God is very near. The priest burnt the incense and prayed that he would be more aware of God's presence. He decided to seek for God until he knew him better and then he would offer incense and himself to God.

The third man was very clever but he was also often very poorly. He knew all about medicines and sometimes used myrrh to take his pain away. He prayed that one day his pain would be taken away and that he would enjoy life more. He knew the closer he got to God, the less his pain would bother him and one day God would take it away. He decided that he would go and seek for a better awareness of God and when he came to him he would offer himself and his myrrh.

God sent a star to guide each of the seekers. As it was the same star they followed, they soon joined together in their seeking. They journeyed a long way until at last they came to Bethlehem and to Jesus. Here they bowed before him and offered their gifts of gold, frankincense and myrrh. They gave thanks that they saw God in the face of Jesus.

Activity

Play 'pass the parcel'. Let there be three boxes – one gold, one silver and one plain white. Tell the children that when the music stops, whoever is holding the parcel is out. When the group is down to six or less, tell them that the people holding the parcels when the music stops will become the three seekers.

Then, remembering the story, they have to say why they are seeking Jesus.

After this encourage the children to talk about why they come to seek Jesus.

Prayer

O God, we seek you until we find you.
When we find you, help us to know you
for when we know you, then we can love you.
Help us to come before you
through Jesus Christ our Lord.
Amen.

Song

We are marching in the light of God

TORCHES

Aim

To encourage them to see that they should offer themselves to God.

Teaching

Have you received any Epiphany cards this year? You will find them among your Christmas cards. Epiphany means 'manifestation' or 'revealing' and it is about God being revealed to the world. Over the next three weeks we will look at three different revelations of God in Jesus Christ. The first is to the wise men, the second is the Baptism of Jesus, the third is the first miracle recorded by St John of Jesus turning water into wine. Christmas and Epiphany are really one great festival about God coming to earth and revealing himself to us in Jesus.

The wise men are described as Magi. Nowhere in the Bible are they described as kings. The Magi belonged to a tribe of priests – like the Levites in Israel. They were teachers and instructors of the kings of Persia (Iran). They were known to be men of holiness a well as wisdom. In Persia there could be no offering of sacrifice unless a Magi was present. What is important for the story is that they were not Jews. The story of the wise men is about God being revealed to the world. God is not just the God of the Jews, he is the God of all peoples: he is our God.

We do not know that there were just three wise men seeking Jesus but we guess by the number of gifts that there were three. Sometimes tradition makes one black, one oriental and the third white. This is to show that God seeks to be known by all peoples.

What do you think the gifts meant?

Gold is a symbol of wealth and power. Gold is the gift for a king.

Frankincense is used by priests and is a symbol of the presence of God. Frankincense declared the priesthood of Jesus and that God is seen in him.

Myrrh is a painkiller and used for embalming bodies. Myrrh tells us that Jesus will free us from our troubles and bring us to life eternal.

(Use the hymn 'We three kings' to explore the themes.)

Now what would you offer to Jesus as an expression about your life and what you hope from him?

(Use the last verse of 'In the bleak mid-winter' to explore the idea of offering ourselves.)

How can we offer ourselves daily to our Lord?

Activity

Cut out of card the letters for GOLD, FRANKINCENSE, MYRRH and OURSELF. Spread the letters face down around the room.

Now ask the group to search for GOLD. They must look for letters to make the word but not reveal any letter to anyone else. The first to find an O or an L must declare, 'I have an O' or 'I have an L'. Other Ls or Os will then be put back as they are found.

FRANKINCENSE – there are extra Rs and Es, so the first one with either of these letters must declare, 'I have an R' or 'I have an E', and the rest of the Rs and Es must be put back.

MYRRH – there is an extra R so the first two who find an R must declare, 'I have an R'. This means a third R will be returned to the pile.

Now ask what word is left. There are seven letters, so get seven people to collect the letters and make the remaining word.

Prayer

God, who by the leading of a star
brought the wise men to Jesus,
guide us in our lives
and bring us to give our love to you.
Amen.

Song

Riding high and low

First Sunday of Epiphany
The Baptism of Christ

Aim
To affirm our belief in the Holy Trinity and in the mission of Christ.

Preparation
Have the Advent/Christmas candles ready to be lit near the font. Decorate the font with flowers and with symbols of the Trinity.

Opening activity
Have five people process from different parts of the church to the font to light the candles. A fifth person carries a ewer of water to the font. Get the congregation to repeat the words of each candle-lighter.

1 We light this candle for God the Creator of light.
2 We light this candle for the light coming into the world.
3 We light this candle for the gifts of the Holy Spirit.
4 We light this candle for the grace of our Lord Jesus Christ.
5 We light this candle for the Word made flesh.

Leader
We rejoice in the light,
we rejoice in the love
we rejoice in the leading
of Father, Son and Holy Spirit.

The water is poured into the font and blessed. The congregation can now renew their baptismal vows around the font and be sprinkled with water.

Opening prayer
Blessed are you, Father, Son and Holy Spirit,
three Persons and yet one God.
We give you thanks and praise
for your presence, your power and your peace
in our lives and in the world.
We come to worship and adore you.

Opening song
Do not be afraid

Readings
Isaiah 43:1-7
Psalm 29
Acts 8:14-17
Luke 3:15-17, 21, 22

Thought for the day
Someone counted the phrase 'Do not be afraid' 365 times in the Bible – one for each day of the year. God says to each of us, 'Do not fear, for I have redeemed you; I have called you by your name, you are mine'

(Isaiah 43:1b). God cares for us as individuals: He loves each of us personally. He is with us in our joys and in our sorrows. God never leaves us but is always with us.

Baptism not only celebrates our commitment to God; it also celebrates God's own commitment to us. Baptism is not just being immersed in water; it is affirming the reality of being immersed in the presence of God the Father, Son and Holy Spirit. A good way to start the day is to affirm:

I am immersed in the light of God the Father.
I am immersed in the love of God the Son.
I am immersed in the leading of the Spirit.
I am immersed in the Three in One.

We can use this affirmation with our children and god-children.

The baptism of John was for the forgiveness of sins. Jesus did not need forgiveness but he needed to express his oneness with us. There are certain turning points in all our lives. St Luke shows Jesus as a man, 12 years old, deciding he needed to do his Father's – that is, God's – work. His baptism is another turning point: Jesus is now 30. Throughout the country, due to John the Baptist, there is a movement towards God. Jesus identifies himself with these people.

At the baptism of Jesus something special happens. There is the voice of the Father speaking personally to Jesus and saying, 'You are my Son, the Beloved; with you I am well pleased.' These words can come from two texts. 'You are my Son' is from Psalm 2:7 and is understood to be the description of the Messianic King. 'Beloved, with you I am well pleased' is part of Isaiah 42:1, which is about the Servant of God and the description of the Servant reaches its peak in Isaiah 53 with the Suffering Servant. Jesus would have the dual role of King and Suffering Servant. Cross and crown go together.

It is worth noting that one of the few images of the Trinity is to be found in the baptism. There is the voice of the God from the heavens, Jesus coming up out of the water and the Holy Spirit descending in the form of a dove.

Question time
Why do you think Jesus came to John for baptism?

How do you show that your life is immersed in the Father, Son and Holy Spirit?

Illustration
There is a species of water fly which flies in the air but dives into the water for its food. It can survive in the water because, as it dives, it takes an air bubble with it. It moves around inside the air bubble until it gets what it wants and then returns to the air. It survives in the water because it is surrounded by air.

Our God surrounds us; we are immersed in his presence. St Paul tells us this when he says 'In him we live and move and have our being' (Acts 17:28). In baptism, our being immersed in water is an outward sign of our total immersion in the presence and power of God.

Intercessions

Blessed are you, Father, Son and Holy Spirit,
for you are ever with us and never leave us.
You are our Creator, Redeemer and Guide.
We come from you.
We belong to you.
We will return to you.
Blessed are you, Father, Son and Holy Spirit.

We give thanks for all your baptised and faithful people.
May we all rejoice in your presence and in your power.
We ask your blessing on all who are being prepared
for baptism, confirmation or ordination.
We pray for Church schools and Sunday schools,
for Bible classes and study groups.
We remember all who are seekers
and long to know you.

Silence

Hear us and help us,
Father, Son and Holy Spirit.

We pray for all who are beginning new work
or new ventures.
We remember especially
any who are leaving home for the first time.
We ask your blessing
upon those forming new relationships
and all who are newly married.
We pray for those who have the care of young families
and we remember any who are struggling at this time.

Silence

Hear us and help us,
Father, Son and Holy Spirit.

We give thanks for our own homes and loved ones.
We ask your blessing upon our parents and godparents,
upon our children and godchildren.
We pray for all who influence our lives
by their teaching or by their example.

Silence

Hear us and help us,
Father, Son and Holy Spirit.

We pray for all who are struggling with life,
those who are burdened with guilt or anger,
all who have memories that disturb them.
We remember all who are ill at home or in hospital,
especially any who feel lonely or unwanted.
We pray for all who have been taken into care this week.

Silence

Hear us and help us,
Father, Son and Holy Spirit.

We give thanks for all who have enriched our lives
by their goodness and care.
We pray for friends and loved ones
who are departed from us.
May they know your love in the fullness of life eternal.

Silence

Merciful Father,
accept these prayers
for the sake of your Son,
our Saviour Jesus Christ.
Amen.

Memory verse

Do not fear, for I have redeemed you; I have called you by your name, you are mine.
Isaiah 43:1b

Suggested music

Hail to the Lord's anointed
Spirit divine, attend our prayers
Spirit of the living God (Iverson)

CANDLES

Aim

To help the children to know that God is always with us.

Teaching

Everyone has a name. Let me tell you about someone in the room and see if you can guess their name. (Say what colours the person is wearing, what their hair is like, etc.) Once a name is guessed, describe someone else. After a while get everyone to say their name and see how many of the children can write their name.

Ask them if they know when they got their name. Tell them your name and that you got it when you were baptised. Talk about baptism. Look at the font or show a picture of a font. Ask what you need for baptism. You need water and some special words and you need your name. God knows us all by our names because he loves us. The special words are 'I baptise you (say your Christian name) in the name of the Father, the Son and the Holy Spirit.

Baptism tells us:

- God the Father loves us and is with us.
- Jesus loves us and is with us.
- The Holy Spirit loves us and is with us.

(Get the children to say each of the three sentences after you.)

To remind us we sometimes say:

The Lord is here:
his Spirit is with us.

If I say the first bit, you say the second. Now let us say it louder.

Activity

Have a small bowl – or better still, a portable font if the church has one – and tell them you are going to show them how a baby is given its name. Choose a group to bring the doll to the font. You can have two parents and godparents. The children need to decide if it is a boy or a girl and what the name is. Get the children to start with:

The Lord is here:
his Spirit is with us.

Tell them to be very quiet and know that God loves them and is with them. Get them to close their eyes and then say quietly:

The Lord is here:
his Spirit is with us.

Now we want the baby to know God is with her/him. So we will say its name and 'I baptise you in the name of the Father, and of the Son, and of the Holy Spirit.'

We might not remember it but we were baptised like this and given our name.

Let us hold the baby up high and say:

The Lord is here:
his Spirit is with us.

Prayer

God, we thank you for loving us.
You know us by our name
and care for each one of us.
Amen.

Song

Father, we adore you

LAMPS

Aim

To get the children to look at the baptism of Jesus according to St Luke.

Teaching

Many people were making their way to the river Jordan where John the Baptist was at work. Who knows what John was doing? Baptist is not an English word; if it was translated, it would probably mean 'the Dipper' because he dipped or plunged people in the river. Can you invent another nickname for him – 'the Plunger', 'the Soaker', 'the Washer'? Not one of them sounds as good as 'the Baptist', though my favourite is 'John the Dunker'. Do you know what dunking is? It is when you dip a biscuit in your drink until the biscuit takes up some of the liquid: biscuit and liquid become one. If you leave it too long, the biscuit will become too much like liquid. (You could demonstrate this!)

John was dunking people in the river Jordan. He was dipping them in the water to wash away any sin or wickedness they had done, so that they could have a clean start. This is why he was called 'the Baptist'.

People from all over the area were coming to John to be baptised, to be washed in the Jordan. Tax collectors, soldiers and all sorts of people came. He was making people think about God and his love.

Jesus came. He had done no wrong but he wanted to share with the people in their turning to God. He was baptised by John in the Jordan. When he came out of the water and was praying, the heavens opened and the Holy Spirit, in the shape of a dove, came upon Jesus.

Then there was a voice from the Father in heaven saying to Jesus, 'You are my Son, the Beloved; with you I am well pleased.'

Jesus was now 30 years old. All this time he had been at Nazareth. Now his new work would begin. He knew by his baptism that he was ready to start his new work.

Activity

Play 'In the Jordan and out the Jordan'.

Get the children to stand in a line. At the command 'In the Jordan' they jump forward. If they are already in the Jordan, they stand still. At the command 'Out the Jordan' they jump backwards on to the bank. If they are already on the bank, they stand still.

At the commands 'On the Jordan' or 'In the bank' they are not to move at all. Anyone who moves when they should not is out – even if it is just a good wobble.

Prayer

God, we thank you for our baptism
and that you are always with us,
Father, Son and Holy Spirit.
Amen.

Song

Father, we love you

TORCHES

Aim

To see the baptism of Jesus as manifesting his relationship with the Father.

Teaching

Show a glass of water and ask the group what water can do. Write up on a board the powers of water.

- Water gives life.
- Water washes.
- Water provides power.
- Water destroys.

If possible, you could have illustrations or headlines of water in these various modes. You could explore the need in much of the world for clean water and water available on tap.

John the Baptist wanted people to turn to God. He wanted them to know forgiveness of sins.

He wanted them to know the power of God and that God gives life. He decided the best way he could do this and get people to understand was to immerse them in water, the water of the river Jordan. Here their sins could be washed away and they could walk in newness of life. Here their past wrongs would be destroyed and they would know of the love and power of God. Soldiers and tax collectors came, as well as lots of other people. All wanted to turn to God and have their sins forgiven.

Jesus came. He did not need to come for forgiveness but he came because so many people were turning to God. Jesus came to be immersed in the love of God the

Father. John was surprised that Jesus came to him but he baptised Jesus, dipping him in the Jordan. When Jesus came out of the water and was praying he knew the Spirit of God was with him, just as the dove at that moment descended on him. He then heard the Father speak to him, saying, 'You are my Son, the Beloved; with you I am well pleased.' The baptism of Jesus reveals – manifests – his special relationship with the Father. Jesus is God's Son and beloved by God the Father.

Jesus knew that his life in Nazareth was now at an end. He was 30 years old and now his special work to show the love of God was to begin.

Activity

Explore the uses of water and relate them to baptism. Then explore the images of the Trinity as found in the baptism of Jesus.

A cloud and a voice often represent the hidden presence of the Father. The Father is heard but not seen. Sometimes the drawing of a hand at the edge of the cloud represents the hidden presence.

Jesus is represented as a human; it is only after the resurrection that his hands bear the print of nails.

The dove represents the Holy Spirit. At other times the Spirit is represented by fire and wind, symbols of power.

Draw the baptism of Jesus and include the symbols for the Father and the Holy Spirit.

Prayer

Father, Son and Holy Spirit,
we give thanks to you for our baptism
and the knowledge that you are always with us,
loving and caring and guiding us at all times.
Amen.

Song

Have you heard the raindrops

Second Sunday of Epiphany

Aim

To show that the presence of Jesus transforms our lives.

Preparation

Have the Advent/Christmas candles at the front ready to be lit.

Opening activity

Let five people speak and be given a lighted taper to light one of the candles.

I am empty and need filling with something.
Come, Lord, fill me with your love.
(*Light candle 1*)

I am drained out and need new power.
Come, Lord, fill me with your power.
(*Light candle 2*)

My batteries are flat and I cannot go.
Come, Lord, fill me with your life.
(*Light candle 3*)

I feel I am scraping the bottom of the barrel.
Come, Lord, fill me with your joy.
(*Light candle 4*)

The box is empty and I am in the dark.
Come, Lord, fill me with your light.
(*Light candle 5*)

Opening prayer

Come, Lord of light and love,
change us and we shall be changed.
Fill us with your peace and with your power
that we may rejoice in your presence
and live to your glory.
Amen.

Opening song

I, the Lord of sea and sky

Readings

Isaiah 62:1-5
Psalm 36:5-10
1 Corinthians 12:1-11
John 2:1-11

Thought for the day

Epiphany is about Jesus being revealed to the world as someone special.

To the wise men he was revealed as 'the king of the Jews', a title used by Herod but kept by the Jews for the Messiah, the Christ, the Holy One of God.

The Baptism revealed Jesus as the Son of God, another title for the Messiah; and through the quoting of Isaiah 42 and 53 Jesus is also revealed as the Suffering Servant. With Jesus, Cross and Crown go together.

This week is the third part of the manifestations and that is through signs of power – what we usually call miracles. Miracles are wonderful events that defy full explanation – if they can be explained, then they are not miracles. Miracles point to Jesus as God's agent – as God himself – at work on earth.

Today's setting for the miracle is a wonderfully ordinary event, a wedding. Cana is a village near Nazareth and here a young couple are celebrating. It is good to know that Jesus, together with his mother and his disciples, is there and enjoying the wedding. For Jewish celebration, wine was essential. There was a saying of the Rabbis: 'Without wine there is no joy.' For the wine to run out was a disaster for the couple. The joy and celebrations would drain away: the party would be over.

Into this situation Mary invites Jesus to do something. Jesus looked at the six water jars that were used for washing. Each jar held between 20 and 30 gallons. Jesus asked the servants to fill the jars and they did so. Now they were to carry them to the steward of the feast. Again they obeyed Jesus. When the steward tasted the water it had become good wine. A miracle! The steward did not know it was a miracle; only the servants knew. The steward congratulated the bridegroom on keeping the best wine till last.

Jesus could take ordinary water from the well and through his power it would become wine. He seems the sort of person a lot of people would like to follow. But we must not lose sight of the sign. The miracle points to Jesus doing only what God can do. This miracle and all miracles point to Jesus as the Son of God; that is, Jesus *is* God.

Question time

Three weeks in a row we have had a revelation of who Jesus is. Can you tell of the three events?

Which revelation do you like best as a pointer to Jesus as God?

Illustration

The car was running well, there was nothing wrong with the engine or the electrics but it suddenly came to a halt. It had juddered for a while and then came to a standstill. There was no way it would start again for it had run out of fuel.

The driver had to sit there on a lonely country road hoping for help. Fortunately there came a farmer on a tractor and he offered to give the car a tow. The driver was not keen as this was quite a new car. When the farmer looked he realised the car had run out of petrol. He had a full can on the farm, so he went away but soon returned and poured the petrol into the tank. He gave the petrol to the driver as a gift and said as he saw him off, 'None of us can run on an empty tank.'

There are times in life when our human resources run out. Then the harder we try, the worse it gets. There are many people who are drained or running near empty; now and again we all need our batteries recharged.

Listen to these words: 'Those who wait for the Lord shall renew their strength' (Isaiah 40:31); or these words of Jesus: 'Come to me, all you who are weary and are carrying heavy burdens, and I will give you rest' (Matthew 11:28).

Intercessions

Blessed are you, Lord our God,
giver of joy and life.
To you be praise and glory for ever.
In your presence is the fullness of joy.
With you is life and life eternal.

Lord God, strength of the weak
and light to all who walk in darkness,
help us to proclaim your saving power
not only in words but also by our lives.
Help us to reveal the joy
of knowing you and your love.
We ask you to bless all preachers and teachers of the faith.
Guide all who study Scriptures
and all who are learning through the example of others.
We pray for all who are being prepared for Confirmation
at this time.

Silence

Lord of life and love,
renew and refresh us.

Lord, we pray for the world
and a right use of its resources.
We ask your blessing
upon any who are suffering from natural disasters,
upon those suffering from famine or flood.
We remember all whose resources are running low
and we pray for the world poor
and all who are without work or proper shelter.

Silence

Lord of life and love,
renew and refresh us.

We give thanks
for all who have supplied us with our daily needs,
for our homes and for our loved ones.
We ask your blessing on homes
that are suffering from great debt
or where the household is unable to cope
through various troubles.

Silence

Lord of life and love,
renew and refresh us.

We give thanks for our well-being
and we pray for all who are struggling at this time.
We remember those who are suffering
from physical disability or weakness,
all who are losing agility or mobility.
We pray for all who do not have the strength
to cope on their own.
We ask your blessing
upon all who have been taken into care.

Silence

Lord of life and love,
renew and refresh us.

We give thanks for the resurrection of our Lord
and for the promise of life eternal.
We pray for our friends and loved ones departed
and ask that they may know
newness and fullness of life in your kingdom.
We rejoice in the fellowship of all your saints
and pray that we may share with them in glory.

Silence

Merciful Father,
accept these prayers
for the sake of your Son,
our Saviour Jesus Christ.
Amen.

Memory verse

With you is the fountain of life, and in your light we see light.
Psalm 36:9

Suggested music

Jesus the Lord said: 'I am the Bread'
Give me joy in my heart.
Joy to the world

CANDLES

Aim

To show Jesus can change things for the better.

Teaching

(Cut out a large water pot from thick paper or card, using the template on the worksheet.)

Show a picture of a wedding. Here is a picture of something special. Who knows what is happening? It is a wedding. Has anyone been a bridesmaid or a pageboy? Tell us what you had to do. What happened after the marriage ceremony? Was there a wedding party with lovely things to eat and drink?

Jesus was invited to a wedding. His mother was there helping and his disciples went with him. It was at a place called Cana (let us all say 'Cana'). The roads to Cana were hot and very dusty. This meant that their feet in sandals got very dirty. So when Jesus and the disciples got to the door of the house, a helper came from the house and they poured water over their hands and feet. They did not have water from a tap. The water was from a well and was in six very big water pots. Let us count the water pots: 1, 2, 3, 4, 5, 6. Soon the water pots were nearly empty

Once they had washed, they all joined the wedding party and there were lots of lovely things to eat and wine to drink. After a while Mary heard the servants saying, 'I cannot find any more wine. There is no wine left and we cannot give people the water to drink because it is dirty water.'

When Mary heard this she went to Jesus and said, 'Please help, for they have run out of wine.' Do you think Jesus could help? Yes, he could. Then Mary said to the servants, 'Do whatever Jesus tells you.'

Because Jesus loves people and does not want them to be sad, he decided to help out at the party. Jesus said to the servants, 'Fill the water pots with water', and they did, right to the top. (Colour the water pot blue right up to the top.)

They did what Jesus asked them. When he asked them to take it to the person in charge of the wedding they obeyed Jesus again. Then the person in charge tasted what was in the water pots and he was surprised. It was lovely wine. (Colour the other side of the water pot red right up to the top.)

He did not know that Jesus had changed the water into wine. But he thought it was very good wine.

Jesus did not want the party to be a sad one. He wanted the people to be happy. He did not want them to run out of what they needed so he turned the water into wine. He was able to do it because the servants obeyed him.

Activity

Play 'Simon says'. You must do whatever Simon tells you to do if he starts with the words 'Simon says'. If I say, 'Simon says: run', you must run. If I say, 'Simon says: stand still', you must stand still. But if I tell you to do something without saying 'Simon says', you must not do it. If you even begin to do it, you are out. The one who stays in the longest is the winner.

(Practise this once or twice before anyone goes out.)

There is a big water pot to colour. We begin with it empty and so it is just white. As the servants draw water from the well the pot is filled so colour it blue. When Jesus tells them to take it to the person in charge and the servants obey, it becomes wine – so colour the other side red.

Prayer

Jesus, you do wonderful things
when we obey you.
We thank you for making us happy today.
Amen.

Song

Jesus' love is very wonderful

LAMPS

Aim

To show how Jesus changed water into wine.

Teaching

What do you like drinking best of all? Tea? Coffee? Cocoa? Milk? Orange? Water?

Who can tell the difference between orange and water? Who can tell the difference between lemonade and water? (You might like to blindfold someone and see if they can tell the difference between orange and water or coke and water by the smell alone and then by taste.) We can tell the difference by how it looks, by its smell and by its taste. You would not make a mistake.

Once there was a village wedding in a place called Cana. It was in the middle of a hot dusty country. When people arrived at the house for the wedding party it was the custom for their hands and feet to be washed at the door of the house. For this purpose, there were six large water pots near the door of the house. They were filled with water for washing; it was not drinking water, though sometimes the animals drank it. By the time all the guests had arrived the water pots were getting low on water.

Jesus was at the wedding and so were some of his disciples and his mother, Mary. After they had been enjoying the party for a while, Mary heard someone say that the party was running out of wine. The poor bride and bridegroom would be really embarrassed. But Mary told Jesus and asked him to help and told the servants to obey Jesus, no matter what he asked. 'Do whatever he tells you.' The servants were used to being obedient and were ready to do whatever Jesus asked them.

Jesus asked them to go to the well and get enough water to fill all six water pots right up to the brim. This took a little while but they obeyed Jesus. Then he asked them to give some water from one of the pots to the governor, the man in charge of the wedding feast. Again the servants obeyed, though they wondered what the governor would say to them when he was given washing-up water to drink. The governor took the water, drank it and smiled. 'This is really good wine,' he said. The servants smiled also because they knew they had taken it from one of the washing-up pots. They would have to look at it, smell it and maybe even taste it. Jesus had made the water turn into wine. Nobody knew about this; only the servants who obeyed him knew – though everyone was happy drinking the wine.

This was the first miracle that Jesus did. It was a sign that Jesus was the Son of God. It was also a sign of how much Jesus loved and cared for people.

Activity

Play 'Simon says'. You must do whatever Simon tells you to do if he starts with the words 'Simon says'. If I say, 'Simon says: run', you must run. If I say, 'Simon says: stand still', you must stand still. But if I tell you to do something without saying 'Simon says', you must not do it. If you even begin to do it, you are out. The one who stays in the longest is the winner.

Have the group act out the miracle at Cana and get them to understand the words of Mary: 'Do whatever he tells you.'

Prayer

Lord Jesus, help us to know
that in obeying you
our lives are enriched and changed
into something precious and wonderful.
Amen.

Song

Rejoice in the Lord

TORCHES

Aim

To show that when our resources run out, God's resources do not.

Teaching

Imagine going on a journey to one of the planets. You will need a good power supply, as well as plenty of air to breathe, food to eat and something to drink. People can last quite a long time without food, less time without water and a lot less time without air. For such a long journey you need to make sure that all the supplies are in sufficient quantities. (You might like to plan what you need.)

For any event we need to plan our resources. If you were going to have a party what would you plan to have for 20 people? What would happen if 50 turned up? You would most likely run out of supplies.

Planet earth has limited supplies of many things – fossil fuels (coal, oil, gas, petrol) are all in limited amounts. If we use them up, another generation will have to find different sources of energy (atomic, wind, waves and, we hope, new forms not yet discovered). In the same way, food is in limited supply, as is water in some areas. Sometimes supplies become limited through natural disasters – such as floods or droughts. It is wonderful when we who have plenty can help to meet the needs of those who have run out of resources. (Look at examples of famine relief.)

Jesus went to a village wedding celebration in Cana of Galilee. His mother was there and so were some of his disciples. The bride and groom wore crowns for the party. The party itself could go on for a whole week and anyone who was in the area could just drop in. It was hard to plan how much you might need. Suddenly Mary heard the servants say, 'We are running out of wine.' This would be very sad for it meant the end of the party. People did not drink water because it was not safe to drink. Wine was their only drink and it was running out. It was sad and rather embarrassing for the couple.

Mary told Jesus about it and said to the servants, 'Whatever he says to you, do it.' The servants were used to obeying, so it was not difficult for them.

Jesus told them to fill the large water pots that were used for washing. The servants obeyed and filled the six pots right up to the brim. They were used to this and it was easy. Next Jesus asked them to do something harder: take some of the water to the person in charge of the party. What would he say when he tasted the washing-up water? The servants were not sure but they obeyed Jesus.

When the person in charge tasted what was given him, he looked at the servants and smiled. This was good wine, the best wine. He even went and congratulated the bridegroom on keeping the best wine till last. He did not know where the wine came from. Only the servants who obeyed Jesus knew of this wonderful transformation.

St John tells us this is the first miracle that Jesus did – and what a wonderful miracle. Water turned into wine. Who can do that? Only God can do it, usually by a slower method of rain and grapes growing. We see Jesus coming to the aid of people whose resources are low. In the same way, he heals the sick, he brings joy to the sad, he brings life to the dead. Jesus can do this because he is God. The same Jesus brings strength to our weakness and is always ready to renew and refresh us.

Activity

Explore areas where resources run low and see how they can be restored. Get them to understand that if you constantly pour something out, it will run dry unless it is replenished in some way. The charging of a car battery as it goes is a wonderful example. If it goes flat, then it needs to be put on a charger.

Discuss the text: 'Those who wait for the Lord shall renew their strength' (Isaiah 40:31).

Prayer

Come, Lord, to our weakness
and fill us with your power.
Come to our weariness and renew us.
Come to our troubles with your peace.
Come, Lord, change us and we shall be changed.
Amen.

Song

Jesus put this song into our hearts

Third Sunday of Epiphany

Aim
To show how Jesus begins his ministry through the Church and the Scriptures.

Preparation
Have the Advent/Christmas candles ready and ask five people to light them.

Opening activity
Light the candles with the five people coming from different areas of the church.

> I light this candle for Jesus who has come to bring us Good News.
> (*Light candle 1*)
>
> I light this candle for the freedom that Jesus brings to the world.
> (*Light candle 2*)
>
> I light this candle for Jesus, the Light of the World, who opens the eyes of the blind.
> (*Light candle 3*)
>
> I light this candle for Jesus our King; his kingdom has come.
> (*Light candle 4*)
>
> I light this candle for the Good News that Jesus is here.
> (*Light candle 5*)

All five say: The Lord is here.
Response: **His Spirit is with us.**

Opening prayer
O God, who has given us the Holy Scriptures
for our learning,
may we read, study and learn your Holy Word
and obey your will,
that your kingdom may come in us and through us
in the power of Jesus Christ our Lord.
Amen.

Opening song
God's Spirit is in my heart.

Readings
Nehemiah 8:1-3, 5, 6, 8-10
Psalm 19
1 Corinthians 12:12-31a
Luke 4:14-21

Thought for the day
Jesus was baptised by John and then spent 40 days in prayer and fasting. He was now ready to begin his mission and there were certain decisions to be made.
Where would he start, in what place?
What would he use for guidance?

Jesus began in Galilee. This was probably the least conservative area of Palestine because Gentiles, people of other nations, surrounded it. It was also very heavily populated: from here Jesus could reach many people and meet many needs. Josephus, who had been governor of Galilee, says it had 204 villages and towns and none with a population of less than 15,000. This means there could have been about three million people in Galilee. Jesus began where life was busy and there were many people. The beginning of his mission in a Gentile-friendly area points the way to the mission to the Gentiles in Acts.

He began by teaching in the Synagogue. The synagogue was the regular place of worship for every Jew. The law said that wherever there are ten Jewish families there must be a synagogue. The synagogue service was divided in three parts: worship, Scripture reading and teaching. Because there were no professional ministers anyone could be invited to teach. Here Jesus began and we are told all held him in high esteem. The positive reaction of the Jews shows that many of them were ready to embrace the Good News that Jesus brought.

He came to his hometown. Nazareth could not be called a village as it had a population of about 20,000. He went to the synagogue 'as was his custom'. The ministry and teaching of Jesus did not break with Judaism but grew out of it. There in the synagogue Jesus read Isaiah 61:1, 2 and 58:6 from a scroll, about God restoring the broken world and bringing in his kingdom:

> The Spirit of the Lord is upon me,
> because the Lord has anointed me
> to bring good news to the oppressed:
> to bind up the brokenhearted,
> to proclaim liberty to the captives
> and release to the prisoners,
> to proclaim the year of the Lord's favour.

When we are told Jesus 'sat down', this is what a Rabbi, a teacher, did; he sat down to teach and that is why all eyes are upon him. How surprised they must have been when he said, 'Today, this Scripture has been fulfilled in your hearing.'

Do we see these words as the mission of the Church and the sharing with Christ of bringing in God's kingdom? Like Jesus we should start in our own area and bring the Good News to bear on what we do.

Question time
Are we attentive to the Scriptures in a way that allows them to speak to us, or do we bring our prejudices and set patterns to them and so not allow them to move us?

Are we aware enough of the 'today' element in God at work, or do we put it off to some mysterious future?

Illustration
There is the story of a Celtic monk who decided to give up study and only to pray. His abbess asked how his mind would be fed if he gave up study. The monk persisted and said that he would leave where he was

and go and search for God overseas. The abbess replied, 'If God cannot be found on this side of the sea, by all means let us journey overseas. But since God is near all those who call on him, we have no need to cross the sea. The kingdom of God can be reached from every land.'

There is a great need for us to know that God is with us today and God desires to bring in his kingdom through us today. Psalm 95 need always be heeded: 'O that today you would listen to his voice!' (verse 7).

Intercessions

Blessed are you, Lord our God,
for by your Word all of life came into being.
You are the Creator, Redeemer
and Sustainer of our world.
Today we rejoice in your presence and in your love.
May we heed your guidance through the Scriptures
and work for the coming of your kingdom.

We give thanks
for all who preach and teach the Good News.
We ask your blessing upon all who translate
and publish the Scriptures,
upon those who provide Bible notes and commentaries.
We pray for all who study and read the Scriptures
and for any who meditate upon your word.
May we at all times be open to your presence
and your love.

Silence

Lord, your word
gives life to us and to the world.

We give thanks for all who strive
to bring freedom and well-being to peoples and nations.
We remember any who are struggling
under oppression or captivity,
all who live in poverty or are homeless.
We pray for those who suffer from injustice or violence,
all who are victims of greed or insensitivity.
We ask you to bless the work of the United Nations
and all peacekeeping forces.

Silence

Lord, your word
gives life to us and to the world.

We give thanks for our homes
and for all who have cared for us and taught us.
Help us to be aware of your presence
in our homes and our loved ones.
We pray for any children who have been taken into care
or who are separated from their parents
due to illness or family problems.
We remember all who struggle with bad housing
or live in deprived areas.

Silence

Lord, your word
gives life to us and to the world.

We give thanks for our vision, our sight and insight.
We pray for all who suffer from blindness
or restricted vision.
We remember those who have lost sight of you
or have no hope for the future.
We ask your blessing upon all who are ill,

who are in pain or in sorrow at this time.
We pray for all who are bereaved
and all who are lonely.

Silence

Lord, your word
gives life to us and to the world.

We give thanks for the gift of life and life eternal.
We rejoice in the fellowship of all your saints in glory.
We remember friends and loved ones
who are departed from us.
May they share with your saints
in that life and love which are eternal.

Silence

Merciful Father,
accept these prayers
for the sake of your Son,
our Saviour Jesus Christ.
Amen.

Memory verse

Today this Scripture has been fulfilled in your hearing.
Luke 4:21

Suggested music

We have a gospel to proclaim
Lord, thy word abideth
O for a thousand tongues to sing

CANDLES

Aim

To encourage the children to see that Jesus came to do special work.

Teaching

Who can remember where Jesus grew up? It was Nazareth. Let us all say 'Nazareth'.

At Nazareth, Jesus worked with Joseph in his workshop as a carpenter. Who knows what a carpenter does? Yes, he makes things with wood. The mother of Jesus looked after them and made sure they had plenty of food and that the house was always tidy. Everyone in Nazareth knew Jesus and that he worked as a carpenter. Every Sunday they all went to church. Does anyone know the name of the church Jesus went to? It was called a synagogue. That is a hard word to remember. Let us say it together: 'Synagogue'.

One day after he had grown up to be a man and been away from home for some time he came back to Nazareth and went to the synagogue to pray. Jesus went to the synagogue every week. It was probably here that he learnt to read. Now he stood up to read. He was given a scroll to read from. (Explain how a scroll is like a rolled-up book, and show them one you have made. Tell them we can all make scrolls afterwards.) Jesus had to unroll the pages until he came to the place where it was written: 'The Spirit of the Lord is upon me.'

Jesus read to them about how the blind would be able to see and how prisoners would be given freedom. Then Jesus sat down. Everyone waited for him to say more and while he sat he told them how he had come to heal the blind and to free the prisoners. People could not believe it. They thought, 'We know him. He is only a carpenter. Where did he learn to do such things?'

But Jesus was now ready to do the work God the Father had sent him to do. Jesus had special work to do that no one else could do. After John had baptised Jesus, Jesus was ready to do this work. (Explore with the children some of the things Jesus did. See if they know of any of the healing miracles.)

Activity

Let everyone make a scroll. On the scroll they can draw a picture of Jesus helping people. Those who are able to could copy the prayer and put it on the scroll to be used at home.

Prayer

Jesus, you are very special.
You care for all people
and want to help them.
Jesus, we thank you.
Amen.

Song

Jesus' hands were kind hands

LAMPS

Aim

To discover that Jesus had special work to do.

Teaching

Who knows what the Rescue Services do? They are the fire brigade, the ambulance workers, the police, the lifeboat people. Get the children to add other names and groups of people. If someone fell down a deep hole, how would they be rescued and by whom?

After Jesus had been baptised, he knew that his special work had to begin. He started by teaching in the synagogues of Galilee. The synagogue was where every Jew met to pray and where people were invited to speak about the Scriptures. Jesus was beginning to tell them of his rescue mission, that he was sent by God and anointed by God, to bring the people back to God. He was aware that the Spirit of God had come upon him in baptism. (Review this and see that the children are aware of the baptism of Jesus, with the descent of the dove and the voice from the cloud.)

When Jesus went to Nazareth, where he grew up, he went to the synagogue on the Sabbath as he always did. (Check that they all understand these terms.) When it came to reading the lesson, Jesus was given a scroll of the prophet Isaiah. He unwound the scroll and read from near the end of it. He read, 'The Spirit of the Lord

is upon me.' Because he knew this was about him, he wanted to tell all the people. After he read it he sat down and began to teach them. He told them how God had chosen him to bring Good News to people. He was sent to give sight to the blind and to bring freedom to people who were captives to sickness or evil. It was all very exciting. Jesus was a special rescue service sent by God. Some people thought it was wonderful.

There were others who could not believe it. They said, 'Is not this Mary's son? Did he not work as a carpenter with Joseph? We know his family and the school he went to. How can he be God's Chosen One?' They refused to listen to Jesus and so he was not able to help them.

Jesus does not force himself upon people. He does not bully. He gives us the choice to listen to him and love him or refuse to be bothered. Jesus wanted to be friends with them all but some would not listen. Are you ready to listen to Jesus and to love him? Let us play a game about listening and see if you are good listeners.

Activity

Play 'Chinese whispers' and see how well the group can pass around a simple message.

Pass around the words 'Jesus loves you'. Then send around 'Jesus wants us to listen to him and love him'. Try a few messages for the fun of it. 'The fire-brigade is a rescue service' or 'Rescues at sea are done by the lifeboat people'.

Prayer

Lord Jesus, help us to be quiet
and to listen to what you say to us.
Let us be ready to share in your work
of rescuing any who are in trouble or need.
Amen.

Song

The image of the invisible God

TORCHES

Aim

To explore the idea of the God of today.

Teaching

When you talk of God, what tense do you use? Most people talk of what God has done and their God is often a God of the past. Sometimes it sounds as if God finished his work some time before we were born! Others talk about what God will do at the end of the world. Their talk is all about the future and into it they project their hopes and their fears. Because we believe we are dealing with the living God, we should make sure we talk of the God who is, who is present, who is with us, who hears us and who answers our prayers. The great revelation to Moses was God saying, 'I AM' (Exodus 3:13, 14). God is not a theory but a person and we meet him and make friends with him in our daily lives.

When Jesus read the passage from Isaiah in the synagogue he sat down and then he said, 'Today, this Scripture has been fulfilled in your hearing.'

What the Scriptures talk about when they talk of God are not past events but events that are happening now. They are events that are eternal and that means we can experience them today. Look at:

- Psalm 95:7 – 'O that today you would listen to his voice!'
- Isaiah 43:18, 19 – 'Do not remember the former things, or consider the things of old. I am about to do a new thing; now it springs forth, do you not perceive it?'

Think what it means when God says to Joshua, 'As I was with Moses, so will I be with you; I will not fail you or forsake you' (Joshua 1:5).

Talk of how our God is the living God and is always present in our lives. Ask the group to express this in any ways that they can.

Activity

Have Bibles and a concordance and explore the idea of the 'God of today'. Seek to help the group to understand that if God is eternal, he *is always*. Get the group to make a prayer or creed affirmation which starts each sentence with 'God is . . .' Let each in turn say, 'God is . . .' and add a word. Once a word is used, no one else in the group must use that word. You can then say, 'Jesus is . . .' and add a word or 'The Spirit is . . .' and add a word.

You may prefer to start each sentence with 'Today' – so, for example, 'Today God is . . .'

Prayer

O God, unseen yet ever-present,
help us to know you are with us
and that you give us power and courage
to do what you would have us do today.
Amen.

Song

This is the day, this is the day

Fourth Sunday of Epiphany

(Also for use on the Feast of the Presentation)

Aim

To rejoice in the light of Christ that has come into our world.

Preparation

This, or the feast of the Presentation is the last Sunday for the Advent/Christmas candles. If possible, have candles for everyone, or at least a representative from each family, to light during the service.

Opening activity

The Advent/Christmas candles are lit by five people coming from different areas of the church. As they light the candles each has a sentence to say:

Jesus Christ is the Light of the World.
(Light candle 1)

Jesus Christ is the Light that scatters the darkness.
(Light candle 2)

Jesus Christ is the Light to show us the way to the Father.
(Light candle 3)

Jesus Christ is the Light that leads us to eternal life.
(Light candle 4)

The Good News is that Jesus, the Light of the World, is with us now.
(Light candle 5)

All five say: The Lord is here.
Response: **His Spirit is with us.**

Let everyone receive a light from the main candles or from each other as the opening song is sung.

Opening song

The Lord is my light, my light and salvation

Opening prayer

Blessed are you, Lord our God,
for you have called us out of darkness
to share in your light.
The bright light of Christ scatters the darkness from within
and is a lantern to our path.
Bless these lights that we carry,
that they may remind us
of your presence and your saving love
revealed through Christ our Lord. Amen.

Readings

Ezekiel 43:27–44:4
Psalm 48
1 Corinthians 13:1-13
Luke 2:22-40

Thought for the day

(If you want the Jewish background to this visit to the Temple, read Leviticus 12.) Forty days after Jesus was born, as was the custom, Joseph and Mary presented Jesus to the priest in the Temple. This is a service of thanksgiving for the birth of a child and an offering to God. As they are not rich, Joseph and Mary do not bring a lamb as an offering but two doves instead. This is all quite normal and every Jewish family in their time could be found doing this. Suddenly into the normal comes something strange. Simeon is a devout man who looked forward to the time when the Messiah would appear. He has spent his life in prayer and waiting for the promised time; he has waited patiently for the coming One. How wonderful that he is present when Joseph and Mary present Jesus. Simeon takes the baby in his arms and in an instant knows this is the Chosen One. A thrill runs through his whole being; what he has waited for is now fulfilled. The words of Simeon have become known by the Latin translation of the words he starts with – Nunc Dimittis – and have become one of the great songs of the Church.

In verses 32 and 34 Simeon gives a summary of the work and the actions of Jesus: 'a light for revelation to the Gentiles and for the glory to your people Israel . . . this child is destined for the falling and the rising of many in Israel and to be a sign that will be opposed.'

Here is another Epiphany, another revealing of Jesus and who he is. Jesus is not only for the Jews but for the Gentiles too. Yet this will meet opposition.

Let us this day rejoice in the light of Christ, the light that scatters the darkness of sin and death, the light that leads us to eternal life. Let us make sure we place our lives in that light each day and that we live by that light.

Question time

Do we let the light of Christ transform the darkness of our life and our world?

How do we place ourselves each day in the love and light of Christ?

Illustration

As Simeon waited, his life was one of watchfulness and patience. We see a similar watchfulness in bird watchers. They place themselves where they believe things will happen. They prepare themselves with binoculars or telescopes. Then they wait, often in silence. This is an attentive waiting, a watchful waiting; they are alert and focused on their hoped-for sighting. There was a man who went in search of a rare owl this way. He waited for three days before it appeared. He saw it only for a few moments but he said he would remember it for the rest of his life. He just had to close his eyes to see it again. He knew what it really looked like. Many of us could learn to be more attentive and watchful towards our God.

Intercessions

By the mystery of the Word made flesh,
Lord, make yourself known to us.

By the coming of Christ, the Light of the World,
Lord, make yourself known to us.

By the birth of Jesus in Bethlehem,
Lord, make yourself known to us.

By his revealing to the shepherds and wise men,
Lord, make yourself known to us.

By his baptism, the voice from the cloud and the dove,
Lord, make yourself known to us.

By his changing water into wine,
Lord, make yourself known to us.

By his proclaiming of the Good News,
Lord, make yourself known to us.

God of light and love,
we remember before you
all who seek to proclaim the Good News.
We ask your blessing
upon all ministers of the word and the sacraments,
upon all who teach and preach in your name.
We pray for all who are striving
to bring the light of Christ to darkened lives.

Silence

Light of God,
shine upon us.

We remember all who live in darkness and in fear.
We pray for the persecuted and the homeless,
for all who are captives or suffer from war or terrorism.
We ask your blessing
upon all who are anxious for their lives.

Silence

Light of God,
shine upon us.

We pray for all who suffer from blindness
or impairment of their sight,
for those who suffer from river blindness.
We ask you to bless
all who seek to relieve their suffering
and to restore sight.
We pray for any who have lost vision
of you and your love.

Silence

Light of God,
shine upon us.

We remember all who are in the valley
of the shadow of death,
all who have passed beyond it
to light and life eternal.
We pray for our loved ones departed from us.
May we all come to rejoice
in the fullness of your kingdom.

Silence

Merciful Father,
**accept these prayers
for the sake of your Son,
our Saviour Jesus Christ.
Amen.**

Memory verse

The Lord is my light and my salvation.
Psalm 27:1

Suggested music

Lord, the light of your love (*Shine, Jesus, shine*)
Faithful vigil ended
Christ is the world's true light

Just before the Peace get everyone to extinguish their candles. Then say:

> We turn away
> from the Christmas and Epiphany season
> and look towards Lent and the Passion of Christ.
> May the light of Christ ever shine
> within us and about us.

There should be enough action to keep all the young people in church today and let them enjoy and experience the lighted candles.

CANDLES

Aim

To show Simeon as one who waited for the coming of God's Chosen One.

Teaching

Have you ever had to wait a long time for anything? Tell me how long you have waited. Did you stand in a queue, or were you waiting at home? We have to wait for lots of nice things. Mothers have to wait until their baby is born. Is anyone here waiting for a baby brother or sister? Sometimes people have to wait for work or just wait for a letter in the post.

I want to tell you about someone who waited a long time to meet Jesus. His name was Simeon. Say that name after me: 'Simeon.' God had promised Simeon that one day he would meet the Christ. Simeon did not know what the Christ would look like but he was sure that he would know him if he ever met him. He knew God would help him. Then one day he felt that God wanted him to be in the Temple at a special time.

While he was there he saw Joseph and Mary and the baby Jesus. He took the baby in his arms to say thank you to God for the baby's life. As soon as he took hold of Jesus he knew he was holding a very special baby. He was holding the Christ, the One that God had sent. He stood looking at the baby and was very happy. He saw that Jesus would bring light and love to the world. Simeon told Joseph and Mary how wonderful the baby Jesus would be. Mary and Joseph did not know what to say. They were amazed at the words of Simeon and would not forget them.

Activity

Have a doll for Jesus and dress up a Joseph, a Mary and a Simeon and let the children act this story. There is a candle to colour and to use as a reminder that Jesus is the Light of the World.

Prayer

Jesus, be our friend.
Bring your love and your light into our lives.
Help us to know that you are always with us
and that you look after us.
Amen.

Song

This little light of mine (chorus)

LAMPS

Aim

To introduce them to Simeon and Anna.

Teaching

After Jesus was born Joseph and Mary took him to the Temple in Jerusalem. They were going to give thanks for the birth of Jesus and say how he belonged to God. They travelled all the way from Nazareth to Jerusalem. Jesus was only 40 days old. (Who would like to count to 40?) That means Jesus was still a very small baby. Mary would wrap him up well for the journey and then she would ride on a donkey carrying Jesus. Joseph walked in front of them. It would take them a few days to get there, so they probably camped at night.

When they came to the Temple there was a man called Simeon (let us say his name together). Simeon was a very holy man. God had told him that before he died he would see the Christ, the Chosen One of God. Simeon had waited a long time for this to happen. He did not know what the Christ would look like but he waited patiently and prayed to God. Mary and Joseph gave Jesus to Simeon so that he could say thank you to God for the baby. As soon as Simeon held Jesus he knew that this was the one he had been waiting for. Maybe he was a bit surprised that it was only a little baby but he knew that this was the Christ he was holding in his hands. This was the one chosen to be a light for the whole world. Simeon was very excited and told Joseph and Mary how special the baby Jesus is.

Not long after this there came a very old lady called Anna; she was 84. She never left the Temple but spent a lot of time praying, serving God and waiting for the Christ to come. She also started to talk to them of the Christ.

Joseph and Mary were amazed at what was said. When they left for home they talked about it on the way. They were now sure that Jesus was someone very special.

Activity

Act out the story. Dress children up as Joseph and Mary and have a doll for Jesus. Let them travel around the room for their journey. Get Simeon to meet them and let him get excited. Then get Anna also to meet them and get excited.

Prayer

Lord Jesus, it is wonderful to know you.
You are our friend and you are the Light
that chases away the darkness of our world.
Help us to love you every day. Amen.

Song

Jesus bids us shine

TORCHES

Aim

To think of the importance of waiting upon God.

Teaching

Forty days after Jesus was born Joseph and Mary took him to the Temple at Jerusalem. This was what every Jewish parent did when their child was 40 days old. They took him to the Temple to give thanks to God for his safe birth and to present him to God in thanksgiving.

In the Temple were a lot of very holy and good people. There were some special people who were called the 'quiet ones' or sometimes 'the quiet in the land'. These were people who spent a lot of time in prayer and who waited quietly and patiently on God. They believed that one day God's Anointed One, the Christ, would come. Simeon was one of the quiet ones. He believed that before he died he would actually see the Christ.

When Mary and Joseph brought Jesus to the Temple, Simeon was there. They gave the baby to Simeon so that he could give thanks to God for the baby's birth. As soon as Simeon took the baby in his arms and looked into his face he got very excited. He knew that in this little baby he was holding the Christ. What he had waited for all his life was here in this little baby. Holding the baby in his arms, Simeon praised God. Get someone to read, as dramatically as possible, Luke 2:29-32.

Joseph and Mary were amazed at these words. They would talk about them all the way back to Nazareth. As Simeon handed the baby Jesus back to them, another one of the Quiet Ones, this time a woman, came up to the family. Anna was very old; she was 84. She came to them and talked about the Christ who was to save his people. Joseph and Mary were not sure what to say. But they would remember their visit to the Temple. They would remember Simeon and Anna and that Jesus was called 'a light for revelation to the Gentiles'.

Activity

Look at the Nunc Dimittis (Luke 2:29-32) and get the group to discuss its meaning, verse by verse. See if they can write it out in their own words. Let them talk about the reaction of Simeon and Anna to the baby Jesus and what it meant.

Prayer

Jesus Christ, Light of the World,
scatter the darkness from about us and within us
and help us to walk as children of the light.
Help us to know that you love us
and are with us always. Amen.

Song

Colours of day

ORDINARY TIME
Proper 1

Sunday between 3 and 9 February inclusive
(if earlier than the Second Sunday before Lent)

Aim

To show that if we are faithful in small things, then we will be trusted to do greater things.

Preparation

Display alongside each other posters about vocations and notices about small jobs needing to be done in the church and community.

Opening activity

Voice 1 Would you help me to sweep the floor?
Voice 2 I have important things to do.
Voice 1 Would you give a hand with the dishes?
Voice 3 I have a lot on my plate at the minute.
Voice 1 Could you move that rubbish?
Voice 4 Who, me? You must be joking.
Voice 1 Would you help me to tidy up this mess?
Voice 5 Gladly. I cannot see it will take long.
Voice 1 At last someone I can depend on. I am sure we will do great things together.

Opening prayer

O God, as you have called us to work for you,
help us to be content to do small things
until you ask us to do something greater.
May we learn to do the little things
to your glory and for the joy of serving you.
Amen.

Opening song

Will you come and follow me

Readings

Isaiah 6:1-8 (9-13)
Psalm 138
1 Corinthians 15:1-11
Luke 5:1-11

Thought for the day

Luke never calls the 'Sea of Galilee' a sea (thalassa) but only a lake (limne). He calls it the Lake of Gennesaret. It is also known as the Sea of Tiberias. This lake is 13 miles long and about 8 miles wide. The river Jordan flows into it from the north and it flows out to the Dead Sea in the south. In the time of Jesus there were at least nine cities around the lake with a population of more than 15,000. Josephus records that on one expedition he was able to commandeer 240 fishing boats. Fish was sent from Galilee to Rome.

Today we hear of Jesus taking the Good News outside the synagogue. He sits in a boat to teach because the crowd had been pressing in on him. The boats belong to Simon Peter (and his brother Andrew who is not mentioned) and to the brothers James and John.

Notice how gently Jesus deals with people. From most of us he asks small things first. It is only if we are willing in the small request that can we expect Jesus to ask us to do something greater. Jesus gets into Simon Peter's boat and says, 'Put out a little way from the shore – just a little way from the land.' It is not asking much, yet the tired fisherman could have said, 'No'.

After speaking to the crowd Jesus turns to Simon Peter and says, 'Put out into deep water.' This was only possible after being in the shallows. The word for 'deep' is 'bathos' and it is a symbol for chaos (Genesis 1:2; Psalm 66:6; Isaiah 5:30). The deep sea was a fearful thing for many Jews, an element that cannot be controlled. Yet God calls into the deep of life and from the depths of our own being. Again Simon Peter could have refused. Discipleship comes through obedience.

Now Jesus says, 'Let down your nets for a catch.' Maybe at this moment the fisherman Simon Peter wonders what this carpenter knows about the sea. Fishing is done at night, and Simon Peter and his fellow fishermen have been out all night and caught nothing. It is interesting to discover how often God calls us through our emptiness or the fruitless tasks we have performed. (Isaiah experienced the empty throne before it was filled with the Presence.) Simon Peter answers, 'Master, we have worked all night long but have caught nothing.' How often is there a feeling of life slipping through the nets or through our fingers; is it all a waste of time? Yet Simon Peter continues: 'Yet if you say so, I will let down the nets.' Though reason and habit say, 'No', Simon Peter still obeys, and through obedience comes the miraculous catch of fish. A more miraculous catch is that of the fishermen. Once Simon Peter, James and John (and Andrew?) came to land their fish, Jesus said, 'Do not be afraid; from now on you will be catching people.' And they left everything and followed Jesus.

We must see this as a 'call narrative', where God calls someone to work for him (see Exodus 3:1-22; Isaiah 6:1-13; Jeremiah 1:4-13). The call authenticates the person and their vocation. This will remind the readers after the death and resurrection of Jesus that the apostles had been called by him.

Question time

Do you know that God calls us all, though only some of us respond?

Can we discover some small tasks we could do for the benefit of others and for the glory of God?

Illustration

Denzil was always talking of giving glory to God. The house he lived in was a tip. Every room was untidy if not unclean. Denzil continued to talk of praising God but gave little respect to the people around him. He seemed unaware of his surroundings or of others, only full of himself. One night he heard God in his dreams saying, 'If you want to serve me, start where you live. Give glory to me by tidying up your part of the world. You will hear me better if you learn to listen to others.' Denzil awoke, aware of how ugly his room looked. That day he started to clean up and get rid of rubbish. Soon he redecorated the room and added fresh curtains. He scrubbed himself and got new clothes. He seemed to be a different person: he actually glowed. If someone needed a person to listen or to care, Denzil was the one. By being attentive to small things, God had called him to do greater things for him.

Intercessions

Blessed are you, Lord our God,
for you have called us to know you,
to love you and to serve you.
We rejoice in your presence
and in your love for us.
Blessed are you, Father, Son and Holy Spirit.

We give you thanks, O God,
for all who have served you faithfully
throughout the ages.
We thank you especially today
for the prophet Isaiah and for the disciples.
We ask your blessing upon all who are called
to preach the word and to celebrate the sacraments.
We pray for theological colleges and their students
and for all your people in their various vocations.

Silence

Father, as you have called us,
give us the power to serve you.

We ask your blessing upon all who feel drained
of resources or energy.
We remember those who are handicapped
by poverty or by the prejudice of others.
We pray for people who feel they have lost their way
or who have been cast aside by society.
We remember the street children of the world
and those who live in slums.

Silence

Father, as you have called us,
give us the power to serve you.

We give thanks that you have called us to know you
and we pray that we may live to your glory.
May our homes and our relationships
reflect our love for you.
We remember before you
homes where there is tension or violence
or where there is neglect
and a lack of respect for each other.

Silence

Father, as you have called us,
give us the power to serve you.

We pray for all who are called to the healing professions.
We ask your blessing on doctors and surgeons,
on nurses and on ambulance crews.
We pray for all who are ill at home or in hospital

and we remember those who are unable to cope
on their own.

Silence

Father, as you have called us,
give us the power to serve you.

We give thanks that you have called us to life eternal.
We remember in your presence
friends and loved ones who are departed from us.
May they share with your saints
in the glory of your kingdom.

Silence

Merciful Father,
**accept these prayers
for the sake of your Son,
our Saviour Jesus Christ.
Amen.**

Memory verse

Here am I: send me.
Isaiah 6:8

Suggested music

I, the Lord of sea and sky
Jesus calls us: o'er the tumult
Follow me, follow me

CANDLES

Aim

To show how Jesus called the fishermen to be disciples.

Teaching

Who has been to the seaside? Did you walk along the beach? You may have seen some fishing boats. Has anyone been in a fishing boat?

Once Jesus was walking along the seashore. It was in the morning and there were crowds of people following him because they wanted to hear what he was teaching. Jesus wanted a place to sit where he could teach without the crowd squashing him. He saw some fishermen who were mending their nets beside their boats. He came to Simon Peter and asked if he could borrow his boat. He just wanted to sit in it and to teach the people. Would Simon Peter just push it out a little from the shore? Simon Peter was tired because he had been trying to catch fish all night but, because Jesus asked him, he let Jesus get into his boat and pushed it into the water. Simon Peter sat in the boat and kept it still while Jesus spoke to the people. Simon Peter listened to every word Jesus said.

After Jesus had finished speaking to the people he asked Simon Peter and Andrew, his brother, to take their boat out to sea into the deep water. They did what Jesus asked them. Then Jesus said, 'Throw out your net to catch the fish.' Simon Peter told him they had fished all night and caught nothing – not even one fish. But if Jesus wanted them to, they would do what he asked. Peter and Andrew threw the net into the sea (keeping one end fastened in the boat) and straightaway it was full of fish. There were so many fish in their net that the boat was tipping to the side. It was too heavy for them to pull all the fish in. So they signalled for help, and asked their friends, James and John, to come in their boat and help them. Soon they filled both boats with so many fish that they were nearly sinking in the water. They had never caught so many fish. They were amazed at the wonderful catch. They would be able to sell the fish for a lot of money.

When they came to land, Jesus asked them to leave all their fish, to leave their boats, to leave their homes and to follow him. He said to the fishermen, 'Come with me and from now on you will be catching people.' Simon Peter, Andrew, James and John left their boats and their fish with their families and they went with Jesus. These were the first disciples. (Let us say 'disciple'. It means someone who followed Jesus and learnt from him.) How many fishermen disciples were there? Let us say their names: Simon Peter, Andrew, James and John. Who was Andrew's brother? Who was the brother of James? Soon Jesus would have more disciples and there would be twelve.

Activity

Make some fish for a fishing competition and see who can catch the most (see the activity sheet). There is also a net on the sheet to fill with fish.

Prayer

God, we thank you
that Jesus called four fishermen to follow him.
Help us to follow Jesus each day
and to do what he would like us to do.
Amen.

Song

Wide, wide as the ocean

LAMPS

Aim

To show how the fishermen obeyed Jesus and caught a wonderful catch.

Teaching

A long time ago many people who lived beside the Sea of Galilee made their living at fishing. Some of the fish would be sent to Rome to feed the thousands of people who lived there. Fishing was a good way of earning money – as long as there were plenty of fish. Four fishermen – Simon Peter and Andrew, who were brothers, and James and John, who were also brothers – had been working all night, for that is the best time to catch fish. They had thrown their net out to the right side of the boat, waited a while and then hauled it in. They had caught nothing. They sailed along in their boat and then threw out their net on the left side of the boat, waited a

while and then hauled it in. They had caught nothing. (Repeat this sequence another couple of times and get the children to complete the sentence, 'They had caught . . .') By the time the sun was rising over the sea the fishermen gave up. It was as if there were no more fish in the sea. All they had caught was a few rocks; now they needed to go to the shore to mend their nets and then have a sleep.

While Simon Peter, Andrew, James and John were mending their nets Jesus came. He wanted to teach the people who were following him and he needed somewhere to sit. He asked Simon Peter if he could borrow his boat and if they would just push the boat out a little from the shore. Simon Peter did as Jesus asked even though he was now tired. The fishermen listened to the wonderful teaching of Jesus. Once he had finished, Jesus asked Simon Peter to go into the deep water and let down his net for a catch. Simon Peter felt like saying he was tired and they had fished all night. There was not much chance of catching anything. But again he obeyed Jesus and they let down their net. Immediately they felt a tug. There were fish in the net, lots of fish – so many fish their boat could not pull them in on its own. Peter and Andrew signalled to their friends (do the children know their names?). James and John came and they were amazed at the weight of the net because there were so many fish. They filled their boats with fish until the boats were so heavy they were nearly sinking. What a wonderful catch! They would be able to sell the fish for a lot of money. But Jesus had other ideas. These strong fishermen had done all that he asked them. He would like them to work with him. He would like them to leave the fish and their boats and help to catch people instead. Jesus said to them, 'Follow me; from now on you will help me to catch people.' The four fishermen (do the children remember their names?) left their boats and their homes to obey Jesus. They left everything and followed him.

Activity

Play 'Simon says'. Whenever the leader says, 'Simon says do this . . .' you are to do it. If the leader does not say, 'Simon says' and just says, 'Do this' or 'Do that', you are not to do it and whoever does it is out.

Prayer

Lord Jesus,
as the fishermen listened to you
and obeyed you,
help us to be ready to do what you want us to do.
Amen.

Song

Fisherman Peter on the sea

TORCHES

Aim

To explore how Jesus deals with the fishermen and how Simon Peter reacts.

Teaching

Read today's Gospel, Luke 5:1-11. (See how much drama you can get into the reading.) Now act out the events to show how Jesus calls the fishermen and how they react, especially Simon Peter. (It would be good if the final result could be videoed and watched later.)

Actors
Jesus, Simon Peter, Andrew, James and John. The rest can be the crowd.

Scene 1
It is night and the fishermen are trying to catch fish. Act the throwing out of the net and catching nothing. Do this several times and let them make comments about catching nothing.

Scene 2
The fishermen are sitting on the shore mending their nets. Jesus and a crowd appear. Jesus asks to use Simon Peter's boat. He sits in it and teaches the crowd. The boat is on the water and being controlled by Simon Peter and Andrew. Jesus asks them to go into the deep.

Scene 3
In the deep, Jesus asks them to throw out the net. Simon Peter tells him how they have worked all night and caught nothing. Andrew whispers, 'Jesus is a carpenter – what can he know about fishing?' But they do what Jesus asks. It is important for them to say, 'We will do what you say.' Then there is an amazing catch of fish. The boat cannot cope and they signal to James and John for help. They fill both boats until they nearly sink.

They have never had a catch like this. Simon Peter realises something special is at work and that Jesus is not just an ordinary person. He and all the disciples are afraid. Simon Peter says, 'Go away from me, I am not worthy.' But Jesus wants people like these fishermen who obeyed him to follow him.

Scene 4
When the fishermen come to land they are interested in their fish. All this fish means a lot of money. Jesus says to them, 'Follow me, from now on you will help me to catch people.' The fishermen look at their fish, look at their boats, and then give them to others in their family. It is important for them to show that they leave everything and follow Jesus.

Activity

The activity is the making of the video and the 'Look at Luke' on the activity sheet.

Prayer

Lord Jesus, as you called the fishermen
and they obeyed you,
help us to do what you would have us do
and to seek to be the people
you would have us be.
Amen.

Song

A stranger walked along the shore of Galilee
(verse 1 and chorus)

Proper 2

Sunday between 10 and 16 February inclusive
(if earlier than the Second Sunday before Lent)

Aim

To show that God is our key to happiness.

Preparation

Have pictures of happy people and a few pictures of people in the depths of despair (or drunk). Have a few captions with 'I would be happy if . . .'

Opening activity

Give everyone a piece of paper on which is written, 'I would be happy if . . .' Everyone fills these in. Some of them can be read out at the beginning of the service. Choose funny ones and sad ones as well as the obvious.

Opening prayer

O God, you are the giver of life and happiness,
on you our well-being depends.
Help us to know you are always present,
that you love us and offer us your strength.
Let us rejoice in you and in your care
as shown in Jesus Christ our Lord.
Amen.

Opening song

Seek ye first the kingdom of God

Readings

Jeremiah 17:5-10
Psalm 1
1 Corinthians 15:12-20
Luke 6:17-26

Thought for the day

There is a sequence that is very like that of Moses in Exodus. Jesus is in the wilderness and he then goes up a mountain to be alone with God. By going up the mountain Jesus is saying, 'Pay attention, for the words I am going to speak to you are special.' We are meant to encounter the word of God in the teaching of Jesus and to receive the light of God's presence. Jesus comes down and chooses the twelve disciples (like the twelve tribes of Israel). Jesus gives the twelve the title of 'apostles' for they are not only to be learners; they are to be sent by him. In the same way as Moses (Deuteronomy 1:1). Jesus addresses the crowd on the plain. In Matthew, what follows is known as the 'Sermon on the Mount'; in Luke, it is the 'Sermon on the Plain'.

People had come to Jesus for teaching and for healing and they were aware that power came out of him. In Jesus there were signs of the kingdom of God at work.

Jesus tells them of the 'blessed'. Blessed is a good translation of the Greek word 'Makarioi', which can simply mean 'happy', though 'blessed' is also connected with the last times and the favour of God.

Jesus connects some strange things with happiness or the blessed, and the oddness of what he says should bring us up with a jolt. Happy are the poor, happy are the hungry, happy are those who weep, happy are those who are hated on account of the Son of Man. We make happiness dependent on external circumstances – 'I would be happy if I won the lottery'; 'I would be happy if I had a good drink'. Jesus wants us to know that true happiness comes from something deep within us. It is not about 'having' or even 'not having'; it is about our relationship with God. True happiness is not dependent on outward things, though they can help – happiness is dependent on God. The danger with riches or plenty is that they can make us self-sufficient and make us forget God and think we can provide for ourselves. Happiness comes from knowing that God provides for us and loves us (see Deuteronomy 8:1-18; 1 Corinthians 6:10).

Question time

How can we persuade a self-made, self-sufficient society that happiness does not lie in possessions or success alone?

Where do you think true happiness is found?

Illustration

It is amazing how many products offer us more happiness, when in fact they are only seeking to fulfil our consuming passion to have more. The notice of 'Happy Hour' at some places is always amusing, for if that is the 'happy hour', what is the rest of the time?

There are many stories of people who have sold their heart or their soul to make money. At first it is wonderful, for money can buy all sorts of things. But possessions alone cannot fill our inner emptiness; we also need love and to know we are of some value. There is nothing worse than the person that has made it in the world but is poor in the sight of his neighbours or God. There is a very telling story from Matthew 19:16-22: the rich young man sought eternal life (did he think he could buy it?) but 'he went away grieving, for he had many possessions' (verse 22).

Intercessions

Blessed are you, Lord our God;
in your presence are joy and peace.
You never leave us or forsake us,
so help us to rejoice in you,
in your love and in your saving power.
Blessed are you, Father, Son and Holy Spirit.

God, we give you thanks
for all who show a radiant faith,
for those who show that in your presence
is the fullness of joy.
Help us also to show the joy and wonder of your love
and to find happiness in your service.
We pray for all who preach the word
and administer the sacraments,
that they may reveal the delight of knowing you.

Silence

Lord, bless us with your presence
and the joy of knowing your love.

We pray for all who are homeless, hungry
or unemployed.
We remember the deprived and poor peoples of our world.
We ask your blessing upon all who suffer
from violence or from war.
May they all know the joy of your love
and that you value each of them.

Silence

Lord, bless us with your presence
and the joy of knowing your love.

We give thanks for our homes and our loved ones.
We remember all who have enriched our lives
by their love or their friendship.
We pray for homes where there is little love or joy
or where there is neglect or abuse.

Silence

Lord, bless us with your presence
and the joy of knowing your love.

We give thanks for all who work as healers
and ask your blessing upon all who are doctors, nurses
or part of the caring and healing professions.
We remember all who are ill at home or in hospital,
all who have been injured
or rushed into hospital this week.
We pray for those who have lost loved ones and friends.

Silence

Lord, bless us with your presence
and the joy of knowing your love.

We rejoice in the gift of eternal life
and we pray for our loved ones departed.
May they share in the happiness of your saints in glory.

Silence

Merciful Father,
accept these prayers
for the sake of your Son,
our Saviour Jesus Christ.
Amen.

Memory verse

Happy are the people whose God is the Lord.
Psalm 144:15

Suggested music

Blest are the pure in heart
A new commandment I give unto you
Blessed assurance, Jesus is mine

CANDLES

Aim

To show Jesus needs friends to work with him.

Teaching

Who helps Mum or Dad at home? What do you do? There are always lots of things to do and we can all help.

Mime some jobs and see if the children can guess what they are: hoovering, sweeping, drying dishes, for example. Maybe a child would like to mime how they help.

Jesus needed people to help him do his work. One day he went up a mountain, so that he could be alone and speak to God. After being on the mountain he came down and chose his disciples. (Do you know how many? Twelve. Do you know any of their names? See Luke 6:12-16.)

Now, with his helpers, Jesus was ready to teach people and to heal people. Crowds of people came to Jesus to learn from him. All who were learners from Jesus were called disciples. We are disciples. (Let us say 'disciple'. Now let us say 'We are disciples of Jesus.') Jesus got the people to sit down so that he could teach them, so that they could learn what God wanted them to do. He had special work for his friends, the twelve he had chosen. Jesus called them 'apostles' because he would send them to teach as he was teaching and to make people well again as he was making people well. (Let us say, 'twelve apostles'.) The twelve apostles would have to listen carefully because they would be asked to do what their leader Jesus was doing. Let us think about what they would do. They would tell people about God. They would tell people about Jesus. They would teach people to do good things. They would make ill people better. And so they would do what Jesus wanted them to do.

Activity

Play 'Do as I say'. Whatever the leader tells everyone to do, they must do it. They must not copy the leader's actions if they are different from what she says. For example, if she says, 'Smile', you must all smile. If she jumps up and down and says, 'Stand still', you must not jump up and down. Anyone who does not do what she says is out.

Prayer

Jesus, help us to be good disciples
and to work for you.
Let us help at home
and be kind to others.
Amen.

Song

Jesus' hands were kind hands

LAMPS

Aim

To look at what makes us happy.

Teaching

Think about Mr Grumpy and Mr Greedy and try to find out why they are never happy. Mr Grumpy is always complaining, he is never satisfied, never pleased with people. Mr Greedy always wants more; the more he gets, the more he wants. Sometimes once he gets something he wanted he then wants a better model or something even more up to date. I know people like that. Do you?

There is a story that when God made the human being he made the human heart so big that it could hold him. The human heart was able to hold the eternal. That means no matter how much we pour into our hearts we can never fill it; only God can fill our hearts. Many people say they are bored. Well, when you bore a piece of wood it has a hole in it. Bored people are recognising a hole in themselves but if they try and fill it just with noise, action or things, they will fail, for it is a space big enough for God and was made for him. When we are unhappy, dissatisfied, grumpy or greedy, it could be God calling to us and saying, 'Make room in your heart for me.' God calls us often and we do not notice. If you really want to be Mr/Miss Happy, you need to learn the secret of happiness. It is not having lots of things (though that can be nice). It is not being always busy (though that can be fun). It is knowing that God is with you and God loves you always. Let us make sure we know this.

Activity

Ask all in the group to make a sad face and then to pass a smile round the circle. As it goes round let everyone smile. Now let everyone smile and let a sad face be passed round to music. Once you pass the sad face on, you have to smile. When the music stops the person with the sad face is out.

Prayer

Lord God,
you have made our hearts big enough to hold you.
We welcome you into our hearts, our lives,
our homes.
Amen.

Song

I am H. A. P. P. Y.

TORCHES

Aim

To show how Jesus gives guidance to his people, as Moses did to Israel, and how we should let Jesus send us.

Teaching

Look at Luke 6:12-16.

Whenever Jesus has something important to do, he goes away to be alone with God the Father. Before any major decision it is important to pray.

St Luke wants us to know that Jesus went up a mountain to pray after he had been in the wilderness. You can compare this to Moses who went up a mountain in the wilderness to pray. Moses went up Mount Sinai and when he came down he gave the twelve tribes of Israel the law. Jesus came down from the mountain and chose twelve disciples to be apostles. The twelve were not only to be learners; they were to be 'sent' by Jesus to do his work. Then he got the people to sit down and gave them guidance on how to live. Jesus wanted to bring them to the freedom of the kingdom of God. Jesus healed people of their diseases and brought peace to those troubled in spirit. People wanted to touch Jesus because power came out from him.

Note in the Gospel there are crowds of people; there are disciples and there are apostles. Well, we are all people who need to come to Jesus. Some of us become disciples and learn about Jesus and his love. It is more exciting when we are 'sent' by him.

Talk about what happens when someone is 'sent' by a pop star. We want to be near that person as much as possible, we want to hear that person, we want to tell others about that person. We collect information about that person and we think about them often. If we can, we spend a lot of time in their presence. That is being 'sent' and that is what an apostle is: one 'sent by Jesus'.

Activity

Ask people to talk for 30 seconds about their favourite pop star or footballer. Afterwards, ask them to talk for 30 seconds about Jesus. Get each of them to talk about how much time they spend copying or listening to their pop or sports idol (good word) and how much time they spend listening *about* Jesus or *to* Jesus. Discuss how we can serve Jesus better and become apostles.

Prayer

Lord Jesus, you called us to know you
and to love you.
Send us out in your power
to tell others of your love
and of your salvation.
Amen.

Song

The kingdom of heaven

Proper 3

Sunday between 17 and 23 February inclusive
(if earlier than the Second Sunday before Lent)

Aim

To show that Jesus wants us to have the glorious freedom of the children of God.

Preparation

Have pictures of people in prison or people who look imprisoned within themselves. Include people in refugee camps. Among the pictures have posters with the words 'Imprisoned by guilt', 'Imprisoned by greed', 'Imprisoned by hatred' and 'Imprisoned by war'.

Opening activity

(To be said slowly)

Voice 1	All who harbour anger or resentment
Voice 2	have become prisoners.
Voice 1	All who are unforgiving and merciless
Voice 2	have become prisoners.
Voice 1	All who are greedy and selfish
Voice 2	have become prisoners.
Both	Jesus has come to set us free.

Opening prayer

Lord God, you sent your Son
to lead us into the glorious freedom of your kingdom.
Change our hearts and our attitudes
that we may share even now
in your kingdom and in your love.
Amen.

Opening song

Praise to the holiest in the height

Readings

Genesis 45:3-11, 15
Psalm 37:1-11, 40
1 Corinthians 15:35-38, 42-50
Luke 6:27-38

Thought for the day

In today's Gospel, Jesus continues his teaching after coming down from the mountain. Like Moses, he wants to lead his people to the freedom of the Promised Land. That freedom will involve a change in our attitude – a change of heart – towards much of life. We are to learn to love and not to hate. The word used for love is not 'eran', which is passionate love, or 'philien', which is family love, but 'agapan' – an active benevolence towards each other. This love is more about our will than our heart, though both are involved. If we are not to become slaves to hatred, greed, anger or resentment, we will have to have a positive attitude of will towards all people. This means whatever people do to us, we will seek to react in a good way to them; we will go out of our way to be kind and generous. Jesus gives us a summary of this attitude in the positive commandment 'Do to others as you would have them do to you' (Luke 6:31).

It is so easy to give up our freedom and become slaves to bad attitudes. We can become consumed by harbouring anger or resentment towards people who have done us wrong. Anger and hatred can use up so much of our time and energy and stop us from enjoying the freedom that God gives to us. We need to learn to be merciful as our Father is merciful; to forgive as we are forgiven. A critical attitude towards others can be so destructive to the community and us. It does not mean acting without discretion; it *does* mean an act of will that seeks the good for the person and in the person. Forgiveness can so often bring us to a new freedom. Possessiveness of things or of people can so easily enslave us; if we cannot give away, if we cease to be generous, then life no longer seems to be generous towards us. It is by giving that we make room in our lives to receive.

Let us seek to learn the glorious freedom of the children of God.

Question time

Have we learnt to exercise the freedom that Jesus offers to us or are we captives to hatred, resentment and greed?

How can we show in our lives the generosity of God towards us?

Illustration

In the Holy Land there are two seas, the Sea of Galilee and the Dead Sea. The same river, the Jordan, feeds both of these seas. The Sea of Galilee teems with life: there are fish in its waters, trees grow near its shoreline, birds visit it and their singing can be heard. The Dead Sea lives up to its name: it does not sustain life, it is too salty to allow plants to thrive and the birds do not like its saltiness. One sea has life and the other is dead, yet the same river feeds both. What is the difference? The answer is quite simple: the river Jordan flows into one end of the Sea of Galilee and out of the other. As the Sea of Galilee receives, so it gives out. The Dead Sea does not have an outlet. All the water that flows into the Dead Sea is kept; it does not give out. The sun evaporates the water and the salts are left behind. Because the Dead Sea does not have an outlet, it dies. By keeping all that it receives, it chokes itself of life. Sadly there are people just like that.

Intercessions

Blessed are you, good and generous God,
for you give us life and all that we have.
Help us to be as generous and forgiving
as you are with us.
May we appreciate all that you have given us
and all that you have done for us throughout our lives.
Blessed are you, Father, Son and Holy Spirit.

We give thanks for all who have shown your ways
by their love and generosity.
We give thanks for all who give their lives
in your service.

We remember today all who seek to maintain worship
in dangerous or difficult places.
We pray for prison chaplains and prison visitors.
We remember those who are persecuted
or imprisoned for their faith.
We pray for all who strive to love
in areas of hatred and resentment.

Silence

God of goodness and love,
give us a loving and courageous heart.

We ask your blessing
upon all who seek to bring peace and unity to our world.
We pray for the work of the Red Cross
and all relief agencies.
We remember all who are suffering
from natural disasters or war at this time.
We pray especially for those who have lost loved ones
or are separated from them.

Silence

God of goodness and love,
give us a loving and courageous heart.

We give thanks
for the protection and love of our own homes.
We ask your blessing upon all who are homeless
or who have been taken into care.
We pray for all who are lonely
and those who are finding it difficult to cope
on their own.

Silence

God of goodness and love,
give us a loving and courageous heart.

We give thanks for our own well-being,
that in you, Lord, we are forgiven
and freed to live life to the full.
We pray for all who are prisoners
of their own greed or unforgiving hearts.
We remember all who are consumed
with rage or violence.
We pray for all who are ill at home or in hospital,
especially those who are not at peace with themselves.

Silence

God of goodness and love,
give us a loving and courageous heart.

We give thanks for the gift of life and life eternal.
We remember in your presence
the generosity of your saints
and of our benefactors who are departed from us.
May our loved ones who are gone from our sight
rejoice with them in your glorious kingdom.

Silence

Merciful Father,
**accept these prayers
for the sake of your Son,
our Saviour Jesus Christ.
Amen.**

Memory verse

Do to others as you would have them do to you.
Luke 6:31

Suggested music

Brother, sister, let me serve you
O Lord, all the world belongs to you
One more step along the world I go

CANDLES

Aim

To tell the story of Joseph and God's care for him.

Teaching

Today we are going to hear about Joseph. (Get them to repeat his name.) Joseph had ten big brothers and one little brother. (How many brothers did that make altogether? Twelve.) Their daddy's name was Jacob. He loved Joseph and gave him a coat of many colours. The ten older brothers were jealous and were not happy with Joseph.

One day Jacob sent Joseph to see his brothers and take a message to them. They were in the desert looking after sheep. It was a very lonely place and they saw Joseph coming across the sands. They recognised him because of his coat. When he came to them they were cruel to him. They took off his coat and put him in a deep hole in the ground. Poor Joseph would not be able to get out. But not long after this the brothers saw some rich travellers and they decided to sell their brother to them. They took Joseph out of the hole and sold him for twenty pieces of silver. Poor Joseph was taken away to a strange land. But he need not have worried because God was looking after him.

The wicked brothers took Joseph's coat and tore it. They dipped it in some blood. Then when they got home they told a lie. The told their father they thought a wild animal had killed Joseph. This made their father very sad. He did not know that Joseph was alive and that God was looking after him.

After many years Joseph became a very important man in Egypt. He looked after the food for the whole country. He stored corn in barns during seven good years of harvest. Egypt had lots of corn, thanks to Joseph. Then there came a time when all the countries were not growing enough corn and so the people could not make bread and were hungry. People came from all over to buy corn from Joseph.

One day ten brothers came looking for corn. They were Joseph's brothers who had been unkind to him. They did not recognise Joseph because he was rich and famous, but Joseph recognised them. Do you think he would give them food? Would he be kind to them?

Joseph still loved his brothers. He gave them all the corn they wanted. He made a present of it. Joseph wanted to see his little brother Benjamin so he told them to bring him the next time they came for more food. So Benjamin was brought. All this time the brothers did not know the rich man was their brother. When Joseph told them who he was they were scared. They had been unkind to him; now he could get his own back and put them in prison. But Joseph told them how God had taken care of him all of the time. Now God would take care of the brothers as well because Joseph had plenty for them all. Joseph still loved his brothers.

Joseph sent his brothers to bring his old father to Egypt. How happy they all were when they met again. And they knew that God looked after them and loved them all.

Activity

This is a good story to get the children to act. A coloured bathrobe or towel will do for Joseph's coat. Or you can make Joseph and his brothers out of pegs and then get the children to go through the story using the pegs for the actions.

Prayer

God, we know you cared for Joseph
and his brothers.
Help us to know you love us
and that you are always ready to care for us.
Amen.

Song

Gives! gives! gives!

LAMPS

Aim

To encourage the children to be generous as God is generous to them.

Teaching

Once upon a time in a high valley in Switzerland there was a poor peasant woman. She lived in a wooden house – in fact, all the houses in the village were made of wood. One cold night a fire swept through the village burning houses, destroying homes. Most people were poor but what they did have they had lost. The families that escaped the fire were afraid to give to their neighbours because it would only make them much poorer. They gave only what was old and unwanted. But the poor peasant woman gave away all that she had, keeping only the fewest essentials. The next night the wind got up and spread the fire to the other houses in the village. These people had now lost all they had. But the poor peasant woman began to receive from others: they were giving her the things that were hers and even more. She could have been better off but she shared out again what she had been given. This was a poor woman who was rich in the eyes of God because she was rich in her spirit.

Mr and Mrs Greedy, on the other hand, never really enjoy life, for the more they get, the more they want. Jesus watched the merchants measuring out cloth and food in the market place. He saw that they were cheating. But when people knew who was cheating, they would not go to them; they went to people who were generous in their measuring. Jesus says to us, 'Forgive and you will be forgiven, give and it will be given to you. A good measure, pressed down, shaken together, running over,

will be put into your lap; for the measure you give will be the measure you get back' (Luke 6:38). (Spend the rest of the lesson talking about what Jesus meant by these words.)

Activity

Have the children read the story of the widow's mite, preferably in a Children's Bible. Then let them act it out. Have plenty of rich men and women giving with show, and the widow quietly giving all that she had.

Prayer

Lord God, we thank you
for all that you have given us
in this wonderful world.
Help us to share with others
and to care for those in need.
Amen.

Song

Two little fishes

TORCHES

Aim

To show how Jesus wants us to be generous as our God is generous.

Teaching

No doubt Jesus had been watching the market traders, how clever they were. They measured cloth by an arm's length. If their arm was shorter than yours, they would measure it if you were buying, but if you were selling, they would get you to measure it. (Demonstrate with two people of different arm lengths.) Or a neighbouring stallholder would slip a weight in the food pan when he was selling and hide it underneath when he was buying.

So many people deal with life like that, wanting to get more than they give. They want to gain and have a big balance at the end of the year. Jesus wanted a change of heart and attitude from such people. He wanted them to learn to be generous, as their Father in heaven is generous to them. Jesus said, 'Forgive and you will be forgiven, give and it will be given to you. A good measure, pressed down, shaken together, running over, will be put into your lap; for the measure you give will be the measure you get back' (Luke 6:38).

It is interesting that mean people usually get mean treatment in return; aggressive people get a return of aggression. Jesus wants us to break that circle of action and reaction by being generous in our attitude, by being forgiving and giving as our Father forgives and gives to us.

The people who are afraid to give are poor indeed. It is no use collecting money or treasure if you are afraid to use it. A lovely ceremony was always performed by the Blackfoot Indians. The way the Blackfoots gained prestige or respect was by how much they could give away. They were only counted rich if they could be truly generous. Some worked the whole year to obtain a pile of blankets and food to give away at the ceremony. The rich were those who could give away a lot of their possessions. At the end of the ceremony a person might have no money left and few possessions but if he had given away a lot then that person was rich indeed.

Jesus knew you couldn't touch a person's pocket if you are unable to touch their hearts. If we are to be like the God who gives us life, who gave us his Son, if we are to be like Jesus who gave his life for us, then we need to learn to give also. If we are unwilling to give, God finds it hard to give us more.

Activity

Ask everyone to clench their hands and pretend they are full of coins. Now pass around a piece of paper. Tell them this paper is a £1000 note. They must pass it around quickly and whoever drops it is out (usually both the person passing and the one receiving the note); those who are caught with it when the music stops are also out. At all times must they keep their hands clenched, pretending to hold on to money.

Get the group to talk about how they can show they are generous.

Prayer

God, you have given us many good things;
our lives are rich because of you.
Help us to be generous with what we have
and to be willing to give to others.
Amen.

Song

Make me a channel of your peace

Second Sunday before Lent

Aim

To show that Christ is our peace among the storms of life.

Preparation

Have pictures of stormy seas and lifeboats. Contact the Royal National Lifeboat Institution for posters and information (West Quay Road, Poole, Dorset BH15 1HZ). You could also have information on the Mission to Seafarers (St Michael Paternoster Royal, College Hill, London EC4R 2RL).

Opening activity

Read out headlines of people lost at sea or overwhelmed by life. Play a recording of 'When you walk through a storm (You'll never walk alone)' as people say over the music:

Voice 1 I was overwhelmed by sickness.
Voice 2 I was sunk deep in debt.
Voice 3 I was struggling in the depths of despair.
Voice 4 I could not cope with all that was being thrown at me.
All Because of our relationships with Jesus we are not conquered by the storm.

Opening prayer

Lord our God, when the storms come over us
and the way is dark,
help us to know that we have a loving Saviour
who is with us always.
Amen.

Opening song

Will your anchor hold

Readings

Genesis 2:4b-9, 15-25
Psalm 65
Revelation 4
Luke 8:22-25

Thought for the day

Jesus is very like Moses who led the people to the Promised Land.

- Jesus receives a call at his Baptism (Luke 3:21, 22).
- Jesus is in the wilderness (4:1-12).
- Jesus goes up a mountain to be alone with God (6:12-15).
- Jesus comes down and teaches the people (6:17-49).
- Jesus rescues his disciples from an overwhelming sea (8:22-25).
- Jesus feeds people in the wilderness (9:10b-17).
- Jesus is leading his people to the promised kingdom of God. Jesus seeks freedom for his people.

Throughout all of this there is a feeling that Jesus is more than a second Moses, more than a good leader or a good teacher. He is the 'Son of God' (Luke 3:22). When the disciples are caught in the storm and Jesus brings calm, they ask the question, 'Who then is this, that he commands even the winds and the water, and they obey him?' (Luke 8:25). The answer can be found in the psalm chosen for today. Psalm 65, verse 7 is addressed to God alone and it says:

'You silence the roaring of the seas,
the roaring of their waves,
the tumult of the peoples.'

And the next thing Jesus does after the stilling of the storm is to heal the mad man of the Gerasenes.

The same verse from Psalm 65 in the Book of Common Prayer is even more fitting:

'Who stilleth the raging of the sea: and the noise of the waves, and the madness of the people.'

The only answer to their questions is, of course, God. It is important for the disciples and for us to realise that Jesus is God and not just a wonder-worker. As God, Jesus is able to control the chaotic elements of this world and to help us survive amid the chaos and dangers that life sends to us. Jesus reveals to us that in him light conquers darkness, order conquers chaos, love conquers hatred and life is stronger than death. In the power of Jesus we are able to survive whatever this world throws at us. We are given strength by having him as our constant companion (if we do not let him just slumber in our lives). To have faith is to have a relationship with him and then to be able to say with St Paul, 'I am convinced that neither death nor life, nor angels nor rulers, nor things present, nor things to come, nor powers, nor height, nor depth, nor anything else in all creation, will be able to separate us from the love of God in Christ Jesus our Lord' (Romans 8:38-39). (You may like to begin at verse 18.)

Question time

Are you aware of the presence, the power and the peace of Jesus in your life?

Can you say how Jesus brought peace to you?

Illustration

There was a man who, for some reason, raged against life. Because he did not start off with riches, he was angry with all rich people. He did not make friends easily and often got into trouble by his aggressive attitude. Everything he gained he kept to himself. Soon he was well-off and successful – but not happy. It seemed storms followed him around. He was not comfortable to be with. He was also very lonely. Then he became ill and he began to struggle; he needed the care and attention of someone. He could afford it and hired a group of carers. One was a nurse who was willing put herself out to help him. She did errands and stayed with him for company. She also told him that she gained great peace of mind from knowing Jesus. The man was embarrassed at first but then wanted to know more. He wanted to know why she cared for him and how Jesus brought peace. In time, as his health improved, he no longer needed carers but he felt he needed this nurse; in fact, he loved her and proposed to her. She accepted him, they married and lived very happily together. He also had a living relationship with Jesus and so he knew of love and peace in his life.

Intercessions

Blessed are you, Lord our God,
for you created the world out of chaos
and when chaos seeks to overwhelm us
you offer us your presence and your peace.
You are ever with us in the storms of life
and we know you as our Saviour.
Blessed are you, Father, Son and Holy Spirit.

Lord, your ship the Church is often buffeted
by storms of oppression and violence.
At all times may we affirm your abiding presence
and your lasting peace.
We remember all who are struggling with their faith,
all who do not know you or love you.
May your Church bring to them
the knowledge of your love
and of your Almighty Power.

Silence

Holy and strong One,
grant us your peace.

We give thanks for all who seek
to bring your peace to the world.
We pray for the work of the United Nations
and peacekeeping forces.
We remember all who are caught up
in the violence of war or tyranny.
We ask your blessing
upon those who are being overwhelmed by life,
upon all who feel they cannot survive on their own.

Silence

Holy and strong One,
grant us your peace.

We pray for our homes and our loved ones.
May we here reveal your peace in our dealings
and in our relationships.
We ask your blessing on homes
that are sinking into deep debt
or where families are unable to cope with each other.

Silence

Holy and strong One,
grant us your peace.

We give thanks for our peace of mind
and we pray for all who are disturbed or distressed.
We remember those who have had a traumatic experience
and those how have suffered from betrayal or violence.
We pray for all who are not at peace
with themselves or with others.

Silence

Holy and strong One,
grant us your peace.

We rejoice that nothing can separate us
from the love of God in Christ Jesus,

that through him life is eternal.
We pray for friends and loved ones
who have passed beyond the storms of life:
may they rejoice in the joy of your presence
and in your everlasting peace.

Silence

Merciful Father,
**accept these prayers
for the sake of your Son,
our Saviour Jesus Christ.
Amen.**

Memory verse

Who then is this, that he commands even the winds and the water, and they obey him?
Luke 8:25

Suggested music

Do not be afraid
What a friend we have in Jesus
Eternal Father, strong to save

CANDLES

Aim

To show that Jesus is our God and Saviour.

Teaching

Jesus and his disciples had been working very hard looking after lots of people. Now they were tired and wanted to get away for a while. They decided to go to sea in a boat and escape from the crowds. They could have a rest as the boat bobbed up and down on the sea. The sail was raised and soon they were right out at sea. Jesus was so sleepy that he was soon asleep in the back of the boat.

While all the disciples were resting, Peter was a little worried. The sea can be a very dangerous place and he noticed that the clouds were increasing and the wind was getting stronger. The wind was making big waves on the sea. (At this point talk about the sea, about waves and how powerful the sea is. Get the children to tell you about trips to sea and about any sea stories they know.)

Now we come back to the disciples in the boat and Jesus asleep. Suddenly with a swoosh the wind hit the little boat hard and it nearly tipped over. (Tilt your body to show the listing of the boat.) Then – whoosh – another great blow of wind, and the little boat rocked in the sea. And then another whoosh (get the children to say, 'Whoosh' three times and rock each time they say it). Now it was hard to stand up in the boat. Peter was struggling to get the sail down so that the boat would not blow over. The wind blew again three large blows (get the children to say, 'Whoosh' very loudly three times). Now it was blowing waves into the boat and the disciples were getting wet. The wind still blew (three more 'Whooshes'). The disciples were frightened because lots of water was coming into the boat. What happens if a lot of water comes into the boat? Yes, it will sink, and then what will happen to the disciples? They would sink in the sea and drown.

All this time Jesus had been asleep in the back of the boat. He must have been very, very tired. Now the disciples shook him and shouted to wake him. They were shouting, 'Master, Master we are perishing.' They thought they were all going to die. The wind was so strong and the waves so big and there was a lot of water in the boat. Jesus woke up and looked at the disciples. Then he stood up in the rocking boat and spoke to the wind and the waves. He told them to be quiet and still. Suddenly the boat stopped rocking, the wind was quiet and still, the waves were gentle. The wind and waves had done what Jesus asked them. The disciples were amazed. Jesus had saved them in the storm. He had saved their lives. But they were also a little afraid and asked, 'Who then is this, that he commands even the winds and the water and they obey him?'

We cannot command the wind or the waves. No one can. Only one person can make the wind and waves do what he wants. Who is that? Yes, only God. Only God can make the wind and waves obey him. So we are learning that Jesus is God, just as the Father is God. Jesus is our Saviour and Jesus is God. Let us all say together, 'Jesus is God.'

Activity

Re-enact the story with lots of wind and waves using a model of a boat. On the activity sheet there is a boat to be coloured with Jesus standing in it.

Prayer

Jesus, you are always with us
and will help us
when the days are stormy and dark.
We thank you for your love and care.
Amen.

Song

Wide, wide as the ocean

LAMPS

Aim

To show the disciples experience Jesus as Saviour and begin to learn he is God.

Teaching

When there is trouble at sea, who helps to rescue people? The lifeboats go out to help and so do helicopters. Other ships also help. Sometimes the helicopter lifts people off the ship if they think they are in danger and the ship might sink. The helicopter crew lower a man on a winch (a strong rope) so that he can be where the people are. Then he straps a person to the same winch and they are raised to safety. He will then go down and rescue another until all are safe. (If possible, show pictures of the Air Sea Rescue at work.) In many ways Jesus came down to rescue us and lift us up into his kingdom. (Read John 3:16 to the children and try to discover what they think it means. God does not want us to perish.)

Once Jesus was very tired after teaching and healing people. He and the disciples decided to cross the sea to somewhere quiet. It would be quieter on the sea than being with the crowds. They got into a boat, raised the sail and set out. The sea was calm and the sky bright. Jesus was so tired that the gentle rocking of the boat soon sent him to sleep. He was curled up in the back of the boat, sound asleep.

Suddenly, as if from nowhere, there was a mighty wind. The waves rose to great heights and the little boat was soon in danger of sinking. Peter lowered the sail and tried to make the boat face the wind because that was the safest thing to do. But waves pounded the little boat and water swept in. With water coming into the boat it got heavier and lay lower and lower in the water. Soon they were in danger of sinking. Even the fishermen disciples were now afraid. The sea was so wild and violent no one would survive for long in it.

All this time Jesus slept. He must have been very tired. They shook Jesus and shouted at him to waken him, saying, 'Master, Master, we are perishing.' Jesus awoke, stood up in the rocking boat and told both the wind and the waves to stop being so violent. Suddenly there was a great calm. The disciples were very relieved; Jesus had saved their lives. But now they were a little troubled for a question about Jesus bothered them. 'Who then is this, that he commands even the winds and the water and they obey him?' There is only one Being in the whole universe that can command wind and waves, the same one that created them, the same one that brought order out of chaos. Who is that? Only God. So that means the disciples were learning again, through his acts of power, that Jesus is God.

Activity

Let the children mime a rescue at sea by a helicopter and its crew. Then they could mime a fireman rescuing someone from a house. They could show a policeman rescuing someone from criminals. After each rescue, talk about the bravery and the risks taken by the rescuers.

Then mime the rescue of the disciples by Jesus.

Talk about John 3:16 and what it might mean for us.

Prayer

God, we thank you
for all who work in the rescue services
and we remember their bravery.
We thank you that Jesus came
to rescue us from death
and to bring us to eternal life.
Amen.

Song

With Jesus in the boat

TORCHES

Aim

To show that Jesus is our God and our Saviour.

Teaching

The Breton fishermen have a prayer which says, 'The sea is so large and my boat is so small.' The sea is definitely mightier than we are and we should treat it with care. Though humans have learnt greater control over the world, they still cannot control the elements. We still hear of destruction by mighty winds, tornadoes and hurricanes. We still read of the sea overwhelming little boats and sometimes villages. We should treat such strong forces with respect.

Fishermen respect the sea and try not to go out when gales are forecast or if they think a storm is imminent. Yet every now and again even the fishermen are caught out. Sometimes it is because the storm was sudden or they had been to sea for a few days and the storm caught them away from the safety of a harbour.

Jesus was once caught in a storm. Jesus and the disciples had been very busy. For a while they wanted to escape the crowds, so they put to sea in a fishing boat. At first all was calm and bright. Jesus, soothed by the gentle rocking of the boat, was quickly asleep in the stern.

The fishermen were the first to notice the change in the weather. The wind was rising and a storm was coming. Before it got too bad they lowered the sail and hoped they could ride out the storm. They turned their boat to face the waves, as this was the safest. But soon the boat was being tossed about and waves were breaking over its bow. Every time some water came into the boat it settled lower in the water. If this went on for long, they would sink and lives could be lost.

Jesus continued to sleep. Suddenly the disciples turned to him for help, shouting to wake him, 'Master, Master, we are perishing.' Jesus woke, calmly stood up and commanded the storm to cease. He spoke to wind and waves. That was strange but, stranger still, there was a sudden calm. The wind and waves obeyed him. The disciples were still afraid and were also amazed, wondering who it was they had in their boat, for even the wind and the waves obeyed him. No one can command wind and waves – only God. No one can make the sea obey him with only a word – only God. Look at Psalm 65:7 and say how these words can only relate to God who is in control. So who, then, is Jesus? (Let the group discuss this.)

Activity

Play 'Storms' which is a variation of 'Battleships'. Everyone will need two pieces of squared paper (12 squares by 12 squares). Number the squares across 1 to 12 and down A – L. Now divide the group into pairs. On one paper they must place three ships of two squares each. Your opponent must not see this.

To begin, one player says, for example, 'Storm on C4', because he thinks there might be a ship there. To remember he will mark the square on his piece of paper. A ship will only sink when both squares have been hit.

His opponent will say if a score has been made on a ship; if it has, that square is crossed off. It is now the other's turn to send a storm.

The game will continue until one player sinks all three ships of his or her opponent and so becomes the winner.

Prayer

Lord Jesus, we thank you
that you have rescued us
from the darkness of sin and death
and opened up for us
the peace and joy of your kingdom.
Amen.

Song

Calm me, Lord

Sunday before Lent

Aim

To show that in Jesus is revealed the full glory of God, for Jesus is God.

Preparation

Have a poster in the porch saying, 'Come here to have your eyes tested', and a second one saying, 'Vision is about seeing clearly'.

Opening activity

Voice 1 Will you open your eyes? You are not aware of what is around you.

Voice 2 Wake up, will you? You miss a lot with your eyes closed.

Voice 3 Do not blame anyone else. You came into this with your eyes shut.

Voice 1 I think you must be blind not to have seen that.

Voice 2 You should get your eyes tested.

Voice 3 Did you know vision is about seeing?

All Lord, open our eyes to your presence that we may behold your glory.

Opening prayer

Lord God, ever present,
open our eyes to your glory
and open our hearts to your love,
that we may rejoice
in knowing you and your power.
Amen.

Opening song

Be still, for the presence of the Lord

Readings

Exodus 34:29-35
Psalm 99
2 Corinthians 3:12–4:2
Luke 9:28-36 (37-43a)

Thought for the day

The story of the Transfiguration is the story of the disciples seeing Jesus for what he really is. The story begins eight days after Peter saying that Jesus is 'the Messiah of God' and Jesus telling them how he must undergo suffering, death and resurrection (Luke 9:18-22).

The place of the Transfiguration has by tradition often been Mount Tabor but this is unlikely as there is a fortress on the top of it. It is more likely to have been Mount Hermon – 9,400 feet high and 11,000 feet above the Jordan valley. Hermon can be seen from the Dead Sea, a hundred miles away. If it is Hermon, then the action probably happened somewhere on the mountainside rather than the top.

The reason for going up the mountain was for Jesus to be alone to pray to God. This also reflects the time when Moses went up the mountain to talk with God and to receive the Law. When Moses came down from the mountain he did not realise that his face shone (Exodus 34:29).

Jesus took with him Peter, James and John. We are told that the disciples were weighed down with sleep. It seems they were often tired. It could also be that here is an attempt by Luke to show how the disciples' eyes were opened to the glory of Jesus: it is when their eyes are opened – 'when they are fully awake' – that they behold his glory.

With the vision of Jesus in his glory, the disciples see Moses and Elijah in glory. Jesus fulfils both the Law as given by Moses and the prophets as represented by Elijah, the greatest of prophets. Both Elijah and Moses had encounters with God on mountains. Moses departed this life on Mount Nebo, and Elijah went up to God in the whirlwind with chariot and horses of fire (see Deuteronomy 34:5, 6 and 2 Kings 2:11).

These two great leaders talk with Jesus of his 'departure'. It would be better to keep the word without translating it, for it is his 'exodus'. Like Moses, Jesus is going to go through a time of trial to bring his people to the Promised Kingdom.

The cloud that overshadows them is like the 'Pillar of Cloud' that went with Moses and the Israelites through the desert (Exodus 13:21, 22). Like the cloud that covered the Tent of Meeting, when the glory of the Lord filled the Tabernacle (Exodus 40:34), this luminous cloud is known as the 'Shekinah' and it represents the hidden glory of God. It is the cloud that hides the glory, for humans cannot bear too much of the glory of God. As if to confirm this there is also the voice from the cloud, the 'Bath Qol'. The voice says, 'This is my Son, my Chosen: listen to him.' Once again it is affirmed that Jesus is the Son of God, that Jesus is therefore God in human flesh. 'Listen' has with it the implication of 'Listen and obey'.

Now the disciples are suddenly alone with Jesus. Everything is back to normal and yet the disciples who had seen this can never be the same again. You might like to look at statements like 'We have seen his glory, the glory as of a father's only son' (John 1:14) or 'The light of the knowledge of the glory of God in the face of Jesus Christ' (2 Corinthians 4:6).

Question time

Are you aware that vision is how we see the world and our God within it?

In what way can we improve our vision so that we see more clearly the glory of God?

Illustration

On the night of 31 August 651, the young man Cuthbert was guarding sheep against robbers and wild animals. He was only 16 years old but possessed a spear and a horse. While he stayed alert and watching, the shepherds slept. The night was clear and full of stars. During the night Cuthbert suddenly saw angels descending to the earth and then ascending, taking with them a holy soul to heaven. Cuthbert sought to awaken the shepherds but they missed seeing what he saw. This made Cuthbert say, 'What wretches we are, given to sleep and sloth, so that we never see the glory of those who watch with Christ unceasingly.' The next day Cuthbert learnt that Aidan had died and he then went and offered himself to become a monk at the monastery of Melrose. True vision nearly always demands obedience and a change of direction.

Intercessions

Blessed are you, Lord our God,
for you have revealed yourself
through Moses and the prophets.
You have made yourself known to us
through your saints
but, above all, you show us your glory
in the face of our Lord Jesus Christ.
Blessed are you, God, for ever.

We give thanks for men and women of vision,
for all who have shown us of you and your love.
We ask that your Church may continue
to show forth your glory in the world.
We seek your blessing upon preachers of the word
and ministers of the sacraments,
upon all who teach and speak in your name.

Silence

Wonderful God,
reveal in us your glory.

We give thanks for artists and craftspeople,
for all who give us a vision of beauty and wonder.
We ask your blessing upon all architects and planners,
upon councils and governments,
that they might keep a clear vision
of what is good for our world.
We pray for all who make decisions
that will affect the future of the human race.

Silence

Wonderful God,
reveal in us your glory.

We give thanks for those who have cared for us
and taught us.
We ask your blessing upon our homes,
our friends and families.
We pray for all homes where there is little sense of love
or where there is neglect or abuse.
We ask you to guide all who have the care of families,
who are struggling with their relationships.

Silence

Wonderful God,
reveal in us your glory.

We give thanks for all
who have made discoveries in medicine
and all who are responsible for the care of human life.
We pray for all doctors and nurses
and our own local health centres.
We ask your blessing
upon all who are suffering at this time,
especially any who feel
they no longer have any value or influence.

Silence

Wonderful God,
reveal in us your glory.

We give thanks for all who have witnessed
to your love and saving power.
We rejoice in the fellowship of all your saints
and pray that our loved ones departed
may share with them
in the fullness of your eternal kingdom.

Silence

Merciful Father,
accept these prayers
for the sake of your Son,
our Saviour Jesus Christ.
Amen.

Memory verse

And the Word became flesh and lived among us, and we have seen his glory, the glory as of a father's only son, full of grace and truth.
John 1:14

Suggested music

Christ, whose glory fills the skies
Lord, the light of your love (*Shine, Jesus, shine*)
God of mercy, God of grace

This is a good Sunday to use the 'Peruvian Gloria'.

CANDLES

Aim

To show that God's glory is seen in Jesus.

Teaching

Show pictures, Christmas cards and Easter cards of Jesus that show him brighter than his surroundings. Get the children to talk about why Jesus is shown with light around him or coming from him. It is to show that Jesus is very special and that he is not just an ordinary person. (Give the children the opportunity to pick out Jesus from other people in paintings or cards, and ask them if they can say how they know.)

Once Jesus wanted to talk with God the Father but he wanted some friends still to be with him. So he took Peter, James and John (get the children to say the names of the disciples and to say how many there were). Jesus and his three friends went up a mountain. They climbed up a long way and the three disciples were tired. They could hardly keep awake. Jesus went just a little way off and began to pray to the Father. Suddenly the disciples noticed that Jesus was shining like a light would shine in the dark. His clothes and his face looked very bright. They realised that Jesus was very special. Then, while they were watching, a cloud came down. It was a dark cloud. Jesus was still shining brightly in the dark. Suddenly they heard a voice from the cloud. They could not see anyone but out of the cloud came a voice and it said some words about Jesus. The voice said, 'This is my Son, my Chosen; listen to him.' (Get the children to repeat this in sections and then again in two sentences.)

Who do you think was speaking from the cloud? Yes, it was God the Father. The three disciples did not see him but they heard his voice. They knew God had spoken to them and they also knew something about Jesus. What did they know? What did God ask them to do?

Then suddenly the cloud was gone. When they looked at Jesus he was not shining any more. But they knew he was special and that, whatever happened to him, God the Father loved him. They knew a secret about him because he is God's Son. They also knew from God that they had to listen to him and do what he asked them to do.

Activity

The children dance to music or run around. When the music stops the children must go to a corner. In each corner there is a person with a card. One side of the card is black and the other is light (it can have the drawing of a light on it). The person holding the card has it hidden before the music stops. When the children are in the corners the cards are revealed. All who have the dark side are out. Those shown the light side continue to dance or run around until the music stops. The last one or ones still in are the winners.

Prayer

God, we thank you
for sending Jesus your Son
to be a shining light
in the darkness of the world.
Amen.

Song

Jesus bids us shine (verse 1)

LAMPS

Aim

To explore the hidden glory of God.

Teaching

If you lost something in a dark room, what would you do to help you find it? Yes, you would put on a light. If you lost something outside in the dark, what would you use to help you find it? You would use a torch and shine it in all the dark places. Searchlights seek out people or things hidden in the dark. (You can demonstrate this by shining on someone after naming them. Keep the light off their faces.) Some lights are used for revealing, for showing things. Spotlights do this and they are very bright. You can use a torch to reveal something hidden under a cupboard or a bed. All of us see by the brightest light of all. What do you call that light? The sun. Why do we not look at the sun? It is too bright to look at and would harm our eyes. If we are to look at the sun, we have to use something to cover our eyes and even then be very careful.

God knew that people could not look at him. He was too wonderful to look at, so he protected people from

seeing him by often speaking from behind a cloud. We can look at the sun when it is behind a cloud. God often spoke to people from a cloud. He was with them but they could not see him. So that we could know better what God was like, he sent his Son to show us. Jesus came to show us how God loves us.

One day Jesus took three of his disciples with him up a high mountain. He took Peter, James and John (get the children to repeat the names). Jesus wanted to spend some time talking to God. While he was doing this, the disciples saw how special Jesus was. Suddenly Jesus and his clothes became shining bright, as bright as a bright light. They were surprised and wondered what it meant. Then a cloud came around them and out of the cloud they heard a voice. Whose voice do you think it was? Yes, it was God speaking to them and he was talking about Jesus. God said, 'This is my Son, my Chosen; listen to him.' After God had spoken to them, the cloud went away and the disciples saw only Jesus standing there. He looked quite ordinary: he was no longer shining. But the disciples knew what they had seen and heard. They knew that Jesus was special. They knew that Jesus is God's only Son and they were to do what he asked them. They kept this a secret for a while, but *we* know their secret. Let us say, 'Jesus is the Son of God.'

Activity

Play 'Light and dark'. Someone goes out of the room and while they are out something in the room is chosen. They then come back in and have to guess what it is. If they are a long way from the object everyone says, 'Dark'. If they move further away, the group says, 'Darker'. If they move towards it, the group says, 'Light', and if they get closer, everyone says, 'Lighter'. If the person comes alongside it, everyone says, 'Dazzling'. The seeker is allowed three guesses, so it is better to wander around until he/she hears the word 'Dazzling' and then guess. Once it is guessed someone else is sent out and it begins again.

Prayer

Jesus, you are the Light of the World.
When we know you,
you bring brightness and hope to our lives.
We know that you are God's Son
and we love you.
Amen.

Song

Sing the second verse of the 'Peruvian Gloria'

TORCHES

Aim

To see how Jesus reveals God to us.

Teaching

Whenever Jesus had something important to do he prayed (see Luke 4:42; 6:12; 22:39-46). He saw that, to do what the Father required, he needed to keep contact with him through prayer. On this occasion, Jesus took three of his disciples up a mountain. This reminds us of how Moses went up a mountain to receive directions from God, and how Elijah heard the voice of God on the mountain telling him what to do. The disciples were very tired, or perhaps St Luke was telling us they were about to have their eyes opened in a new way: they would soon see Jesus like they had never seen him before.

While Jesus was praying, the disciples saw a change in him. It was as if he shone with brightness, like Moses' face had shone when he came down from Mount Sinai. Then the disciples could see two people with Jesus: the giver of the Law from God and the greatest of the prophets – Moses and Elijah. The disciples began to realise that Jesus was the Promised One that was sent to bring freedom to his people. Then a cloud came round them like a mist. From the cloud came a voice – just as there had been a voice at Jesus' baptism. The voice said, 'This is my Son, my Chosen; listen to him.' They were in no doubt that it was the voice of God. The Father was saying Jesus was his Son, the Chosen One, the Messiah. They were also commanded to 'listen to him', and listening implied obeying.

Suddenly life returned to normal. The cloud was gone, and so were Moses and Elijah. Jesus was no longer shining. But they knew they had seen the glory of God revealed in the face of Jesus. They knew they had heard the voice of God from the cloud. Now they were prepared to face Jerusalem where Jesus would suffer, die and rise again. They knew that, whatever happened, God would be with them.

Activity

Encourage the group to write code messages to each other where the word 'glory' is a hidden word. 'Giving love out reveals youth' may not make a lot of sense but the first letters of the five words spell 'Glory'. 'I give you 7-12-15-18-25' is also the gift of 'glory' if the alphabet is simply replaced by numbers with A as 1 and Z as 26. Get the group to discuss when they think the hidden glory of Jesus is revealed.

Prayer

Good and gracious God,
you give us a glimpse of your glory
in the life and love of Jesus Christ.
Help us to live and work to your glory
every day of our life.
Amen.

Song

Glory, glory in the highest

LENT
First Sunday of Lent

Aim

To encourage people to see Lent as a time for improving their lives and their worship.

Preparation

Have pictures of targets around the entrance – dartboard, goal posts, archery target and rugby posts, for example – with the following captions displayed among them: 'If there are no targets you cannot score'; 'Without goal posts there can be no goals'; 'Lent is a time for setting goals for improving our aim.'

Opening activity

Print out the following and give a copy to everyone:

> AIMS FOR LENT
>
> I will seek to be generous towards others in thought, in action and in giving.
>
> I will cut back on what stops me achieving and doing what I am able to do.
>
> I will keep in daily contact with God who is ever with me.
>
> Signed .... Date ....

(These are the traditional aims for Lent and are usually seen as Almsgiving, Fasting and Prayer.)

Opening prayer

Lord Jesus, who walked the way of the cross
and gave your self willingly for us,
help us to be generous in our living
and to give ourselves to you.
Amen.

Opening song

Forty days and forty nights

Readings

Deuteronomy 26:1-11
Psalm 91:1, 2, 9-16
Romans 10:8b-13
Luke 4:1-13

Thought for the day

Jesus is full of the Holy Spirit after his Baptism, and it is this Spirit who leads him into the wilderness. It is the Spirit who initiated the encounter with evil. In the same way, the Church and its people need to confront evil as a witness to God. Too often the Church seems silent in the face of evil.

The wilderness is a dangerous place where food and water are scarce and wild beasts roam; it was also thought to be where evil powers roam – maybe a place for some to avoid. But God is also to be found there, as he was with Moses and the people of Israel in the desert; as he was with Elijah in the wilderness. The number forty implies a long time but it is also symbolic. The flood lasted for Noah for forty days (Genesis 7:4). Moses was on Sinai for forty days and nights (Exodus 34:28). Elijah travelled for forty days in the wilderness (1 Kings 19:8). Israel was in the wilderness for forty years (Exodus 16:35; Deuteronomy 2:7). On all these occasion we are told of the care and protection of God

Testing or temptation often comes when our resistance is low. Then comes the desire to give up the struggle against evil and to give up striving for God's kingdom. We lower our sights and our aims and so miss the target. In the New Testament one of the words for sin means 'missing the target'. For Jesus the desert is where he sorts out his aims and priorities.

'Command this stone to become a loaf of bread' is a great temptation for a hungry man. More subtle is the implication: look after yourself. Fill yourself with the things you desire, for you have the power to do it. We spend much of our lives filling ourselves with one thing or another. Jesus reminds us that we are dependent on God for life.

Jesus says, 'One does not live by bread alone.' All his hearers would understand by knowing the full quotation that continues, 'but by every word that comes from the mouth of God' (Deuteronomy 8:3).

Jesus is then offered the whole world. Was it the devil's to give? All Jesus had to do was compromise a little; accept the 'fallen' life as normal. Jesus replies with Deuteronomy 6:13: 'Worship the Lord your God and serve him only.' Jesus rejects false worship. What we worship determines our character, whether it is footballers, pop idols, models, or soap stars. Only the worship of God is the road to eternal life.

The devil then uses the holiest of places and quotes Scripture to lead Jesus astray. Nowhere or nothing is safe in the struggle against evil. Scripture can be misused and so can the Church, as history often shows. Jesus replies from Deuteronomy 6:16: 'Do not put the Lord your God to the test.'

It is too easy to jump just because the suggestion seems to come from good quarters; we have to use our hearts and minds and seek to serve our God.

Notice the devil leaves 'until an opportune time'; the battle is not over. It never is, as long as we are alive. The struggle against evil continues.

Question time

Are there areas where you feel the Church should speak out more against evil?

What do you feel are some of the false gods and idols of today?

Illustration

Anyone who is still alive is tempted, so do not say you are not tempted. If you are not tempted, you have never lived or you have let something in you die. There is always a tug of war between good and evil, between achieving and failing to do so. There is no place or person free from this battle. In the book *Rogue Herries*, Hugh Walpole tells of how Herries had come to the wild and lonely Lakeland where he met a travelling preacher called Robert Finch. Herries asked:

'How shall I like this place? It is cut off from the world.'

There was a sudden odd note of scorn in the little man's voice as he answered, 'It is the world, sir. Here within these hills, in this space of ground is all the world. I thought that while I was with my Lord Petersham that the world was there, but in every village I have passed since then I have found the complete world – all anger and vanity and covetousness and lust, yes, and all charity, goodness and sweetness of soul. But most of all, here in this valley I have found the whole world. Lives are lived completely . . .The mountains close us in. You will find everything here, sir. God and the devil both walk in these fields.'

Rogue Herries, Part 1, by Hugh Walpole

Intercessions

Blessed are you, Lord our God,
for you never leave us or forsake us.
When we wander away from you, you keep with us.
When we turn our backs on you,
you wait patiently until we turn again.
You are a loving and a forgiving God.
Blessed are you, Father, Son and Holy Spirit.

God, we thank you for our talents and abilities
and for all the people who help us to achieve in life.
We ask your blessing
upon all who set high ideals and hopes
for our society and the world.
We pray for all who are striving to improve their lives
and the communities in which they live.
We give thanks for the Church and its ministers
and ask your guidance and grace to be upon it.
We remember all who are struggling
against evil and wickedness at this time.

Silence

Lord, as you forgive and offer us newness of life,
help us to forgive.

We remember in your presence
all who have given their lives
in the service and care of others.
We pray for those who seek to keep law and order,
all who influence the minds of the young
and all who shape our society by their actions.
We ask your blessing especially
on those who stand against evil
at the risk of their own lives or well-being.

Silence

Lord, as you forgive and offer us newness of life,
help us to forgive.

We give thanks for our homes and our loved ones.
Lord, may we make our homes fit for your presence
and able to reveal your love.
We pray for all who harbour anger, resentment
or hatred in their hearts.
May they learn the joy and freedom
of forgiveness and mercy.

Silence

Lord, as you forgive and offer us newness of life,
help us to forgive.

Lord God, we thank you
for your loving kindness towards us.
We pray for all who are caught up in crime,
in violence or in drugs,
for all who have lost hold on a good way of life.
May they discover a new way and a new freedom in you.
We pray for victims of crime
or any who have been injured
through the carelessness of others.
We remember also all who are ill at home or in hospital,
especially those known to us.

Silence

Lord, as you forgive and offer us newness of life,
help us to forgive.

We rejoice in the witness of the saints
who sought to live holy and righteous lives.
We pray for our loved ones departed:
may they know newness of life in your kingdom
and enjoy your presence and love for ever.

Silence

Merciful Father,
accept these prayers
for the sake of your Son,
our Saviour Jesus Christ.
Amen.

Memory verse

You are my refuge and my fortress; my God, in whom I trust.
Psalm 91:2

Suggested music

Take my life, and let it be
Father, hear the prayer we offer
Lead us, heavenly Father, lead us

CANDLES

Aim

To show there is a battle between good and evil.

Teaching

Have you ever been told not to do something and then you have done it? All of us are able to be good or naughty. We can choose to do what we are asked or we can disobey. By doing wrong we can hurt and upset our parents. We are lucky that our parents love us, and love us even when we have hurt them.

Jesus wanted to do what God the Father sent him to do but the devil wanted to stop Jesus and make him do other things. Jesus went into the desert to pray to God the Father and to decide what he should do. There was no one else to be seen but the devil was there seeking to make Jesus go the wrong way.

Jesus had not eaten food for a long time and was hungry. The devil said, 'Look at these lovely round stones – you could make them into bread. You could have lots of food.' Jesus was hungry but he knew it was a trap. The devil wanted him to look after himself and make food just for himself. Jesus reminded the devil that God gives us life and what we need. We depend on God for everything.

The devil then said, 'I will give you the whole world, if you bow down and worship me.' He wanted Jesus to turn away from giving all his love to God. Jesus knew that the world belonged to God: the devil was telling him lies. Jesus said to the devil, 'You should worship God and only work for him.'

The devil was a bit angry by now and took Jesus right to the top of the Temple. It was really high up, a long, long way to fall. The devil said to Jesus, 'Jump! God and his angels will protect you.' What do you think might have happened if Jesus had jumped? He could have been killed. The devil was trying to get him do wrong things. Jesus knew he was being tricked by the devil and said, 'No, I will not jump. You should not do things to make God have to save you.' The devil was very cross but Jesus had won. Jesus would do what God wanted him to do. But the devil would be back to try and trap Jesus again.

Activity

Play 'Directions'. In each corner of the room is a direction – North, South, East and West.

The children dance or run around until the music stops and then they run to a corner. The leader has four cards, one for each direction, face downwards. After moving the cards around she asks one of the children to pick a card. The card is looked at and then it is announced, 'Everyone who has gone east (or whatever the card is) has gone the wrong way.' This group are then out. The last one or two in are the winners.

Prayer

God, help us to do what is right and good
and not to upset our parents or you.
Amen.

Song

We are marching in the light of God

LAMPS

Aim

To show that we have to aim for the good if we are to do it.

Teaching

Begin by playing 'Bean toss' (see Activity). Ask what happens if you miss. No points. You could try again. You could practise until you got better. Now if you take away the bucket, what happens? No one could score. You need a target if you are to score. If there are no goal areas, you cannot score goals. The game would become boring if there were no goals to aim at or targets to hit.

Ben wanted to learn to play the keyboard. He even had some lessons but he did not practise. He did not try to learn more; he did not aim to be a better player and after a while he gave up. When he grew up he wished he had learnt to play the keyboard. He was wrong to believe there was no need to practise.

Hannah wanted to be a ballet dancer. She went to classes and practised every day. Even when she didn't feel like bothering she made sure she practised. When she was older she became a very famous ballet dancer and yet she still practised every day. She always aimed to do her best.

Jesus wanted to do good work for God the Father. He went away to a quiet place to decide what God wanted him to do. Evil tried to make Jesus do wrong things and stop him serving God.

'Why do you not make these stones into lovely bread? I know you are hungry.' Evil knew that all of us like filling ourselves with nice things. Jesus replied that we do not live by bread alone. It is God who gives us life. We must never forget that our lives come from God.

Then Evil offered Jesus the whole world if only he would worship something other than God. Do you think the world belonged to Evil? I don't. I think the world really belonged to God. Evil often tells lies. Jesus said we are to worship only God. Let us remember it is God who is the Creator of the world.

Then Evil took Jesus to the top of the Temple and said, 'Jump. God loves you and cares for you. He will send his angels to protect you.' What do you think would have happened if Jesus had jumped? He would probably have died. Then Evil would have won. But Jesus said we are not to tempt God by doing such things. We are not to try and force God to do things, but we are to do what God would like us to do.

Jesus had beaten the powers of evil three times, so they left him but they would be back when they had a chance.

Activity

Play 'Bean toss'. Divide the group into two teams. Each team needs five beans and a bucket to throw them into. Let someone keep the score for each team. It is not a race. The teams give everyone a turn of throwing the five beans, one at a time, into the bucket. A point is scored for every bean that stays in the bucket. Do not make the distance too far between bean thrower and bucket.

Prayer

Lord God,
when we fail to do what you want us to do
forgive us and help us then to do what is right.
Give us strength to do what is good.
Amen.

Song

We don't believe the devil's lie

TORCHES

Aim

To show that life is a battle between good and evil, and because Jesus is human it is the same for him.

Teaching

Have you ever done something that you should not have done? Often by doing what others do not want us to do, we upset them. Sometimes friends fall out for ever. Everything we do, even in secret, has an affect on us and on others. We need to learn to do good and to avoid evil. We need to learn when we do wrong to say sorry and, if possible, to put it right.

Although Jesus is the Son of God, he was tempted as we are. Like every human, Jesus had the opportunity to do right or to refuse and just do what he felt like. Jesus had to decide what his aims were and how he would achieve them.

Before he began his teaching and healing ministry, Jesus went into the desert to work out his priorities and how he could serve God the Father. In this lonely place he would have time and space to think. Yet, like us all, it was when he had the time to think that he was tempted to go wrong.

Jesus had been fasting for forty days so he was truly hungry. It is not surprising that the first temptation is food. Lots of people are tempted by food. The devil says, 'Look after yourself, no one else will. Turn these stones into bread and feast yourself.' Jesus was hungry but he knew that food would not fill him. Jesus knew that God made a space in every person to be filled by God alone. He knew that God gives life even more than food, though he knew that we all need to eat.

Jesus was now offered all the kingdoms of the world (they were not really the devil's to give). All Jesus had to do was stop worshipping God. There are many things in the world that will stop us from praying. We will say we are too busy or we have something else we need to do. Jesus saw that God was the only One to worship, the only One to trust fully, the only One to give life.

Jesus replied, 'Worship the Lord your God and serve him only.'

Maybe it is because Jesus used the Scriptures to guide and help him that the devil tried to use them too. Jesus was next taken to the highest point of the Temple. Now the devil said, 'Jump!' The devil even quoted the Scriptures (Psalm 91): 'He will command his angels concerning you, to protect you', and 'On their hands they will bear you up, so that you will not dash your foot against a stone.' Jesus knew the love and protection of God but he also knew we should not seek to force God to do things for us. Jesus said, 'Do not put the Lord your God to the test.'

The devil had been defeated three times: three rounds to Jesus. But do not think the fight was over; the devil will return. In our own lives, as long as we live, we will meet temptation.

Activity

Have a dartboard with some Velcro darts. See who can score and who has difficulty. Alternatively have a plastic bucket and a few table tennis balls and see who can throw the most to stay in the bucket. As soon as a person misses two they are out. Talk about goals and scoring, the need to practise and the need to try again and again if we miss. Show how most of us need another chance.

Give this group the 'Aims for Lent' that was given out in church.

Prayer

Lord God,
on the way of goodness,
when we fall,
forgive us and lift us up.
Help us to do your will
and to seek to bring in your kingdom.
Give us the strength to resist temptation
and to do what is right and good.
Amen.

Song

He who would valiant be

Second Sunday of Lent

Aim

To show how God can be trusted to keep his promises.

Preparation

Collect advertisements of 'Special Offers' – the more absurd or unlikely, the better. Place them in the church entrance.

Opening activity

Voice 1 I bought 40 boxes of sweets because if you collect the wrappers from 40 you get a free CD.

Voice 2 It would have been cheaper to buy the CD. You've been had.

Voice 3 I get my petrol at the village filling station because it offers a reward of £5 once you have bought 500 litres.

Voice 2 That is a penny for every litre and they charge 2p a litre more for their petrol. You've been had.

Voice 4 I was told I had won a free holiday in a luxury hotel; all I had to pay for was my meals.

Voice 2 I know, but the meals cost more there than anywhere else and you had to pay dearly for anything you used. You've been had.

(Pause)

You can depend on God: when he makes promises they have real value and he always keeps them.

Opening prayer

O God, you have promised to be with us always,
in the dark to be our light
and to be our salvation.
Help us to put our trust in you
and your everlasting love.
Amen.

Opening song

The God of Abraham praise

Readings

Genesis 15:1-12, 17, 18
Psalm 27
Philippians 3:17–4:1
Luke 13:31-35

Thought for the day

In today's Gospel we see that not all Pharisees were opposed to Jesus. Here we have some Pharisees warning Jesus that Herod is out to kill him and advising him to flee for safety.

The very mention of Herod must have made the disciples quake with fear. Herod had already ordered the beheading of John the Baptist. He had shown disrespect for the dead by building Tiberias on tombs. Herod could easily have had Jesus killed.

Jesus shows no fear. He sends a message to Herod, saying, 'Go and tell that fox.' Now to the Jew the fox was a symbol of three things: it was the most cunning of animals, it was more destructive than other animals as it killed for pleasure, and it was a worthless and insignificant creature. Herod did not intimidate Jesus. As the devil could not sway Jesus from his course, neither could this tyrant. Jesus continues the work of the kingdom of God and says Herod cannot stop it (Luke 13:32, 33). The reference to the 'third day' contrasts Herod who puts to death, with God who brings to life, even from the dead.

Although Herod destroyed John the Baptist, and although by the time Luke was writing the Temple built by Herod had been destroyed, the movement towards bringing in God's kingdom will not cease. God's promises will be fulfilled. In a time when the idolatry of Rome, its destructive power and its injustices were rife, it is important to know God's promises will still be fulfilled. The outward symbols, even the officers of the church, may be attacked and destroyed, but God will still be there and continue his work.

The lament of Jesus over Jerusalem is that it has rejected his offer: God's offer of love. Like Herod, the city of Jerusalem had a destructive side: it rejected and killed the prophets. Jesus wanted to take Jerusalem 'under his wing', to give it love and protection, but it was unwilling. God fulfils his promises but he will not force them upon us. God offers us his kingdom but it is up to us to accept it and give it our allegiance.

Question time

God offers us his kingdom. Are we willing to live in it and by its rules?

Jesus offers us his presence. Do we take this offer up and have a relationship with Jesus, or do we ignore him?

Illustration

In a dream a man was told where there was treasure hidden in a nearby castle under a blue stone. The dream was quite clear and he could remember every bit of it. Yet he did not bother even to see if the stone was there in the castle. He told his dream to a friend. His friend went immediately and found a great treasure under the blue stone. He became very rich and although he was generous toward his friend, his friend realised that because he had not bothered when an opportunity was offered him he had missed out in a big way.

How often do we miss out on the fullness of life because we do not take up the promises of our God?

Intercessions

Blessed are you, Lord our God,
for you give us life and promise us life eternal.
In your Son you have shown us
the joy and the fullness of your kingdom.
Throughout our lives you offer us
your light and your salvation.
Blessed are you, Father, Son and Holy Spirit.

Father, as we give you thanks
for our freedom and ability to choose
we pray for all who are being persecuted for their faith.
We remember those who live in homes
where faith is discouraged or scorned.
We ask your blessing
on all who are struggling with their faith
or who are tempted to turn their back on you.

Silence

Lord, we come to you:
you are our light and salvation.

We rejoice in the good things of our land.
We pray that justice and freedom will be for all peoples.
We remember today all who are imprisoned
for speaking out against evil
or for resisting a corrupt regime.
We also pray today for the peace of Jerusalem.

Silence

Lord, we come to you:
you are our light and salvation.

We give thanks for our homes
and for those who have provided us
with love and security.
We ask your blessing upon our families and our friends.
We pray for homes where there is division and violence.
We remember especially today
children who are taken into care
and children who are in danger.

Silence

Lord, we come to you:
you are our light and salvation.

We pray for all who work in the healing professions,
all who do research in medicines
and all who care for ill people.
We pray for friends and loved ones who are ill
at home or in hospital.
We pray especially today for . . .
We ask your blessing upon all whose illness finds no cure.

Silence

Lord, we come to you:
you are our light and salvation.

We give thanks for the gift of eternal life
and we pray for friends and loved ones
who are departed from us.
May we rejoice with them
in the fellowship of all your saints.

Silence

Merciful Father
**accept these prayers
for the sake of your Son,
our Saviour Jesus Christ.
Amen.**

Memory verse

The Lord is my light and my salvation; whom then shall
I fear? The Lord is the stronghold of my life; of whom
shall I be afraid?
Psalm 27:1

Suggested music

The Lord is my light and my salvation (Rizza)
Have faith in God, my heart
Lord, you call us to a journey

CANDLES

Aim

To show how God keeps his promise.

Teaching

Abram was a very rich man. He had lots of sheep and
he had servants to look after him. He had a very nice
wife called Sarah but he was not happy. What do you
think might have made him sad? (Explore this idea and
help the children to talk about what makes people
happy and sad.)

Abram was sad because he did not have any children.
He was getting old and would have liked at least a son
so that he could hand on his farm, his sheep and all his
riches. But he did not have a son and it made him very
unhappy. Abram would really have liked to have a son
so he talked to God about it.

God asked Abram to go out into the night and look at
the stars. God had made all of them. God said to Abram,
'Count the stars, if you are able to count them.' Abram
started to count the stars, but soon he lost count. He
could not remember which ones he had counted. Some
twinkled on and off and were hard to count. After a
while Abram gave up trying to count them. Why do
you think he gave up? There were too many stars to
count: there were thousands of stars.

God knew that Abram could not count the stars for
there were too many. Now God said to Abram, 'You
shall have as many children as there are stars. From you
will grow a big family. It will be so big that you would
not be able to count it.' Abram believed because he
knew that God kept his promises. God always keeps his
promises. The Bible tells many stories of how God has
kept his promises, so we know when he makes a promise it is true.

Abram and Sarah had a baby boy when they were
very old. Sarah and Abram believed God could do anything and Sarah laughed for joy when she held her son
in her arms. She said, 'God has made me laugh.' They
called their son Isaac which means 'laughter' or 'laughing
boy' because they were so happy that God's promise
was beginning to come true.

Isaac would have twins called Jacob and Esau. So as
a grandfather Abram had more children. Jacob has 12
sons, so as a great-grandfather Abram had even more
children. And so Abram and Sarah's family grew and
grew until there were so many they could not be
counted. It came true, just as God had promised them.

Activity

Play a version of 'The farmer's in the dell'.

Abram's on the farm,
Abram's on the farm,

heigh-ho, heigh-ho,
Abram's on the farm.

Abram wants a wife,
Abram wants a wife,
heigh-ho, heigh-ho,
Abram wants a wife.

Sarah wants a child,
Sarah wants a child,
heigh-ho, heigh-ho,
Sarah wants a child.

We laugh with the child,
we laugh with the child,
ha, ha, ha, ha,
we laugh with the child.

The game ends with the laughter. The child becomes the next Abram and starts again.

Prayer

God, we know that you are always with us
and that you love us
because you have promised us –
and you always keep your promise.
Thank you.
Amen.

Song

Who made the twinkling stars

LAMPS

Aim

To show how God keeps his promises.

Teaching

Abram was very well-off, a rich man. He had lots of sheep, lots of servants and he had a beautiful wife called Sarah. As Abram and Sarah got older, Abram often became sad. There was one thing he wanted that money cannot buy: he wanted a son. He wanted a son who could work with him and to whom he could give all his riches one day. Abram badly wanted a son but it seemed he could not have a son.

Abram was a man who loved God and trusted in God. Already God had given him great things. Abram knew God quite well because they often spoke to each other in prayer. So Abram went to God in prayer and said how he was not happy. 'God, I have a lovely wife and great riches, but I am not happy because I do not have a family. I would like a son. If I do not have a son, all my riches will go to someone else and not to my family. I really would like a son.'

God listened to Abram as he always listens to prayers. God said to Abram, 'Go outside into the dark night and tell me what you see.' Abram went out and looked all around. He could see the shapes of sheep in the darkness – is that what God wanted to show him? Then he looked up at the stars – they were so beautiful. There

were hundreds and thousands of stars, and God had made every one of them. God is so wonderful. God asked Abram, 'Can you count the stars?' Well, Abram tried. He tried but he kept losing count – there were so many stars and some twinkled on and off. There were too many to count.

'Can you count the stars, Abram?'

'No, Lord, there are far too many and I keep losing count.'

'Abram, I who made all the stars will give you a son. You will not have to leave your riches to any other. Your son will have sons, and those sons will have sons . . . until your family is like the stars and it cannot be counted.'

'Thank you, Lord, I know that what you promise comes true. I will wait for what you have promised, for the time when Sarah gives me a son.'

As God promised, the time came and Sarah gave birth to a boy. The child made them both so happy that they called him 'laughing boy' or, in their language, Isaac. To Isaac twins would be born – Jacob and Esau. To Jacob twelve sons would be born, and so Abram's family began to grow just as God had promised. Abram knew that what God promised would happen.

Activity

Look at a chart of the night sky and suggest the children might like to count the stars! On the activity sheet cover the words 'God keeps his promise' with small sticky stars (available from most stationers). There are instructions for making a sky at night for Abram to look at.

Prayer

God, you keep your promises
and listen to all who call upon you.
Let me come to you in prayer
and to know that you are always ready
to help me and protect me.
Amen.

Song

Can you count the stars?

TORCHES

Aim

To show that God's work cannot be stopped, even through persecution and death.

Teaching

In today's Gospel we learn that not all Pharisees are against Jesus. In fact, many Jewish people followed Jesus. Here was a group anxious for Jesus. They were afraid Herod was out to kill him. Herod was afraid that Jesus was getting too popular and he wanted to stop him. The Pharisees were afraid *for* Jesus. Herod was afraid *of* Jesus. Jesus was not afraid. Jesus said, 'Go and tell that fox for me.' I should imagine no one dared to tell Herod

SECOND SUNDAY OF LENT

and no one would call him 'a fox'. The fox is the slyest of creatures. It kills for the pleasure of killing and it is counted worthless. No one would dare call Herod a fox. Yet he was sly and he killed for the pleasure of killing. He had already killed John the Baptist.

Jesus was not afraid because he knew that Herod could not stop his work even if Herod did kill him. God's kingdom will come, no matter what wicked men and women do. God had promised that his kingdom would come and that promise would be fulfilled. Perhaps in verse 32 Jesus used words that could be linked to his resurrection when he says, 'On the third day I finish my work.' Jesus was well aware that he was likely to die and that is why he went towards Jerusalem. In Jerusalem, Jesus would come up against the powers that wanted to stop him.

It saddened Jesus that Jerusalem was where prophets and holy people were killed: Jerusalem, which was meant to be the Holy City and the place of peace. He had tried to bring it protection and love but many people – not only Herod – were rejecting him. Jesus tells them their house is left to them, for in rejecting him they are rejecting the love of God and God himself. Yet God's promise will be fulfilled no matter what is happening upon the earth. God's kingdom will come.

Many earthly kingdoms have persecuted the Church and its saints. These kingdoms have come and gone. God's kingdom still remains and waits for us to enter.

Activity

Spend a little time looking at the 'Aims for Lent' and see how the group are trying to keep them. Talk about promises and the need to keep them. How much do we trust in God? There is an opportunity to affirm God's love and his kingdom on the activity sheet.

Prayer

Lord God, we pray that your kingdom will come
on earth as it is in heaven.
May we be part of your kingdom
and seek to do your will in all that we do.
Through Jesus,
who died and rose again for us.
Amen.

Song

God is faithful

Third Sunday of Lent

Aim

To show how our lives have purpose and are meant to be useful.

Preparation

Have pictures of trees and their fruit. Display a sign saying, 'By their fruits you shall know them.'

Opening activity

See how many fruits people can match with their trees. If possible, include a fig tree and its fruit, or even a fig or two, to see if people actually know what they are.

See how far down the alphabet the congregation can go naming fruit – apple, banana, cranberry, date, elderberry . . . This is quite hard. How far can you go?

Opening prayer

Lord, to turn away from you
is to enter into the darkness
and to fall.
To turn to you
is to rise and come to the light.
To abide with you
is to live in love and peace.
Lord, as we come to you
give purpose to our days.
Amen.

Opening Song

As the deer pants for the water

Readings

Isaiah 55:1-9
Psalm 63:1-8
1 Corinthians 10:1-13
Luke 13:1-9

Thought for the day

To understand the parable of the fig tree, we need to know two things. We need to know that all parables are about us and the way we live. We also need to know something about the importance of the fig tree in the Promised Land.

In many ways the fig tree was the most popular of trees. The picture of the Promised Land was 'a land of wheat and barley, of vines and fig trees, of pomegranates, a land of olive trees and honey' (Deuteronomy 8:8). When the spies looked over the land to see how fertile it was, they brought back grapes, figs and pomegranates as proof (Numbers 13:23). When the Old Testament wanted to describe peaceful times and prosperity it is of someone sitting under his own vine and fig tree (1 Kings 4:25; Micah 4:4; Zechariah 3:10). The fig tree was used as a symbol for the covenant between Israel and God (1 Kings 4:25; Isaiah 36:16; Jeremiah 24:4-7; Joel 2:22). The lack of fruit was a symbol of a lapse in faithfulness (Jeremiah 5:17, 8:13, 24:8-10; Joel 2:12).

The fig tree is a lovely tree, though not terribly tall – it grows to about 15 to 20 feet high. The spread of its branches can be up to 30 feet and so it provides good shelter and shade. Jesus had seen Nathanael under the fig tree's shade. But, more than shade, the tree was valued for its fruit and it cropped twice a year. The first crop comes off the old wood in June and the second off the new wood in September. A fig tree takes about three years to reach maturity; if by then it has not fruited, it is not likely to. From a fig tree the owner expects figs; if it does not produce, it does not fulfil its purpose. A tree that does not fruit is taking up room, feeding off the land and not giving in return. In the parable the tree is given another chance but it will not go on for ever, for there will be a day of reckoning.

The fig tree in the parable was all promise and no performance. It had its leaves, maybe even flowers, but it did not produce fruit and that was its main purpose. To give shelter from the heat was not enough; it was there to produce figs and if it failed to produce fruit, then it was useless. Uselessness invites disaster, for all things have a purpose – and that includes us. The church is not only a place of shelter; we have to produce the fruits of the Spirit.

Profession without practice is condemned. It is no use saying we are Christian if it does not show in the way we live.

Thank God for the second chance. We are still here for another year. Heed the words of Jesus to repent: we are to turn around (Luke 13:5) and not proceed in the wrong direction. Let us bring forth fruit.

Question time

If we played the game 'The Weakest Link', where do you think you would be when it comes to bearing fruit?

What do you consider your purpose to be on this earth?

Illustration

Abraham Lincoln triumphed over many adversities to become the President of the United States. Here are some of his words and they are about all of life and not just gardens:

Die when I may, I want it said of me that I plucked a weed and planted a flower wherever I thought a flower would grow.

Think of the purpose of our existence as expressed by The Shorter Catechism of 1647:

What is the chief end of man?
To enjoy God and to glorify him for ever.

Intercessions

Blessed are you, Lord our God,
for you are our Creator.
You have made us out of your love and for your love.

You have created us to enjoy this earth
and to bring forth the fruits of the Spirit.
Blessed are you, Father, Son and Holy Spirit.

We give thanks for your Church throughout the world,
that it is a place of shelter and security,
that it offers sanctuary and peace to many.
May the Church be a place where talents are developed
and your purpose fulfilled.
May we each show in our lives the fruits of the Spirit
in love, joy and peace.
We pray especially
for any who are struggling with their faith
and for those who are learning to turn to new ways.

Silence

Lord, you are our helper:
your hand holds us fast.

We thank you for all who provide us
with food and the essentials of life.
We ask your blessing upon all who grow crops
and care for sheep and cattle,
and upon fishermen.
We pray today for all who are unemployed
or have been made redundant,
all who are unable to work through illness.
May they still know they have a purpose in life
and that they are useful members of our communities.

Silence

Lord, you are our helper:
your hand holds us fast.

We give thanks for our parents
and all they have done for us.
May we be useful members of our home and community.
We pray for all who are struggling with debt
or with division within the family.
We ask your blessing upon our loved ones and friends.

Silence

Lord, you are our helper:
your hand holds us fast.

We remember before you, O Lord,
all who feel that they are unwanted or rejected.
We pray for those who suffer from a disability
and those who are unable to cope on their own
through illness or through becoming weak and frail.
May they know they are respected and loved members
of our communities.
Lord, give them courage and hope in their troubles.

Silence

Lord, you are our helper:
your hand holds us fast.

We rejoice in the gift of eternal life.
Help us to live that life as fully as we can now
to your glory and to the benefit of others.
We remember all who have improved our world
by their lives and their attention.
We give thanks for all your saints
and we ask you to bless our loved ones
who have departed from us.

Silence

Merciful Father,
**accept these prayers
for the sake of your Son,
our Saviour Jesus Christ.
Amen.**

Memory verse

Seek the Lord while he may be found, call upon him
while he is near.
Isaiah 55:6

Suggested music

For the fruits of his creation
To everything there is a season (*Turn, turn, turn*)
Give me joy in my heart

CANDLES

Aim

To show how God loves us and gives us another chance
to love him.

Teaching

Once upon a time there was a man who got a gardener
to plant a tree near his house. He hoped that when it grew
he would be able to sit in the shade and be comfortable
in the bright sunshine because where he lived was very
hot and sunny. Most of all, the man hoped that he would
get some fruit from his tree. The tree was a fig tree, so
what sort of fruit would you expect him to get? That's
right: figs. Who has tasted a fig? Maybe some of you
would like to try one now. (Figs are readily available
from fruiterers or supermarkets – see if you can provide
a few fresh figs.) The man wanted the tree to give him
figs but he would have to wait. The first year the tree
was just growing and there were no figs. The second
year the man hoped there might be some figs. But there
were no figs. (Get the children to repeat it each time you
say, 'But there were no figs.') He waited yet another
year – he was sure the tree would give him figs. But
there were no figs. For three years the tree had been
looked after; it had been watered and cared for. The tree
was in good soil and taking strength from the soil. But
there were no figs.

The owner was not very happy. The tree was well
looked after – it was producing leaves and giving
shade. But there were no figs. What do you think he
decided to do? Cut it down. But the gardener who cared
for all the trees said, 'Give it another chance. Maybe
next year it will do better and produce figs.' The owner
agreed and the tree was given another chance.

Now God wants us to love him and to talk to him in
prayer but we often forget. Yet God does not get angry
with us because he loves us and he always gives us
another chance. Even when we have done what God
does not like, he gives us another chance. We can begin
again because God still wants us to love him.

Activity

Play a game of 'Second chance'. Have corners of two different colours and four different shapes (playing cards could produce this). Use a pack of cards and when the music stops the children run to a corner. The cards are cut and it is announced that black (if that is the colour revealed) is out. After a pause say that the black ones shaped like a club (if the spades were cut) are given a second chance. When only two are left have only one colour and the one that avoids the shape cut is given a second chance and becomes the winner. The game can then start again.

Prayer

God, we thank you
for your love and care.
When we do wrong
you are always ready to give us another chance
to turn and give our love to you.
Amen.

Song

Gives! Gives! Gives!

LAMPS

Aim

To show that God wants us to be useful.

Teaching

In the land where Jesus lived there were two very popular things to grow – vines and fig trees. What do we get from vines? Grapes. (You may like to produce enough grapes for every one to have one.) What do fig trees produce? Figs, of course. Who has tasted figs? (If possible, provide a piece of fig for everyone to try.)

In the country where Jesus lived people liked to grow fig trees near their house to give them shade from the heat. But they also chose the fig tree because it would give them fruit in the early summer and in the autumn. People enjoyed coming out of their house and picking some figs to eat.

One man got his gardener to plant a new fig tree. In the first year he did not expect any figs for the tree was too young. In the second year he hoped it might produce one lot of fruit – but there was none. In the third year he looked forward to figs. The tree had been well looked after and watered, and it should now produce figs – but there was none.

The man decided this was not a very good tree; in fact, it was a useless tree because it did not do what it was expected to do. So he decided to have the tree cut down. It was no use wasting time on something that did not respond to attention. It might as well be scrapped. He went to the gardener and said, 'Cut that useless tree down; it is a waste of space.' The gardener knew the tree should have produced fruit by now but he didn't want to cut it down. He asked that the tree might have another chance. He said, 'Give the tree

another chance. Leave it just one more year and let us see if it produces fruit.' The tree was saved for a while longer and was given the chance to bear fruit and be useful.

We are all meant to be useful people – useful at home, useful at school and useful in serving God. We are lucky because when we fail to be useful, those who love us and care for us give us another chance. (Seek examples of this from the children.) We are given the chance to start again or to try again because none of us is useless. We are all useful because God made us to be useful.

God wants us to love him and to speak to him. This is one of the big reasons we are here on the earth – so that we might give our love and our prayers to God. If we fail, God does not say we are useless; he gives us another chance to love him. God wants us to turn to him each day and to be useful people on the earth. Let us promise to try and do what God wants.

Activity

Divide the group into pairs and teach them to play 'Scissors, rock, paper'. Point out how scissors are useless against rock, paper is useless against scissors, and rock is useless against paper. The aim is to choose something useful and so win the game.

Prayer

God, you have made us for a good purpose
and to be useful to you and each other.
When we fail to do what you want
forgive us and help us to start again.
Amen.

Song

For the fruits of his creation

TORCHES

Aim

To encourage the group to be useful members of church and society.

Teaching

Most gardens in the Holy Land were planted with vines and fig trees. If a person had a large garden, they would have a vineyard and a group of fig trees. Very often fig trees were planted near a well or near to the house because in full leaf the tree provided shelter from the heat. It was good to be able to sit under a fig tree and to eat its fruit. It took a fig tree only two years after it was planted to start fruiting; if it did not fruit by the third year, there was something wrong and it was not likely to produce fruit.

Jesus told a parable about a fig tree. It was planted by the gardener, well cared for and watered. It took nourishment from the soil and took up space near the house. But it did not produce fruit, not in its second or even in its third year. Because it didn't produce anything it was useless. It was good at taking up nourishment and space, good at taking the time of the gardener but not at giving out any fruit. It was all take and no give. The owner decided that the tree was useless. It could be cut down and replaced with another. He told the gardener to cut it down. The gardener was used to caring for the tree and he thought it should be given another chance. 'Please give it another year,' he said. The owner agreed with the gardener and for a while the tree was given another chance.

Jesus was not teaching us about fig trees; he was talking about our lives and us. We are meant to be able to give as well as receive. People who just take are not living as God meant them to. We are not meant to be useless members; we are meant to be useful at home, at school, at church. We all have something we can give to the world around us. If we fail, God does not write us off or cut us down. God loves us and gives us another chance. God wants us to love him and to give ourselves to him. When we fail to do this, God does not decide to wipe us off the face of the earth; he gives us another chance. God is always willing to forgive and to accept us.

We must look carefully at the end of the parable. The tree is given another chance but not for ever – a chance to do what it was made to do; it must not go on being useless. We must not test God's love by failing to turn to him and by not doing what he wants us to do. This is why Jesus often says to the people, 'Repent.' If you are going the wrong way, 'turn around', accept the chance you are given. (Spend the rest of the time talking about being given another chance and exploring the 'fruits of the Spirit' in Galatians 5:22.)

Activity

Look again at the 'Aims for Lent' and see who needs to start again. Encourage the group to explore the idea that no one is useless.

Place various fruit in a bag and see if the group can recognise them by touch. (Apple, pear, orange, banana, peach, grape are all reasonably easy to recognise. You might like to add a fig and even a tennis ball to make life a little difficult!)

Prayer

God, we thank you for your love.
When we are down you lift us up,
when we stray you seek to bring us back,
when we fail you forgive us.
Lord, help us to lead useful lives
and to serve you faithfully.
Amen.

Song

The fruit of the Spirit (Jackson)

Fourth Sunday of Lent
Mothering Sunday

Aim

To give thanks to God for our mothers and for all who have mothered us. We also give thanks to God for his loving care.

Preparation

Give everyone or every family a prayer for their mother and a candle to light as a 'thank you'. Have a large box filled with sand that can hold the candles in an appropriate place when they are lit. Remember, all people who come in have had or have mother; let no one be excluded. You may like to give them a printed copy of the opening prayer that will be sung.

Opening activity

Invite all to come forward in family groups or, if they are on their own, all individuals with their candle to light as 'thank you' for their homes and especially their mothers. While this is being done, or afterwards, sing the opening prayer.

Opening prayer

Bless our mother, Lord, every day. (3)
O Lord, bless her now.

Keep her safe, O Lord, every day. (3)
O Lord, bless her now.

Give her joy, O Lord, every day (3)
O Lord, bless her now.

(Tune: 'Kum ba yah')

(If there are lots of candles to light, different groups of children could sing this throughout the candle lighting.)

Opening song

Our Father, God in heaven

Readings for Mothering Sunday

Exodus 2:1-10 or 1 Samuel 1:20-28
Psalm 34:11-20 or Psalm 127:1-4
2 Corinthians 1:3-7 or Colossians 3:12-17
Luke 2:33-35 or John 19:25-27

Readings for Fourth Sunday of Lent

Joshua 5:9-12
Psalm 32
2 Corinthians 5:16-21
Luke 15:1-3, 11b-32

Thought for the day

What does every living creature have in common? They have a mother. If there were no mothers there would be no people to know of in the Bible. Moses, Samuel and Jesus all had mothers who cared for them and protected them. Do you know the name of the mother of Moses? She was called Jochebed (Exodus 6:20). His mother hid him from the soldiers of Pharaoh at great risk to herself.

Who was the mother of Samuel? She was called Hannah (1 Samuel 1:20). For a long time she had no children and promised if she had a child she would raise him to do the work of God. When Samuel was born Hannah sang a song for joy. When Samuel was old enough she took him to the priest Eli, so that Samuel could learn to work for God.

Who was the mother of Jesus? Mary; without her saying 'Yes' to the angel that visited her, without saying 'Yes' to God, the baby Jesus could not have been born into the world. In caring for Jesus, Mary helped to bring to the world a loving Saviour.

All of us are fortunate if we have a mother who has loved us, cared for us, fed us, worked for us and protected us. Even when we have done wrong things, our mothers still love us. Most of us can depend on the love of a mother.

Today we seek to give thanks for the constant love and care of our mother. We also give thanks for the care and nourishment we have received from the Church.

Let this be the day when we thank our mother by trying to make her work easier, by taking our share of the work at home, by washing up and tidying our room. Let it be a day when we give her a card, a letter of love, a posy or some present as a sign of our gratitude and love in return for her love.

Question time

When did we last openly express our love and gratitude for our mother? This is a good day to begin again if we have been slow in expressing our love.

You cannot pay for love or buy it. How can we give thanks for the love of our homes?

Illustration

I want to tell you of a mother who had no children, yet she had a big family. Her name was Teresa and she was born in Albania. She became a nun and her work took her to one of the largest towns in the world, Calcutta. There are many people in that city and it is overcrowded. Many poor people have nowhere to go and they feed off scraps thrown out by others, often out of rubbish bins. They sleep on the streets, in doorways, under bridges. If they are ill, no one cares for them; there are not enough doctors and nurses. They have no home to go to and no mother to look after them. Teresa tried to help as many as she could and they knew her as Mother Teresa.

One day Mother Teresa saw a woman lying in the road. People were just walking past and ignoring her. Mother Teresa saw the woman was very ill. She tried to get people to help but no one wanted to know. Mother Teresa tried to get her into hospital but the doctor said there was no room for people so poorly. She went to see the health officer and he offered her two very small rooms where she could live with the woman and look after her. She did that until the woman died.

Mother Teresa got lots of women, mothers and nuns together and founded the Missionaries of Charity to care for the ill, the unwanted, for the old, for babies and for unwanted children. Mother Teresa may not have had any children of her own but many people called her Mother and she had one of the largest families on earth.

Mother Teresa often said, 'Let us do something beautiful for God', and this she did time and time again.

Intercessions

(Let families pray the intercessions today. The first part is devised for younger children to pray. Remember they need rehearsing and need to be heard.)

For our parents and the love that they give to us,
God, we thank you
and we praise you.

For our mother's love and care,
God, we thank you
and we praise you.

For our father's love and protection,
God, we thank you
and we praise you.

For the love we share with our brothers and sisters,
God, we thank you
and we praise you.

For our homes and all that you give us,
God, we thank you
and we praise you.

We pray for Mother Church
that helps us to grow in the faith,
for our clergy and all who minister to us and care for us,
for all who help us to know and love God.

Silence

Loving Father,
hear us and help us.

We remember today all homeless peoples,
all who are separated from their loved ones
through war or troubles.
We pray for any who are taken into care,
whether they are young or old.
We ask your blessing
upon all who have lost loved ones this year
and upon all who are feeling lonely or unwanted.

Silence

Loving Father,
hear us and help us.

We give thanks for our own homes
and ask your blessing upon our family and friends.
We ask you especially
to bless our mother at this time.
We pray for mothers throughout the world;
may they never be taken for granted
and always be respected.

Silence

Loving Father,
hear us and help us.

We pray for all who are ill at home or in hospital.
We remember families where the mother is ill
or where she is tending an ill child.
We ask your blessing upon families
where there is poverty or the inability to cope.

Silence

Loving Father,
hear us and help us.

We give thanks, O God, for your loving care
and we ask your blessing
upon all our loved ones and friends
who have departed this life
and are at peace in your kingdom.

Silence

Merciful Father,
**accept these prayers
for the sake of your Son,
our Saviour Jesus Christ.
Amen.**

Memory verse

You are a hiding place for me; you preserve me from trouble; you surround me with glad cries of deliverance.
Psalm 32:7

Suggested music

God is love: his the care
For the beauty of the earth
Bind us together, Lord

CANDLES, LAMPS and TORCHES

Today is a day for the family to worship together, to rejoice in being a family and to give thanks for their mutual love. Involve as many of the children as possible in doing things. Let them bring up the bread and the wine, and take the collection. The children could carry banners expressing thanksgiving for the love of their homes and the love of God. Children could be encouraged to bring a photograph of their mother and bring it with them when they come to the altar rail. Let children lead some of the intercessions and some of the readings. It should be possible for a mother and a child to share in a reading. If flowers or cards are given out, remember all of us have a mother. Encourage all to come forward. Some may like to place their flowers or card near the candles if their mother has died and is now in God's kingdom and love.

Fifth Sunday of Lent

Aim

To rejoice in the sacrificial love of Mary, which is a foretaste of the sacrifice of Christ the 'Anointed One'.

Preparation

Have statements about love in the entrance – 'Money can't buy you love'; 'Love changes everything'; 'Love ever gives and gives'; 'Love is priceless'. Include pop song titles.

Opening activity

If possible, let the 'Torches' sing 'Said Judas to Mary'. Alternatively, this can be sung by three people each taking a part. If this is not possible, let three people read the various parts – the more dramatic, the better.

Opening prayer

O God, who through Jesus
revealed your great love for the world,
help us to give ourselves in love and service
to you and to each other,
so that the world may know we are your disciples.
Amen.

Opening song

A man there lived in Galilee

Readings

Isaiah 43:16-21
Psalm 126
Philippians 3:4b-14
John 12:1-8

Thought for the day

St John tells us it is only six days to the Passover, the time of sacrificing the sacrificial lamb. All male Jews who lived near enough were expected to go to Jerusalem for the Passover. Because the city was so crowded, Bethany was counted as part of the outer limits of Jerusalem and a place that could accommodate pilgrims. Jesus had been condemned by Caiaphas and 'outlawed' by the Pharisees (see John 11:47-53, 57). Jesus was not put off and went towards Jerusalem at great risk to his life. He stayed at the home of Lazarus, whom he had raised from the dead, and Lazarus sat at table with him.

Martha loved Jesus and served him as best she knew how by looking after his need for food and comfort. People like Martha made the ministry of Jesus possible.

Mary was an impetuous person and not afraid of showing that she loved Jesus. She came into the room and gave him the most precious thing she had – a pound of costly perfumed oil. She poured this perfume over the feet of Jesus. She did not presume she could anoint his head with oil (Psalm 23:5). She did the unusual act of anointing his feet.

As Messiah, or Christ, means the Anointed One, Mary's act has special significance. It is an act of love, and in love nothing is too costly to give to the beloved. Mary then probably scandalises some by wiping the feet of Jesus with her loose hair. (In Palestine no self-respecting woman would appear in public with her hair loose; this was a sign of a loose woman.) Jesus accepts this attention as a sign not only of her love but also as a preparation for his burial (John 12:7). He is in no doubt that his time is now limited. Love makes it possible to face the task ahead. Pain can be borne as long as we know we are not totally on our own. The extravagance of love enriches giver and receiver.

When we are told the house was filled with the fragrance, it is a little detail that must be obvious. Perhaps John wanted us to realise that the whole Church would be filled with the memory of this act (see Mark 14:9).

Judas then costs Mary's act of love. You can never do that – love cannot be measured by money. Here is a hint that some of the women understood Jesus better than some of the apostles.

Question time

Do you think the perfumed oil should have been sold, as Judas suggested, or can you see that love must not be measured by cost, especially someone else's love?

How did different people give their love and attention to Jesus during his stay at Bethany?

Illustration

A nurse in hospital described how humans have a great capacity for accepting what is happening to them and for enduring pain as long as they have loved ones about them and people who truly care. Pain can be borne as long as we are not left alone. We need to know in our troubles that we are still loved and cared for. Worse than pain is the feeling of separation from loved ones or a feeling that we are no longer wanted.

When many were beginning to go against Jesus – including Judas – it is good to see the expression of love and affection that is shown him from the whole household at Bethany.

Intercessions

Blessed are you, Lord our God,
for you love us with an everlasting love;
you never leave us or forsake us.
You have given your only Son for our salvation
and to bring us to eternal life.
Blessed are you, Lord God, now and for ever.

Father, we give you thanks
for all who have given their lives
in love and service of humankind.
We remember today all who quietly live sacrificially
so that others may enjoy the fullness of life.
We ask you to bless all who risk their lives
to bring the Good News to others.

We pray for any who feel that their ministry
is a lonely and unrewarding task.

Silence

Help us, Lord, to serve you,
to give and not to count the cost.

We give thanks
for all who have offered their talents and time
without questioning the cost.
We pray for all who work in the emergency services,
for all who look after our needs and well being.
We ask you to bless all who are seeking
to relieve poverty and oppression in the world.

Silence

Help us, Lord, to serve you,
to give and not to count the cost.

We praise you for our loved ones
who have enriched our lives
by their care and goodness.
We ask your blessing upon our families and friends,
upon our teachers
and all who have been our benefactors.
We pray for all who feel neglected and unwanted.

Silence

Help us, Lord, to serve you,
to give and not to count the cost.

We give thanks for all you have given us, O God.
We remember in your presence
all who are suffering,
all who are being persecuted,
all who are oppressed.
May we help where we can
to ease their pain or their troubles.

Silence

Help us, Lord, to serve you,
to give and not to count the cost.

We give thanks that through the love of Christ
and his offering of himself on the cross
you have opened to us the way to life eternal.
We ask your blessing upon your saints
and upon all our loved ones departed.
May we rejoice with them
in your love and in your kingdom.

Silence

Merciful Father,
**accept these prayers
for the sake of your Son,
our Saviour Jesus Christ.
Amen.**

Memory verse

I want to know Christ and the power of his resurrection.
Philippians 3:10

Suggested music

Ubi caritas et amor
And now, O Father, mindful of the love
Have faith in God, my heart

CANDLES

Aim

To show the importance of being a friend of Jesus.

Teaching

Everyone needs some friends they can talk with and share with. Tell me the name of one of your friends. Friends are people we can go to when we need help or looking after. Perhaps some of you have stayed with a friend at their house.

Jesus had his special friends. We call them disciples. Do you know the names of any of the disciples? What were the names of the fishermen disciples? Jesus loved to visit his friends and to hear what they were doing. We know he had three friends in a village near Jerusalem called Bethany. Here lived a brother and two sisters. The brother was called Lazarus. Does anyone know the names of the sisters? They were called Martha and Mary. Let us say the names of the friends of Jesus. Lazarus, Martha and Mary. Let us say them again. Whenever they knew Jesus was coming they would be busy getting ready for him. Lazarus probably collected and chopped wood for the fire to cook on. Mary and Martha would be busy around the house.

Perhaps you help your mummy when you are having visitors. Then while mummy is getting a meal ready, other members of the family can talk to the visitors.

It was like that in the house at Bethany. When they heard that Jesus was coming they got everything ready for him. Lazarus stopped work and came to talk to Jesus. He would sit with him and have a meal. Jesus liked to be able to talk to Lazarus.

Martha did what she was good at – she cooked a meal for Jesus. Martha knew that Jesus was often travelling and needed something good to eat. Jesus enjoyed eating what Martha cooked for him.

Mary wanted to give Jesus a special present but the only precious thing she had was a box of perfume. It had a beautiful smell and was very expensive. She was saving it for a special occasion. Then she thought, 'This is a special occasion.' She went in to where Jesus was sitting on the floor with Lazarus and poured the perfume over the feet of Jesus. Jesus knew that Mary did this to show that she cared for him and he was very pleased.

Jesus had three good friends at Bethany – let us say their names. Each of his friends gave him something special and spent time with him. When do we spend time with Jesus? Yes, when we pray. Jesus likes to know that we are his friends and that we speak to him each day.

Activity

Make the house at Bethany by laying a shoe box on its side. Have plasticine or cut-out figures to represent Jesus, Lazarus, Mary and Martha. Show the work that the three did around the house to get ready for Jesus. The children could mime Lazarus chopping wood, Mary sweeping and Martha cooking. Let them also show Mary putting the nice smelling perfume on the feet of Jesus.

Prayer

Jesus, we thank you for being friends
with Lazarus, Martha and Mary.
We would like to be your friend
and to meet you every day.
Amen.

Song

Jesus' love is very wonderful

LAMPS

Aim

To show that we can all have something to offer.

Teaching

Jesus wanted to be at Jerusalem for the feast of the Passover. Jerusalem would be full of people from all over the land, so Jesus decided to go and stay with his friends at Bethany, a village just outside Jerusalem. He had been there on other occasions, and no doubt his friends looked forward to seeing him. Not long ago he had gone to Bethany when Lazarus became ill and died. Jesus brought Lazarus back to life again. For doing this, his friends would be for ever grateful and sought to make Jesus really at home.

Lazarus stopped what he was doing so that he could sit with Jesus, to talk to him and listen to him. Because Jesus was a friend, Lazarus wanted to spend as much time as possible with him. As was the custom, they sat on the floor of the house.

While they talked Martha was busy cooking. Not only had Jesus come but his disciples were there as well. It was a lot of people to look after and Martha was busy. She was good at cooking and knew that Jesus often needed a good meal. So she did what she was good at and provided the food.

Mary wanted to do something special for Jesus. Lazarus was listening to Jesus. Martha was cooking for Jesus. What could Mary do that was really special? Then she remembered she had a very precious box of perfume, the sort that could only be used for special occasions. Well, this was such a time. She brought the perfume into the room where Jesus was and began to put it on his feet. Soon the whole room was filled with the beautiful smell. Judas began to complain that Mary had wasted a box of perfume and she could have sold it and given the money to the poor. Jesus said to Judas, 'Leave her alone. Do not upset her. She has done a beautiful thing for me out of her own love. What she has done will always be remembered.' Mary was so pleased that she had used the perfume on Jesus. Each of the three had done something different for Jesus.

Let us think about the words from the Christmas carol 'In the bleak mid-winter':

What can I give him, poor as I am?
If I were a shepherd I would bring a lamb;

if I were a wise man I would do my part,
yet what can I give him: give my heart.

Discuss how we can give our heart, our love, to Jesus. Can we seek to give Jesus the best we have to offer? Jesus wants us to give ourselves to him as he gave himself for us.

Activity

Have boxes with various smelly things in them. Provide an opening only big enough to let the group smell what is inside each box. See who can recognise the most smells. Have things like an onion, a chocolate cake, mint, apple, vinegar – anything with a strong smell that they will recognise.

Prayer

Lord Jesus, as you gave your life for us
and offer us your friendship,
help us to be your close friend
and to talk with you each day.
May we give our love and our life
to work for you and your glory.
Amen.

Song

Jesus put this song into our hearts

TORCHES

Aim

Through the song 'Said Judas to Mary', to show the meaning of the act of love by Mary at Bethany.

Teaching

The High Priest and the Pharisees had made Jesus an outlaw and wanted people to tell them where he was, so that they could kill him. Jesus knew that his time on earth was soon to be over. He wanted to be in Jerusalem for the Passover, though he knew the danger in going there. Bethany is a village on the outskirts of Jerusalem and is counted as part of Jerusalem for the festival. At Bethany, Jesus could stay with his friends, Lazarus, Martha and Mary. These three had a very special reason for wanting to show their love for Jesus. Do you know why? (Give a recap of John 11 if they don't remember.)

Lazarus was pleased to see Jesus because, without Jesus, Lazarus would be dead. He stopped all his work to give Jesus his undivided attention. He sat with Jesus, talked to him and listened to him.

Martha, as always, provided for Jesus and his friends. This meant she was busy preparing food and making sure Jesus got enough to eat. Without people like Martha, Jesus could not survive.

Mary wanted to do something special for Jesus. She was so grateful that her brother was alive. But what could she do? Then she remembered the precious oils that she had. (It was more solid than oil and was used as a perfume.) With the oils she came and anointed Jesus. Did you know that 'Christ' means the 'Anointed One'? Who, then, anointed Jesus? Possibly John the Baptist with water, and now Mary with oil. She did it out of gratitude and love. You cannot cost acts of love but Judas tried to. Let us spend the rest of the time looking at the hymn by Sidney Carter about this occasion.

Activity

Act the hymn out with readers. Then, if possible, get three people or groups to sing it:

> Said Judas to Mary, 'Now what will you do
> with your ointment so rich and so rare?'
> 'I'll pour it all over the feet of the Lord,
> and I'll wipe it away with my hair,' she said,
> 'I'll wipe it away with my hair.'

> 'Oh Mary, oh Mary, think of the poor,
> this ointment, it could have been sold,
> and think of the blankets and think of the bread
> you could buy with the silver and gold,' he said,
> 'you could buy with the silver and gold.'

> 'Tomorrow, tomorrow, I'll think of the poor,
> tomorrow,' she said, 'not today;
> for dearer than all the poor in the world
> is my love who is going away,' she said,
> 'is my love who is going away.'

> Said Jesus to Mary, 'Your love is so deep,
> today you may do as you will.
> Tomorrow you say I am going away,
> but my body I leave with you still,' he said,
> 'but my body I leave with you still.'

> 'The poor of the world are my body,' he said,
> 'to the end of the world they shall be.
> The bread and the blankets you give to the poor
> you'll know you have given to me,' he said,
> 'you'll know you have given to me.'

> 'My body will hang on the cross of the world,
> tomorrow,' he said, 'and today,
> and Martha and Mary will find me again
> and wash all my sorrow away,' he said,
> 'and wash all my sorrow away.'
> *Sidney Carter*

Prayer

Lord Jesus, friend of Lazarus, Martha and Mary,
be my friend this day.
May I know of your love and your care for me
and may I give my love and my life to you,
Jesus Christ my Lord.
Amen.

Song

Said Judas to Mary

Palm Sunday

Aim

To rejoice at the entry of Christ into Jerusalem and to share in the Passion story.

Preparation

Make sure there are enough palm crosses for everyone. It is a good exercise to get a few of the older children together and make your own. You may prefer to get palm crosses from Africa and so support a village that spends a good deal of the year making palm crosses. These can usually be obtained from SPCK shops or one of the missionary societies. You can also have palm branches to wave or branches from an evergreen tree. Have a few tambourines, castanets and shakers for the younger children to play during the procession.

Opening activity

Use the Liturgy of the Palms. Have two children to hold the trays of palm crosses and two other children to distribute them. During the distribution all could sing the words 'Praise God' over and over to the tune of 'Amazing Grace'. Get everyone to hold up their palm cross while they are blessed. Now is a good time to have a procession and sing as you go. Have at least one hymn the children can easily sing, such as 'We have a king who rides a donkey' or 'Give me joy in my heart'. If you are fortunate enough to be able to borrow a donkey, the procession could go outside and then around the church. The 'Hosanna' song from *Jesus Christ Superstar* is good for a procession.

Readings

Liturgy of the Palms
Luke 19:28-40
Psalm 118:1, 2, 19-29

Blessing of the Palms

(The congregation hold up high their palm crosses.)

Lord God, whose Son Jesus Christ
rode into Jerusalem as the Messiah,
to suffer and die,
bless these palms
that they may be to us a sign of his victory.
May we who hold them
always accept him as our King
until we rejoice in the kingdom
where he reigns with you and the Holy Spirit,
now and for ever.
Amen.

Let the people move to the entrance of the church with the palm crosses that have been blessed. Use Psalm 24 verses 7-10 (said or sung – if said, let the leader of the worship and the congregation say alternate verses).

7 Lift up your heads, O gates!
and be lifted up, O ancient doors!
that the King of glory may come in.

8 Who is the King of glory?
The Lord, strong and mighty,
the Lord, mighty in battle.

9 Lift up your heads, O gates!
and be lifted up, O ancient doors!
that the King of glory may come in.

10 Who is this King of glory?
The Lord of hosts,
he is the King of glory.

Behold your king comes to you, O Zion,
meek and lowly and sitting on an ass.
Hosanna to the Son of David.
Blessed is he who comes in the name of the Lord.

Processional

All glory laud and honour

Readings

Liturgy of the Passion
Isaiah 50:4-9a
Psalm 31:9-16
Philippians 2:5-11
Luke 22:14–23:56 or Luke 23:1-49

Let the dramatic readings of the Passion narratives replace the sermon today. Allow the Scriptures to speak for themselves. Use as many people as possible to share in the readings. I have provided ideas for the Liturgy of Palms rather than comment on the Passion. I hope Holy Week will be used to do the latter.

Thought for the day

Jesus was travelling from Jericho to Jerusalem, about 20 miles and uphill nearly all the way. This was a rocky and dangerous road, more dangerous for Jesus because the leaders of the church had already outlawed him. There was a price on his head (John 11:57).

Jesus would not be swayed from coming to celebrate the Passover in Jerusalem. It was all planned. He had made arrangements for the ass and the password was 'The Lord needs it'. Bethphage and Bethany were favourite places of Jesus and here he was well known and liked. These places were on the south-east side of the Mount of Olives and were counted as part of Jerusalem for festivals. Here Mary had anointed Jesus. Here he stayed at the house of Lazarus, Mary and Martha. Here he raised Lazarus from the dead. It was also where he had stayed at the house of Simon. And on this hillside was the Garden of Gethsemane. The Palm Sunday events started from here.

Jesus could have slipped into Jerusalem unseen but he confronted the authorities by his action. Many people rode donkeys. The donkey was counted a noble beast. Kings rode horses to war or when they wanted to emphasise their might. When they came in peace they rode upon a donkey. Jesus would enter Jerusalem as the Prince of Peace, the promised Messiah. People would be given the choice to accept him or reject him, as is still the case. Already groups were polarising for or against Jesus. Jesus refused to be a puppet king who would dance at the whims of people. He refused to be a warlord and lead them to battle. He refused false dignity and pomp. Yet he would rule in the hearts of those who would allow him to.

Jesus rode on the donkey to fulfil the prophecy of Zechariah 9:9, 10 (read these verses out). He is your King. Will you accept him? It is by living his way that God's kingdom comes on earth.

Question time

Have we accepted Christ as our Lord and King?

Do we allow the love and peace of Christ to rule in our hearts?

Intercessions

Blessed are you, Lord our God,
for you have redeemed us
by the offering of your Son upon the cross.
Through his death you destroy death
and open to us the kingdom of heaven.
As we seek to welcome Jesus into our lives
with cries of 'Hosanna',
and as we walk the way of the cross,
keep us ever mindful of your love and your peace.
Blessed are you, Father,
with the Son and the Holy Spirit.

Lord God, we thank you
for the coming of Christ into the world
and sharing in our troubles.
We rejoice in your saving power
and in the promise of life eternal.
We pray for all who seek to walk the way of the cross
this week.
We remember pilgrims in Jerusalem
and all who keep this Holy Week.
We ask your blessing
upon all Christians who are facing persecution
and rejection at this time.

Silence

Give thanks to the Lord for he is good;
his mercy endures for ever.

We pray for the peace of the world,
that the nations of the world may come
to find peace through the Prince of Peace.
We remember all who are suffering
through acts of violence and tyranny,
all who are being ill-treated,
the scorned and rejected of the world.

Silence

Give thanks to the Lord for he is good;
his mercy endures for ever.

We give thanks for the love of families and friends
and we ask your blessing upon their lives.
We remember today the homeless
and all who are finding it difficult to cope on their own.
We pray for all who live on the streets
and have no one to care for them.

Silence

Give thanks to the Lord for he is good;
his mercy endures for ever.

We give thanks for the loyalty of friends
and we pray for all who have been betrayed
by friends or loved ones.
We ask your blessing
on those who are deeply hurt
by the actions of others.
We pray for all who harbour hatred and resentment
and ask that they might find the power to forgive.

Silence

Give thanks to the Lord for he is good;
his mercy endures for ever.

As we remember the death and passion of our Lord,
we rejoice in his victory.
We pray for loved ones who have departed from us.
We remember all who have been bereaved recently
and all who have lost their lives
through accidents or acts of violence.
May they know of your love
and the joy of your kingdom.

Silence

Merciful Father,
accept these prayers
for the sake of your Son,
our Saviour Jesus Christ.
Amen.

Memory verse

Blessed is the king who comes in the name of the Lord!
Peace in heaven, and glory in the highest heaven!
Luke 19:38

Suggested music

For the Liturgy of Palms
Ride on, ride on in majesty
Hosanna, hosanna
Hail the coming Prince of Peace

This last hymn, from *Celtic Hymn Book* (Kevin Mayhew) is a wonderfully rousing hymn that captures the welcoming of our King.

For the Liturgy of the Passion
When I survey the wondrous cross
Meekness and majesty
My song is love unknown
There is a green hill far away
Were you there when they crucified my Lord?

CANDLES

Aim

To share in the joy of the entry of Jesus into Jerusalem.

Teaching

Have you ever had a ride on a donkey? Where was that? Most people who have a ride on a donkey in this country do it at the seaside. In many countries the donkey is a very important animal. Kings in some countries ride donkeys to show they are being friendly to the places they visit.

If you look carefully at a donkey, you'll see a dark line running along its back from head to tail. It has another dark line running from shoulder to shoulder. (You can draw these lines on a board or a piece of paper.) What sort of shape do these lines make? They make the shape of a cross. Who can tell me about the cross and what happened to Jesus?

I want to tell you about Jesus borrowing a donkey from a friend. Jesus was going to go to Jerusalem from Bethany. It was not very far so he could have walked, but he wanted to enter Jerusalem as a king coming in peace. So you can guess what he did. He got two of his disciples to go and borrow a young donkey. The man who owned the donkey said, 'What are you doing, taking my donkey?' The disciples replied, 'The Master needs it.' The man then said that they could borrow the donkey. The disciples then put their cloaks on the donkey for Jesus to sit on, and they all set off for Jerusalem.

As Jesus was going up the hill on the donkey people cheered and shouted, 'Hosanna!', which is like us shouting, 'Hurrah', though it really means 'God save us'. Let us all shout 'Hosanna!' together. Hosanna! Let us do it again but louder. Then people began to cut branches off the palm trees. Some branches they laid on the ground so that Jesus and the donkey could walk on them like a carpet. Some branches they held in their hands and waved. When the branches were waved they made a swishing sound. Let us all say, 'Swish, swish.'

The people were very excited because they knew Jesus was very special. They kept shouting, 'Hosanna!' and waving their palm branches and cheering for Jesus. They wanted God, through Jesus, to save them from all evil.

Activity

Now we will act out the story. We will have two disciples to get the donkey. We need two strong people to be the donkey and we need Jesus to ride it. (Cover two of the class with a blanket or large dark towel to be the donkey. Choose someone light and small to be Jesus.) Now I will divide the crowd into three groups. One group will shout, 'Hosanna!' when I point to them, another group will shout, 'God save us.' The last group will wave the branches (made from the activity sheet) and say, 'Swish, swish.' If I point to two groups, they both have to say their words. If I wave my hands, everyone has to say their words. Rehearse this once or twice until there is good sound and movement. Then get Jesus to travel around the room on the donkey (you may have to get someone to support him/her) as the group welcomes him.

Prayer

Jesus, we welcome you
as our King and our God
as we shout Hosanna.
Jesus, we love you
for you are the Son of God.
Amen.

Song

We have a king who rides a donkey

LAMPS

Aim

To show Jesus wants us to accept him as our Prince of Peace.

Teaching

The Chief Priest and the Pharisees had made Jesus an outlaw. They had put a price on his head, which meant if anyone told them where he was, they would be given money. Do you know who betrayed Jesus? Sadly, it was one of his friends, a disciple called Judas. But that is another story.

Jesus wanted to go to Jerusalem but he knew it was dangerous for him. Some people were trying to capture him. At first he stayed with some friends, Lazarus and his sisters. Do you know the names of the sisters? Mary and Martha. Maybe no one knew that Jesus was staying there. Then he decided he would go to Jerusalem. Some of the disciples tried to persuade Jesus not to go, or if he went, to go quietly and well covered up so that no one would notice him. But Jesus was not afraid and he would not sneak into Jerusalem. In fact, he would come to Jerusalem like a king, cheered on by his friends and others.

Jesus planned to do this some time before. Now he was able to say to two of his disciples, 'If you go over to that house, you will find a young donkey tied. Loose it and bring it here. If any one asks you what you are doing, just say, "The Master needs it."' This was the secret password to the owner, and if he heard these words, he would let the donkey go with the disciples. When the disciples were loosening the donkey the owner said, 'What are you doing?' Tell me what the two disciples said. ('The Master needs it.' Let us all say it together). When the passwords were said, the owner allowed them to take the donkey to Jesus.

Now Jesus was ready to enter Jerusalem. He would not sneak in but he would ride in like a king. Not on a warhorse but on a donkey. Kings in the land where Jesus lived rode on donkeys when they came in peace to a place. Jesus wanted to enter the city called the 'Possession of Peace' (which is what the word Jerusalem means) as the Prince of Peace. The disciples put some of their cloaks on the donkey for Jesus to sit on. Now they set off. People became excited when they saw Jesus riding the donkey. They cut down branches from the palm trees and laid them on the ground like a carpet; some even laid their cloaks on the ground for the donkey to walk over. They were welcoming the Prince of Peace.

Soon a shout was heard. The people wanted to thank God for all the deeds of power they had seen. 'Blessed is the king!' Many took up the shout 'Blessed is the king who comes in the name of the Lord.' Let us all say it: 'Blessed is the king who comes in the name of the Lord.' The people were shouting, 'Peace in heaven and glory in the highest.' Others still were cheering and shouting, 'Hosanna', which means 'God save us'.

Jesus entered Jerusalem as the Prince of Peace. Many welcomed him. But the Pharisees were not pleased. They tried to stop him. Before the week was out they would cause his death. We all have to decide whether we are for Jesus or against him, whether we welcome him or reject him. Let us welcome him today by praising him and saying 'Hosanna'.

Activity

The main activity is to be part of the Palm Sunday procession. After the lesson let the group re-enact the movement of Jesus from Bethany to the entry into Jerusalem. Encourage them to know why things were done and how they fulfilled the words of Zechariah.

Prayer

Jesus, we welcome you with joy
and with shouts of Hosanna
for you are our King and the Prince of Peace.
Through you, may we have peace
in our hearts, in our homes and in the world.
Amen.

Song

Give me joy in my heart

TORCHES

Aim

To show we have the opportunity to accept or reject the Prince of Peace.

Teaching

Most people want rulers who will do just what they want. We want all the good things – such as good schools, hospitals, roads – but not to have to pay for them in taxes. We want puppet kings to dance to whatever tune we seek to play. Many people approached Jesus in the same way: they wanted Jesus to lead them in the way they wanted to go. They wanted a leader who would drive out the Romans and give them the land to themselves. They wanted a warlord who would lead a rebellion and drive out the enemy of occupation. Jesus came to do just that but the enemy of occupation was not the Romans; it was the people's own selfishness and greed, their insensitivity and sin. (Discuss this.)

Jesus taught that our approach to God is not 'Do this, give me this', but rather 'Your will be done'. If we are to be part of God's kingdom, we must live by its rules. To go against God's will is to turn our back on his kingdom.

Jesus was unwilling to hide from the authorities even when they had made him an outlaw (John 11:57), although he *did* move with caution and the donkey was borrowed through pre-arranged passwords, 'The Master needs it'. Jesus confronted the authorities, as he confronts all authority, with his offer of kingship and peace. Jesus does not force himself on Jerusalem but gives the people the chance to accept him and his ways or reject him. (He does the same with us.)

As Jesus rides a donkey, he shows he comes not as a warlord but as the bringer of peace. (Let someone read aloud Zechariah 9:9, 10.) Once again Jesus is giving the people the opportunity to accept him and his way. For a moment it seems it is happening. The people welcome him with shouts of 'Hosanna', which means 'God save us.' (Compare Matthew 21:9, Mark 11:9, 10 and John 12:13 with Luke 19:38. Luke is writing for his Gentile readers to understand.)

Sadly the authorities are unwilling to accept Jesus. Jerusalem misses the God-given opportunity for peace and for accepting the Prince of Peace. Jerusalem sets off on its own course which would eventually lead to its destruction by the Romans in AD 70. Let us be aware that our King comes to us and offers us his peace – the choice is ours.

Activity

Play 'Simon says'. Point out that you are only out if you do things that Simon has not said. To do other than Simon says is to put yourself out. After the game talk about how this illustrates our relationship with our God.

Prayer

Lord Jesus,
help us to know you as the Prince of Peace
and to accept your rule in our hearts and lives.
Teach us to pray and live by the words
'Your will be done'.
Amen.

Song

Hosanna, hosanna
or the 'Hosanna' song from *Jesus Christ Superstar*

EASTER
Easter Day

Aim

To enter into the joy and wonder of the resurrection and the presence of the risen Lord.

Preparation

There can be a lot of preparation for Easter and it is good to involve as many children as possible. The church will be decorated with flowers, so invite the children's help with the decorating. Let the children help to prepare the Easter Garden and cover an empty cross in spring flowers. Banners can be made with words such as 'Jesus is risen!'; 'Christ is alive!'; 'Jesus is here!'. If possible, everyone should be able to light a candle from the Easter Candle or from their neighbour's candle.

Opening activity

Let there be a procession where banners are carried and the flower-covered cross leads the way. Stop at the tomb for a rolling-away of the stone (let a child do this). Shout, 'Alleluia, Christ is risen!' with the response, 'He is risen indeed. Alleluia.' Light the Easter Candle (again let a child do this). Once more shout, 'Alleluia, Christ is risen!' and have the same response as before.

Opening prayer

(at the lighting of the Easter Candle)

May the Christ raised in glory
scatter the darkness from our hearts and minds
and from this world.
May the light of the risen Christ
shine upon us this day and always.
Alleluia, Christ is risen.
He is risen indeed. Alleluia.

Opening songs

(for the procession)

Jesus Christ is risen today
Halle, halle, halle

Readings

Acts 10:34-43 or Isaiah 65:17-25
Psalm 118:1, 2, 14-24
1 Corinthians 15:19-26 or Acts 10:34-43
John 20:1-18 or Luke 24:1-12

Thought for the day

After the harrowing events of Good Friday, Mary could not sleep. One of the things that troubled Mary was that Jesus didn't have the usual spices placed by his body. She rose early while it was still dark and made her way to the tomb. Throughout the journey (maybe two miles) Mary kept asking who would roll away the stone. It would take a few men and the tomb was sealed. Who would roll away the stone? Mary wondered who could roll away the sorrow and heaviness that was in her heart; it would take a miracle for the weight to be lifted. Who will remove the stone? (Two or three people could quietly sing a few lines of the hymn 'The angel rolled the stone away'.)

Yet when Mary saw the stone rolled away it caused her to panic. Her reaction was to think that someone had stolen the body. She went to tell Peter. He would be delighted to be woken up before six in the morning! Perhaps Peter feared the authorities were now coming for him.

Now Peter and John run to the tomb. The young John outruns Peter, but is afraid to enter the tomb until Peter arrives. Peter goes into the tomb and so does John. The linen wrappings are there and the cloth that had been around the head. It is as if Jesus had just come through them. As yet they do not understand that Jesus must rise. The disciples return to their home.

Mary stays there weeping and wondering. In a vision of angels Mary is asked, 'Woman, why are you weeping?' She is weeping because she has been separated from Jesus, first by his death and now by not being able to see his body. Now Jesus asks her, 'Woman, why are you weeping?' Mary supposed the speaker to be the gardener as she looked up with tear-filled eyes. When Jesus said, 'Mary', she knew. No one spoke to her like that except Jesus. She replied, 'Rabbouni' (which means teacher) and reached out and clung to him. This was no ghost; this was a solid person. Mary was told not to stay there hugging Jesus but to tell the disciples that he was to be ascending to the Father. Yet another knock on Peter's door and this time the word of Mary astounded them all: 'I have seen the Lord' – and she meant the risen, living Lord Jesus. This new awareness would change Mary, the disciples and then the world.

Question time

Do we realise there are times when questions are of little use and we should stop and bow before the mysteries? The resurrection is a mystery to be enjoyed, not a problem to be solved.

As Christ is risen and alive, do you speak of him in the present tense?

Illustration

High up on the moors in the winter season, men go out and set fire to the old heather. By now the heather is all twisted and gnarled; it no longer produces food for the birds and even the moorland sheep are in danger of pulling their teeth out tugging at it. The heather has become useless to the life it usually sustains. So it is burnt, but with a controlled burning. In the flames it may look as if it is totally destroyed but it is not. Under the ground its roots are safe and the men make sure the fire is not too fierce to reach the roots. In the spring the old heather is gone but little shoots appear. The heather is rising from the earth and soon will appear as fresh and as useful as ever. What was destroyed is back with newness of life.

Intercessions

Blessed are you, Lord our God.
On the first Easter Day
you raised your Son, Jesus Christ,
triumphant over death, sin and evil.
In his death you have destroyed death
and in his rising to life you have opened to us
the kingdom of heaven.
Blessed are you, Father, Son and Holy Spirit.

With the whole Church
throughout the world and in heaven
we rejoice,
for Christ is risen.
Let every Christian rejoice,
let every heart rejoice,
for Christ is risen.
We ask your blessing this day
on all who are celebrating the resurrection.
We pray especially for groups that are persecuted
or oppressed because of their faith.
We remember also all who doubt the Good News
and all who are seekers.

Silence

Jesus, stand among us
in your risen power.

We remember today all who are struggling with life.
We pray for the world's poor, refugees
and all who are used as work slaves.
We ask your blessing upon all who are losing heart
or who feel discouraged and despondent.

Silence

Jesus, stand among us
in your risen power.

We give thanks for those who taught us the faith
and introduced us to the living Lord.
We pray for schools and Sunday Schools,
for all teachers of Religious Education.
We ask you to bless us with your presence
in our homes and in our work.

Silence

Jesus, stand among us
in your risen power.

We pray for all who are terminally ill,
for all who are in a hospice or in care.
We pray also for their loved ones in this time of anxiety.
We remember those who have been bereaved this year,
especially all who are left on their own
and feel lonely or unable to cope.
Lord, bless all whose powers are failing
with your love and strength.

Silence

Jesus, stand among us
in your risen power.

We rejoice in your triumph over death
and we pray for all your saints
and our loved ones who have departed this life.
May they rejoice with us this Easter Day
in the fullness of life eternal.

Silence

Merciful Father,
accept these prayers
for the sake of your Son,
our Saviour Jesus Christ.
Amen.

Memory verse

Why do you look for the living among the dead? He is not here, but has risen.
Luke 24:5

Suggested music

Now the green blade riseth
Thine be the glory
Alleluia, sing to Jesus
We shall go out with hope of resurrection (*Celtic Hymn Book*)

It is a good day to sing an acclamation after the announcement of the Gospel, such as 'Alleluia'(Celtic) from the *Celtic Hymn Book*, and again at its end. You may like to use the Peruvian Gloria to replace the Gloria on this day.

CANDLES

Aim
To enter into the joy of Easter.

Teaching

Who can tell me what happened to Jesus on Good Friday? Jesus died on the cross. It was very sad for his friends and the disciples. It made them all unhappy and frightened when Jesus died. After he died they took his body and put it in a cave and then blocked up the entrance with a large stone. This all happened on Good Friday (Let us all say, 'Good Friday.') On Good Friday, Jesus was crucified, dead and buried.

The next day was the Sabbath and it was a day when people were not allowed to travel or work. No one was able to go back to the tomb or cave where Jesus was buried. Mary wanted to go and be near Jesus but she was not able to because of the Sabbath. If it was the day after Friday, what day was the Sabbath? What was the next day after that? When it was very early on the Sunday morning, while it was still dark, Mary went to the tomb. She got a big surprise because the stone had been moved from the front of the cave. (At this stage use the Easter Garden, or a smaller version of it the children may have made.) This upset Mary and she started to cry. Someone must have stolen the body of Jesus.

Mary ran to tell Peter. Peter and John ran to the tomb. It was empty. Only the cloths that Jesus had been wrapped up in were there. They looked as if Jesus had just come through them. Peter and John were puzzled and they went away.

Mary stayed near the tomb. Her eyes were filled with tears and she could hardly see. Suddenly there was someone near. Mary thought in might be the gardener and she asked him if he knew where the body of Jesus was. It was then he said her name, 'Mary.' She knew that voice. She knew it was Jesus. Jesus was not dead. Jesus was alive. (Let us say, 'Jesus is not dead. Jesus is alive.') This made Mary so happy. She could hardly believe it. Jesus is not dead. Jesus is alive. Mary hugged Jesus, she was so happy. Jesus said to Mary, 'You must go and tell the disciples that I am alive.' Mary would rather have stayed with Jesus but she knew she could not keep this good news to herself. She went to the disciples. She was very excited and said to them, 'I have seen the Lord.' (Let us all say together, 'I have seen the Lord.') That is what happened on the first Easter morning. Mary met Jesus, risen from the dead, in the garden.

Activity

If possible, all the children should take part in the activities in the church.

You may like to have an Easter-egg painting competition or a miniature Easter-Garden competition. Eggs could be brought hard-boiled and decorated during their class if you have one. An Easter-egg hunt is always fun, especially if it can be outside. You could have an egg-rolling competition or even an egg 'jarping' contest (this is a little like conkers: the children clash eggs and see which break first). Easter cards to take home could also be made.

Prayer

God, we thank you for Easter
and that Jesus rose again from the dead.
We know that Jesus is alive and loves us.
Alleluia.
Amen.

Song

(*To the tune of 'Here we go round the mulberry bush'*)

Jesus has risen from the dead,
from the dead,
from the dead,
Jesus has risen from the dead
on this Easter morning.

LAMPS

Aim

To rejoice in the fact that Jesus is alive.

Teaching

Get the group to rehearse the following mini-drama. Encourage them to make the whole event as alive as

possible. Every time the words 'Jesus is alive' are said, the whole group respond, 'Jesus is alive. Alleluia.'

Narrator It is early on Sunday morning and Mary prepares to leave the house. She goes to the tomb. She finds the stone rolled away. She does not find the body of Jesus. She starts to cry because she is so upset. She hurries to tell Peter and John. Peter and John run. John gets there first. Peter goes into the tomb. Then John goes in. After this they go home. They meet Mary on her way back to the tomb. Mary is weeping and she sees someone. She thinks it is the gardener and says to him . . .

Mary Sir, do you know where they have taken Jesus?

Jesus Mary.

Narrator Mary is amazed. Can it be Jesus?

Jesus Mary!

Narrator It is Jesus! Jesus is alive.

Chorus Jesus is alive. Alleluia.

Narrator She runs to him and hugs him. He is not a ghost. He is alive.

Chorus Jesus is alive. Alleluia.

Jesus Do not cling to me. Go and tell my disciples the good news.

Narrator Mary runs to tell Peter and the disciples.

Mary I have seen the Lord. Jesus is alive. Alleluia.

Chorus Jesus is alive. Alleluia. Alleluia.

Activity

If possible, all the children should take part in the activities in the church.

You may like to have an Easter-egg painting competition or a miniature Easter-Garden competition. Eggs could be brought hard-boiled and decorated during their class if you have one. An Easter-egg hunt is always fun, especially if it can be outside. You could have an egg-rolling competition or even an egg 'jarping' contest (this is a little like conkers: the children clash eggs and see which break first). Easter cards to take home could also be made. Perhaps during Holy Week banners could have been made for the church procession.

Prayer

God, we thank you
that Jesus showed himself alive to Mary
and that he is risen from the dead.
Alleluia.
Amen.

Song

This is the day (verses 1 and 2)

TORCHES

Aim

To rejoice in the mystery of the resurrection.

Teaching

Look back over the last few days and see that the group know the basic story of the betrayal, the death and burial of Jesus. They should all know that it was on Good Friday that Jesus died.

Jesus was given a hurried burial on the Friday after he had died on the cross because the next day was the Sabbath. On the Sabbath no work is allowed to be done and no journeys undertaken. This meant that on the Saturday the tomb in which Jesus was buried was unvisited.

As Luke tells the story, we get it from a different standpoint. It is the women – Mary Magdalene, Joanna, Mary the mother of James and other women with them – who go to the tomb first of all (Luke 24:10). Their purpose was to bring the spices they had prepared to give Jesus a proper burial. It does not seem to enter their minds that they cannot roll away the stone. The women are the first to discover the stone rolled away. The women are the first to go into the empty tomb and discover that the body of Jesus was not there. The empty tomb puzzles them; the empty tomb itself does not produce ideas of resurrection. The women are deeply perplexed. Two men, who are later described as angels (24:23), say to them, 'Why are you seeking the living among the dead? He is not here, but has risen.'

At the suggestion of the two men, they recall the words of Jesus that he 'must be handed over to sinners, and be crucified, and on the third day rise again.' These words tell us how they interpreted their initial experience. The women relate this to the eleven disciples (ask why eleven) and the rest. But the male disciples do not believe what they are told and describe it as an idle tale (24:11). St Luke is concerned throughout his Gospel to tell of the faithful women, even at the danger of showing the male disciples looking a little foolish, which their attitude of superiority does here.

To confirm what the women have said, Peter runs to the tomb and sees the empty linen cloths and goes home amazed (24:12).

Although today's Gospel ends there without a sighting of Jesus, Luke continues and tells of the appearance of Jesus to the two on the road to Emmaus and to the disciples (24:13-53).

Activity

The young people should be in church for the whole service unless it proves impractical. They should help in carrying banners, bringing up the bread and wine, perhaps saying a prayer and also taking the collection. You may like to have an Easter-egg painting competition or a miniature Easter-Garden competition. Eggs could be brought hard-boiled and decorated during their class if you have one.

Prayer

Lord God, to you be praise
for through your Son Jesus Christ
you have conquered death
and opened to us the way to eternal life.
We rejoice in your love
and in the resurrection of your Son.
Alleluia.
Amen.

Song

The angel rolled the stone away

Second Sunday of Easter

Aim
To share in the joy of Easter.

Preparation
Have a large candle – the Easter Candle – and 12 smaller candles, plus a sand try or holder to put them in.

Opening activity
Ask a child to light the Easter Candle.

As it is lit, let the child say: 'Alleluia. Christ is risen.' The response by all is: 'He is risen indeed. Alleluia.'

Each of the speakers who has seen Jesus lights a candle and then says they have seen the Lord before placing their candle in the sand tray.

Reader   We light a candle for Mary who said:

Mary   I have seen the Lord. Alleluia.

Reader   We now light ten candles for the disciples who on Easter Day saw Jesus.

(Reader may like to ask, 'Why ten?' – Judas is dead and Thomas is not with them.)

Ten Disciples each lighting a candle from the Easter Candle
    We have seen the Lord. Alleluia.

Thomas   I doubt it. I saw him die. Crucified, dead and buried. I doubt it.

Reader   We will hear in the Gospel today how Thomas stayed with the disciples and that Jesus appeared to them again.

Jesus   Thomas, put your finger here, and see my hands. Reach out your hand and put it in my side. Do not doubt but believe.

Thomas   My Lord (pause) . . . and my God. I have seen the Lord. Alleluia.

Let all sing the 'Celtic Alleluia' (*Celtic Hymn Book*)

Opening prayer
Lord God, we give thanks for the resurrection
and rejoice that Jesus appeared to his disciples.
We give thanks for the doubt of Thomas
that turned into faith.
Though we do not see you, Lord Jesus,
help us to know you and to trust in you.
Amen.

Opening song
Lord, you are in this place (*Celtic Hymn Book*)

Readings
Acts 5:27-32
Psalm 118:14-29 or Psalm 150
Revelation 1:4-8
John 20:19-31

Thought for the day
Some people are fortunate in that they are in the right place at the right time. Others only reach what they seek through their persistence and determination.

Thomas was not with the disciples on Easter Day when Jesus appeared. He could see their joy but he found it hard to enter into it. How could you just believe it if someone told you they had seen a person alive after a cruel death?

Thomas had a few habits that were not useful to his faith. He was a natural pessimist. When Jesus suggested they went to Jerusalem, Thomas said, 'Let us all go and we will die together.' Then he was a sceptic. He would not accept belief because he was told about it. He was aware of the joy of the disciples. They said they had seen the Lord. Thomas coolly said, 'Unless I see the mark of the nails in his hands, and put my finger in the mark of the nails and my hand in his side, I will not believe.'

Thomas stayed with the believers and talked with them. He prayed with them and ate with them. He did not separate himself from them. The surest way to belief is to stay with real believers; not with people who just recite creeds but with those who have met the risen Lord. Regular worship is the way our faith grows and is kept alive.

Thomas was not afraid to say when he doubted. 'Unless I see . . . and touch I will not believe.' Thomas said what he felt and not just what he was expected to say. Of such Tennyson wrote:

> There lies more faith in honest doubt
> than in a thousand creeds.

Thomas doubted but it did not stop him being a seeker. He did not write off the experience of the disciples. He stayed with them and questioned and sought the truth. He found because he was a seeker. Did not Jesus say, 'Seek and you shall find'?

Like Thomas, we need not fear doubts. We do need to fear not testing our doubts within the fellowship of the faithful. We need to seek until we find.

Question time
Do we honestly talk about our doubts with those who know the Lord?

Do we let the risen Lord fill our lives with joy and peace?

Illustration
Archbishop Anthony Bloom was a young atheist but he was a seeker. He heard a lecture on Jesus and just could not believe what he heard. He picked up a Bible and turned to the Gospels. He counted the chapters of each Gospel so that he could read the shortest. He chose St Mark and this is what he said:

I started to read St Mark's Gospel . . . before I reached the third chapter, I suddenly became aware that on the other side of my desk there was a presence. And the certainty was so strong that it was the Christ standing there that it has never left me. This was the real turning point. Because Christ was alive and I had been in his presence.

Intercessions

Blessed are you, God and Father of our Lord Jesus Christ.
To you be praise and glory for ever.
Alleluia.
By the raising of your Son from the dead
you have opened to us the way to eternal life.
You have given us an everlasting joy
and a deep peace
through bringing us to know the risen Christ.
Blessed are you, Father, Son and Holy Spirit.

We give thanks for your faithful people
throughout the world,
for the fellowship of all believers.
We ask you to bless all who preach and teach
the reality of the resurrection.
We pray for all who are struggling with doubt
and for all who are seeking a relationship with you.

Silence

Risen Christ, be known among us
and give us your peace.

We give thanks for the gift of peace
and pray there may be peace in our hearts,
in our homes and in the whole world.
We remember areas where there is warfare and strife.
We pray for all who are not at peace
with themselves or with you.
We ask you to bless all
who are working for peace in our world.

Silence

Risen Christ, be known among us
and give us your peace.

Lord Jesus, as we rejoice
in your risen presence in an earthly home,
make yourself known to us in our homes,
in our fellowship
and in the breaking of the bread.
Lord, teach us to be at home with you in our homes.
May our homes be where your presence is known.

Silence

Risen Christ, be known among us
and give us your peace.

We give thanks for the new hope and courage
that is ours through the resurrection.
We pray for all who are discouraged
or without hope at this time.
We remember those who are seriously ill
and any who are facing death.
We pray for those who are tending the ill
and any who are anxious about loved ones.

Silence

Risen Christ, be known among us
and give us your peace.

We rejoice in the defeat of death
by the resurrection of our Lord.

We pray for all who have given their lives
in the service of humankind,
all martyrs and saints.
We remember our loved ones departed
and ask that they may rejoice
in the fullness of life eternal.

Silence

Merciful Father,
accept these prayers
for the sake of your Son,
our Saviour Jesus Christ.
Amen.

Memory verse

Do not doubt but believe.
John 20:27

Suggested music

This is the day
The Lord is risen indeed
To God be the glory!

CANDLES

Aim

To rejoice with the disciples in the risen Lord.

Teaching

Can you remember how Jesus died? What do we call the day when Jesus died? After Jesus died he was buried in a cave and a big stone was rolled against the opening so that he was closed in and in the dark. When Mary came on Easter Day she found the stone was rolled away. She ran and told Peter. Then Peter and John ran and found the cave was empty. Jesus was not there. Mary stayed near the cave and suddenly she saw Jesus. He was alive. It was lovely. She was so happy and excited. Jesus told her to go and tell the disciples. Mary went and said, 'I have seen the Lord.' (Let us all say it.)

The disciples did not know what to say. Some thought Mary had gone to the wrong place, but Peter and John had seen the empty cave. John noticed that the cloths that had been wrapped around Jesus were lying as if Jesus had come through them. But the disciples did not know what to say. They had seen Jesus die – how could he be alive? Mary told them again, 'I have seen the Lord.' (Let us all say it again.)

The disciples closed the doors of the house where they were. They were frightened that the people who had killed Jesus might come after them too. While the doors were closed Jesus came into the room and said, 'Hello. Peace be with you.' The disciples could hardly believe it. Jesus was there with them – Jesus is alive. Jesus is risen from the dead – They were so excited and so happy. It was wonderful. Thomas was not with them when Jesus came, and the disciples could hardly wait until he returned so that they could tell him. They knew

Thomas would find it difficult to believe that Jesus is alive. When he came they said, 'We have seen the Lord.' (Let us say it.)

Thomas found it hard to believe. He said, 'I will only believe if I see Jesus, if I can put my finger in the nail holes in his hands.' It was a week later that Jesus came again. This time he spoke to Thomas and invited him to put his finger in the nail holes and to know that it is Jesus and he is alive. Thomas said to Jesus, 'My Lord and my God.' (Let us say that to Jesus.) Thomas knew Jesus is alive and it was wonderful to see him.

Now Thomas could say what Mary had said and what the disciples said: 'I have seen the Lord.' (Let us say it once more.)

Activity

Get the children to act out today's story as you retell it. Have Mary, ten disciples and then Thomas all say, 'I have seen the Lord.' Get Jesus to show himself alive and say, 'Peace be with you' to the disciples. Then let Jesus invite Thomas to touch the nail marks in his hands. Get Thomas to say, 'My Lord and my God.'

Prayer

God, we thank you that Jesus is alive
and wants to be our friend.
Help us to know he is with us always.
Amen.

Song

Away in a manger (last verse only)

LAMPS

Aim

To share the wonder of Thomas.

Teaching

Can you tell me what happened to Jesus on Good Friday? After he died on the cross he was buried. Who knows in what sort of place he was buried? On the Sunday something very special happened – what was it? What do we call the day when Jesus rose again? On Easter Day Mary Magdalene saw Jesus alive in the garden near to the tomb where he had been buried. Then two of his friends saw him alive as they walked to Emmaus. In the evening of Easter Day ten of his disciples were meeting together in one room when Jesus appeared again. Why did only ten of the disciples see Jesus? Where were the other two? Judas, who betrayed Jesus, was already dead. The other disciple who was missing was Thomas.

When Thomas came to the disciples they told him, 'We have seen the Lord.' Thomas could not believe it because he had seen Jesus die on the cross. Mary Magdalene was able to say, 'I have seen the Lord', but Thomas could not believe it because he had seen Jesus buried in the tomb. The two from Emmaus had said how Jesus walked with them on the road and explained the Scriptures to

them. Thomas could not believe it because he had seen the large stone rolled against the tomb and he knew Jesus was dead. Thomas wanted to know how it was possible. He stayed with the other disciples and talked with them about Jesus, about what Jesus had said and about what they had seen. Thomas then said to them, 'I will only believe if I can put my finger into the nail holes in the hands of Jesus. Then I will know it is he. I will not believe until I can put my hand into the hole the spear made in his side. Then I will know it is he.'

The other disciples did not think that this was possible, but they were not sure. It was now a whole week since they had seen Jesus. Once again it was a Sunday. The disciples were all together and Jesus was suddenly there with them. The risen Lord was present with them and Thomas could not doubt it. Jesus spoke to all of them and said, 'Peace be unto you.' Then he turned especially to Thomas as he stretched out his hand and said, 'Put your finger here and see my hands. Reach out your hand and put it in my side. Do not doubt but believe.'

Thomas did not know what to say – this was so wonderful, so amazing. Not only was Jesus there in front of him, alive, but Jesus also knew all that Thomas had been saying. Jesus really was special and really was alive. Thomas said to Jesus, 'My Lord and my God.' (Let us all say together to Jesus what Thomas said, 'My Lord and my God.')

Jesus then said to Thomas, 'Have you believed because you have seen me? Blessed are those who have not seen and yet have come to believe.' Who do you think Jesus is talking about when he says this?

Activity

Let us act out the story by encouraging various people to come and say to Thomas, 'I have seen the Lord.' Thomas will say to each, 'I will not believe unless I see, unless I can touch.'
Have a dramatic moment when Jesus appears and says, 'Peace be with you.' Now let him speak to Thomas and get to touch his hands and his side. Let Thomas then kneel before Jesus and say, 'My Lord and my God.'

Prayer

Lord Jesus, risen from the dead,
I believe in you,
I trust in you,
I love you.
You are my Lord and my God.
Amen.

Song

Fisherman Peter (verses 4 and 5)

TORCHES

Aim

To share in the wonder of the resurrection.

Teaching

On Good Friday Jesus was crucified, dead and buried. Disciples and loved ones had seen him die and gone to his burial in the tomb. It all happened so quickly. It was hard for them to believe. But they knew he was dead and when you're dead you're dead. Well, that was on Good Friday and on the Sabbath that followed. It was early on the Sunday that Mary Magdalene went to the tomb and found it empty. She could only believe that someone had stolen the dead body. She ran and told Peter. Peter and John ran and saw the empty tomb. But at this stage they did not see anyone else. Mary stayed at the tomb, weeping. It was there in the garden that Jesus came. Mary could not believe it at first. Then she was so excited. Jesus was not dead: Jesus is alive. She ran to tell the disciples, 'I have seen the Lord.' The disciples did not know what to think and could hardly believe it.

Later that day two friends of Jesus were on the road to Emmaus. They were sad because of the events of Good Friday. They had seen Jesus die. But now he walked with them, talked with them, looked at the Scriptures with them. Yet they did not recognise him immediately. It was when he broke the bread in their house that they knew it was him. They rushed back to tell the disciples, 'We have seen the Lord.'

Meanwhile the disciples had closed the doors of the house where they were. They wanted to lie low, as they were afraid. Maybe the people who had killed Jesus would come for them next. Suddenly they realised that Jesus was there with them. Their hearts were nearly bursting for joy and their minds were full of wonder.

Jesus is risen. What Mary had said is true: Jesus is alive. Now they too could say, 'We have seen the Lord.'

Jesus had now been seen in the garden, on the road and in the room where the disciples were. But Thomas missed out. He was away and missed these amazing events. Thomas refused to believe unless he could see for himself, unless he could actually touch the nail holes and the wounded side of Jesus. During the week that followed Easter the excited disciples talked of how they had seen the Lord. Thomas naturally doubted it. On the Sunday they were all together when Jesus appeared. Again the risen Lord stood among them. He invited Thomas to come and touch his hands, to put his hand in the side that was wounded. There was no doubt: Jesus is alive. Thomas was full of wonder and awe. Jesus had conquered death. Thomas faced Jesus and said to him, 'My Lord and my God.'

Activity

Encourage the group to retell the story of the death and resurrection of Jesus until the events of the Sunday after Easter. Ask them to choose which was the most important moment for them. Perhaps they could mime that moment showing wonder and awe, or, with other members of the group, act it out.

Prayer

Jesus, my Lord and my God,
let me rejoice in the resurrection,
let me know you now by faith.
Jesus, I give thanks to you
for life and life eternal.
Amen.

Song

I believe in Jesus

Third Sunday of Easter

Aim

To see Jesus as the risen Lord on the shore of Galilee.

Preparation

Have the Easter Candle, plus 16 smaller candles for the sand tray.

Opening activity

Ask a child to light the Easter candle. As it is lit, let the child say: 'Alleluia, Christ is risen.' The response by all is: 'He is risen indeed. Alleluia.'

Reader   We light 12 candles (let children come out and do this) – one for Mary, ten for ten disciples, and one for Thomas.

(When the children have placed their candles in the tray they face the congregation and say:

11 disciples and Mary
> We have seen the Lord. Alleluia.

Cleopas and companion
> Do not forget, Jesus appeared to us on the road to Emmaus and in the breaking of the bread. (Two candles are lit and placed in the tray.) We have seen the Lord. Alleluia.

Reader   Today we hear how Jesus appeared to Saul on the Damascus Road and to Ananias in Damascus.

Paul and Ananias
> We have seen the Lord. Alleluia.

Reader   His disciples see Jesus again whilst they are at work and on the seashore. The light is spreading. More are able to say, 'I have seen the Lord.'

Let all sing the 'Celtic Alleluia' (*Celtic Hymn Book*) or 'The Spirit lives to set us free'.

Opening prayer

Praise and glory to you, risen Lord.
As you appeared to your disciples on the shore,
be known to be among us today and always.
Amen.

Opening song

Alleluia, sing to Jesus

Readings

Acts 9:1-6 (7-20)
Psalm 30
Revelation 5:11-14
John 21:1-19

Thought for the day

Today's readings are very much about vision, of seeing the Lord. Saul sees Jesus on the Damascus road, and in Damascus, Ananias also sees the Lord. St John the Divine in his revelations sees the 'Lamb that was slaughtered being worshipped by the hosts of heaven'. Then the Gospel is about seven of the disciples seeing the risen Lord. It is wonderful to have a vision but with all visions comes responsibility; at the very least vision needs our attention and usually obedience to the call. See how both Saul and Ananias are asked to do something. Like Isaiah (Isaiah 6) Ananias says 'Here I am.' The Lord says to Ananias, 'Get up and go.'

Today's Gospel reading appears to be an addition to St John for it is almost certain that John's Gospel ended originally with chapter 20. As it has been added, there must be an important message.

Life has a habit of repeating itself. Things that we thought had passed have a habit of returning. We think we are making progress, then suddenly we find ourselves back where we started. H. E. Bates compared life to a game of snakes and ladders: sometimes you are climbing ahead and suddenly you drop back almost to the beginning.

It was like this for the disciples. They had left all to follow Jesus: they left fishing, the tax office and the field to share with him. Then it came to a sudden end with the crucifixion. They were knocked right back. The risen Lord made their spirits soar and they were full of new hope. But how would they make their living now? Naturally the fishermen went back to Galilee. Peter decided to go fishing and with him went six others – Thomas, Nathanael, James and John who were the sons of Zebedee, and two other disciples. They toiled all night and caught nothing. As in all of life, when things go wrong, they go wrong in all sorts of directions. They couldn't even catch fish. There was a feeling that they had been here before.

Just as the new day dawned, Jesus stood on the shore. They did not recognise him at first. He directed their net throwing and they caught so many fish that they could not haul them all in. It was then that John realised who it was and said to Peter, 'It is the Lord.' Peter, who had only been wearing a loincloth as he fished, put on his tunic before he jumped into the sea – odd to put clothes on to jump into the water. Perhaps it can only be understood if you know that the Jews said a man had to be properly dressed to come and worship.

Jesus is not a ghost, not just a vision; he is real and he is solid. He has lit a fire and prepared food for them. He shared bread and fish with them. Now come the challenges of the story. 'Simon, son of John, do you love me more than these?' We do not know if Jesus was talking about the catch of fish or about the other disciples. More likely it was about the promise that Peter did not keep, for three times Peter had denied knowing Jesus. Now three times Jesus asks Peter about loving him. Each time when Peter says, 'Yes, Lord; you know that I love you', Jesus asks him to care for his lambs and sheep. Peter was given his task, his mission to be a pastor, to be a co-shepherd with the Good Shepherd.

The risen Lord brings forgiveness; love restores broken relationships. Peter is affirmed and then is able to affirm his task. If we are to be disciples, we have to listen to and follow the Master (John 21:19).

Question time

Have we taken seriously the call to follow Jesus?

What part do we have in the mission of Jesus to care for his flock and the sheep of his pasture?

Illustration

It is told that when Jesus returned to heaven, the Archangel Michael barred his way. The archangel said, 'How can you return to heaven? Your work is not yet completed. There are many who do not know about or who have not heard of your saving acts.' Jesus said, 'I have left my friends to complete what I have begun.' The Archangel was amazed. 'Do you mean those puny, often straying humans?' 'Yes,' said Jesus, 'I trust them and I know that through following me they will bring my gospel to all the world.'

Intercessions

Blessed are you, Lord our God,
for you have called us out of darkness
into the glorious light of your presence;
you fill our emptiness with the richness of your love.
We rejoice in the power of the resurrection
and in your gift of eternal life.
Blessed are you, Father, Son and Holy Spirit.

Lord, we thank you for calling us to follow you
and to share in your outreach to all peoples.
We ask your blessing
upon all who go out to preach the word,
upon all pastors and shepherds of your flock.
Give us all the wisdom to follow in your steps
and to bring others to know and love you.
We pray for all who are involved in mission
and in spreading the Good News
through teaching and example.

Silence

Hear us, O Lord, and have mercy upon us;
O Lord, be our helper.

We give thanks that you give us strength and courage
through your presence.
We pray for all whose work
appears to be meaningless or fruitless.
We remember those who are virtually slaves
and work for a very small income.
We ask your blessing upon all
who have been made redundant
and all who are unemployed.

Silence

Hear us, O Lord, and have mercy upon us;
O Lord, be our helper.

We praise you, O God,
for the love and protection of our homes.
We ask your blessing upon each of our loved ones,
our families and friends.
We pray for homes where there is little joy or love.
We remember all who are struggling
with their relationships
and all who feel lonely or unwanted.

Silence

Hear us, O Lord, and have mercy upon us;
O Lord, be our helper.

Lord, we ask your blessing
upon all who are discouraged or despondent
at this time,
upon all who feel that life is not worthwhile.
May they know of your love and your presence.
We pray for all who are ill at home or in hospital,
all who are fearful of the future
and anxious about their loved ones.

Silence

Hear us, O Lord, and have mercy upon us;
O Lord, be our helper.

We give thanks for the risen Lord,
ever-present and welcoming us
to the fullness of eternal life.
We pray for our loved ones who are departed from us;
may they share with your saints
in the joy of your kingdom.

Silence

Merciful Father,
**accept these prayers
for the sake of your Son,
our Saviour Jesus Christ.
Amen.**

Memory verse

Follow me.
John 21:19

Suggested music

Hark, my soul, it is the Lord
We have a Gospel to proclaim
You stood there on the shoreline
Will you come and follow me

CANDLES

Aim

To show that Jesus is alive and seen by his disciples.

Teaching

Has anyone gone fishing at the seaside? It is always a little sad if we do not catch anything and exciting if we do. Maybe you have seen the big boats come in with their catches of fish – or sometimes they come back without having caught anything.

Can you remember the names of the fishermen disciples? Peter, Andrew, James and John. Perhaps some of the others went fishing too. In fact, we know that one night (that is the best time to catch fish) six of the disciples of Jesus went fishing with Peter. Peter had suddenly said to them, 'I am going fishing.' The others said they would go with him. Count as I tell you their names: Peter, Thomas, Nathanael, James and John. How many is that? Then there were two more, which makes . . . seven. They all got into Peter's boat and went to fish.

When they were into the deep water Peter threw out his net to catch fish (let us pretend to do it). After a while they pulled it in (let us do that). What did they catch? Nothing. Then they threw the net out the other side of the boat. (Repeat the actions two or three times more.) Every time they caught . . . nothing. They had worked all night and caught nothing. They were going to give up and go home. Then someone on the shore shouted to them, 'You have caught no fish, have you?' They answered, 'No. We have caught nothing.' The man told them to throw out their net once more to the right. They did this and they caught so many fish that their nets were nearly breaking (let us pull in the fish). It was wonderful. This had happened to them once before – it made John think and he said to Peter, 'It is the Lord.' Yes, it was Jesus alive and not dead. Jesus was waiting for them on the beach. Peter jumped out of the boat and waded through the water to get to Jesus first, though soon they were bringing the fish to land. And how many do you think they counted? There were 153 of them.

Jesus had lit a fire on the beach and cooked some fish for them. There was a lovely smell of fish cooking and there was bread there too. Jesus got them to bring some of their fish to cook and they all shared breakfast together. The disciples were really excited because Jesus was alive and still with them.

Activity

Colour in some fish and then use them in the game. The fish are laid on the floor and the children have to use an old magazine or newspaper to waft them into the 'net', which is a designated part of the floor. When all fish are in the net the game is over. There is also the opportunity to make a boat with a fishing net.

Prayer

Jesus, we are happy
that you shared a meal with your friends
and helped them to catch fish.
We would like to be your friend
and talk to you each day.
Amen.

Song

Jesus is a friend of mine

LAMPS

Aim

To show that Jesus is alive and not a ghost.

Teaching

After Jesus died on the cross the disciples stayed in Jerusalem for a while. During that time they saw Jesus alive, risen from the dead. Can you tell me who saw Jesus and where?

1 Mary, in the garden.

2 Cleopas and companion, on the road to Emmaus.

3 Ten disciples, in the room where they were staying. (Who was missing and do you know why?)

4 To the ten disciples again and to Thomas. Can you remember the words Thomas said to Jesus? 'My Lord and my God.'

After this the disciples returned to their homes and to their work. Maybe they were waiting for Jesus to tell them what to do next. In the meantime, Peter decided to go fishing. Six of the disciples decided to go with him. Thomas, Nathanael, James and John. How many is that? Then there were two more, which makes . . . seven, counting Peter. They all got into Peter's boat and went to fish. They went out at night, in the dark, as it was the right time to fish. They worked all night and caught nothing. It seemed a waste of time. But fishermen are used to having to seek for their catch and they are not always lucky. The sun was now rising and dawn was coming. In the low light they saw a stranger on the shore and he shouted, asking them, 'Do you have any fish?' They shouted back, 'No, we haven't caught any.' He then said, 'Throw your net out to the right for there are fish there.' They did this and immediately their net filled. Now, the last time this happened to them it was Jesus who had told them to cast their net. Suddenly John realised it was Jesus and said to Peter, 'It is the Lord.' As they were not far from the land, Peter put on his tunic and jumped into the sea so that he could get quickly to Jesus.

On the beach Jesus had lit a fire. There was a lovely smell of wood smoke and of fish cooking. There was also some bread. Jesus invited the disciples to bring some of the fish they had just caught. Then he said, 'Come and have breakfast.'

None of them dared ask Jesus who he was because they knew it was the Lord. He was alive and not dead. He was not a ghost for he had lit a fire and cooked a meal. He was not a ghost for he was eating with them and talking to them. They were so happy that Jesus was alive and was sharing a meal with them. Jesus still had work for them to do and, even more exciting, he would work with them.

Activity

This is a good story to act out. Have six fishermen toiling all night and catching nothing. Show them casting the net from the boat a good few times. Let Jesus appear as the night ends and shout across to the fishermen. Let them show their amazement and joy at the catch of 153 fish. Then say John's words of awe: 'It is the Lord.' Get Peter to jump into the sea and wade or swim to where Jesus is on the shore. Haul in all the fish. Bring some fish to Jesus. Then let them sit around and share a meal with the risen Lord.

Prayer

Come Jesus,
be known as our companion and friend.
Let us know that you are ever with us
and love us
and help us to work for you.
Amen.

Song

A stranger walked along the shore

TORCHES

Aim

To draw out some of the importance of this third meeting with the disciples.

Teaching

Check that they know the name of the day Jesus died and the name of the day he rose again. See if they can say whom Jesus appeared to (Mary Magdalene, Cleopas and companion, ten disciples). See if they know why just ten.) The second time Jesus appeared to the disciples, whom did Jesus speak to especially? What did he ask Thomas to do? And what did Thomas say to Jesus?

Now we will look at the third appearance of Jesus. Jesus has been seen in a garden, on the road, in a house, and now he will be seen on the seashore. The disciples are slowly learning that Jesus is with them always and that he works with them and through them (see Mark 16:20).

The disciples have gone back to their home area. There are seven of them gathered together – Peter, Thomas, Nathanael, James and John plus two more. Peter decides it is necessary to go fishing – for life must go on. All of them decide to go with him. As is normal, they go out at night to fish. 'That night they caught nothing.' Is there not a feeling we have been there before? (See Luke 5:1-11.) Once again, nets and lives are empty. Does John want us to realise that this is always true? Without Jesus we are in the dark and our lives are not satisfied.

Jesus stands on the shore. So often he is at the edge of our life, waiting for us to hear him, see him, obey him. Jesus stands on the shore of this world and on the edge of eternity.

Jesus calls the disciples and asks them if they have any fish. Then he directs them to where there are fish. Once they cast the net there is a catch in abundance. John is aware of the way life seems to be repeating itself and realises it is Jesus on the shore. 'It is the Lord,' he says to Peter. Peter, also coming to the same awareness, puts on his tunic and jumps into the sea. They were only a hundred yards from the shore. Peter was anxious to get closer to Jesus as quickly as he could.

Jesus has a fire lit and fish cooking upon it. He invites the fishermen to bring some of their catch and they all share a breakfast of fish and bread. The actions of Jesus are not those of a ghost. Jesus cooks and eats, he talks with his disciples and gives them directions. This is not a ghost but the living Lord.

Peter had denied Jesus three times (see John 13:36-38 and 18:15-27). There is no doubt that Peter was full of guilt and remorse. Jesus deals gently with him and asks him three times, 'Do you love me?' Each time that Peter said, 'Yes', Jesus gave him a task to do, to care for his flock. Peter was forgiven and given the opportunity of sharing in the work of the Good Shepherd. The work of Jesus is not done. Like Peter, we are all called by Jesus to work for him and to follow him. We are privileged to be able to share in the work of the risen Lord and in his mission today.

Look again at Mark 16:20 and discuss it.

Activity

Let the group try and use images to describe life with and life without Jesus – for example, night and dawn (light); unrewarding toil and fulfilment; emptiness with life slipping through our fingers and nets, and fullness and purpose. Encourage them to look at the risen Lord and the hope of eternal life.

Prayer

Risen Lord, may we know that you are with us
and seek to be our friend.
Help us to give time and attention to you each day,
that we may share in your mission
and do what you would have us do.
Amen.

Song

Sing out an Easter song

Fourth Sunday of Easter

Aim

To explore our relationship with Jesus through the image of the shepherd.

Preparation

Have the Easter Candle, plus five smaller candles for the sand tray.

Opening activity

At Easter we rejoice that Jesus is alive. Let someone light the Easter Candle and say: 'Alleluia. Christ is risen'. The response by all is: 'He is risen indeed. Alleluia.' In turn, each reader lights a candle from the Easter Candle, faces the front, speaks and then puts their candle in the sand tray.

Reader 1   Rejoice because in Jesus the Good Shepherd 'goodness is stronger than evil'.

Reader 2   Love is stronger than hate.

Reader 3   Light is stronger than darkness.

Reader 4   Life is stronger than death.

Reader 5   Victory is ours through him who loved us.

Sing either the 'Celtic Alleluia' or 'Goodness is stronger than evil' (both from the *Celtic Hymn Book*)

Opening prayer

Lord Jesus, we rejoice in your presence
and that you call us to follow you.
Help us to listen to your voice
and to do what you would have us do.

Opening song

The King of love my shepherd is

Readings

Acts 9:36-43
Psalm 23
Revelation 7:9-17
John 10:22-30

Thought for the day

The tenth chapter of St John is very much about the image of sheep and shepherd. Jesus describes how the shepherd calls his own sheep by name and leads them out. In verse 8 Jesus declares he is the gate for the sheep. This describes not only our entry into his kingdom but also his protection of us, as the shepherd used to lie across the gateway of the fold to safeguard the sheep. This idea is continued in verse 11 where Jesus says, 'I am the good shepherd. The good shepherd lays down his life for the sheep.'

The Jews were arguing about these words. Some thought Jesus mad; others thought him to be wonderful. At this point today's Gospel begins. It is the Dedication Festival, the festival of Hanukkah, sometimes called the Festival of Lights. It was to celebrate the heroic victory of Judas Maccabaeus over the king of Assyria. In 170 BC over 80,000 Jews perished in the attack on Jerusalem and as many again were taken into captivity. Six years later Judas Maccabaeus rescued Jerusalem, and the Temple was cleansed and purified. To celebrate this festival, lights were lit in every Jewish home as well as in the Temple. The festival takes place on the 25th day of Chislev, which corresponds to our December and so is very near to our Christmas. We are told it is winter and Jesus is walking in the portico of Solomon, which is a roofed-over colonnade in the first court of the Temple precincts.

The Jews ask Jesus, 'How long will you keep us in suspense? If you are the Messiah, tell us plainly.' There were two main groups: those who wanted to know and looked forward with joy to the answer, and those who sought to trap Jesus and accuse him of blasphemy or madness. Jesus replies by telling them he has already told them and that his works testify to this. 'But you do not believe, because you do not belong to my sheep.'

Jesus details then what makes believers. 'My sheep hear my voice. I know them and they follow me. I give them eternal life, and they will never perish. No one will snatch them from my hand' (John 10:27, 28).

To hear is to obey. Not only do his believers hear him, they obey him. He knows them. He has a relationship with them. He loves them and cares for them. They are his followers. Just as sheep follow their shepherd to new pastures, we follow Jesus into newness of life. Unlike ordinary sheep, those who follow Jesus will not perish: they receive the gift of eternal life. (Compare John 3:16.)

No one can take them from Jesus, not even death. One of the greatest comments on this is Romans 8:35-39; it would be worth reading this aloud.

Question time

Do we recognise the hallmarks of a disciple as listed in John 10:27, 28?

Are we able to rejoice in the fact that 'nothing can separate us from the love of God in Christ Jesus'?

Illustration

Two flocks of sheep had become intermingled. Night was coming down and it would be very difficult to separate them before it was dark. If men or dogs were sent in, it would cause a lot of fear among the sheep and greater confusion. The shepherd who came to care for his flock said, 'Leave them alone. Wait until it is almost the end of day, then I will call mine. They know me, they will hear my voice and follow me.' As evening came, the shepherd started to call. The reaction among the sheep was interesting, for some heard the voice and wanted to run away because they did not know it. The sheep that belonged to the shepherd recognised his voice. They heard a call that meant safety, shelter and sustenance. They knew of the love of the shepherd and came running to where he was.

Intercessions

Blessed are you, Father, Son and Holy Spirit.
Through Jesus Christ
you have broken the power of sin and death
and opened the kingdom of heaven to all believers.
Through Christ the Good Shepherd
you lead us from darkness into your glorious light;
you lead us from death to life eternal.
We rejoice that nothing can snatch us from your hand.
Blessed are you, One God now and for ever.

Father, we give you thanks and praise
for Jesus the Good Shepherd.
Help us to hear his voice and to follow him.
We pray for all who share his pastoral ministry,
all preachers of the word
and ministers of the sacraments.
We ask your blessing upon all who go out in home visits,
all carers, doctors and nurses and home helpers.
We remember especially
those who reach out to the outcasts and rejected.

Silence

Good Shepherd, guide us
and help us always.

We give thanks for all who seek
to bring peace and unity to our world.
We ask your blessing upon all shepherds,
farmers and fishermen and all who work in agriculture
or to provide us with food and clothing.
We ask you to guide all who have the care of young people,
all teachers, youth leaders and social workers.

Silence

Good Shepherd, guide us
and help us always.

Father, we give thanks
for all who have cared for us and provided for us.
We pray especially for parents and loved ones,
for our families and friends.
We pray for those who have taught us the faith
and been examples to us,
and we ask your blessing
upon all who are still our guides and helpers.

Silence

Good Shepherd, guide us
and help us always.

Father, we pray for all who have lost their way in life.
We remember those who have lost faith
in themselves, in others or in their God.
We pray for all who are finding life desperate
and are disillusioned or fearful.
We ask you to comfort and bless
all who are struggling
with illness or problems that they cannot solve
and those who feel unable to find help or hope.

Silence

Good Shepherd, guide us
and help us always.

We rejoice that the Good Shepherd gives us life eternal
and that nothing can separate us
from the love of God in Christ Jesus.

We join with the fellowship of the saints
and our loved ones departed
to praise you.
We commend them and ourselves
to your unfailing love.

Silence

Merciful Father,
accept these prayers
for the sake of your Son,
our Saviour Jesus Christ.
Amen.

Memory verse

My sheep hear my voice. I know them, and they follow
me. I give them eternal life, and they will never perish.
John 10:27, 28

Suggested music

All people that on earth do dwell
Blessed assurance, Jesus is mine
Faithful Shepherd, feed me

CANDLES

Aim

To show that Jesus the Good Shepherd cares for each of us.

Teaching

Who knows what is covered in wool and says 'Baa'?
Has anyone here seen a sheep? Tell me what a sheep
looks like. Would someone like to come out and draw
one?

If you get a lot of sheep together, what do you call
them? A flock of sheep.

And what do you call the person that looks after
sheep? He is called a shepherd. (Let us all say that
together.) In our country, where does the shepherd keep
his sheep? They are usually in fields and fenced in,
though in some areas the sheep roam freely.

In the land where Jesus lived, to be a shepherd was a
very dangerous job. The shepherd had to protect the
sheep against wild animals, even against wolves and lions
sometimes. He also had to protect his sheep from robbers.
So he had to be brave and strong. The shepherd also led
the sheep to where there was plenty of food for them to
eat and water for them to drink. The shepherd did not
follow his sheep but he led them and they followed
him. He knew each of his sheep – he knew the naughty
ones and the good ones, he knew the poorly ones and
the strong ones – and he looked after them all. He had
names for each of them and they knew when he called.
When the shepherd called they ran towards him
because they knew he loved them and cared for them.

Sometimes a sheep got lost or went astray. Then the
shepherd would look for it and search until he found it.

Jesus wants us to love him and follow him. Sometimes Jesus is called the Good Shepherd and we are his
flock. Jesus rescues us from trouble and danger, and

tries to keep us safe. Whatever happens, Jesus the Good Shepherd loves us. He knows our name and calls each of us to come to him.

Activity

Play 'Simon says'. Get the children to understand they must do what Simon says. If they do something without Simon saying so, they are out. They have to learn to listen and do what they are told.

Prayer

Lord Jesus, help us to be still and quiet,
to know you are with us
and that you love us.
You are the Good Shepherd
and we are your flock.
Let us try and do what you want us to do.
Amen.

Song

Little lamb has lost its way,
lost its way,
lost its way.
Little lamb has lost its way.
Let the shepherd find it.

Little child has lost its way,
lost its way
lost its way.
Little child has lost its way.
Good Shepherd, find it.

(Tune: 'London Bridge is falling down')

LAMPS

Aim

To show that the Good Shepherd loves us and is willing to give himself for us.

Teaching

Some people are very brave and do dangerous jobs. Some even risk their lives for others, and some even die that others might live. Can you tell me of a person who does a dangerous job and why it is dangerous?

(Talk about the Air Sea Rescue, the Fire Brigade, ambulance workers, the police. Tell how sometimes an ordinary person will risk their life to save others who are in trouble. You may like to tell of a sea rescue or of a courageous rescue from a fire or accident.)

Do you think being a shepherd is a dangerous job? Not usually in this country, though some shepherds on the moors have died in winter storms trying to care for their sheep. Normally it is a peaceful job. In the days of Jesus, to be a shepherd was to have a dangerous job. You had to stay with the sheep during the night and protect them from harm. The shepherd had to face wolves and maybe even a lion. Probably they would have no more than a club or a knife with which to defend themselves. Often they would light a fire to scare away the

wild animals. The other danger was from robbers: there were groups that would snatch sheep away from the flock and kill them. The shepherd had to be brave enough to keep these wicked people away.

Jesus compared himself to a shepherd. In fact, he called himself the Good Shepherd. Who do you think he saw as his sheep? Jesus was willing to die for his sheep – and he did die upon the cross. Jesus died that we might have eternal life. Jesus was brave enough to fight against darkness and death, so that we might be able to have light and life. Jesus did not want anything to snatch us from God and his love. Jesus said that, like a shepherd, he knows each of us by name, we are all important to him. He calls us to follow him and not to be afraid.

Would someone like to read Psalm 23? Perhaps if there are enough people we will read a verse each and say what we think it means.

Activity

Play 'Do as I say'. Everyone sits facing the shepherd and they must do what the shepherd tells them and not copy his or her actions if they are different from what is said. If he lifts one arm and says, 'Lift one arm', you must do the same. If he jumps up and down and says, 'Stand still', you must not move or you will be out. The last person in becomes the next shepherd.

Prayer

Jesus, you look after us
as a shepherd would look after his sheep.
We thank you for your love and care
and ask you to protect us in all dangers.
Amen.

Song

Loving Shepherd of thy sheep

TORCHES

Aim

To understand more of the love of Jesus as revealed in the Good Shepherd.

Teaching

Do you know any stories that Jesus told about sheep? There is the story in St Luke 15:3-7. (Let the group either read the story or retell it.) In St John's Gospel, Jesus calls himself the Good Shepherd (John 10:11). Explore with the group what they think this means about their relationship with Jesus. (The group may like to read John 10:11-15.)

In today's Gospel, which comes from the same chapter, Jesus says important things about his relationship with believers: 'My sheep hear my voice. I know them, and they follow me. I will give them eternal life, and they will never perish. No one will snatch them out of my hand' (10:27, 28).

If we are to be believers, we need to listen to what Jesus says. More than listen, we need to do what Jesus wants us to do. We learn to say with Jesus to the Father, 'Your kingdom come, your will be done.' To listen properly is to do what God wants us to do.

Jesus says, 'I know my sheep.' Think about what that means. He knows our foolishness and our weakness as well as our strong points. Jesus knows when we stray away from him and when we fail him. But as the Good Shepherd he seeks us out and wants us to come back to him.

Sometimes sheep get into trouble. They go where they are not meant to go and do what they are not meant to do. Who gets the blame but the shepherd? It is the shepherd who gets the abuse and has to pay for any damage or loss. Jesus cares for the wandering sheep and says, 'I will lay down my life for the sheep.' Jesus has a gift for those who believe in him and follow him: 'I give them eternal life, and they will never perish.' Jesus leads us to eternal life and will not allow anything to stop this as long as we follow him. Many Christians faced torture and death without fear because they knew that life in Jesus is eternal and that nothing – not even death – can separate us from the love of God in Christ Jesus. (One of the greatest comments on this is Romans 8:35-39. Get a few to read these verses aloud and then have the whole group comment on this passage.)

Activity

Get the group to read Psalm 23 dramatically and then put it into their own words.

Let them explore the idea that the Good Shepherd gives us eternal life.

Prayer

Lord Jesus,
you are the Good Shepherd.
You seek and save the lost.
You care for the fallen and restore the sick.
You call each of us by our name
and you offer us eternal life.
Lord, help us to know you
and to follow you day by day.
Amen.

Song

The Lord's my shepherd

Fifth Sunday of Easter

Aim

To explore how God's glory is revealed in the death and resurrection of Jesus.

Preparation

Have the Easter Candle, plus four smaller candles for the sand tray.

Opening activity

Let someone light the Easter Candle and say: 'Alleluia. Christ is risen.' The response by all is: 'He is risen indeed. Alleluia.' In turn, each reader lights a candle from the Easter Candle, faces the front, speaks and then puts their candle in the sand tray.

Reader 1   Glory be to God.
Glory to the Father for the beauty
and wonder of creation.
Glory be to the giver of life.

Reader 2   Glory to Jesus who, in bitter pain,
poured for us the life-blood
from his sacred vein.
Glory be to Jesus,
risen from the dead and with us now.

Reader 3   Glory to the Holy Spirit,
within us and around us.
Glory be to the Holy Spirit, the Breath of life.

Reader 4   Glory to God for his never-failing love.
Glory to God for loving you and me.

Sing the opening verse and chorus of 'To God be the glory' or the 'Peruvian Gloria'.

Opening prayer

Glory to you, Father, Son and Holy Spirit,
for you have revealed your love for us
through the death and resurrection of Christ our Lord.
As you love us with an everlasting love,
help us to love you more and more each day.
Amen.

Opening song

Love divine, all loves excelling

Readings

Acts 11:1-18
Psalm 148
Revelation 21:1-6
John 13:31-35

Thought for the day

John reminds us that Judas has left the company. In a very telling way John declares Judas went out and 'it was night' (13:30).

Judas chose to go out into the dark rather than stay with the Light of the World. Jesus does not exclude Judas. Judas walks away from him and excludes himself. Judas excused himself from the company and went into the dark. Jesus knew what Judas was about to do and yet did not stop him. Jesus never forces any of us to stay against our will. The choice is ours. The dark clouds had been building and what was about to happen could be easily predicted. There was already a price on Jesus' head. Jesus wanted the disciples not to lose heart but to see that through the events that followed the glory of God is to be revealed.

The glory of Jesus is revealed on the cross. Jesus lays down his life for all who are willing to be his friends. St Paul tells us that while we were yet sinners Jesus died for us. Glory is seen through the willing sacrifice of his life for our lives. In the field of medicine we remember not those who make a fortune but those who gave their lives that others might live. The researchers into radiation, Pierre and Marie Curie, are a good example of this.

The glory of the Father is revealed in that he gave his Son for our salvation. God cares for the world and the state of the world. He is not unmoved by our troubles and sorrows. God loves us so much that he would go to extremes to help us and reveal his love. This is the love that is seen on the cross, yet is there for us to see from the incarnation through to the ascension. God's glory awaits us in all creation.

God will glorify Jesus in that the cross is not the end. Death is not the end. Jesus wins the victory over death. In the cross the glory of God is revealed but it is seen again in the resurrection and the ascension. Soon the disciples would be separated from Jesus by death but it is only for a little while. This farewell is only for the moment.

As part of his bequest, Jesus leaves the disciples a commandment: 'that you love one another, just as I have loved you'. And it is by this that people will know that we are his disciples: by our love for one another. If this is how our discipleship is measured, how our life is measured, we need take heed how we react to each other.

Question time

Do we regularly give thanks to God for his creation, salvation and inspiration?

Do we make sure our church and community show the love that Jesus asks of us?

Illustration

Over 150 years ago no one cared for the lepers on the Hawaiian islands. They were driven out of their homes and even off their island. The lepers were taken to a special island called Molokai. Here they were abandoned on the beach, left to suffer and to die.

One man was anxious to do what he could. He was a Roman Catholic priest, Father Damien. He went to Molokai and was shocked at the state of the lepers. A collection of filthy ramshackle huts housed over 800 lepers. Many were helpless, weak and unable to do anything. Yet in their troubles they had built a small chapel.

Father Damien set to work. He encouraged those who were able to tidy up the mess they lived in, to build better homes and to provide a decent water supply. For 13 years he stayed with the lepers and in the end caught the disease himself. He said he was proud and privileged to be one of them. They wanted him to leave Molokai and receive better attention but he refused. Even in his last illness he gave his blankets to others in their need. He continued to show to the end his love of others, that they were not without hope and that the glory of God was for them as for others.

Intercessions

Blessed are you, Father, Son and Holy Spirit,
our Creator, Saviour and Inspirer.
We give thanks for your love and glory
revealed in the death and resurrection of Jesus.
We rejoice in his love for us
and seek to be his friends always.
Blessed are you, One God for ever.

We give thanks for the faithfulness of your disciples
and the love of your saints throughout the ages.
May your glory be revealed through your Church today.
We ask your blessing upon all who proclaim
your love and your saving power,
upon all who are seeking
to bring reconciliation and peace to the world.
We ask you to bless all who translate
and publish the Scriptures
and all who reach out in mission.

Silence

Lord, in your love,
renew and restore us.

We praise you, Lord, for your renewing powers
and we ask your blessing upon areas
that have been marred and spoiled by greed or war.
We pray for all who live in deprived or slum areas.
We remember those who have lost their homes
through debt or violence.
We remember all who are refugees
or victims of terror.

Silence

Lord, in your love,
renew and restore us.

We give thanks for all who have been our friends
and helpers throughout our lives.
We ask your blessing upon our homes and our loved ones.
We pray for friends whom we have not seen for a while
and for all who share our daily lives.
We remember any who are lonely
and feel unloved or unwanted.

Silence

Lord, in your love,
renew and restore us.

Lord, we remember your suffering
and we pray for all who have been betrayed with a kiss
or deserted by friends.

We remember those
whose relationships are breaking down
and those separated from their loved ones
due to illness or infirmity.
We pray for all who are suffering at this time
either at home or in hospital.

Silence

Lord, in your love,
renew and restore us.

We give thanks that by your death you destroyed death
and by your rising to life again
have restored us to eternal life.
We remember in your presence
the saints known and unknown
who have been loyal to you to the end.
We ask that our friends and loved ones departed
may share with them in the glory of your kingdom.

Silence

Merciful Father,
accept these prayers
for the sake of your Son,
our Saviour Jesus Christ.
Amen.

Memory verse

I give you a new commandment, that you love one another. Just as I have loved you, you also should love one another.
John 13:34

Suggested music

Hark, my soul
A new commandment I give unto you
Christ's is the world in which we move

CANDLES

Aim

To talk about friends of Jesus and show how we can be friends.

Teaching

When we start school or playschool we meet lots of new people and we make friends. Some become special friends. Who would like to tell me the name of one of their friends?

Friends like doing things together. They go out together, they play together. They like to sit together and sometimes they share a meal or some sweets together. Friends are special because we can share secrets with them and we help each other. Tell me some of the things you like doing with your friends.

Jesus had many friends. Sometimes he stayed at their homes and ate a meal with them. He had three friends who lived at Bethany. Does anyone know their names?

They are called Mary, Martha and Lazarus. When Lazarus was ill his sisters sent a message to Jesus to tell him that his friend was ill. By the time Jesus arrived, Lazarus had died and was buried. But his friend Jesus brought him back to life again.

Jesus had 12 special friends. At least four of them were fishermen. Do you know their names? Do you know the names of any more of the disciples? Jesus shared with the disciples. They talked to him and listened to him. The 12 friends helped Jesus in his work and they told other people about him. His friends loved being with him. Sadly one of his friends did things that were not good for Jesus. Jesus had taught him many things and shared meals with him but Judas went and told the enemies of Jesus where he was and they came and captured him. Jesus wanted to be friends with Judas but Judas walked away from him.

Today Jesus has lots of friends and he gives his love to them. He has friends all over the world. Do you know what they are called? They are called Christians, like you. You are a Christian because you are a friend of Jesus. Let us all say, 'I am a Christian, I am a friend of Jesus.' Now let us say it again. The friends of Jesus like to spend time with him and talk to him. How do you talk to Jesus? By praying. Jesus is always with us and never leaves us; he loves us and wants us to love him and be his friends.

If possible, get one of the older children to read this and get them all to say, 'Jesus is my friend' when the reading is finished:

Jesus is my friend and I'm a friend of Jesus.
Jesus is my friend and I'm a friend of his.
I can talk to him anytime I like.
He is always listening,
that's how I know that Jesus is my friend
and I'm a friend of his.

Julia Plaut
© Copyright 1995 Kingsway's Thankyou Music

Activity

Play an elimination game where the children have to gather into groups of 12, 8, 7, 5, 4, 3, 2. When the groups are formed let them hold hands in circles. The first two times when people are out, have the group invite them in as 'friends'. When there are only two left, let them invite everyone to join them as friends. Let the two go round the circle in opposite directions shaking hands with all and saying, 'Welcome, friend.'

Prayer

Jesus, I am happy that you are my friend
and that you never leave me.
Help me to remember you each day
and to speak to you in my prayers.
Amen.

Song

Jesus' love is very wonderful

LAMPS

Aim

To encourage the children to accept the friendship of Jesus.

Teaching

Jesus was special to many people. He often put himself out to help people and to give them the chance to be his friends. Can you tell me the names of any of the friends of Jesus? Let us start with the twelve disciples. Four were fishermen. Do you know their names. What are the names of some of the others?

Jesus had many more friends. There were two sisters and a brother who lived near Jerusalem at Bethany. When the brother was poorly they sent for Jesus to come and help. Can you tell me their names? (Mary, Martha and Lazarus.) Jesus stayed at their house for a meal more than once because they were some of his friends.

Jesus made friends with people that others did not count as friends. Can you give examples? Lepers and tax collectors were some of them. He said, 'Anyone who comes to me I will never drive away (John 6:37). Jesus did not exclude anyone from his friendship, though there was one person who excluded himself. Does anyone know who it was? Judas was a disciple. He worked with Jesus and helped Jesus but because he could not make Jesus do what he wanted, he betrayed him. Jesus sought to be friends with Judas but Judas walked out to betray Jesus the very night Jesus shared a meal with him. Jesus does not force people to love him: you cannot force people to love you. Jesus let Judas go because Judas chose to go. Jesus never excludes anyone from his friendship but some choose not to be friends.

Jesus offers to be our friend. He says, 'Come to me.' He invites us to meet with him each day. He offers us his love and seeks ours in return. We are given the ability to choose whether we will speak to him in prayer or not. Remember, Jesus wants us to come to him and love him. Let us promise to be friends of Jesus and to talk to him each day.

Activity

Divide into teams. One person from each team is blindfolded. There is an obstacle course to travel (use boxes and chairs) and the blindfolded person has to get to the end of the course without bumping into anything. To help them on their journey they have a friend who holds one hand and guides them. Once they are at the end let another member of the team be blindfolded with a friend to guide them. All should have a turn of being blindfolded and of being a friend. This is not so much a competition as to show that we need friends.

Prayer

God, I thank you for all my friends
and for all who share with me.
I thank you that Jesus offers to be my friend.
May I learn to be a friend of his,

to speak to him each day
and welcome him into my life.
Amen.

Song

Jesus is special, special to me

TORCHES

Aim

To look at Judas and to see how Jesus does not exclude him.

Teaching

Everyone needs friends with whom they can share their life. We all need companions to share with us in our joys and in our sorrows. We naturally choose our friends. Then we share part of our life with them. Sometimes they help us to do something we could not do on our own. Friends come to us when we need them.

Jesus, like anyone else, needed friends. He needed people he could share with and who would help him in his work. How many of his close friends did he choose to be his disciples? The disciples travelled with him, supported his work and told others about him. The *twelve* worked well with Jesus. No one was forced to follow him; he invited them and they came.

There was one disciple who was not like the rest. He was trying to force Jesus to do things he did not want to do. Yet Jesus still loved him. At the Last Supper, Jesus shared the meal with his disciples but knew one was about to betray him. I am sure you can tell me his name: Judas Iscariot. Before the meal was over Judas left. He was going to tell the enemies of Jesus where he was in return for 30 pieces of silver. Jesus knew but did not stop him. Jesus knew you couldn't force people to love you or to be your friends; they must choose freely. Jesus did not stop being a friend of Judas. It was Judas who stopped being Jesus' friend. Judas walked out into the darkness and betrayed a friend.

Jesus knew his arrest and even his death were now near at hand. He was aware that his disciples would find it awful. He tried to prepare his friends for what lay ahead. The disciples could not know that through his death Jesus would destroy death and through his resurrection he would offer his friends eternal life. To help his friends he gave them a 'new commandment': 'that you love one another. Just as I have loved you.' And it is by this that people will know that we are his disciples: by our love for one another. (Discuss how our church shows this to its members and the community at large. Are there ways in which we can include new people, as Jesus includes everyone?)

Activity

Draw a square on the floor or use two large sheets of newspaper. Ask four people to stand in the square. It will look full. Let each invite another. Now with eight people, ask each of them to invite another. It is amazing how many you can get into a small space. Tell them that everyone has to have both feet in the square. See if they can invent a way to accommodate everyone.

Prayer

Lord Jesus, you have promised
to accept all who come to you,
and you offer your love and peace.
Help us to live at peace with each other
and not to exclude people
from our care and attention.
Amen.

Song

Jesus is my friend, closer than a brother

Sixth Sunday of Easter

Aim

To show that Christ offers us his peace and his presence.

Preparation

Have the Easter Candle, plus smaller candles for the sand tray.

Opening activity

Let someone light the Easter Candle and say: 'Alleluia. Christ is risen.' The response by all is: 'He is risen indeed. Alleluia.' In turn each reader lights a candle from the Easter Candle, faces the front, speaks and then puts their candle in the sand tray.

Reader 1 I light this candle to remind us that Jesus is present and with each of us always. The Lord be with you.

Reader 2 I light this candle to remind us that the risen Lord offers us his peace. The peace of the Lord is always with you.

Reader 3 I light this candle to remind us that in the darkest of days the risen Lord is there and is our light and salvation. The Lord be with you.

Reader 4 I light this candle for the promise of the Spirit to lighten our days and inspire us. The Lord be with you.

Opening prayer

Lord Jesus, you are with us always
wherever we are and whatever is happening.
Help us to know you and your abiding presence,
to trust you and to live in your love and in your peace.
Amen.

Opening song

Peace, perfect peace, is the gift

Readings

Acts 16:9-15
Psalm 67
Revelation 21:10, 22–22:5
John 14:23-29 or John 5:1-9

Thought for the day

Jesus knows that his time is short. He is aware that there is a price on his head and he knows Judas has gone out to betray him. Soon Jesus will be taken prisoner and killed. All his earthly teaching will apparently come to an end. This must have been a very sad time in some ways. Today's reading sounds a little like the last will and testament of Jesus. He does not have possessions to leave with the disciples; he has no money but what he leaves will enrich them for ever.

First is the promise of the Spirit, 'whom the Father will send in my name'. The disciples of Jesus are not to be bereft for they are to be given the Spirit of God. The Spirit will be their guide and teacher. The Spirit will inspire them. The Spirit will remind them of Jesus, of his teaching and of his calling each of them.

Jesus leaves his disciples the gift of peace. This is not worldly peace, which is usually a cessation of war or when nothing is happening. This is the deep peace of God. This peace cannot be created by stillness or even meditation, for it is not of our making. It is a gift from Jesus: it is his peace. Whatever is going on in the world, even when troubles rage, his peace is there for us to accept. This peace is not dependent on circumstance but on us accepting it from the Lord.

The 'exodus' of Jesus is now near, yet he says to his disciples, 'Do not let your hearts be troubled, and do not let them be afraid.' This must have reminded the disciples of the words from Isaiah 43:1: 'Do not fear, for I have redeemed you; I have called you by your name, you are mine.'

Jesus tells them how he is going back to the Father and suggests they should be glad. Jesus is trying to widen the vision of the disciples. Life is larger than we can see. Though Jesus is going away from our sight, he still comes to us as he promised the disciples. The gifts of peace and the Presence are Christ's gifts to us all.

Question time

Do we spend enough time enjoying the presence of the risen Lord? There is always more need to talk *to* Christ than talk *about* him.

In our striving for peace do we ever accept it simply as a gift that is offered to us? We cannot make peace unless we accept it.

Illustration

In the old days crossing the Atlantic in a sailing boat left everyone to the mercy of the wind and waves. How those old wooden boats rocked about! People not used to the rolling of the boat could not walk on deck. Many had to spend most of their voyage below deck. Everything that could be was fastened firmly down to prevent it from being washed overboard. Today's journeys are a great contrast. Waiters can carry soup and children can play on deck. People lounge in the sun and hardly notice the rising and falling of the waves. Even in a storm the main body of the ship remains relatively calm – all because of the unseen gyroscope that maintains the balance of the ship. We have been offered the power of peace and calm in our lives through the presence of Christ. Do we accept this offer or neglect it at our peril?

Intercessions

Blessed are you, Father, Son and Holy Spirit.
In your presence is the fullness of joy.
You are our light and our salvation.

In you is our peace,
the peace that the world cannot give.
Blessed are you, one God now and for ever.

Lord God, we give you thanks for your peace
that you offer to us and to all people.
May your church be a true instrument of your peace,
bringing love where there has been hatred,
and fellowship where there has been division.
May your peace be seen in our actions
and within our community.
We pray for all who are not at peace
with themselves, with each other or with you.

Silence

Good and gracious God,
give us your peace.

We pray for the world
divided by strife and suffering from disunity.
Help us to know the peace we should accept,
the peace we should give
and the peace we need to forego.
We pray for the United Nations
and for peace-keeping forces throughout our world.
We remember all who are suffering
from war or political unrest at this time.

Silence

Good and gracious God,
give us your peace.

We thank you for our homes,
for their comfort and their security.
We pray for homes where your peace is not easily found.
We remember families divided by hatred and violence,
all who have little or no peace in their hearts or lives.
We pray for all who are suffering
from stress or tension within their relationships.

Silence

Good and gracious God,
give us your peace.

Lord, we remember all disturbed and distressed people,
all who have suffered from traumatic events
or who are troubled in spirit.
We pray for all who are exhausted or depressed
at this time,
for all who can find no rest.
We ask your blessing upon all who are ill or in pain,
upon those in hospital or being cared for at home.

Silence

Good and gracious God,
give us your peace.

We give thanks that through your love we have life eternal.
We pray for friends and loved ones departed;
may they rejoice in your presence and in your peace.
We commend ourselves and your whole world
to your peace and your unfailing love.

Silence

Merciful Father,
**accept these prayers
for the sake of your Son,
our Saviour Jesus Christ.
Amen.**

Memory verse

Peace I leave with you; my peace I give to you. I do not give as the world gives. Do not let your hearts be troubled, and do not let them be afraid.
John 14:27

Suggested music

O let the Son of God enfold you
Peace, perfect peace, in this dark world of sin
Longing for light

CANDLES

Aim

To show Jesus as a healer and as caring for the ill.

Teaching

Jesus went up to Jerusalem for a special festival of the Temple. He was walking around the city on his own and he came to a part of the city known as Bethzatha (let us say it together). There at Bethzatha was a way into the city called the Sheep Gate and near that was a pool. The pool was big enough to swim in. Around the pool there were five groups of arches to shelter those who came to the pool. Lots of people came to this pool because they believed that it could make them well again if they were ill. But only sometimes would the pool make people better and then only one at a time. Let me tell you how it happened.

Under the five arches were lots of people who were ill. There were blind people, people who had a hurt arm or hand, people who could not speak, people who could not hear, and people who could not walk. Some of these people came or were brought every day. Some had been ill for a little while, others had been ill all their lives. They were all waiting until they saw the water in the pool starting to bubble and move about. If the water moved in this way the first one into the pool could be healed. But sometimes people thought the waters were being moved and it was only the wind blowing the water. Someone could only be made better by the waters bubbling up from underneath. Some people would be able to get into the pool much quicker than others. Which of those who are ill do you think would not get there first? Sometimes people had friends to help them to get into the pool and so they got there faster.

Jesus walked by the pool and saw a man who was not able to walk. He knew the man had been there a long time. He had been ill for 38 years, probably all his life. (He was older than many of your mothers and fathers and he had always been ill.) Jesus asked him, 'Do you want to be made well?' The man explained he had no one to help him into the pool. He had come often but he could not get there first. Someone always went down the steps into the pool before him.

Jesus looked at the man and was sorry for him. Jesus said to him, 'Stand up, take your mat and walk.' The man had never been able to do this before but he stood up because Jesus said so. He stood up and walked. He was so excited. He could stand on his own two legs and he could walk. Wouldn't his family be surprised when he walked into the house! Jesus had made him well. This is what Jesus did to many ill people. Do you know what we call it when Jesus does something wonderful? It is a miracle. (Let us say it together: 'A miracle.') Can you tell me of any other miracles that Jesus did?

Activity

Play 'In the river, on the bank'. Have a river (a pool) and tell the children if you say, 'In the river', they have to jump in quickly. If you say 'On the bank', they have to jump out quickly. If you say, 'On the river' or 'In the bank', they must not move at all. Anyone who makes a wrong action is out.

Prayer

Lord Jesus, we thank you for your miracles,
for making ill people better
and for the love you show to them.
Help us to give our love to you
and to come to you each day in prayer.
Amen.

Song

Praise him, praise him, all his children praise him.

LAMPS

Aim

To show Jesus as a miracle worker and healer.

Teaching

When there was a special service in the Temple of Jerusalem all the grown men were expected to go to the service if they lived in the city or were within 15 miles of it. There were three special services each year – Passover, Pentecost and Tabernacles. The Passover was the first one of the year and Pentecost was 50 days later. Jesus often came to Jerusalem for these festivals.

This time we think Jesus was on his own as there is no mention of his disciples. He was not very far from the Temple and walking near the gate called the Sheep Gate in the city walls. He went to see a pool called the Pool of Bethzatha. He knew that a lot of ill people and poor people would be there.

The pool was deep enough to swim in and had steps down into it. It also had five groups of arches with a cover over them for people to shelter under. Most of the people who were there were ill or suffering from a disability. There were blind, lame and paralysed people there, all hoping to be healed by the waters of the pool. The people believed that if the waters were bubbling up and were disturbed, the first person into the water would be healed. Sometimes there was probably a false alarm when it was only the wind disturbing the water. Sadly only the first in would be healed; for anyone else

it was too late. This meant that some people had a better chance than others. The blind could not see it, the lame could not run to it and the paralysed did not really have a chance.

As Jesus walked around he noticed a man lying on a mat. The man looked frail and as if he had been there a long time. Jesus stopped and talked with him and discovered the man had been ill for 38 years. That must have been nearly all of his life. Jesus asked the man, 'Do you want to be made well?' The poor man explained that he had no one to help him and that he could not get to the pool quickly enough on his own. When the waters were stirred up, someone else always stepped down into the water before he could make it.

Jesus looked at the man and simply said, 'Stand up, take your mat and walk.' The man trusted in Jesus and in his words and stood up. As asked, he took up his mat and began to walk. Just with a few words Jesus had made the man better. It was a miracle. Can you tell me of other miracles that Jesus did? What is your favourite miracle and why?

Activity

This is a good story to act out. Let the children be the ill people, the blind, the lame and the paralysed. Let them all sit or lie near an area designated as the pool. Announce that the waters are troubled. Only the first one in is healed and can sit out. You may like to allow another two stirrings of the water before Jesus arrives. Let Jesus speak to the man lying on the ground and ask, 'Do you want to be made well?' Let the man explain his situation. Then Jesus will say to him, 'Stand up, take your mat and walk.' Get the man to do this cautiously and slowly before he walks away.

Prayer

Lord Jesus, we give thanks for your healing power
and for the peace you bring to so many lives.
Help us to know you are with us always
and that you care for us.
Amen.

Song

Praise him, praise him, praise him in the morning

TORCHES

Aim

To get the group to realise that if we want to know the gift of peace we have to use it.

Teaching

(Start with the activity.)

When we are given presents, it is quite interesting to guess what they are if they are well wrapped. Usually presents are for our pleasure or benefit. They will be no use to us if we leave them wrapped up. Presents are to be used and enjoyed. We should get pleasure out of opening the gifts and then using them. Now if I gave you a £100 note I am sure you would be excited. Suppose you put it in a photo frame and showed it to people. It might be fun but the money is useless unless you use it.

When Jesus knew that he was soon to be betrayed and handed over to the authorities he was worried for his disciples. He knew they would be distressed and troubled. During his last day with the disciples he tried to warn them of the trouble ahead. He had already told them that he would be put to death and even said how he would rise again, but they understood very little of this. Jesus then told them of certain things that would be given to them when he was gone from their sight.

God would send the Holy Spirit to be their teacher and guide. The Holy Spirit would remind them of all that Jesus had said and done. What is the name of the day when we remember the coming of the Spirit upon the disciples? Pentecost. The gift of the Spirit is given to us. We are inspired and guided by the same Spirit. This is a wonderful gift and we must not fail to walk in the Spirit and live by it.

Jesus also gives the disciples his peace. This is not like worldly peace that often means a gap between wars. The peace of Jesus is the power to live in harmony with all of creation. The peace of Jesus gives us the power to live a full and exciting life. This is a gift and given to us. We cannot make this peace; we can only accept it and enjoy it. This gift is freely given but if we do not use it, we can lose it. Let the peace of Jesus fill our hearts and minds. The deep, deep peace which the world cannot give and which we cannot create – the deep, deep peace of Christ – fill our lives and our actions. Let the peace of the Lord be always with you.

(Spend the rest of this session talking of how we can benefit from the gift of the Spirit and the peace of Christ.

Activity

Wrap up various objects and say how they are gifts. Ask the group to guess what each of the gifts is. Have obvious gifts like a football, a tennis racquet, a cricket bat, a baseball bat and a golf club wrapped. Say how all the gifts are useful and once unwrapped should be used. If you tell them all the gifts are to do with sport, it might help. Then pass around a mystery gift – an envelope and inside a piece of paper with the word 'PEACE'. Let them all guess what it is. Tell them it is a gift and it is to be used. Finally open the envelope.

Prayer

Lord, make me an instrument of your peace.
Where there is hatred, let me sow love.
Where there is injury, pardon.
Where there is discord, union.
Where there is doubt, faith.
Where there is despair, hope.
Where there is darkness, light.
Where there is sadness, joy.
For your mercy and for your truth's sake.
Amen.

Attributed to St Francis 1181–1226

Song

Peace is flowing like a river

Ascension Day

Aim

To rejoice in the presence of the ascended Lord.

Preparation

Light the Easter Candle.

Opening song

Hail the day that sees him rise

Activity

This takes place after the Gospel at the Easter Candle. It replaces the Opening activity and prayer and also the intercessions. There is a diagram of a traditional Easter Candle at the end of today's resources. If you want to add the crown of thorns, the nails and the spear hole to the candle before the service, you could use five drawing pins. Different people could do a section each. You can have also (or instead) five people ready to show and dispose of a crown of thorns (which could be made from barbed wire), two nails for the hands, a spear, a single nail for the feet.

Affirm the Alpha and Omega
God, you are the beginning and end of all things.
All things are made by you and for your love.
You are the Alpha and the Omega;
Creator of time and space;
Saviour beyond time and space;
Spirit within time and space.
We worship and adore you.

Withdraw the incense grain for the crown of thorns (or touch the top of the candle)

The head that once was crowned with thorns
is crowned with glory now.

(Show the crown that is to be put on a table for display)

Lord, we remember before you
the troubled in mind,
all who have painful memories,
the depressed and the despairing,
the mentally disturbed.
Lord, keep our hearts and minds
in the knowledge and love of God.
Ascended Lord, may we, in heart and mind,
ascend to where you are in glory.
Alleluia.
Alleluia.

Withdraw the grains of incense for the hands (or touch two places further down the candle)

(Show the two nails and place them with the crown of thorns)

We are in our Lord's nail-torn hands.

'Jesus' hands were kind hands doing good to all,
healing pain and sickness, blessing children small,
and my hands should serve him, ready at his call.
Jesus' hands were kind hands doing good to all.'

The hands fastened by hatred and nails
are freed by the love of God.
We remember in your presence all whose hands are idle.
We pray for the unemployed and redundant,
the handicapped and all with waning or failing powers.
We remember all who are tempted
to misuse the power that God has given them.
We are in the hands of God.
Alleluia.
Alleluia.

Withdraw the incense grain for pierced side of Christ (or move further down the candle)

(Show the spear and then place it with the crown and the nails)

Time and again the humans break the heart of God.
Yet God never ceases to love us.

'He comes the prisoner to release
in Satan's bondage held;
the gates of brass before him burst
the iron fetters yield.

He comes the broken heart to bind,
the bleeding souls to cure,
and with the treasures of his grace
to enrich the humble poor.'

God, we remember before you
all who are betrayed in love,
the broken-hearted and the deserted,
the rejected and the lonely.
We thank you for our loved ones and our friends.
The Ascended Lord loves us with an everlasting love.
Alleluia.
Alleluia.

Withdraw the incense representing the feet (or place your hands near the bottom of the candle)

(Show the nail that held his feet and place it with the other symbols of Christ's death)

He who was firmly fixed is set free.
Hail the day that sees him rise. Alleluia.

See, he lifts his hands above! Alleluia!
See, he shows the prints of love! Alleluia!
Hark! His gracious lips bestow, Alleluia!
blessings on his Church below. Alleluia!

Lord, we remember before you
all who are striving for freedom,
all who are held captive.
Rejoice, for death is conquered.
We are free.
Christ has won the victory.
Alleluia.
Alleluia.

Extinguish the candle.
(Place the unlit candle with the other symbols)

The Lord has gone up on high.
Alleluia.
Alleluia.

Lord, though parted from our sight,
far above the starry height,
grant our heart may thither rise
seeking thee above the skies.

Jesus said, 'I am with you always.'
Alleluia.
Alleluia.
'I go to prepare a place for you
that where I am you may be also.'
Alleluia.
Alleluia.

Lord, we remember in your presence
all who are in the dark.
May they come to your love and light
and know you as their ascended Lord and friend.
We remember all our loved ones departed
and rejoice that we are all united in you.
The Lord is here. Alleluia.
Alleluia.
His Spirit is with us. Alleluia.
Alleluia.

Readings

Acts 1:1-11* or Daniel 7:9-14
Psalm 47 or Psalm 93
Ephesians 1:15-23 or Acts 1:1-11*
Luke 24:44-53

* The reading from Acts must be one of the readings for the day.

Thought for the day

'While he was blessing them, he withdrew from them and was carried up into heaven. And they worshipped him.'

Some things defy description and the Ascension is one of them. I do not like the paintings that look as if Jesus is levitating a little off the ground. I prefer to see the disciples and a bright cloud that represents the hidden glory of God. I do not like the idea of Jesus taking off as if rocket-propelled. The Ascension is not about having lost Jesus but of us having gained the way into heaven: it is about the eternal presence of Jesus in our lives.

Jesus had to be freed from the restrictions of space and time. There are examples in the Gospels of Jesus being needed but not being there. Mary and Martha were upset that Jesus was not there when Lazarus was dying. He did not even arrive in time, though the raising of Lazarus made a great difference. When the disciples were at sea in the storm Jesus had to go to them. The Ascension frees Jesus from the restrictions of time and space. Jesus can say at the end of St Matthew, 'I am with you always.' Though departed from our sight, Jesus is ever-present and with us. We should rejoice in the company of the risen and ascended Lord.

Jesus ascended because he had descended. He came down to walk among us as man but not just to be a friend. He came down with the purpose of lifting us up. He descended so that we might ascend and be part of his everlasting kingdom. He became man so that all of humanity might share in the Godhead. He seeks to lift those that are down. May we, in heart and mind, ascend to where our Lord is.

Question time

Do you realise that the risen and ascended Lord, though unseen, comes to you?

How can you show that in Christ we have a share in his eternal kingdom?

Illustration

A man was wandering carelessly without looking where he was going. The result was he fell into a well. The well was deep and dark, and the dirt and slime clung to the man. He knew that he could perish in this horrible place.

The God of the Old Testament, the God of the Law, came and said, 'If you had kept to the right path, you would not have ended up like this. You have strayed from the straight and narrow and now you are suffering for it. One day you will be given a rescuer.'

Allah then came and looked down at the man and said, 'It is the will of Allah. Fate has brought you here. You could not escape from this whatever you did. But it may be my will that you get out again.'

Buddha looked down on the man and said, 'Smile, for it is all in the mind. Cleanse your mind and everything will be all right.'

Jesus said nothing. He descended into the mud and mire. He experienced the dark, the pain, the discomfort. He was there in the depths taking hold of the man. Then, through great efforts that cost him dearly, Jesus rose and when he ascended he took the man with him.

Memory verse

He was lifted up and a cloud took him out of their sight.
Acts 1:9

Suggested music

Alleluia, sing to Jesus
The head that once was crowned with thorns
He is Lord, he is Lord

CANDLES, LAMPS and TORCHES

As this is a working day and a school day, I have assumed there will be no separate teaching for the children and young people. However I feel, if the opportunity is there, the children should be encouraged to go up into the church tower or a high place and release balloons with tags on them celebrating the Ascension. Included in the Candles, Lamps and Torches books are suggestions for tags and banners that could be made during the sermon if the young people have the opportunity to withdraw. I have also included a hymn for each group. This is an important event and if missed on Ascension Day the material could be used on the Sunday following.

Song

Candles – I'm singing your praise
Lamps – Jesus isn't dead any more
Torches – Great is he who is King of kings

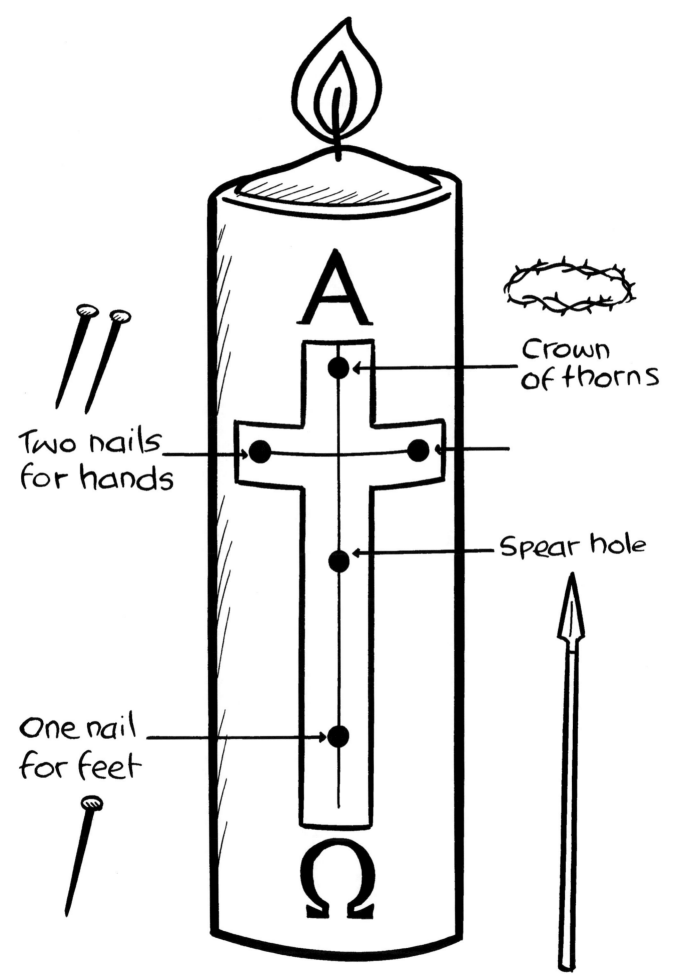

A

Crown
of thorns

Two nails
for hands

Spear hole

One nail
for feet

Ω

Seventh Sunday of Easter

Aim

To rejoice that we dwell in God and he in us.

Preparation

Have a large vase with some horse chestnut blossom in it. Beside this have an empty cross. Have a card with the words: 'I am with you always.'

Opening activity

What happened to the Easter Candle on Ascension Day? It was put out and removed.

What sort of blossom is this? Chestnut. In the country-side it is sometimes called the 'candle tree'.

A folk tradition tells us that when the Easter Candle was removed from the church, the chestnut tree put forth its candles in praise of the Ascension. We have the blossom beside an empty cross because Jesus is ascended into heaven.

How many ways can you say 'Goodbye'?

Cheerio, TTFN, Ta-ta, bye-bye, etc. Jesus did not use any words like these when he entered the cloud. He was not leaving the disciples, only being hidden from their sight. He said, 'I am with you always.'(Show the card and place it beside the chestnut blossom.) So we can say:

The Lord is here:
His Spirit is with us.

Opening prayer

Eternal God, by raising Jesus to life
you have given us victory over death.
By his Ascension into heaven
you have opened your kingdom to us all.
We lift our hearts and minds to you
and pray that we may share in your love for ever.
Amen.

Opening song

Praise, my soul, the King of heaven

Readings

Acts 16:16-34
Psalm 97
Revelation 22:12-14, 16, 17, 20, 21
John 17:20-26

Thought for the day

Today's Gospel has the last words of Jesus before he goes out to the Garden of Gethsemane, to his arrest and crucifixion. This is a prayer of Jesus for his disciples and for all who come to believe through the disciples and the outreach of the Church. The prayer shows the trust Jesus puts in the disciples and in us. He knew the frailty of the disciples and that they hardly understood what he was saying. He still handed his work on to them and put his hope and confidence in them as he does in us.

Jesus prays for our unity but it is not a unity of our making; it is a unity through our dwelling in God and God dwelling in us. It is a unity that is about relationships, not only with each other but with God. It is a unity of love, that we love each other as Jesus loves us. Unity comes not through schemes and meetings but through heart-to-heart relationships.

Jesus prays, 'As you, Father, are in me and I also in you, may they also be in us.' The great gift of God to us is that we dwell in him and he in us. We are never without the presence of God, for in him we live and move and have our dwelling. This is expressed well in the 'Prayer of Seven Directions' (a good prayer to start and end each day with):

God before me: God behind me.
God on my right and God on my left.
God above me: God beneath me.
God, this day within and about me.

Because God is greater than we are, there are six directions saying that we are in God and one direction saying that God is in us. We are more God-possessed than possessing God! This is the Glory and the love that we share: we can meet God in others and be God to others. The unity that we have is God-given. The joy we have is from our indwelling and it is something we need to take time to know and enjoy.

Question time

Does you life show that you are in the presence of God and that nothing can separate you from him?

Is your prayer life about indwelling or is it more like a long-distance phone call?

Illustration

There is an old story about God and the humans after the Fall. Because man had separated from God through disobedience, God decided to hide from humans. He asked his angels where he should hide. 'Hide in the heights of heaven,' said the first angel. God replied, 'The humans would expect me to be in the high places and they will find me in their own high experiences.' The second angel said, 'Then why not hide in the depths?' God replied, 'Again, all human beings descend into the depths from time to time and they will discover that I am there.' One little angel had bided his time and he saw the mistakes of others. He said to God, 'Why not hide in the human heart? They will never find you there.' God smiled and said, 'How true', and from that day hid in each human heart. Yet there are so few humans who seek his presence in their lives.

Intercessions

Blessed are you, Lord our God.
To you be praise and glory for ever.
You have become one with us
in taking our humanity into the Godhead.
Now we are one with you
and share in your love and glory.
May we rejoice that we dwell in you
and you are in us
this day and for ever.
Blessed are you, Father, Son and Holy Spirit.

Let us rejoice with the whole Church
in the Ascension of our Lord.
May the lives of all who are Christian
reveal your presence and your love to others.
Bless all preachers of the word
and ministers of the sacraments.
We pray for all who lead retreats and quiet days,
all who teach Religious Education
and all who are training in theological colleges.

Silence

Risen and ascended Lord,
hear us and help us.

We give thanks for men and women of vision.
We pray for all who are doing scientific research,
all who are exploring
into the depths and mysteries of creation.
May we learn to use all new discoveries with wisdom
and with respect for the earth and all its creatures.

Silence

Risen and ascended Lord,
hear us and help us.

We give thanks for the love we have received
at home and through our friends.
We ask your blessing
upon all who seek to strengthen family life
and to improve the surroundings
of those who live in deprived or run-down areas.
We pray for any who are tempted by drugs or vice,
that they may have a vision of a better way of living.

Silence

Risen and ascended Lord,
hear us and help us.

We remember all who are struggling to survive.
We pray for the world poor,
the homeless and the war-torn.
We ask your blessing upon all who are refugees
or who suffer from famine.
We pray for all who are ill
and unable to enjoy life to the full.

Silence

Risen and ascended Lord,
hear us and help us.

We give thanks that we have a great High Priest
who has entered into the heavens,
even Jesus our Lord.
May the faithful departed,
in fellowship with all your saints,
rejoice with the ascended Lord in glory.

Silence

Merciful Father,
accept these prayers
for the sake of your Son,
our Saviour Jesus Christ.
Amen.

Memory verse

As you, Father, are in me and I am in you, may they also be in us, so that the world may believe that you have sent me.
John 17:21

Suggested music

All honour and power
Christ be with me, Christ within me
Rejoice, the Lord is King

CANDLES

Aim

To ensure the children understand the events of the Ascension.

Teaching

(Start with the activity, repeating it three or four times so that the children begin to see the sequence.)

Once Jesus died on the cross, what happened to him next? He was buried in a tomb – that is, in a cave – and a big stone was rolled against the entrance. They thought that no one could get in or out. After three days – Friday, Saturday, Sunday – what happened to Jesus? He rose again. Jesus was alive and seen by many of his friends.

Mary saw him in the garden and she was very happy. Two disciples met Jesus on the road. Ten disciples met Jesus in the room where they were staying. A week later Thomas was with the ten and they all saw Jesus. Thomas touched the hands of Jesus, where the nails had made holes. Then they met Jesus again at the seaside; while they had been working, he cooked breakfast for them. Jesus was seen in all sorts of different places but the time had come for him to be with more people. To do this he had to be hidden from the sight of the disciples: he had to return to heaven.

Jesus met the disciples on the mountain. He talked to them and then a cloud came and hid Jesus from their sight. They could not see him any more. When a cloud covers the sun, where is the sun? It is still there. Even on a very cloudy day the sun is still there. It is the same with Jesus: a cloud hid him but he is still with his disciples and he is still here with us. The disciples did not wave goodbye. They did not say, 'Cheerio', because Jesus had not left them. The very last words Jesus said to them were 'Remember, I am with you always' (Matthew 28:20). Let us say what Jesus said and remember he is with us.

Activity

Encourage various actions as you tell of Jesus:

Jesus dies on the cross (*stand still with arms outstretched*).

Jesus is buried in the tomb (*curl up on the ground as if asleep; be as still and quiet as possible*).

Jesus rises from the dead (*stand up, show your hands and say, 'Peace to you'*).

Jesus ascends into heaven (*jump as high as you can and shout, 'Alleluia'*).

Jesus is with us always (*run around the room until signalled to stop; stop and say, 'Jesus is with us always'*).

Prayer

Jesus, you are always with us.
You love us and seek to help us.
Let us give our love to you every day.
Amen.

Song

Jesus is a friend of mine, praise him

LAMPS

Aim

To show the meaning of the Ascension.

Teaching

Have you ever wanted to be in two places at once? Maybe you had to go to school but at the same time you would have liked to be outside playing a game. Wouldn't it be wonderful if we could be in two places at once? You could be sitting at your desk and going to a party at the same time. But we cannot; we can only be in one place at a time.

There was a man who lived in the country. He wanted to tell over 500 people at the same time some good news. He could rush around from house to house but it would take hours. The people lived a long way apart and he could not get them all together. Instead he left where he lived and went into the town. There he went to a television studio. He appeared on television in every home he wanted to visit. By going away from his friends and being out of their sight he was able to be seen by all of them at the same time and tell them the good news.

The disciples saw Jesus in many different places after his resurrection. Can we make a list of them?

In the garden, on the road, in a house, in a room where the ten disciples met, again when Thomas was present. Then he was seen by the Sea of Galilee as he prepared breakfast for the disciples. Jesus wanted the disciples to know that he is with them always. It was necessary to be seen to be alive and not to be a ghost. This is why we are told of Jesus eating. But Jesus wanted to be free from the restriction of space and of time. He wanted to be with all his disciples and he wanted to be with people in every age and in every land.

Jesus led his disciples up a mountain. He loved mountains and he often went into the hills to pray. It was on a mountain that the disciples saw him shining white and then hidden by a cloud. Now on this mountain, Jesus spoke with them and told them of his departure. He did not say, 'Farewell.' They did not say 'Goodbye.' Because Jesus promised them something special. He said to them, 'Remember I am with you always.' Those were not words of someone going away. It was only that he was now hidden from their sight. If Jesus kept turning up, everyone would be forced to believe. You cannot fail to believe if you see him. Jesus wanted us to believe even though we cannot see him. He wanted the disciples to know he was with them and would work with them. When the cloud hid Jesus from sight it meant he was free from the restrictions of space and time.

Jesus is with us. That is why at nearly every service we say words like 'The Lord is here. His Spirit is with us' or 'The Lord is with you. And also with you'. It is to remind us that the Lord is always there.

Activity

Play 'Glory'. Make a circle with everyone facing into the centre. Everyone keeps their hands behind their backs. One person is put in the middle. A ball of tennis ball size to represent the sun is given to one person. Everyone making the circle represent clouds. The ball is passed from one person to another. The person in the middle has to watch carefully until he spots the movement or the ball. Once he is sure where the ball is, he cries, 'Glory', and points at whoever has the ball. If he is correct, then the person with the ball has to go into the centre. If he is incorrect, the game recommences.

Prayer

(To be learned by heart)

Dear Lord, for these three things I pray:
that I may know you more clearly,
love you more dearly,
and follow you more nearly
day by day.

After Richard of Chichester (1197–1253)

Song

Alleluia, alleluia, give thanks to the risen Lord

TORCHES

Aim

To explore the Ascension through the eyes of Peter.

Teaching

Reporter Hello, Peter. I am told you were with Jesus on the mountain when he returned to the Father.

Peter Yes, I was there but so were the ten other disciples. We all saw Jesus enter into the cloud.

	Jesus loved mountains and high places. He often went alone into the mountains to pray.
Reporter	I thought Jesus was crucified, dead and buried.
Peter	He was all of that but he rose again. Thank God. Mary Magdalene saw him first. We could hardly believe her. Then two on the road to Emmaus saw Jesus. He appeared to ten of his disciples, including me, later the same day. Thomas was away and did not see him until a week later.
Reporter	Was Jesus seen again?
Peter	Once, when we went fishing on the Sea of Galilee. We saw him there in the early morning light on the shore. He had started cooking breakfast for us and he told us where there were fish to catch.
Reporter	He was not a ghost, then?
Peter	No, Thomas had touched him. Mary had clung to him. Now he was eating fish with us. This was no ghost.
Reporter	Tell me about the Ascension.
Peter	We were with Jesus on Mount Olivet. He loved this place. Here is the Garden of Gethsemane. At one side of the hill is Bethany and at the other Jerusalem. Jesus talked to us and told us of the gift of the Spirit. He asked us to wait in Jerusalem. Then he moved a little way from us, and a cloud hid him from our sight.
Reporter	Do you mean like a bit of fog?
Peter	You could say that. But I think it is the cloud that hides the glory of God. Like the cloud that filled the tent of meeting when Moses spoke with God. Like the cloud on Mount Sinai when Moses went up to meet God.
Reporter	Have you seen Jesus since then?
Peter	No. But do you know his last words were not 'Goodbye'. He said, 'Remember I am with you always.' He is not restricted any more by space or time. He is with each of us.
Reporter	Where do you think he is now?
Peter	Let loose in all the world. (*Pause*) The Lord is here. Alleluia, alleluia.
Reporter	His Spirit is with us. Alleluia, alleluia.

Activity

Get two readers to read the above script. Tell them to put as much feeling as possible into it. Then get the rest of the group to act as the other disciples. They have to say what they feel about the Ascension and what it means for people today.

Prayer

Lord unseen, yet ever near,
help us to know your presence
and to believe in you.
Lift our hearts and minds,
that we may be at home with you in your kingdom
and enjoy your love for ever.
Amen.

Song

King of kings and Lord of lords

Pentecost

Aim

To know the Spirit as our strength and our guide.

Preparation

Have the names of the twelve disciples (Matthias having been chosen to replace Judas) on separate cards. Give twelve small children the cards, and red and white streamers to wave. Give twelve more children balloons to carry. Then have twelve people with lit candles. There should also be a sand tray for the candles.

Opening activity

Let this group (and the rest of the congregation, if possible) process around the church waving banners and carrying candles. Have the names of the disciples placed near a sand tray. Let the balloons be tied to the corners of the altar rail. As each candle carrier comes to the sand tray, let them announce: 'The Lord is here.' Have the whole congregation reply: 'His Spirit is with us. Alleluia.'

Opening prayer

Breathe in us, Holy Spirit,
that we may think what is holy.
Move in us, Holy Spirit,
that we may do what is holy.
Attract us, Holy Spirit,
that we may love what is holy.
Strengthen us, Holy Spirit,
that we may guard what is holy.
Guard us, Holy Spirit,
that we may keep what is holy.

St Augustine of Hippo (354–430) (adapted)

Opening song

Love divine, all loves excelling
or The Spirit lives to set us free (good for procession)

Readings

Acts 2:1-21* or Genesis 11:1-9
Psalm 104:24-34, 35b
Romans 8:14-17 or Acts 2:1-21*
John 14:8-17 (25-27)

* The reading from Acts must be one of the readings today.

Thought for the day

The disciples had shared in the ministry of Jesus. They had experienced his healing miracles and his teaching. True, they had suffered the trauma of the crucifixion, death and burial, but they had also seen the risen Lord. He had appeared to them two or three times, assuring them of his love and his presence. In story fashion you would expect these men to be bold and able to do anything, but in fact we find them hesitant and fearful, once again behind closed doors. Not a very inspiring display, yet typical of much of human nature: locked in and afraid of life.

It seems the resurrection was not enough in itself to get the disciples going. This wonderful event did not seem to make them braver or stronger. There was still an emptiness within. Jesus had understood this well and told them to wait in Jerusalem where they would be baptised by the Holy Spirit (Acts 1:4, 5) and then they would receive power to become witnesses (Act 1:8).

What exactly happened at Pentecost we will never know. The disciples could only describe their experience in terms of wind and fire, two of the strongest elements of the world. Their emptiness was changed and charged with power. The sound, the Spirit, filled the house. It was as if each received a flaming light and the Spirit filled each of them (Acts 2:1-4). The God who seemed to be outside of them was now also known to be within. In the first 13 chapters of Acts there are more than 40 references to the Spirit. The Spirit is experienced as power from on high (Acts 1:8, 4:31, 13:9). The Spirit is experienced as guidance (Acts 8:29, 10:19, 11:12, 11:28, 13:2-4, 15:28, 16:6, 20:23). Through the indwelling Spirit the disciples are changed for ever and it is the selfsame Spirit that fills the Church of today and each of us. Let us wait upon the Spirit each day for strength and guidance.

Question time

Have you learned to wait each day on the power of the Spirit?

Does you church show that it is Spirit-filled and that its strength and power come from God?

Illustration

There are lots of ancient stories about werewolves and creatures that come in the night and steal away your life powers. You wake in the morning feeling drained and half-dead. Well, you might not believe such tales but it is still possible to awake short on energy and resources, and the more we try to put it right, the more in danger we are of becoming exhausted. When our batteries run low we need a charge from outside of ourselves. Too many of us think we are self-sufficient, able to go in our own strength, when we need to learn to wait upon the Lord for renewal and for guidance. Just as we would not drive around all day with a flat tyre, so we should make sure we begin the day filled with the power and love of God.

Intercessions

Blessed are you, Lord our God.
To you be praise and glory for ever.
Your Spirit moved over the face of the deep
at the beginning
to bring order out of chaos
and light and life into the world.
Pour your Spirit into our hearts
and kindle in us the fire of your love,
that we may reveal your power in our lives
and walk in the joy of your presence.
Blessed are you, Father, Son and Holy Spirit.

Come, Holy Spirit, fill our lives
which without you would be dull and cold.
Fill our Church
which without you would be an empty shrine.
We ask you to guide and strengthen
all who preach the word,
all who teach the faith.
We pray for all who are preparing
for Confirmation or for Ordination,
for all who are seeking to grow in the faith
and in a relationship with you.

Silence

Come, Holy Spirit, fill our hearts:
renew and refresh your creation.

We give thanks for all who are inspired and guided by you.
We ask your blessing upon all artists, musicians,
writers and craftspeople.
We pray for all who influence the minds of others
through broadcasting or through their example of living.
We remember today
all who live in deprived or depressing surroundings.

Silence

Come, Holy Spirit, fill our hearts:
renew and refresh your creation.

We give thanks for the coming of the Spirit
and the filling of an earthly home.
We ask your blessing upon our homes
and our relationships.
We pray that our friendships enrich each other
and help us to be more aware of you.
We pray for all who are taken into care
and all who lack the love of a stable home.

Silence

Come, Holy Spirit, fill our hearts:
renew and refresh your creation.

We remember all exhausted peoples,
the world-weary, the depressed and the discouraged.
We pray for all who despair
and all who feel they can no longer cope with life.
We ask your blessing
upon friends and loved ones who are ill
and upon all who have been involved in accidents
this week.

Silence

Come, Holy Spirit, fill our hearts:
renew and refresh your creation.

We give thanks for the gift of the Spirit
and the promise of eternal life.
We remember all who have served you faithfully
and are now at rest in your kingdom.
We pray for loved ones and friends
who are departed from us,
that they may rejoice in life eternal.

Silence

Merciful Father,
accept these prayers
for the sake of your Son,
our Saviour Jesus Christ.
Amen.

Memory verse

All who are led by the Spirit of God are children of God.
Romans 8:14

Suggested music

O Breath of Life
Spirit of the living God (Iverson)
Breathe on me, Breath of God

CANDLES

Aim

To show how the disciples were filled with the power of the Spirit.

Teaching

Start with the making of streamers and crowns for the activity.

Have a radio-controlled car or some power-driven toy. Take the battery out and show that it will not work. Talk about how it needs a power source and how sometimes the power source runs out. If possible, put some old batteries in and show that it will still not work. Now put some new batteries in. We cannot see the power but we know it is there. (Let the children make the toy work for a while.)

The disciples were in Jerusalem, in a house, and they were waiting until they received power from God. They were doing what Jesus asked them: waiting for new power. Suddenly there was a sound like the wind (let us make the sound of the wind). The sound filled the house where the disciples were. They could not see the wind but they heard it and felt it. The power was all around them. They knew something special was happening.

Next they saw flames of fire in the room, not burning anything but dancing around the room. The fire seemed to touch each of them. They were not afraid because they knew it was God giving them the power of the Spirit. The Spirit of God came upon each of the disciples and gave them new strength and the power to go out and tell of Jesus. The disciples had not been brave enough to go out and speak to the people before, but now they were because they had new power. God's Spirit gave them power to go out and to speak.

Get the children to act this out. Have a group that are disciples and get them to sit quite still. Tell them they are not to move until they are given a crown of flames. Let there be a 'visitor' for each disciple. This group makes the sound of the wind and runs around the room waving streamers. Then they go and get a crown for each disciple and place it on the disciple's head. Now all jump up and dance and shout.

Activity

Use red, yellow and white crêpe paper to make cheerleader streamers. Get the children to stand still until they are given a streamer. Then they must dance and jump about to show they have power. A single streamer could be passed around a circle and only after it is received can that person jump up and down before passing it on to the next. Alternatively you can use a fiery crown – and only when it is on a head can that person dance.

Prayer

Dear God, we thank you for your Spirit
which gives us power
and makes us able to do
all that we are able to do.
Amen.

Song

I'm a pow, pow, power pack

LAMPS

Aim

To encourage the group to know that the Spirit gives us power.

Teaching

In the olden days ships did not have motors and they had to depend on the wind to make them move across the sea. Sometimes when they were in the middle of the ocean the wind dropped and the sails went limp. The sailors could not do anything but wait. They had to wait until the wind blew again. Sometimes they had to wait for days and they became excited when the wind at last began to blow. Once the wind filled the sails they were able to get going.

Jesus wanted his disciples to tell the world about his resurrection and his love for all people. But the disciples did not seem to have the power or the energy to do what Jesus wanted them to do. At the feast of Pentecost, the twelve disciples met together in Jerusalem. Judas was not there because he had died. A new disciple was now in his place. The new disciple was called Matthias. He was chosen because he had followed Jesus from the beginning and he was also a witness to the resurrection. Now the twelve were waiting until God sent them power from on high. They were waiting for the coming of the Holy Spirit.

Suddenly there was a sound like a mighty wind. The disciples felt the wind was filling the house. They could not see the wind but they knew it was there. They felt something special was happening to them. God was sending his Spirit to fill them and to move them. God was sending his Spirit to give them power. Then it was as if fire was filling the house but the house was not burning. The whole house was full of light. The fire then seemed to come upon each of the disciples. They felt its warmth and its power. They knew that God was filling them with his Spirit and with his power. Now they had power and the courage to go out and tell others about what was happening to them and to tell them about Jesus.

Activity

Get the children to act this out. Have a group that are disciples and get them to sit quite still. Tell them they are not to move until they are given a crown of flames. Let there be a 'visitor' for each disciple. This group makes the sound of the wind and runs around the room waving streamers. Then they go and get a crown for each disciple and place it on the disciple's head. Now all jump up and dance and shout.

Prayer

Come, Holy Spirit of God,
fill our lives with your presence and your power.
Give us the courage and the power
to tell of you and of our Lord Jesus Christ.
Amen.

Song

Spirit of God, unseen as the wind

TORCHES

Aim

To seek to understand the events of Pentecost.

Teaching

Begin with Peter outside and speaking to the people about what has happened to the disciples. Explain that the prophet Joel looked forward to a time when the Spirit of God would come upon all flesh. Look at the reading from Joel 2:17-21 as quoted by Peter. (Get someone to read this.)

Now go back to the disciples before the coming of the Spirit. They are all together in one room. It is Pentecost, only 50 days since the Passover and the death of Jesus. In those 50 days the disciples had seen Jesus two or three times; they had experienced the resurrection. They had also seen Jesus ascend into heaven by entering the cloud. They had experienced many wonderful things, but as yet they did not have the power or the ability to proclaim them. Jesus asked them to wait in Jerusalem until they had received this power from on high. In the meantime, the disciples had made up their number to twelve again; they had chosen Matthias to replace Judas Iscariot. Now in Jerusalem for the feast of Pentecost, they waited upon God.

Suddenly there was a sound and a movement. Nothing could be seen but it was like a rushing mighty wind and it filled the house where they were. (The Jews use the same word for wind, breath and for spirit.) Something wonderful was happening. The disciples were being moved by a power that they could only describe as the power of God. Then it was as if the room was filled with light and fire. There seemed to be tongues of flame dancing around the room and each of the disciples seemed to receive a touch of that flame. They knew

God had not only visited them but also filled them with his power and his Spirit. Now they could go out and tell the world about Jesus and the Spirit. These were now Spirit-filled men and they wanted the world to know that God gives his Spirit to all who seek him.

Activity

Have a tray with 12 candles on it waiting to be lit Let us light a candle for each of the disciples (you might like someone to read out their names from Acts 1:13 and add 1:26 for Matthias). Now produce extra candles, one for each person. Tell them as the Spirit of God is given to us all, we can add our names and a candle to the tray. Let each light a candle and add it to the tray as they say their name. And so the light spreads from person to person and from age to age.

Prayer

Spirit of the living God, fall afresh on me.
Spirit of the living God, fall afresh on me.
Melt me, mould me, fill me, use me.
Spirit of the living God, fall afresh on me.

Daniel Iverson (1890–1972)

Song

For I'm building a people of power

ORDINARY TIME
Trinity Sunday

Aim

To rejoice in the presence and power of Father, Son and Holy Spirit.

Preparation

Have the font filled with water and a decoration of flowers near it. You may like to have shamrock or clover leaves to give to each member of the congregation after they acknowledge that they are immersed in Father, Son and Holy Spirit.

Opening activity

Let the people profess their faith:

Do you believe in God the Creator, who made heaven and earth, who made us out of love?
I believe and trust in him.

Do you believe in God the Son, who shared in our humanity, who died and rose again for us?
I believe and trust in him.

Do you believe in God the Holy Spirit, who is the Lord and giver of life and sustains us in our need?
I believe and trust in him.

This is the faith of the whole Church.
I believe and love one God, Father, Son and Holy Spirit.

Now have a procession to the font, which should contain some water. Let everyone dip their fingers in the water and then sign themselves on their forehead with the sign of the cross. Encourage them all to say, 'I am in the presence and love of God – Father, Son and Holy Spirit.'
For the Gloria sing the 'Peruvian Gloria'.
For the Creed sing 'We believe in God' (Graham Kendrick).

Opening prayer

Blessed are you, Father, Son and Holy Spirit.
You have created the world
out of your goodness and love.
You have redeemed us from death and sin
by your grace and love.
You are our Guide and our Strength
through your presence and your love.
Blessed are you, Three Persons in One God,
for ever and ever.
Amen.

Opening song

Father of heaven, whose love profound

Readings

Proverbs 8:1-4, 22-31
Psalm 8
Romans 5:1-5
John 16:12-15

Thought for the day

There are some things that we cannot put into words no matter how skilled we are. It is difficult to capture a sunset in words, though it is not hard to enjoy the sunset. A meaningful relationship cannot be tied down by a description, yet it is still good to say why some relationships are meaningful to us. Love cannot be fully expressed in words – it is beyond mere expression – but it would be a sad world if we gave up trying to tell of our love. In the same way, when we try to explain the Trinity we find that words fail us. The mystery of Godhead cannot be contained in a neat formula or grasped by our minds. The majesty of God is beyond our comprehension. Yet we need to communicate our experience and tell of the things of our heart. Often what the mind cannot comprehend the heart can grasp.

The word 'Trinity' does not appear anywhere in the Bible, yet the Bible is full of accounts of the Creator, Redeemer and Comforter. The reading from Proverbs hints at 'wisdom' being God's co-worker from the beginning: 'I was beside him, like a master worker; and I was daily his delight, rejoicing before him always, rejoicing in his inhabited world and delighting in the human race' (Proverbs 8:30, 31). For God to have a personality there needs to be at least another personality to relate to. Personality is of the utmost importance because it is of the essence of the Godhead. The way we reflect God's image is through our personality.

In Romans, St Paul tells us, 'We have peace with God through our Lord Jesus Christ' (5:1). A little later St Paul declares, 'God's love has been poured into our hearts through the Holy Spirit that has been given to us' (5:5).

In St John's Gospel we have Jesus talking of the 'Spirit of truth' who 'will guide you into all truth' (16:13). He also tells us of the Father and how he had given all to his Son (16:15).

There are only hints and expressions of the Trinity but there is no doubt that our God is a triune God. We believe in God the Creator who made the world and all that is in it. God created the world out of his own love and for his love. We believe that God revealed himself to the world in Jesus. Jesus is God incarnate. When the world strayed away from God and got lost in sin and death, Jesus came to redeem the world through his love and to bring us to eternal life. Once Jesus ascended into the heavens, the Holy Spirit of God came to us and gave us strength and guidance. The Spirit is ever-present and fills us with his power and his love. The Holy Spirit is God. Yet there are not three Gods separate from each other but One God. Hard to grasp with the mind, but the heart will begin to understand if we give our attention to each person of the Trinity.

Question time

What signs are used to represent the Trinity? Can you find such signs in your church?

Are you sure you have a relationship with the Three Persons of God and not just one or two?

Illustration

To understand the Three in One is quite difficult. St Patrick suggested the shamrock with its three shapes that made one leaf. Clover is much the same. Others have suggested the human being as made up of body, mind and spirit: three parts that you cannot fully separate and yet one being.

You might like to think of the sun. You can see it in the sky and yet it is too bright to look at. In its glory you may like to compare the sun to God the Father. Even when the sun is hidden we know it is still there.

The sun provides the world with light. This light gives life to the world and in the light we can live and move. Let the light remind us of Jesus who is the Light of the World. Even on the dullest of days the sun still provides us with light.

The sun also provides us with warmth. Without the warmth the world would be cold and dead. In the warmth we grow and live. Let the warmth remind us of the Spirit.

Glory, light and warmth – we can talk of them as separate things and yet they are bound together. One would not exist without the other.

Intercessions

Blessed are you, Father, Son and Holy Spirit,
Three Persons in One God.
To you be praise and glory for ever.
In your goodness you have revealed yourself to us
and invited us to share in your glory.
Blessed are you, God, for ever.

Father, we give you thanks for your creation,
for the beauty and wonder of our world.
We ask your blessing
upon all who work in caring for the earth
and who labour to provide us with our daily needs.
May your Church lead others
to respect the world and each other.
We ask your blessing upon family life
and upon all relationships.

Silence

Holy, holy, holy God,
hear us and help us.

Jesus Christ, Son of God, we give thanks
for your love revealed in our salvation.
May we share with you
in the bringing of all people to a greater freedom.
We pray for the emergency services
and for all who risk their lives on behalf of others.
We ask your blessing upon all who are caring
for the ill and hungry of our world.

Silence

Holy, holy, holy God,
hear us and help us.

Holy Spirit of God, may we know your presence
with us and within us.
We give thanks for the talents and the abilities
you give to us.

We pray for all scientists and research workers,
for all artists and craftspeople.
We ask your blessing upon all who teach
and those who learn.

Silence

Holy, holy, holy God,
hear us and help us.

Holy and blessed Three,
we wonder at your unity and diversity.
We pray for our families and our homes.
We remember before you
all who are having difficulties in their relationships
and all who suffer from mental illness or autism.
We pray for all who are separated from loved ones
through illness.

Silence

Holy, holy, holy God,
hear us and help us.

You, Lord, are our Creator, Redeemer and Guide.
As you have made us and redeemed us,
you offer us new life and life eternal.
We remember in your presence
all our loved ones and friends who are departed from us.
May they rejoice in your love and presence
now and for evermore.

Silence

Merciful Father,
**accept these prayers
for the sake of your Son,
our Saviour Jesus Christ.
Amen.**

Memory verse

We have peace with God through our Lord Jesus Christ . . . God's love has been poured into our hearts through the Holy Spirit that has been given to us.
Romans 5:1, 5

Suggested music

Thou, whose almighty word
Holy, holy, holy, Lord God Almighty
Lead us, heavenly Father, lead us

CANDLES

Aim

To introduce the children to the idea of Father, Son and Holy Spirit.

Teaching

Start with the activity. Get the children familiar with the shapes of circles, squares and triangles. Help them to see a square has four sides and a triangle three. Draw a triangle and write along the sides, 'The Father, the Son and the Holy Spirit.' In the centre write, 'God'. Ask a child to read down the sides. Turning the triangle around if necessary. Now get three people to read one side each. When a side is read, get the whole group to respond, '. . . is God'.

How many make God? Three.

Who are they? Father, Son and Holy Spirit.

We will divide into three. I will be group one. The class will be divided into groups two and three. I will say something about the Father. Group two will repeat it but about Jesus. Then group three will repeat it but about the Holy Spirit.

Leader	The Father is God.
Group 2	Jesus is God.
Group 3	The Holy Spirit is God.

Leader	The Father is strong.
Group 2	Jesus is strong.
Group 3	The Holy Spirit is strong.

Leader	The Father loves us.
Group 2	Jesus loves us.
Group 3	The Holy Spirit loves us.

Leader	The Father is here.
Group 2	Jesus is here.
Group 3	The Holy Spirit is here.

Leader	Father, we love you.
Group 2	Jesus, we love you.
Group 3	Holy Spirit, we love you.

Activity

Play 'Circles, squares and triangles'. The children run around. When you call, 'Circles', they have to make circles of five people. When you call, 'Squares', they have to make groups of four in the shape of a square. When you call, 'Triangles', the groups have to be of three and make the shape of a triangle. It is useful to start this game by making sure the children know these shapes. Let three different people come out and draw them. The game is not an elimination game. If there are spare children who cannot make up a shape let them try to make it by drawing it with their hands in the air.

Prayer

Father, you are always with us.
Jesus, you are always with us.
Spirit, you are always with us.
We thank you, Father, Son and Holy Spirit.
Amen.

Song

Father, we adore you

LAMPS

Aim

To introduce the group to the idea of the Trinity.

Teaching

Who knows the difference between a circle, a square and a triangle? Without drawing them or using your hands

it is quite difficult to describe them. It is more difficult to describe a human being. We are more than just bodies. What else makes us what we are? We have a mind and it needs feeding like our bodies. How do we feed our minds? We are often in danger of giving our minds junk food or food that is bad for us. There are some things that are harmful to our minds, just as there are some things that are harmful to our bodies. We have a body and a mind. What else makes us what we are? We have a spirit. We are more than just mind and body. Our spirit needs attention and care, just as our bodies and minds do. How do we care for our spirit? We care for it by making contact with our God and by praying to him regularly. We are body, mind and spirit, and yet we are just one person, one human being.

God is much greater than we are. God is three persons and yet only one God. Just as we are body, mind and spirit, God is made up of three persons: The Creator, the Maker of all things; then the Redeemer, the Saviour of the world; then the Guide and the Strengthener. When we were baptised we were baptised in the presence and the power of the three. We were baptised: In the name of . . . ? And of . . . ? And of . . .? Everyone who is baptised is baptised in the name of the Father and of the Son and of the Holy Spirit. Our God, in three persons, is always with us and is ready to help us.

Spend what time is left talking about the Creator God, the Redeeming God and the Guiding God.

Activity

Have a selection of three different colours of wool cut into long lengths. Give each child a single colour and get them to team up with two others who have different colours. Show them how to knot the three strands together at one end and then to plait the wool into one. Once the three are one, get them to knot the wool at equal distances, so that it can be cut and made into three bracelets, one for each of them to wear. (Note: there will have to be two knots close together for the cuts in between them.)

Prayer

Father, we thank you for the creation of the world
and for giving us life.
Jesus, we thank you for living and dying for us,
that we may share in life eternal.
Spirit, we thank you for your power
and that you are always ready to guide us.
We give our love to you, Father, Son and Holy Spirit.
Amen.

Song

Father, we love you

TORCHES

Aim

To look at symbols of the Trinity.

Teaching

Let us imagine we are going to design a stained-glass window in praise of the Trinity. What do we mean when we talk of the Trinity?

We mean we believe in three persons in one God. How do we usually describe these persons?

First is God the Father, who we think of as the creator and maker of all things. This includes giving us life and the world around us.

Next is Jesus Christ, the Son of God, who came down to earth and shared in our humanity. Jesus was crucified, died and was buried. He rose again and through his rising offered us the hope of eternal life.

The third is the Holy Spirit, whom Jesus promised would be given to us as our Guide and would bring us new power and abilities.

The Three together are a unity. Tri-unity: Three in One and One in Three. Tri-unity is usually shortened to the word 'Trinity' and this is shorthand for Father, Son and Holy Spirit: Three persons in One God.

Activity

Design a window depicting the Trinity and write a prayer that expresses the Triune nature of God. It could be a prayer where each person of the Trinity is addressed in the same way. For example:

Father all loving,
Jesus all loving,
Spirit all loving,
we give our love to you.

Prayer

We rejoice in your creation,
in your saving power
and in your presence within us.
We seek to give ourselves to you,
Father, Son and Holy Spirit.
Amen.

Song

Father God, we worship you

Proper 4

Sunday between 29 May and 4 June inclusive
(if after Trinity Sunday)

Aim

To encourage people in their use of intercessory prayer.

Preparation

Give everyone a piece of paper on which they can write the name of someone they want to pray for.

Opening activity

Tell the congregation you are not going to read out all the requests for prayer. God already knows what each of us is asking. Two young members of the congregation will come around with collection plates and bring the prayers to the sanctuary during the first hymn. The prayers will be on the altar throughout the service.

Opening prayer

Lord God of all power and might,
you know our needs before we ask.
We ask you to hear our prayers,
to come to our help
and to give us your peace,
through Jesus Christ our Lord.
Amen.

Opening song

O for a thousand tongues to sing.
or O Lord, hear my prayer (Taizé)

Readings

1 Kings 18:20, 21 (22-29) 30-39
or 1 Kings 8:22, 23, 41-43
Psalm 96 or Psalm 96:1-9
Galatians 1:1-12
Luke 7:1-10

Thought for the day

Capernaum means 'the village of compassion'. Here Jesus has shown compassion for Peter's mother-in-law, for the man with the troubled spirit in the synagogue and for the ill people who were brought to him.

In Capernaum there was a centurion who asked Jesus for help. A centurion is like a company sergeant major. He would look after a hundred soldiers. He was a man used to authority and to being obeyed. We know he was a man of means for he had built a synagogue for the Jews in Capernaum. He was a Gentile but obviously had a good relationship with the Jews. Not all Roman soldiers or their leaders were disliked. The centurion was a man of compassion for he was concerned for one of his slaves. Under Roman law a slave was not counted of any value. The owner of a slave could discard a useless slave. He could actually kill a slave of his own and would incur no charge. Often a slave who was ill or old was thrown out to die. We are told the centurion valued his slave highly and was concerned that he was ill.

In his compassion for his slave, the centurion sent word to Jesus through some of the Jewish elders, asking him to come and heal his slave. He was used to delegating authority and asked the Jewish elders to intercede on his behalf. Perhaps the centurion did this because he knew that a strict Jew had no dealings with Gentiles and would not enter a Gentile house. Yet he was sure Jesus could heal his slave.

When the centurion saw that Jesus was on his way to his house he sent a message through friends, saying, 'Lord, do not trouble yourself, for I am not worthy to have you come under my roof; therefore I did not presume to come to you.' Here you see the humility of the man in his respect for Jesus and the high regard he had for the power of Jesus. The messengers continued with the words of the centurion, 'But only speak the word, and let my servant be healed. For I also am a man set under authority, with soldiers under me; and I say to one, "Go", and he goes, and to another, "Come", and he comes, and to my slave, "Do this", and he does it.' The centurion had others to intercede for him and he believed that Jesus could heal without having to go to the person: distance was not a barrier. The centurion believed he had only to ask and he would receive. This Roman soldier knew about the power of prayer and of others interceding on behalf of him and his servant.

Such a deep understanding and faith amazed Jesus. Here was a Gentile who put to shame so many who called themselves believers. Jesus said, 'I tell you not even in Israel have I found such faith.' Faith does not belong to a certain group or nation. Faith is revealed in the living relationship that a person has with God. Faith is not restricted to Jews or Christians. It is no use claiming to be part of the Church unless we show a living relationship with our God. The centurion put his faith in Jesus. He believed that Jesus would respond and could heal. He did not have to see Jesus but he believed in him and his power. Without ever meeting Jesus, through his own faith and the intercession of others, the centurion had the joy of seeing his servant healed.

Question time

Do we take seriously the power of intercession and speak to Jesus on behalf of others?

What do you understand by 'faith'? Do you see it as a set of beliefs or as a living personal relationship with our God?

Illustration

Martin's father was a tribune in the Roman army. This meant he was a man of authority and had charge over six centurions and 600 men. When Martin was 10 years old he went to church and declared he wanted to learn the Christian faith. His pagan parents were not well pleased. The church was attractive to this young mind as the church often is to young folk. By the time he was 15 Martin was often engaged in church work. Not long after this the recruitment age for the Roman army was lowered to 16. Martin's father saw this as an opportunity and got the recruitment officer to call. He came unannounced and with manacles to take Martin off to the army. Now he would have to spend the next 25 years as a soldier. This was not a barren time for Martin. Here he would learn of discipline, obedience and orderliness. He would learn of the need to travel lightly without too many possessions, and because they were often on the move celibacy was the ideal. As the son of an officer he was soon given a commission and was allowed a servant. He shocked others by taking it in turns with his servant to clean their boots. He gave his money to the poor and cared for the needy. It was at the city gates of Amiens that Martin cut his cloak in half and gave half to a beggar.

That same night in a dream he heard Christ say to the angels in heaven, 'Look what Martin, who is still a catechumen, has given to me this day,' and showed them the cloak. Only later would Martin be baptised. Here was a Roman soldier who showed a living faith and a vital relationship with Jesus.

Intercessions

Blessed are you, Father, Son and Holy Spirit.
You hear our prayers
and are ever ready to help us.
May we live in awareness of your presence
and your peace
and rejoice in your abiding love
and in your power.
Blessed are you, one God for ever.

We give thanks for all who have sustained us
through their prayers,
who have interceded on our behalf.
We ask you to bless
all who exercise a ministry of intercession.
We pray for religious communities.
We ask you to guide all who are concerned
with the outreach and mission of the Church
and we ask for your blessing
upon the outreach of our church
to the local community.

Silence

Lord of all power,
hear us and help us.

We give thanks for all who are involved
in communication and education.
We pray for schools, colleges and universities,
those who teach
and all who are learning new things.
We ask your blessing upon those involved
with broadcasting and the press.
We pray for freedom of the press
and freedom of speech for all peoples.

Silence

Lord of all power,
hear us and help us.

We give thanks
for those who have given us of their love,

who have spent time and their lives in caring for us.
We ask your blessing upon our homes
and all whom we love.
We pray for homes where there is little love
and poor communication.

Silence

Lord of all power,
hear us and help us.

We give thanks for our lives
and all who have enriched them.
We pray for all who suffer from autism
or have problems communicating.
We remember those who suffer from deafness
or the inability to speak.
We pray for those who are suffering
from Alzheimer's disease
and all who are too frail or ill to look after themselves.

Silence

Lord of all power,
hear us and help us.

We give thanks for the communion of saints
and rejoice that we have a share with them
in your kingdom.
We remember before you our friends and loved ones
who are departed from us.
May they rest in peace and rejoice in glory.

Silence

Merciful Father,
**accept these prayers
for the sake of your Son,
our Saviour Jesus Christ.
Amen.**

Memory verse

Ascribe to the Lord honour and power.
Psalm 96:7

Suggested music

We have a gospel to proclaim
Give thanks with a grateful heart
To God be the glory!

CANDLES

Aim

To show how Jesus cares for the centurion's servant.

Teaching

There was a Roman soldier who lived in Capernaum by the Sea of Galilee. He had a hundred soldiers to look after and he was called a centurion (let us say this together: 'centurion'). The centurion was a very kind and rich man. He paid for a church to be built for the Jews in Capernaum. But something made the centurion sad. He had a servant who was ill. He had asked the doctors to make his servant better but they could not.

He would have spent a lot of money to make him well but his money could not help. He was sad because his servant was so ill and he could not help. Then someone told him that Jesus was in Capernaum. The centurion thought if anyone could help his servant, Jesus could. He sent some of his friends to tell Jesus that his servant was ill and to ask if he would heal him.

What do you think Jesus said? Yes, Jesus is always ready to help those who ask him. Jesus set off for the house of the centurion. All the time since he sent his friends the centurion was watching to see if Jesus would do anything. He knew Jesus could make his servant well without even coming to the house. Jesus just had to say the words and the servant would be healed. When he saw that Jesus was coming along the road with a crowd of people, the centurion sent another group of friends with a message to Jesus. He said, 'Lord, do not trouble yourself to come to my house. I did not feel it was right for me to ask you so I sent some of my friends. My friends asked you for my sake to heal my servant. I am in charge of men and if I say to this one, "Go", he goes; if I say to that one, "Come", he comes. If I say to a servant, "Do this", he does it. I know that you can just say that my servant should be made well and he will be.'

Jesus was amazed how much this centurion understood about his power and how he could heal his servant. He was pleased to heal the servant of the centurion – and, as asked, he did not even go to the house. He made the servant better because he was asked to by the friends of the centurion. Jesus and the centurion never met but Jesus knew the centurion believed in him.

Activity

Play 'Simon says'. Get the children to understand the need to obey orders and only to do what Simon says. You may like to use a helper so that you can hide Simon behind a screen and so show that orders can be issued without the person being seen.

Prayer

Lord Jesus, we cannot see you
but we know that you love us
and are always ready to help us.
Thank you, Lord Jesus.
Amen.

Song

Jesus' hands were kind hands

LAMPS

Aim

To show how Jesus cares for all people.

Teaching

The Jews were not usually friends with the Roman soldiers because the soldiers had taken over their country.

But there were some soldiers they liked because they were kind and generous. In Capernaum, where Simon Peter lived, there was a Roman soldier who was in charge of 100 soldiers. Do you know what you call a Roman soldier in charge of 100 soldiers? A centurion.

This centurion was a rich man and he built a synagogue for the Jews who lived in Capernaum. What is a synagogue? It is a church for Jewish people to pray in. The centurion paid builders to build a new church for the Jews. The centurion was friendly with a lot of the Jewish people, though they did not go to his house because Jews did not usually go into houses that are not Jewish houses. (Do you know what you call people who are not Jews? Gentiles.)

The centurion was rich and powerful but there was something he could not do. He had a servant who was ill and he could not make him better. He had spent a lot of money and had doctors to look at his servant but no one could make him well again.

One day he heard that Jesus was in Capernaum. He knew that Jesus had made other ill people well again and thought perhaps Jesus would make his servant well again. The centurion sent some of his Jewish friends to Jesus to ask if he would heal his servant. Because he was not a Jew the centurion did not come by himself but sent Jewish friends. What do you think Jesus did when they asked him? Jesus went with them and started to go to the house of the centurion. The centurion had been watching and waiting to see if Jesus would do anything. When he saw Jesus and a crowd coming up the street, the centurion was bothered. He felt that he was not worthy for Jesus to come into his house. So he sent another group of friends as messengers to Jesus. They came to Jesus as he was on the way to the house and said, 'The centurion has sent us and has said, "Lord, do not trouble yourself for I am not worthy to have you come under my roof. Only speak the word and my servant shall be healed."' Jesus was amazed that the centurion understood how much power Jesus had and how he could heal without going to the house. He understood so much about Jesus and what he could do.

Then the friend told Jesus more: 'The centurion has said, "Only speak the word and let my servant be healed. I also am a man with authority, with soldiers under me; and I say to one, "Go", and he goes; to another, "Come", and he comes; and to my slave, "Do this", and the slave does it.'

Jesus was amazed by the centurion's trust in him and his power to heal just by a word and even from a distance. There was no way the centurion doubted his power. The centurion was a true man of faith. Jesus sent the friends back to the centurion's house and when they got there they found the servant was well again.

Activity

Let the children act out this story. Have an ill servant at one end of the room and Jesus at another. Get messengers to come from the centurion. As Jesus gets halfway, let the centurion send out his new message. (Let the children discuss why he did this and how he believed in the power of Jesus.) You may like Jesus to raise his hands towards the servant and say a few words as the servant rises from his bed.

Prayer

Jesus, we thank you for your love
towards all people and us.
We pray to you for all who are ill or troubled
at this time.
May they know you are with them
and want to help them always.
Amen.

Song

Jesus' hands were kind hands

TORCHES

Aim

To be aware of the faith of the centurion.

Teaching

To understand today's story we need to know two things that had an effect on the events which took place.

The first is that Jews usually avoid dealings with Gentiles (non-Jews) and especially the Roman army. Often relationships with the Roman army were strained, although many Jews were Roman citizens, as was St Paul. Strict Jews did not enter a non-Jewish house for if they did, it rendered them unclean. For some even contact with a Gentile made them unclean. We must remember that Jesus was a Jew.

The second is that slaves are usually counted as dispensable. You could dispose of an ill, old or useless slave by throwing them out on to the street. The owner of a slave was allowed to kill the slave without fear of prosecution. More than one writer advises if you have an ill slave to get rid of him. There are always plenty of other slaves.

The centurion of today's Gospel is obviously different from many. He has Jewish friends. He built a synagogue in Capernaum for the local Jewish community. He is also deeply concerned about an ill servant. For all his money and power the centurion could not heal his servant. No doubt he had tried local healers and doctors but to no avail.

As a Gentile, he does not approach the Jewish teacher and healer, Jesus. Instead he sends Jewish friends to seek healing for his servant. They come and intercede on behalf of the centurion and the servant. As ever, Jesus is ready to hear requests. We must remember prayers can only be answered if they are prayed. Jesus sets off with the friends of the centurion.

Watching from his villa, the centurion is bothered that Jesus is willing to put himself out so much. He is worried about Jesus entering his house. Now he sends another message with friends. 'Lord, do not trouble yourself, for I am not worthy to have you come under my roof; therefore I did not even presume to come to you.' Jesus is aware of the humility and of the vision of this man of authority. His request is not a command but asked with an awareness of his own unworthiness. Here is faith indeed.

The centurion's message continues, 'But only speak the word, and let my servant be healed. For I also am a man set under authority with soldiers under me; and I say to one, "Go", and he goes, and to another, "Come", and he comes, and to my slave, "Do this", and the slave does it.' The centurion was aware of the command and the power of Jesus. He did not need to see him. He only wanted Jesus to respond to his plea. He believed if he asked of Jesus, he would receive. No wonder Jesus was amazed at such faith – even today many Christians are not as strong as this in their faith. Jesus sent the friends back to the centurion and when they arrived they found the slave in good health.

Activity

Spend time talking about intercession and the need to pray for others as well as ourselves. Make an intercession book to be used throughout the week.

Prayer

Lord, you know our needs
and you are ready to answer our prayers.
We ask your blessing
upon all who are ill or in distress at this time.
May they know your presence and your peace
and rejoice in your saving power.
Amen.

Song

Go, tell it on the mountain

Proper 5

Sunday between 5 and 11 June inclusive
(if after Trinity Sunday)

Aim

To show Jesus is the Lord of life.

Preparation

Have posters showing how Sight Savers restore sight to many people, enabling them to live a fuller life (Sight Savers International, Grosvenor Hall, Bolnore Road, Haywards Heath, West Sussex RH16 4BX). You may like to add two texts: John 3:16 and John 10:10.

Opening activity

Ask everyone to close their eyes and shut out the light. They are to keep them closed for about a minute. Then, as they are touched by a neighbour, they should open their eyes and give thanks quietly for light and life. (You can get a child to go down each row and touch the person at the end of the row. Once they open their eyes they can pass the touch on to the rest of their row. Or you can get the front row to pass the touch to the row behind them until all rows have received their sight again.)

Opening prayer

Blessed are you, Lord our God.
You are the giver of light and life;
in you is our salvation.
We come to you for wholeness and well-being,
for renewal and for strength.
In you, O Lord, is our trust:
through Jesus Christ our Lord.
Amen.

Opening song

My Father, for another night

Readings

1 Kings 17:8-16 (17-24) or 1 Kings 17:17-24
Psalm 146 or Psalm 30
Galatians 1:11-24
Luke 7:11-17

Thought for the day

Jesus has left Capernaum and gone to Nain. This is a day's journey of about 25 miles. Nain is not far from Nazareth and not far from Shunem where Elisha brought a child back from the dead (2 Kings 4:18-37). As Jesus, the Lord of life, and those with him approached the gate of the town, they met a procession coming the other way. Leading the procession out was a group of professional mourners, playing instruments and weeping and wailing. A man who had died was being carried out on a bier. The bier was like a wicker basket and open so that the body was visible. The dead man had been the only son of a widowed woman. In this sentence we hear of a double if not a treble tragedy that is still common in many countries. The woman had lost her husband. That was hard enough but now she had lost her only son. What pain there is when a parent loses a child. To make matters worse, because the economy was based on men, the woman was likely to face isolation and poverty. She would become one of the marginalised people of the world, and so would her daughters if she had any.

Once again we see the compassion of Christ. When the Lord saw her he had compassion for her. The word St Luke uses to describe compassion means 'being moved to the depths of his heart'. This is not a God without feeling or a Christ beyond our pain. He feels our sorrows. 'In every pang that rends the heart, the man of sorrows has a part.'

Jesus said to the woman, 'Do not weep.' Then he approached the bier and touched it. For a Jew to touch a dead body made him unclean. The bearers stood still. Jesus had halted the procession towards death. The Lord of Life stood in the way of the grave. Now he spoke to the man and said, 'Young man. I say to you, rise!' The dead man sat up and began to speak. Jesus gave him to his mother. Death had taken the young man but the Lord of Life gave him back to his mother. Here is the mission of Jesus: he came that we should not perish (John 3:16); he came that we should have life and life in all its fullness (John 10:10). He is the Good Shepherd who rescues us from death. St John says of Jesus, 'In him was life, and the life was the light of all people' (John 1:4). By his death he destroyed death, and by his rising to life again he opens to us the way to life eternal (Hebrews 2:15).

Question time

Do we accept that in Jesus death is defeated and that he is the Lord of Life?

Does our church express its concern for the marginalised people of our land and the world?

Illustration

Pasha lived in India and his world was slowly getting darker and darker. This was hard enough to bear because his oncoming blindness meant he was losing the ability to enjoy the light of day. Even worse than this, however, was the fact that he would soon be without work due to his loss of sight. Not only Pasha but all his family would suffer. They would join the many poor and marginalised people of India. Then one day it was announced that an 'Eye Camp' was coming to his village. This was run by Sight Savers and was producing wonderful results all over India. Pasha was accepted for what was a relatively simple operation. Afterwards his eyes were bandaged for a few days and, in a sense, he felt worse off. Then came the wonderful moment when the bandages were taken off and he could see. Not only had his sight been saved but also his family had been rescued from poverty. The healing was one for the whole family and they were able to live a fuller life once more.

Intercessions

Blessed are you, Father, Son and Holy Spirit.
You have created light and life
and you offer to us your light and your life.
In you we triumph over death
and are given the gift of eternal life.
Blessed are you, one God for ever and ever.

We give thanks to you, O Father,
that in Jesus is the resurrection and the life,
and that through him we have the victory over death.
We give thanks for the Good News of the Gospel
and pray for all who seek to proclaim
your love and salvation.
We ask your blessing on all who preach the word
and who administer the sacraments.
We pray especially for those
who are working with the under-privileged
and marginalised of the world.

Silence

Strong and saving God,
hear us and help us.

We give thanks for our lives
and we remember before you
all who suffer from poverty, from war
or from prejudice.
We ask your blessing upon all homeless people
and all who are out of work.
We pray for those who are unable to cope
with their circumstances
and whose lives are spiralling out of control.

Silence

Strong and saving God,
hear us and help us.

We remember before you
our homes and our loved ones.
We ask your blessing upon our families and friends.
We pray especially for homes
where there is illness or poverty
and any home where there has been a recent death.

Silence

Strong and saving God,
hear us and help us.

We rejoice in the gift of life
and ask that you will protect us and help us
at all times.
We pray for all who are suffering
from a debilitating illness.
We remember those who are suffering from blindness
and all who through illness can no longer work.
We pray for loved ones
who are separated through illness
and for all who are in a hospice at this time.

Silence

Strong and saving God,
hear us and help us.

We ask your blessing
upon our loved ones who have departed this life,
that they may live with you
and know your peace.
We rejoice in the gift of eternal life
and in the fellowship of all your saints.
May we share with them
in the fullness of your kingdom in glory.

Silence

Merciful Father,
**accept these prayers
for the sake of your Son,
our Saviour Jesus Christ.
Amen.**

Memory verse

O Lord my God, I cried out to you, and you restored me to health. You brought me up, O Lord, from the dead, and you restored my life as I was going down to the grave.
Psalm 30:2, 3

Suggested music

When days are touched with sadness
The King of love my shepherd is
O Lord, all the world belongs to you

CANDLES

Aim

To show how Jesus makes sad people happy and gives a young man life again.

Teaching

Once there was a very sad woman. She was crying and a lot of people with her were crying. She lived in a place called Nain. Now she was leaving Nain and going out of the town by the large gateway in the walls of the town. She was going to bury her son who had died. This is what made her sad. She was very sad because not long ago the boy's father had also died. Now she was without her husband and her son. As she walked out of Nain, musicians were playing sad music on flutes; people were crying out loud. Everyone was unhappy. Her son was being carried out in what looked like a large basket. He was lying there as if he was just asleep but they knew he was dead. This was all very sad indeed.

Coming the other way towards the gate was a crowd of people. It was the disciples of Jesus and some of his friends. Jesus was there with them. Jesus came to where the sad people were and where the young man was being carried out and he stopped them. Some people wondered what he was doing. He looked at all the sad people and he was sorry for them. He went over to the man who was lying so still and said, 'Young man, I say to you, rise.' The dead man opened his eyes, sat up and began to speak. Everyone was amazed. Jesus helped the young man to get up and he gave him to his mother. Now all the tears had gone. The sad music stopped and everyone was very happy. Their sad faces were now happy faces. Jesus had made them glad and had made the young man alive again.

Activity

There is an opportunity to make sad and happy faces on the activity sheet. Once this is done the children could all show the sad faces and walk slowly around with them until they meet Jesus. Then let them show the happy faces and jump up and down with joy.

Prayer

Jesus, we know that you love us
and care for us.
You want us to be happy and to enjoy life.
We thank you, Jesus.
Amen.

Song

Jesus' love is very wonderful

LAMPS

Aim

To show Jesus reaches out to help those in trouble.

Teaching

If you were sad or in trouble, whom would you go to for help? We go to our mother and father, sometimes to a sister or brother and sometimes to a friend. If you have something that you cannot do by yourself, is there someone you would ask to help you?

Our story today is about a very sad woman, and what she wants, it seems, no one can do for her. Not long ago her husband died and that made her very sad. She had a son who was just a young man but he did his best to work for the home and to look after his mother. Then one day the son took ill and it was not long before he died too. The woman was very sad indeed as she prepared to bury her son.

The woman lived in Nain. She was now going towards the cemetery outside the town to bury her son. There was a procession of people. At the front were musicians who were playing very sad music and with them were people who were making sad sounds and crying. Then followed the young man who was carried by some of the men. They carried him in what looked like a large wicker basket. There was no top on the basket and you could see the dead man who was being carried. Next to him was his mother and friends and everybody was very upset. It seemed there was no one to help them. The young man was beyond help. The town of Nain had a wall around it and now the procession had reached the town gate.

Coming in the other direction was another group of people. It was a small crowd and they seemed to be very happy. Here were the disciples and followers of Jesus, and Jesus was with them. The sad group and the happy group met at the gates of Nain. Normally the happy group would stand aside and let the sad group

pass but Jesus went up to the sad group. He went right to the dead man who was being carried and touched the bier – that is the name given to the basket the man was in: it is spelt B I E R. Still touching the bier, Jesus spoke to the man lying in it. He said, 'Young man, I say to you, rise.' Jesus was speaking to a dead man but the young man heard him and came back from the dead. Jesus had brought him back to life again. The young man sat up. Everyone was amazed and probably some were a little frightened. All the sad sounds had stopped. The people carrying the bier put it down on the ground. Jesus helped the young man out of it and then gave him back to his mother. Her sadness had gone: Jesus had made her glad. Even more wonderful, Jesus had given new life to her son. Jesus had made him come alive. No wonder everyone was happy. Jesus is the Lord of Life. All the people gave thanks to God and said, 'A great prophet has risen among us.' They told everyone they met what a wonderful saviour Jesus was.

Activity

Play 'Sad and happy faces'. Get everyone to stand in a circle. Someone has to make a sad face and then they run their hands down their face and it changes to a smile. Then they throw the sad face to someone else in the circle. That person then shows a sad face, takes it away and throws it to someone else. (Get the children to exaggerate happy and sad as much as possible.) Then everyone shows a happy face. The last person with a sad face throws it out of the circle. Talk about how we can make others happy or sad.

Prayer

Lord Jesus, you came
that we should enjoy living
and to give us life that is eternal.
We thank you for your power and presence
with us always.
Amen.

Song

I believe in Jesus

TORCHES

Aim

To show how Jesus breaks through barriers and gives life to a young man who had died.

Teaching

Again we must remember that Jesus was a Jew. If you remember last week's story it was about Jesus helping a Gentile; he would even have visited his house. Strict Jews do not have dealings with Gentiles: to enter a Gentile house would make a strict Jew unclean. Jesus broke through this barrier and helped the Roman centurion.

This week we see Jesus breaking another barrier. It was thought that if you touched a dead body, you were made unclean and so could not enter into the life of the community. There was some wisdom in this. Can you think of reasons for not touching something dead? (Talk about infection and contamination.)

Jesus had travelled from Capernaum to Nain. That is a journey of about 25 miles. With him were his disciples and other people.

Nain is not far from Shunem which was famous for a healing miracle by Elisha. (Get the group to read 2 Kings 4:18-37.) In Nain was a woman who probably wished she had lived at the time of Elisha. Her husband had recently died and now her only son had died. If only there had been some prophet that could have saved him. She had prepared for the young man's funeral. She had hired the professional mourners who played sad music and made loud weeping and wailing sounds. She had arranged for her son to be carried by some friends. They would probably carry him in a wicker basket shaped like a coffin but with no lid. His body would be buried without the wicker basket and it would be used again. As the procession set off you could see the dead man being carried and all the people weeping and wailing – it was a picture of sorrow and sadness. Without her husband or her son, the woman wondered who could help her. The procession reached the gates of the town on their way to the cemetery. They were moving towards the place of the dead.

Jesus and his group were just about to enter into the life of the town through its gates. It is at this point that the Lord of Life is faced with the body of this young man. Normally people would stand aside and let the dead and mourners pass. Jesus goes up to the group and touches the bier (that is the name of the basket the man is carried in). Everyone stops and wonders what he will do. Jesus may be ready to offer sympathy to the group for he obviously showed great compassion. But he does not speak to them. He speaks to the dead man and says, 'Young man, I say to you, rise!' The dead man sat up and began to speak. Then Jesus took him and gave him back to his mother. Everyone was asking themselves, 'Who is this with such power over death?' Fear and awe came upon the people. Jesus reminded them of Elisha and they said as they glorified God, 'A great prophet has risen among us.' Everyone was so excited by this and they went around telling others what Jesus had done. They were beginning to discover that Jesus is 'the resurrection and the life'.

Activity

Look at the song 'Now the green blade riseth'. Get the group to relate this song to the life and death of Jesus and to the power he has to give life and joy. They may like to act out or dance the events portrayed in the song.

Prayer

Lord Jesus, we rejoice in your power.
In you, light conquers the darkness;
joy replaces sadness;
life defeats death.
In you, victory is ours.
Alleluia.

Song

Now the green blade riseth

Proper 6

Sunday between 12 and 18 June inclusive
(if after Trinity Sunday)

Aim

To encourage people to make contact with Jesus.

Preparation

Have a poster that says, 'SIN SEPARATES.' If possible, show two people going in opposite directions. Have another poster of a couple hugging each other with the words, 'LOVE FORGIVES AND UNITES US.' A third poster can have a mobile phone and a note which says, 'URGENT. MAKE CONTACT WITH GOD.'

Opening activity

Remember someone you have lost contact with and pray for them. (*Pause*)

Remember someone you find hard to forgive and pray for them. (*Pause*)

Remember your own sins and ask God to forgive you. (*Pause*)

Opening prayer

God, you welcome us with open arms
and when we turn to you,
you are there ready to forgive us.
Forgive us when we ignore you
and do what we should not do.
Give us today your peace
through Jesus Christ our Lord.
Amen.

Opening song

Dear Lord and Father of mankind

Readings

1 Kings 21:1-10 (11-14) 15-21a
or 2 Samuel 11:26–12:10, 13-15
Psalm 5:1-8 or Psalm 32
Galatians 2:15-21
Luke 7:36–8:3

Thought for the day

Because the story of the woman who anoints the feet of Jesus is given a different emphasis in all four Gospels, it is important to see what Luke is trying to tell us.

We are told it is the house of Simon, a Pharisee. In Mark, Simon is described as a leper. Luke uses the story to criticise the Pharisees, as he was doing in 7:30-35. The scene is likely set in a central courtyard. Maybe there was a fountain. In good weather meals were often eaten outside in the courtyard. It was the custom that when a Rabbi visited a house such as this, people from round about came and listened to him. This explains the presence of the woman – although Simon was not pleased that she was there. Luke calls the woman a sinner to make a point about forgiveness and possibly about contact, for Jesus has just been described as 'a friend of tax collectors and sinners' (7:34).

Simon invites Jesus but when Jesus comes Simon seems to ignore him. When a guest enters a house three things are normally done. The visitor is welcomed with a kiss of peace. In the case of an important visitor or rabbi, this would not be omitted. Because roads were dirty, water was poured over the feet of the visitor to cleanse them and to cool them from the heat. Then it was usual to burn some sweet-smelling incense or to place a few droplets of attar of roses on the visitor's head. Simon did none of these things and obviously did not instruct his servants. Jesus was in his house; Simon could boast of a visit by this interesting rabbi. But Simon did not really make any contact with Jesus. Jesus was there but Simon ignored him.

The woman was just the opposite to Simon. As Jesus reclined at the low table, she came and stood over him. She stood there weeping, and large tears were dropping on to the feet of Jesus. Jesus was aware of this and did not move. The woman loosened her hair and used it like a towel to rub the feet of Jesus. By now the righteous people were scandalised. There was still more to come. The woman had a phial of sweet-smelling scent. She broke open the scent and anointed the feet of Jesus with the perfume. Jesus accepted all of these actions and the contact the woman had made with him. Simon could not hold back any longer. He said to himself, 'If this man were a prophet, he would have known who and what kind of woman is touching him – a sinner.'

Jesus was aware of this and talked to Simon about forgiveness. Obviously this was a subject that Simon found hard, yet he did understand about forgiveness. Simon had kept his distance from Jesus and from this woman. Jesus then asked Simon to look at his actions and the woman's. 'You gave me no water for my feet, but she has bathed my feet with her tears and dried them with her hair. You gave me no kiss, but from the time I came in she has not stopped kissing my feet. You did not anoint my head with oil, but she has anointed my feet with ointment.' Simon was told how he had avoided making contact but the woman had made immediate contact. Simon did not show love or respect towards Jesus but the woman did. Jesus turned towards the woman and said to her 'Your sins are forgiven.' Those at the table began to ask, 'Who is this who even forgives sins?' They were talking *about* Jesus rather than *to* him. There was an answer. He is the Christ, the Saviour, but many would not accept this. The woman made contact – a living relationship with Jesus – and that is what you call faith. Jesus said to her, 'Your faith has saved you. Go in peace.'

Question time

We come to church but do we really seek to make contact with our God?

Do we approach God knowing we need forgiveness, and rejoice that God is willing to give it?

Illustration

Someone was described as 'a self-made man worshipping his own creator'. Think about this for a moment. Often what keeps a person from God is the illusion of self-sufficiency. Some say they have grown up and do not need such a Father figure. Yet none of us will survive without God. The strange thing is the closer someone comes to God, the more aware they are of their own weakness and sin. St Paul spoke of sinners and said, '. . . of whom I am the chief'. St Francis said, 'There is nowhere a more wretched sinner than I.' God can deal with those who are aware of their sins. He can reach out to them in forgiveness. He can reveal his love in accepting the sinner. The self-righteous and the self-sufficient set up their own barriers and are far harder to approach. Those who come to God aware of their sin and weakness are the ones who discover his power in their lives and his love.

Intercessions

Blessed are you, Father, Son and Holy Spirit,
for you welcome us into your presence.
You forgive our sins and give us the power,
through contact with you,
to walk in newness of life.
In your love you accept us and offer us eternal life.
Blessed are you for ever.

We give thanks for all who have come to know
the joy of your forgiveness
through the ministry of your Church.
Help us to know that, though you do not love the sin,
you do love and accept the sinner.
We pray for all who share in healing and forgiveness.
We ask you to bless all who care for others,
all who preach the word,
those who administer the sacraments
and those who counsel any who are in trouble.

Silence

Lord, we come to you:
hear us and help us.

We give thanks for your forgiveness
and we pray for all who are consumed
by guilt and bad memories.
We pray for all who are unable to forgive others
or themselves.
We remember all who are surrounded by self-righteousness
and feelings of self-sufficiency.
We ask your blessing on all who find it hard
to make contact with others,
all who are lonely and all who feel unwanted.

Silence

Lord, we come to you:
hear us and help us.

We give thanks for all who have shown us
love and forgiveness,
for those who loved us
even when we hurt them by our actions.
We pray for all who love us and share our lives.

We remember friends and loved ones
with whom we have lost contact.
We pray for all who suffer from relationships
that are broken by past sins
and cannot find healing.

Silence

Lord, we come to you:
hear us and help us.

We pray for all who are ill or suffering at this time.
We ask your blessing upon all who suffer
through the sin and violence of others.
We pray for all who are caught up
in vice, drugs and addiction.
We ask for your healing upon our society and our lives.

Silence

Lord, we come to you:
hear us and help us.

As we affirm the forgiveness of sins
and the resurrection of the body,
we pray for our friends and loved ones
who are departed from us.
May they know the joy of your forgiveness
and rejoice with your saints in life eternal.

Silence

Merciful Father,
**accept these prayers
for the sake of your Son,
our Saviour Jesus Christ.
Amen.**

Memory verse

Happy are they whose transgressions are forgiven, and whose sin is put away. Happy are they to whom the Lord imputes no guilt.
Psalm 32:1, 2

Suggested music

Just as I am, without one plea
Praise, my soul, the King of heaven
There's a wideness in God's mercy

CANDLES

Aim

To show how those who love us accept us.

Teaching

Once there was a man who invited Jesus to his house. The man was called Simon. Because Jesus was special, the man invited Jesus for a meal. But when Jesus came, Simon did not look after Jesus. Simon did not welcome him into his house. He did not offer Jesus water to wash with and he did not give him any sweet-smelling water to put on his head. Because he did not do these things, he was being rude to Jesus and not really caring.

A woman came to the house where Jesus was and she stood beside Jesus. Jesus was sitting on a carpet on the ground. Soon Jesus felt water dropping on to his feet and when he looked up he saw that it was tears from the woman's face as she was crying. She felt that no one really loved her. When Jesus' feet were really wet, the woman bent down and dried the feet of Jesus with her hair. Simon was not pleased about this. Then the woman took a bottle of scent and rubbed it on the feet of Jesus. Jesus could see the woman was sad because she had done some wrong things and she was troubled with remembering them. Jesus said to her that what she had done wrong was forgiven; she should go home in peace. Because she had come to Jesus and cared for him, she knew he cared for her and forgave the wrong she had done.

Sometimes we do wrong things, naughty things, and it upsets our mother or father or our teacher. But they still care for us and want us to do better. God also cares when we do wrong. What are some of the wrong things we can do? (This could bring out some interesting thoughts from the young children.)

When we do wrong, what should we say to our mothers and fathers and to our friends? We should say we are sorry. We can also say to God that we are sorry when we have done things that we should not do. Because, like our parents, God loves us. God will forgive us and still care for us.

Activity

Play 'Stuck in the mud'. This is a game of tag. If the person is tagged, they have to stay where they are, stuck in the mud with legs apart and arms outstretched and shouting for help. A player who has not been tagged can crawl between the person's legs and set them free again.

If you have only one 'it', it is very easy to be set free. Choose two or three 'its', so that it is easier to catch more people.

Prayer

God, we know that you love us.
We are sorry when we do wrong.
We ask you to forgive us
and keep us in your love.
Amen.

Song

Father God, I know you love me so

LAMPS

Aim

To invite the children to understand the need to say 'sorry'.

Teaching

Some people think that they are always right and never do anything wrong.

Like Little Jack Horner, they sit in a corner and say 'What a good boy am I'!

Yet all of us have done wrong things at some time and upset those who love us by what we have done. Just as we do not always get our sums right or our spellings right, we make mistakes in what we do and sometimes it hurts people. Some people do not seem to care if they hurt others, like Mr Nasty or Mr Greedy. But if we care for those who love us, what do we do when we have done wrong? We say we are sorry and put it right if we can. Though often those who love us are upset by what we do, they still love us. God loves us and when we do wrong we can say sorry to him. He may not like what we have done but he will forgive us if we are sorry.

There is a story about Jesus and a man who thought he was very good and a woman who had done wrong things. The man was called Simon and he invited Jesus to his house. Because Jesus was a teacher, other people would come to the house to hear him. Simon seemed to ignore Jesus when he came to the house. He did not welcome him or give him water to wash with. It was usual to give a guest some sweet-smelling water to put on their head. Simon did not offer any to Jesus.

The woman who came to the house had done some wrong things and Simon did not like her. Jesus was sitting on the ground with other guests when the woman came and stood behind him. Suddenly Jesus felt warm drops of water falling on his feet. He looked up and saw it was the woman's tears. Then she bent down and wiped away the tears with her hair, using it like a towel. After she had done this she took out a bottle of perfume and broke it open and poured it over the feet of Jesus. Again Simon was not pleased. He felt that Jesus should have chased the woman away. But Jesus knew the woman was sorry for the wrong she had done. He said to Simon, 'Do you see this woman? I entered you house; you gave me no water for my feet; she has washed my feet with her tears and dried them with her hair. You did not welcome me with a kiss, but from the time I came in she has not stopped kissing my feet. You did not anoint my head with oil, but she has anointed my feet with ointment. I tell you her sins are forgiven.'

Then Jesus turned to the woman and said, 'Your faith has saved you; go in peace.'

There was Simon and the woman. One made contact with Jesus and the other did not. Which do you think was the happiest one?

Activity

Play 'Simon says'. Let them see how wrong actions put you out. Give everyone another chance when they do wrong and then say, 'Sorry'. If they do not say, 'Sorry', they are out. See if they can understand they put themselves out by their actions and attitudes and that no one else wants them to be out.

Prayer

God, we thank you that you always love us.
When we do wrong you do not like what we do
but you still love us.
Help us to say sorry when we do wrong
and to give our love to you.
Amen.

Song

Friend of sinners, Lord of truth

TORCHES

Aim

To explore the need for and the idea of forgiveness.

Teaching

Stand up, anyone who has never done anything wrong. I did not expect anyone to stand up because all of us have at one time or another done things that upset or hurt others. Doing wrong things is called 'sin' and sin separates us from each other as it breaks down trusting relationships. Can you give examples of sin separating us from each other?

If you are trying not to do wrong again and want to make friends again, what must you do? (Explore ideas of saying 'sorry' and, if possible, putting things right.)

Some people believe they are much better than others, and for that reason God and other people are bound to love them. But self-righteous people are often quite off-putting and frightening. Surely we all need other people's forgiveness and to know that we are loved even when we are not perfect.

To understand today's story we have to know a few things. Simon, who is a Pharisee, has invited Jesus to his house. It is likely they would meet in a central courtyard – that is, in the open. There would be no chairs to sit on. The guests would sit on low sofas or more often on a carpet on the ground. They would lean towards the food that was in the middle. They would rest on their left hand with their feet pointing away from the table.

When someone came to a house certain things were expected out of politeness. The owner of the house would welcome his guest with a kiss of peace. He would then make sure that there was water for the guest to wash his feet after walking on dusty roads. Then, as a sign of respect, sometimes the guest would be anointed with some sweet-smelling rose water on their head. Simon did none of these things and so was quite rude to his guest. He did not make any real contact with Jesus.

Because Jesus was a rabbi, a teacher, the courtyard would become open to anyone who lived near to come and listen to the teaching. When a certain woman came in, Simon was not pleased because she was known as a 'sinner'.

The first contact the woman made with Jesus was that she stood behind him and let her tears fall on his feet. Jesus could have moved his feet and it would have been a sign to the woman that she had to stop. But Jesus accepted her as she was. When the feet of Jesus were quite wet with her tears, the woman bent down and wiped them dry with her hair. This really upset Simon. It got even worse because she then poured a sweet-smelling scent over the feet of Jesus. Everyone could smell it. Simon said, 'If this man were a prophet, he would have known what kind of woman this is who is touching him – she is a sinner.' Simon was stern in his righteousness and unforgiving. Jesus does not like sin – he spent his life battling against sin and evil – but he loves the person even though they have done wrong. Jesus is accepting and forgiving. Simon had kept his distance; the woman, in her need, made contact. It is to the woman that Jesus says, 'Your faith has saved you; go in peace.'

(Spend the rest of the session talking about forgiveness and the love of God.)

Activity

Look at John Donne's poem entitled 'Love' (let two people read it dramatically).

> Love bade me welcome, yet my soul drew back,
> Guilty of dust and sin.
> But quick-eyed Love, observing me grow slack
> From my first entrance in,
> Drew nearer to me, secretly questioning
> If I lacked anything.
>
> 'A guest,' I answered, 'worthy to be here.'
> Love said, 'You shall be he.'
> 'I, the unkind, ungrateful? Ah, my dear,
> I cannot look on Thee.'
> Love took my hand, and smiling did reply,
> 'Who made the eyes but I?'
>
> 'Truth, Lord, but I have marred them: let my shame
> Go where it doth deserve.'
> 'And know you not,' says Love, 'who bore the blame?'
> 'My dear, then I will serve.'
> 'You must sit down,' says Love, and taste My meat.'
> So I did sit and eat.

Prayer

God, we thank your for the forgiveness of sins
and the opportunity to start again.
We are sorry for when we have done wrong
and gone against your love.
Forgive us and help us to do better.
Amen.

Song

Oh! Oh! Oh! How good is the Lord

(Add a verse: 'He gives me forgiveness')

Proper 7

Sunday between 19 and 25 June inclusive
(if after Trinity Sunday)

Aim

To show that Christ is the Prince of Peace.

Preparation

Have a poster that says, 'Christ the Prince of Peace'. You may like to show Jesus standing in the middle of a storm or show a picture of a stormy sea. Have below the poster the words from Psalm 65:7: 'You silence the roaring of the seas, the roaring of their waves, the tumult of the peoples.'

Opening activity

Ask everyone to clench their fists tightly until they almost hurt, to curl their toes tightly and to screw up their faces. Now when I say, 'Peace be with you', relax. Let go of all tension; know that peace is a gift. Allow God's peace to flow into you and around you. Know the choice is yours: you can stay uptight or accept the love and peace that God gives you. The peace of the Lord is always with you; rest in that peace. (Have a short silence.)

Opening prayer

Lord Jesus, you stilled the raging storm
and the madness of the man in the tombs.
Give us your peace.
Let there be peace in our hearts,
in our lives
and in all our dealings.
Amen.

Opening song

Peace, perfect peace, is the gift

Readings

1 Kings 19:1-4 (5-7) 8-15a
or Isaiah 65:1-9
Psalms 42, 43 or Psalm 22:19-28
Galatians 3:23-29
Luke 8:26-39

Thought for the day

The disciples have just been in a storm at sea and think they could have perished. Jesus stills the storm and also their fears and anxieties. Possibly the storm had driven them off course. They landed on the south-eastern edge of the lake. Perhaps they were hoping for a rest, a peaceful time. As Jesus stepped on to the land a madman met him.

The man's mind was in constant turmoil. He thinks he is a whole Legion, an army of demons. People have driven him out of the city and he lives among the tombs. He has been chained up but in his fury he broke the chains – perhaps they are still partly attached to his wrists and he waves them about like a weapon. Because he is not allowed to be with the living, he has made his home with the dead. A madman having lost contact with others now lives alone with his demons. His life is a mini-hell – though for him it *is* hell. He rushed towards Jesus. I am sure that gave the disciples yet another feeling of turmoil. He shouted at the top of his voice, 'What have you to do with me, Jesus, Son of the Most High God? I beg you, do not torment me.' He may have been mad but he recognised Jesus and that Jesus had power.

In contrast to the man, Jesus is quite still – Jesus who stills the storm, who calms the wind, who is the bringer of peace. Can the Lord who brought order out of chaos do anything for this man? We ask with Macbeth: (Act 5 Scene 3):

Canst thou not minister to a mind diseased,
Pluck from the memory a rooted sorrow,
Raze out the written troubles of the brain,
And with some sweet oblivious antidote
Cleanse the stuffed bosom of that perilous stuff
Which weighs upon the heart?'

Jesus can and he will. He asks the man his name.

The man replies, 'Legion.' Perhaps he feels he has a legion of demons in him, or maybe in his early days he suffered a trauma brought on by the atrocities of a Roman legion. The man pleaded for his 'army' and asked that they were not sent to the abyss. Jesus agreed to this and told the man the demons had entered a herd of pigs which were hurtling towards the sea. Perhaps the loud crying of Legion had frightened the pigs. The man was healed, he was clothed and in his right mind when people came out to see Jesus. The man wanted to follow Jesus but Jesus said to him, 'Return to your home, and declare how much God has done for you.' For many of us the telling of the wonderful story of Jesus should begin in our homes and among our friends.

Question time

Do recognise Jesus as the Prince of Peace and the giver of peace?

Do we see that our share in mission begins with our home and our friends?

Illustration

We cannot create peace but we can accept it. Peace is a gift from God to us. We can accept it by living in a peaceful way. The mind can often be in turmoil like a raging sea and yet God is there and offering us his peace. Peace is not an absence of activity but rather a working in harmony with the world around us. Peace comes through a right relationship between others and us, but, above all, between God and us. Peace is God's gift and will help us to get back in tune with everything, but if we persist in staying out of tune with others or the world it is hard for God's peace to get to work in us.

Intercessions

Blessed are you, Lord our God,
for you created order out of chaos
and the world out of your love.

You offer peace and well-being to all of your creation.
Blessed are you, Father, Son and Holy Spirit.

We give thanks to you, O Lord,
for all who help to bring healing and peace to your world.
May the Church be seen as an instrument
of your peace and of your love for all peoples.
May all who are distressed and disturbed
come to know the peace of Christ and his love.
We ask your blessing upon all meditation groups
and all who help others to live in harmony.

Silence

Christ, our Lord,
grant us your peace.

We pray for peace in the world:
peace between nations,
peace within all communities,
peace in our hearts and in our lives.
Lord, show us the peace we should accept,
the peace we should give,
the peace we need to work for
and the peace we should forego.

Silence

Christ, our Lord,
grant us your peace.

We ask your blessing upon our homes,
that they may be full of your love
and that we may live in harmony with each other.
We pray for families suffering
from broken relationships or violence,
and for those who just cannot cope with life.

Silence

Christ, our Lord,
grant us your peace.

We remember all who are suffering from mental stress,
all who are experiencing a breakdown
of their lives or their personalities.
We pray for those taken into care
and those who are a danger to themselves or others.
We ask your blessing upon those
who are suffering from mental anguish or trauma.
We pray for all who are seeking to restore
health and peace to individuals or communities.

Silence

Christ, our Lord,
grant us your peace.

We rejoice in the peace that passes all understanding
and pray that our loved ones departed
may know the peace and joy of eternal life.

Silence

Merciful Father,
**accept these prayers
for the sake of your Son,
our Saviour Jesus Christ.
Amen**

Memory verse

You silence the roaring of the seas, the roaring of their waves, the tumult of the peoples.
Psalm 65:7

Suggested music

What a friend we have in Jesus
This is my story, this is my song
Peace, perfect peace, in this dark world of sin

CANDLES

Aim

To show that Jesus brings peace.

Teaching

The disciples had been with Jesus on the Sea of Galilee in a storm. Can anyone tell me what happened? Jesus was asleep during the storm but the disciples woke him up because they thought the boat might sink and they might die. Jesus spoke to the wind and the sea, and the storm stopped and then there was peace. (Spend the activity time now, acting this out.)

After the storm, the disciples had been brought to the other side of the lake. It was a place they did not know. They did not like it because they saw it was a grave-yard. But they pulled the boat up and came ashore. As soon as they landed, there was a howling, roaring sound, and they saw a man with chains on his hands, waving his arms and shouting. The disciples were afraid. The man shouted especially at Jesus but Jesus was not afraid. Jesus went towards the man and asked him his name. The man said his name was 'Legion' because his mind suffered from so many troubles. Jesus, who stilled the storm and stopped the wind and waves raging, wanted this man to know peace in his mind and life. Jesus made him well again and healed his troubled mind. After this the man was calm, just like the wind and the sea were calm when Jesus spoke to them. The man wanted to follow Jesus but Jesus told him to go home and to tell other people the wonderful thing that Jesus had done for him.

Activity

Get most of the children to sit on the floor. Tell them they are in a boat in a storm. Let others be the wind and the waves, rising up and down and making roaring sounds like the wind. Let the storm be loud and frightening. Now let them waken the one chosen as Jesus. He stands up and says, 'Peace, be still.' Only then does the storm stop.

Prayer

Lord Jesus,
when we are afraid or in trouble
help us to know you are with us
and that you love us always.
Amen.

Song

Jesus' hands were kind hands

LAMPS

Aim

To show Jesus brings peace to troubled and shattered lives.

Teaching

After the stilling of the storm (you may like to revise this by asking some of the group to tell the story), the boat the disciples and Jesus were in was off course. So that they could have a rest after feeling so anxious and troubled, they made for the nearest bit of land. As soon as they landed the disciples wished they had not. They landed in a graveyard among tombs and they could hear a strange groaning and moaning. The disciples felt there might be demons there and were a little scared. Then suddenly out from the tombs came a man yelling and shouting. He was a very wild-looking man. On his wrists were chains that were once meant to keep him fastened. He was so strong that he had broken the chains. He came towards Jesus, waving his arms and shouting. Jesus did not run away and the man fell at the feet of Jesus and shouted, 'What have you to do with me, Jesus, Son of the Most High God? I beg you, do not torment me.'

Jesus had already commanded the evil to come out of the man. Now he asked the man his name. He said, 'Legion', because he believed many demons had entered him. Jesus wanted to heal the man but he felt the man needed to know that the evil had left him. Jesus looked up and saw a herd of swine on the hillside. He said to the man that he was free from his trouble because it had left him and entered into the swine. At that moment the herd of swine ran down the slope and into the sea. The man was now sure he was healed. When people from the town came and saw the man, they were amazed that he was well and not troubled. Jesus had brought peace to the man. Legion would have liked to follow Jesus but Jesus said to him, 'Go home and tell them how much God has done for you.'

Activity

Have an outline of a human body photocopied about five or six times. Then cut the shape up into random pieces, about eight pieces a body. Try not to make them too alike in the cutting. Tell the group the pieces are like a person who feels he is shattered or broken. See if they can gather up the fragments and arrange themselves in groups with a whole body.

Prayer

Lord Jesus, you are the Prince of Peace.
You stilled the waves, the storm
and the troubled mind of the madman.

Let us live in your peace
and know your power in our lives.
Amen.

Song

Give me oil in my lamp

TORCHES

Aim

To show how Jesus cares for the shattered.

Teaching

There was once a woman who had a beautiful jewel. Sadly one day she dropped it and it got a great crack right through it. It was not totally shattered but it looked spoiled. A friend who was a very good artist asked if he could have the jewel for a while. He took it home and very gently dealt with the crack. He did not make it go away but he carved a beautiful flower on to the jewel and the crack was now part of the beautiful design. The lady said she thought the jewel was now better than it had ever been.

In the Gospels, we see Jesus taking shattered and broken people and mending their lives. We see Jesus restoring people so that they can fully join in life again. Jesus helped them to renew their contact with others. (Look at Luke 7, the healing of the centurion's servant, the restoring to life of the young man at Nain, and the forgiving of the woman who was a sinner. For all these their breakdown became a breakthrough into newness of life.)

Not long after these healings, Jesus is with the disciples on the Sea of Galilee and they are caught in a storm. Jesus stills the waves and the wind, and brings peace in the storm and peace to the troubled minds of the disciples. Now the boat has been blown well off course, so they make for the nearest land. As soon as they step out of the boat they feel like getting back in. They are in a graveyard full of tombs. The disciples believed demons would be here among the graves. So it was hardly a surprise when they heard a howling and saw a man with chains on his wrists rushing towards them. No doubt the disciples were ready to panic. Jesus stood his ground. Could he who brought peace to the raging elements not heal a single madman? Jesus commanded the evil to come out of the man. Strangely, the man knew Jesus and recognised his power. He threw himself at the feet of Jesus and said, 'What have you to do with me, Jesus, Son of the Most High God? I beg you, do not torment me.'

Jesus tried to calm the man and asked him his name. The man replied, 'Legion', because he believed that so many demons had entered him. (A legion is 6000 Roman soldiers.) Jesus could see that he needed to convince the man that he had the power to bring him peace. He told the man that the demons had left and, at his request, had entered into a herd of swine that were feeding nearby. As he said this, the herd of swine ran off into the sea and were drowned. The man knew he was healed and was at peace. He was no longer shattered. He wanted to go with Jesus. Jesus told him to go home and tell people what God has done for him. He did this and told everyone what Jesus had done for him. Once again this is a recognition that Jesus is God.

Activity

Have a meditation of peace. Let the leader use these words and have silences between sentences. You could play a peaceful piece of music at the same time.

> Know that Jesus offers us his peace. He offers his peace to shattered and troubled peoples. Jesus says, 'My peace I give to you, my peace I leave with you, not as the world gives, I give to you.'

> Relax in the presence of Jesus.

> Let all tension go from your body, check each part to make sure you are relaxed. Rest in the deep, deep peace of Christ.

Let your mind think upon a peaceful scene and know that Christ offers you his peace.

Let the peace of Christ be about you, within you and over you. Know it is a gift. Accept it.

The peace of God keep your heart and mind in Christ Jesus our Lord.

Prayer

Lord Jesus, let your peace fill my heart,
my actions and my days.
Let your peace be known in my life,
in my work and in all my dealings.
Help me to be an instrument of your peace
and to share your peace with others.
Amen.

Song

Peace is flowing like a river

Proper 8

Sunday between 26 June and 2 July inclusive

Aim

To show that Jesus calls us to follow him and asks for our commitment.

Preparation

Have posters about vocation. Include posters about mission, ministry and religious communities.

Opening activity

Have someone interviewed about God calling them, and ask them to say what they think God requires of them. You may be able to get an ordinand or a member of a religious community to speak, although anyone who has a sense of vocation would be good.

Opening prayer

Lord, you have called us to follow you.
Make us worthy of our calling.
Help us to be faithful and true
and always ready to serve you in others.
Amen.

Opening song

Jesus calls us: o'er the tumult

Readings

2 Kings 2:1, 2, 6-14
or 1 Kings 19:15, 16, 19-21
Psalm 77:1, 2, 11-20 or Psalm 16
Galatians 5:1, 13-25
Luke 9:51-62

Thought for the day

Elisha's calling is described in both of today's readings from Kings. His vocation is progressive in that he is called first to be a servant and disciple and later to be Elijah's successor. This is the normal pattern of many vocations where there is a time of apprenticeship, training and learning before we enter into the fullness of our calling. In the Kings stories the cloak is important, as it is a sign of authority and power. When Elisha takes up the cloak, he is taking on the work that God gave to Elijah.

In Luke we have the words of Jesus to would-be followers. We hear of three who come to say they will follow him. Jesus does not say it is easy but warns there will be difficulties.

To the first man Jesus is simply saying, 'Count the cost. To follow me is a way of hardship and denial.' Jesus did not want people to come under false pretences: He would offer no easy way, nor freedom from persecution. Jesus respected the person by telling him of the high demands. We need to know that being a member of the Church is demanding, and to follow God's call is not easy. But it will be a great adventure.

Jesus' words to the second man seems really harsh. It is likely the man was a little like St Augustine of Hippo when he said, 'Lord, make me a saint, but not yet!' He was putting off following. In all probability the man's father was not dead, and not thinking of dying. The man was saying, 'Wait until I have no ties' – well, that will never happen.

Jesus is saying there is a crucial moment for us all and if that moment is missed, we may not get another opportunity. The man had stirrings in his heart but could not escape the grip of his surroundings. We must act when the heart is moved: if we put off until tomorrow, it is not likely to happen.

The last comments of Jesus seem hard. The man only wanted to say farewell to those at home. Jesus knew that there are many things that can tie us and hold us back. Many a vocation has been hindered by members of one's own family or by looking back over what has been. Looking backwards to the 'Good Old Days' is often a danger of the Church. Vocation is a call for us to act now. In the words of God to the people through Moses, 'Tell the people to go forward.' Jesus calls us to move forward in faith with him.

Question time

Are we aware that God calls us to work with him and for him: that we all have a share in the mission of Christ?

Are we prepared to sacrifice some things in order that we fulfil our vocation?

Illustration

Dietrich Bonhoeffer was a German Lutheran priest who was executed by the Nazis for his resistance to their evils. He says this concerning the cost of discipleship:

Cheap grace is the deadly enemy of the Church . . . cheap grace is the preaching of forgiveness without requiring repentance, baptism without church discipline, communion without confession, absolution without contrition. Cheap grace is grace without discipleship, grace without the cross, grace without Jesus Christ, living and incarnate.

Intercessions

Blessed are you, Father, Son and Holy Spirit.
You have called us into life.
You call each of us
to reveal your presence and your love.
Make us worthy of our calling
and help us to do what you would have us do.
To you be glory and blessing for ever and ever.

Lord God, may we heed your voice
and obey your commands,
that we may witness to you and your saving power.
We pray that all within your Church
may be enabled to fulfil their vocation.

We remember all who are seeking to serve you
through their baptism, confirmation or ordination.
We pray that your Church may grow
in outreach and in number.
We ask your blessing upon all who are called
to be prophets or priests at this time.

Silence

Lord, you have created us:
make us worthy of our calling.

We give thanks for all who seek to serve others.
We pray for our Queen
and for all who are in government.
We ask your blessing
upon the work of the United Nations
and all who are striving to bring peace to our world.
We remember those who are working with refugees
and the poor of the world.

Silence

Lord, you have created us:
make us worthy of our calling.

We give thanks for those who have helped us
to develop our talents and abilities.
We pray for our homes
and for those who have taught us.
Bless all schools, colleges and universities.
May our homes reflect your grace and goodness,
your love and your acceptance of the needy.

Silence

Lord, you have created us:
make us worthy of our calling.

We give thanks for our freedom
and we pray for all who feel frustrated
and who feel their vocation has been thwarted
through illness, poverty or oppression.
May they know that God always has a calling for us –
even when our first calling is not possible.
We pray for all who are suffering at this time
and ask your blessing upon all who are called
to care for the ill and the lonely.

Silence

Lord, you have created us:
make us worthy of our calling.

We give thanks that you call us to eternal life
and to the joy of your presence in your kingdom.
We rejoice in the fellowship of your saints
and pray for our loved ones departed.
May we all enjoy serving you now and for ever.

Silence

Merciful Father,
**accept these prayers
for the sake of your Son,
our Saviour Jesus Christ.
Amen.**

Memory verse

Whom shall I send, and who will go for us? And I said,
'Here I am, send me!'
Isaiah 6:8

Suggested music

Will you come and follow me
Thou didst leave thy throne
O Jesus, I have promised

CANDLES

Aim

To show how Elisha followed Elijah to do the work of
God.

Teaching

Prepare a drawing of Elijah and stick it on a plate that
you can spin. Have a piece of cloth that represents his
robe. Start the lesson with 'Spin the plate'(see Activity).

Elijah worked for God and told people about God
and what God wanted them to do. (Let us say his name
together: 'Elijah'.) As Elijah got older, God told him that
soon he would go to God in heaven. So Elijah prepared
someone to learn from him and to do God's work. That
person was called Elisha. This is the same sort of name,
so let us say, 'Elisha'. Whom did Elisha work for? Elijah.
Whom did Elijah teach? Elisha.

Elijah knew he was ready to go to heaven when he
was on the road with Elisha. They came near to a place
called Gilgal and Elijah said, 'Stay here; for the Lord has
sent me further on. He wants me to go to Bethel.' But
Elisha did not want to stay behind and said, 'As the
Lord lives, and as you yourself live, I will not leave
you.' So he went on to Bethel with Elijah. When they
got there Elijah said, 'Stay here, for the Lord wants me
to go on to the river Jordan.' But Elisha did not want to
stay behind and said, 'As the Lord lives, and as you
yourself live, I will not leave you.' So the two of them
went to the river Jordan. Fifty other men of God followed
them and watched when they came to the Jordan. The
river was deep and wide. Elijah took off his cloak and
rolled it up and hit the water with it. The water parted,
and Elijah and Elisha went across the river on something like a pathway that had appeared. They walked
across on dry ground.

When they had crossed over the river Jordan, Elijah
said, 'Tell me what I can do for you, Elisha, before I am
taken away from you.' Elisha said, 'Let me receive double
of your spirit, of your power.'

'That is a very hard thing you have asked,' said Elijah.
'But if you see me going away from you, it will be given
you. If you do not see me go, it will not be given you.'

As they walked in the desert there was a whirlwind
spinning and turning and a chariot of fire and horses of
fire. Elisha saw Elijah go away in the whirlwind. He
could not see Elijah any more; he had gone. (Spin the
plate with Elijah on it and make it fall face down. Now
produce the cloak.) Elijah had gone but his cloak was
still there. Elisha picked up the cloak and went to the
river Jordan. He rolled up the cloak and hit the river
with it and the waters parted. Then Elisha knew he had
been given power from God, the power he had asked
for. Now he would do the work that God had asked Elijah
to do.

Activity

Play 'Spin the plate'. Some of the younger ones might not manage to spin it, so give them some help but let them call the name of another member of the group. Tell them how they should watch and catch the plate when it is still spinning for if it stops spinning they are out.

Prayer

God, we thank you for this day,
for our homes
and for all the people who love us
and care for us.
Amen.

Song

We are marching in the light of God

LAMPS

Aim

To get the children to understand they have to make efforts to follow Jesus.

Teaching

Is there anyone here who plays a musical instrument? How often do you have to practise? Lots of musicians practise every day and sometimes for hours before a concert. For most people, to be good at anything only comes with practice. This means we must not let other events and pleasures take away our practice time.

To be a good reader or to be good at sums only comes with practice. If we do not learn now, it is harder later. If we want to be a good footballer, or cricketer or dancer, we will need to play and to practise often. Some runners or jumpers practise every day so that they might win a medal in a race that is over a year away. Such practice calls for dedication, for us to make great efforts.

If we want to be Christians, it is much the same. We need to spend time each day praying and we need to learn more about God. We need to come to church when others are lying in bed or going out to do what they feel like doing. We have to give ourselves to God each day and not just when we feel like it.

When someone wanted to follow Jesus, Jesus warned him of how hard it could be. Listen to Luke 9:37, 38. (Let someone read this.) To follow Jesus meant giving up comfort and security and taking risks. Jesus did not promise it would be easy.

Jesus invited another person to follow him. (Get someone to read Luke 9:39b-40.) This man was saying, 'Not yet', and was putting off following Jesus for the moment. He was not ready to give himself to the work of God.

Then there was another person. (Have someone read Luke 9:61.) It seemed right to go and say goodbye, but Jesus saw the man was putting off, like many of us do. He was saying, 'I would come but I have other things to do first.' Have we decided to put God first and to make sure we give our time and our love to him?

Activity

Explore how we spend time practising and learning – including school time. How do we improve our skills? How do we progress? What do we love doing and are we able to develop it?

Lazy people and those who do not give their time and attention usually make little progress.

Show how God wants us to give our love and our attention to him each day. See if the children can suggest a way to do this. Encourage them to promise to give time each day to God.

Prayer

Dear Lord, for these three things I pray:
may I know you more clearly,
love you more dearly,
and follow you more nearly,
day by day.

Richard of Chichester (1197 –1253) – adapted

Song

I, the Lord of sea and sky

TORCHES

Aim

To look at vocation and commitment.

Teaching

Cuthbert was a young man of 16. He was protecting sheep from wolves and rustlers. This meant he had to stay out on the hills at night. These were the border hills just into what is now Scotland. The night was 31 August 651. While the shepherds slept, Cuthbert kept watch. He had to keep his senses alert. Suddenly in the night sky he saw movement and he said he saw angels coming down from heaven and taking a holy soul to God. He woke the shepherds for them to see but the moment had gone. In their sleep they had missed the vision in the night. The next day Cuthbert and the shepherds heard that St Aidan of the island of Lindisfarne had died. Cuthbert was already a Christian and now decided that the vision was God's call to him. Maybe one day he would succeed Aidan. Cuthbert left the shepherds and the flock and made his way to the monastery of Melrose. There he offered to dedicate himself to God in the religious life. Not only did he do this but in time he became a great religious leader and also went to work on Lindisfarne.

Different people are called to do different things. Not everyone is called to the religious life. Some are called to be teachers and some doctors, some are called to be mothers and some are called to be manual labourers. One thing is sure: we are all called to worship and to give glory to God. The problem is God calls and the individual often stalls: they put off. Sometimes we get another chance but at other times if we miss the chance, we miss it for ever. When Jesus called the fishermen to follow him, we are told that they left their nets, their boats, their catch of fish: they left everything and followed him. Shakespeare expresses the need to grasp the opportunity when it comes in *Julius Caesar* (Act 4 Scene 3):

> There is a tide in the affairs of men,
> Which, taken at the flood, leads on to fortune;
> Omitted, all the voyage of their life
> Is bound in shallows, and in miseries.

Fortunately we are often given a second and even a third chance. Yet it is sad that many young Christians do not dedicate their lives to daily prayer and learning of God. God calls us to have a relationship with him and to tell of his glory. Do we see this as part of our vocation? Today's Gospel shows this does not promise to be easy, but if we are to follow Christ, we must be willing to meet the challenge.

Activity

Spend time discussing how God calls each of us into a relationship with him. How can we improve and develop our faith? Look at the activity sheet and see various people who put off following Jesus.

Prayer

Lord, open our eyes to your presence,
open our hearts to your love,
open our lives to your service,
that we may serve you with joy
and know you are with us always.
Amen.

Song

We have a Gospel to proclaim

Proper 9

Sunday between 3 and 9 July inclusive

Aim

To explore the mission of the seventy.

Preparation

Have two notices in the entrance to the Church. Let the first say, 'We need FAT Christians', and the second, 'Are you part of the TEAM?' Appropriate drawings could be added to each notice.

Opening activity

Have three young people with the letters F, A and T. All should say together, 'We need FAT Christians.' Then each holds up a letter and speaks in turn.

F is for Faithful.
We need faithful Christians.

A is for Available.
We need available Christians.

T is for Teachable.
We need teachable Christians.

Let four more people come out and ask, 'Are you part of the TEAM?' They each show a letter and say in turn:

To
Each
A
Ministry

Then all say together; 'We all share in the mission of Christ.'

Opening prayer

O Lord, as you have called us
to work with you and for you,
make us worthy of our calling
and keep us faithful to you.
Amen.

Opening song

O Lord my God, when I in awesome wonder

Readings

2 Kings 5:1-14 or Isaiah 66:10-14
Psalm 30 or Psalm 66:1-9
Galatians 6:(1-6) 7-16
Luke 10:1-11, 16-20

Thought for the day

The mission of Jesus needs to grow to be successful. The whole Church is in the growth business. Jesus does not work alone: he chooses twelve disciples. Then, as his mission grows, he appoints another seventy to be sent out in twos and prepare for his coming to other places that he intends to visit.

Seventy was a symbolic number. When Moses found he could not cope alone and needed helpers, seventy members were chosen for the twelve tribes of Israel (Numbers 11:16-25). Seventy was also thought to be the number of nations in the world. As St Luke was thinking of the outreach of Christ, it could be he was thinking of the day when every nation and person would be given the chance to know and love the Lord and be ready for his coming to each of us.

Jesus is aware that there are many souls to save: 'the harvest is plentiful'. Sadly the harvest could be lost because the 'labourers are few'. We still need to pray that the Lord will send more labourers who will be willing to say, 'Here am I Lord. Send me.'

Let us look at the instructions Jesus gave to the seventy and see how they still apply to us. His first word to them is 'Go'. So much of mission fails because we do not get going. We never start, never move from out of our security and comfort zones. We need be aware that there are dangers and we will often be like lambs among wolves.

Jesus asks us to travel light. Often we do not get started because our lives are so full of clutter that prevents us. Too often we become possessed by our possessions.

Do not be side-tracked. It is easy for small talk and trivialities to stop you. (See Elisha's instruction to Gehazi in 2 Kings 4:29. This is not a call to be aloof or discourteous but rather to remember our priorities.)

Ask God's peace on what you are doing and offer that peace to others. If they do not accept the peace of God, you have not lost it.

You do this not for what you can get out of it in the way of praise, money or food, but for the sake of the mission of Christ.

Know that you are to bring the wholeness and healing of God. You are to bring his peace and well-being to the sick in body, mind and spirit.

Let people know that the kingdom of God is very close to them. Their God is not a God who is far away but who is close to each of them and loves them.

This is the outreach of Christ through the Church, and you are called to share in it once you know the Christ and his love.

Question time

Are you part of the team and sharing in the outreach and ministry of the Church?

How do you help the mission of Christ to grow?

Illustration

Picture coming home on a dark night. All the lights are out in the whole area. There must have been a power cut. Everyone is in the dark. The only glimmer of light comes from the church. You are a bit nervous and you go in. There is someone sitting in the sanctuary and he is surrounded by light. You sneak forward and see that he has nail marks in his hands and feet. You know it is the Christ but his feet are fastened by chains and his hands are tied. The Christ is unable to move. You come close and ask, 'Lord, your feet are fastened and your hands tied – why?' The Christ replies, 'My feet are fastened and my hands tied because my people do not pray regularly. They do not reach out to others in love. They do not share in my saving works. I have entrusted my work to them and they have not accepted the light I have offered them. Things will only change when you share with me: when you see Christ in others and be Christ to others.' Suddenly you are aware of this truth, and lights start coming on all over the place.

Intercessions

Blessed are you, Lord our God,
for you reach out to each of us
in love and in peace.
You offer us your healing and power
and you call us to share in telling this Good News
to all people.
Blessed are you, Father, Son and Holy Spirit.

We give thanks to you, O Lord,
for the good news of the gospel.
We ask your blessing upon all who seek
to share in the mission and outreach of Christ.
May the Church grow in holiness, in outreach
and in number.
We pray for missionary societies
and for all who are seeking to spread the good news.
Grant that we may share in this mission.

Silence

Lord of the harvest,
may your kingdom come in us.

We pray for those who harvest the crops of the world.
May no one suffer
from the greed and selfishness of others.
We pray that the hungry may be fed
and all refugees and homeless people cared for.
We ask you to guide those who are in charge
of multinational companies,
that their labourers may get fair wages and justice.

Silence

Lord of the harvest,
may your kingdom come in us.

We give thanks for those who have taught us the faith
and shared their love of God.
We ask your blessing
upon our homes and our friends.
We pray for those of our friends
who do not know you
and have not heard the Gospel.

Silence

Lord of the harvest,
may your kingdom come in us.

We ask you blessing upon the hungry of the world,
those who are without food
and those hungry for the word of God.
We pray for all who are ill
and for those who have lost their employment
through illness.
We remember all who are lonely
and all who are in need in any way.

Silence

Lord of the harvest,
may your kingdom come in us.

We give thanks that you offer us eternal life
in Christ Jesus.
We rejoice in the fellowship of all your saints.
Bless our loved ones and friends
who have departed from us.
May they enjoy the fullness and peace
of your kingdom.

Silence

Merciful Father,
**accept these prayers
for the sake of your Son,
our Saviour Jesus Christ.
Amen.**

Memory verse

Bless our God, O peoples,
let the sound of his praise be heard,
who has kept us among the living,
and has not let our feet slip.
Psalm 66:8, 9

Suggested music

We have a gospel to proclaim
Tell out, my soul
Forth in thy name, O Lord, I go

CANDLES

Aim

To show how God heals Naaman through Elisha.

Teaching

Have you ever been away from your mummy and daddy? I'm sure you missed them and they missed you. The little girl in our story was taken a long way from home and made to work in a big house. The lady of the house was kind and talked to the little girl quite often. The house belonged to Naaman. One day the girl saw that the woman was very sad; she had been crying. The girl found out that Naaman was ill – his skin was covered in marks and if he did not get better, he would have to leave home.

The little girl was sorry for the woman and for Naaman and she wondered how she could help. Then she remembered Elisha. (Do your remember Elisha and how he got his power through Elijah from God?) The little girl told the woman all about the wonderful things Elisha had been doing. He had been making ill people well again. Maybe Naaman could go and see him. The woman told her husband and he agreed to go. He said he would try anything to be made better.

It was a very long way to go but Naaman set off and travelled for a long time. Elisha saw Naaman coming and knew why he had come. He sent a messenger to say to Naaman, 'Go and wash seven times in the river Jordan and you will get better.'

Naaman was angry. 'Fancy telling me to wash in the Jordan. I have nicer rivers at home. I thought Elisha would come out and give me something hard to do. I am not going to bother. I will go home.'

Naaman was lucky that some of his servants knew of Elisha's power and how God worked through Elisha. They said, 'Elisha has asked you to do something easy. Why do you not go and do it? We are sure it will not hurt you.' So Naaman went down to the river and stood in it. 'How many times have I to wash?' The servants reminded him, 'Seven times.' (Let us count slowly to seven.) That is how many times Naaman got in and out of the Jordan. Even after six times he was not better. After the seventh God made Naaman better just as Elisha had said he would. Isn't God marvellous! He made this ill man better.

After saying thank you to Elisha, Naaman hurried home. There he said a big thank-you to God for making him better. It made his wife and the little girl so happy to see him and they also said thank you to God. Then Naaman said yet another thank-you. Who do you think he said it to? Yes, to the girl who was one of the smallest people in his house.

God wants everyone to help him and no one is too young or too small.

Activity

Play 'In the river and on the bank'. If you say, 'In the river', everyone must jump forward into the river. If you say, 'On the bank', all must jump backwards on to the bank. If you say, 'On the river' or 'In the bank', no one must move and if they move they are out.

Prayer

God, we pray for all children who are ill
and away from home.
May they remember that you are with them
and that you love them always.
Amen.

Song

God, you can use me

LAMPS

Aim

To show that Jesus seeks our help.

Teaching

Jesus wanted to tell everyone of the love of the Father God but he could not do it by himself. He needed some helpers. The helpers would have to stay with him and learn from him and then he would send them out to tell others. Can you remember how many Jesus chose to be his special helpers? Twelve, like the twelve tribes of Israel. What do we usually call the twelve helpers of Jesus? Disciples, which means those who learn from Jesus, or Apostles, which means those who were sent by Jesus. Jesus could only send them out after they had learnt about him. Jesus sent them out in twos. How many sets of two can you get out of twelve?

When Judas, who betrayed Jesus, died, there were only eleven disciples. How many sets of two were there? It meant that there was one left by himself. The disciples knew that the one needed a partner and that they should really be twelve so they chose Matthias because he knew Jesus and knew that Jesus was risen from the dead (Acts 1:21-26).

But twelve was not enough to tell all the people in the land where Jesus lived. So Jesus chose another seventy and after they had learnt from him like the disciples, he sent them out like apostles. Jesus sent them out in twos. How many twos can you get in 70? They all went out and told people about Jesus and how God was very near.

Now in our country we need people to be disciples and apostles. We need people to learn about Jesus and to know Jesus through their prayers. Then we need to send those people out as apostles. You are already becoming disciples because you are learning about Jesus and speaking to him in prayer. Once you know Jesus and his love, you could become apostles and be sent out to teach others. Jesus needs disciples and apostles. He would like us to tell others about his love and that God is very near.

Activity

Cut out 70 paper people and then number them twice, 1 to 35. Place all of them around the room with their number not showing. Now the children have to collect two people of the same number. They are allowed to pick up one number and then search for the other. They must always replace other numbers so that they cannot be seen. When they have two numbers the same they shout, 'I can go', and then sit to wait for others to be ready. If there are numbers left, say how sad it is that there are not enough people to bring in all the numbers.

Prayer

Jesus, you called twelve to be your disciples
and another seventy to tell others about you.
May we share in telling others the good news
and of your love for everyone.
Amen.

Song

Go, go, go into the world

TORCHES

Aim

To show how Jesus needs us to proclaim his kingdom and bring others to the love of God.

Teaching

When Jesus wanted to reach out to others and to reveal the love of God, he chose twelve followers to be with him and to learn from him. What do we usually call the twelve? They are the disciples. To be a disciple means to be a learner and a follower. To be a disciple of Jesus needs discipline. To learn about Jesus and to get to know him means spending time in his presence and choosing to leave some other things behind, even if just for a while. Once the disciples had been with Jesus they were ready to be sent out to proclaim the good news and bring others to Jesus. A person who is sent is called an apostle. We cannot really be sent unless we spend time with Jesus.

Jesus wanted more and more people to know of him so he chose another seventy and sent them out in twos to prepare the way for his coming. Today Jesus needs us if the good news is to be heard. If people do not commit themselves to speaking of Jesus, how will others hear? If you truly believe Jesus is wonderful, how can you keep this good news to yourself? Listen to these words of St Teresa and know that they apply to you.

> Christ has no hands but your hands
> to do his work today.
> Christ has no feet but your feet
> to lead others in his way.
> Christ has no lips but your lips
> to tell folk how he died.
> Christ has no love but your love
> to win them to his side.

Prayer of St Teresa of Avila – adapted

You are already seeking to be a disciple; become an apostle also and be sent by Jesus. The first word Jesus said to the seventy as he sent them out was 'Go'. Far too often Christians lack the desire to get up and go. Let us look at the activity sheet and see what advice Jesus gave the seventy.

Activity

Explore Luke 10:1-9.

1) Go but with the awareness that the work will not be easy – you will be like lambs among wolves. Caution is needed.

2) Travel lightly. Too many people are hampered by possessions and their attachment to things.

3) Do not get side-tracked by idle chatter. This is not an excuse for ignoring people.

4) Be a bringer of peace and offer peace to people.

5) You are not in it for gain, for money, food or popularity.

6) Share in the healing ministry of Christ.

7) Let people know the kingdom of God is not far from any of them.

Because the seventy heeded these words, Jesus was able to work through them. Are you available to work for Jesus?

Prayer

Lord Jesus,
take our hands and work with them;
take our feet and reach others through them;
take our lips and speak through them;
take our hearts and set them on fire
with love for you and for all people.
Amen.

Song

Colours of day

Proper 10

Aim

To explore the question 'Who is my neighbour?'

Preparation

Display information about the Samaritans, the London City Mission, Christian Aid and the Rescue Services.

If possible, have information of a recent rescue in your area.

Opening activity

Ask everyone to seek out someone in church they do not know or have not spoken to for a long time. They ask them their name and then say, 'May God bless you and your loved ones.' If you already know their name, say it then the words. Once all are back to their seats, ask the congregation if there is someone in the church they would not speak to and, if so, ask them to pray quietly for them.

Opening prayer

Lord God,
you know our needs and our weaknesses.
You love us and reach out to us in power.
Help us to share in your care and love
for all who are in need at this time,
through Jesus Christ our Lord.
Amen.

Opening song

O Lord, all the world belongs to you

Readings

Amos 7:7-17 or Deuteronomy 30:9-14
Psalm 82 or Psalm 25:1-10
Colossians 1:1-14
Luke 10:25-37

Thought for the day

The nature of teachers and students of the law is to question what they are told and to seek clarification from others. This is as true today as it was in the time of Jesus. The lawyer asks, 'What should I do to inherit eternal life?' Jesus asks a question in return: 'What is written in the law?' The reply of the man is part of what is written in a little leather box called a phylactery that is strapped on his wrist. He quotes from Deuteronomy 6:5 which says, 'You shall love the Lord your God with all your heart, and with all your soul and with all your might.' To this the Scribes added Leviticus 19:18 which bids a person to love his neighbour as himself. The Rabbis sought to define who was a neighbour and at their worst limited this to fellow Jews; Gentiles were not counted as neighbours no matter how closely they lived to Jews. The parable of the Good Samaritan is a challenge to our limited care.

The story begins with a man on the downhill road from Jerusalem to Jericho. With his back to the Holy City, he is making his way towards a place that was known for its vice and corruption. Some have seen symbolism in these images. The man is going downhill and alone. Now this road was notorious for robbers and brigands, and it is foolish to travel alone, especially if you have anything precious. Is not life precious? The man is mugged by a band of robbers, stripped of his possessions, his dignity and his health. He is left half-dead and before long he will be three-quarters dead and then finished.

Lucky man: here comes a priest. Help is at hand. But when he sees him, the priest passes by on the other side. Well, if the priest had gone over and touched the man and the man was dead, it would make him unclean and he would not be able to perform his duties for seven days (Numbers 19:11). It would seem the priest was concerned with ceremony rather than charity. You could hear the common cry: 'It's more than my job's worth.'

Well, the next one who comes along is a good church-man, a Levite. Surely there is hope there. The Levite perhaps is frightened that the robbers are still near and the man on the ground is just a decoy. He could use the same excuse of the priest for not making contact. The law was more important than love.

Then comes the Samaritan – a non-Jew. Surely he won't bother. But he does because he is moved with pity for a fellow human being. He goes over to the man and pours oil and wine on the wounds – normal usage for both, though also symbols of peace and joy. He then lifts him up and puts him on his own animal, brings him to an inn and takes care of him. The next day the Samaritan pays the innkeeper and says, 'Take care of him; and when I come back, I will repay you whatever more you spend.'

Jesus then asked which proved to be a neighbour. When the lawyer replied, 'He that showed mercy', Jesus said, 'Go and do likewise.'

We are challenged to accept as our neighbour and to show concern for those we try to avoid; those who get into trouble through their own fault; those who are racially or religiously different; all who are in need or in trouble.

In John 8:48 the Jews called Jesus a Samaritan. Maybe we should heed the words of the Good Samaritan and interpret them as Jesus speaking to us: 'Take care of him; and when I come back, I will repay you whatever more you spend.'

Question time

Do we seek to set limits on who is worthy of help and who is not? Very often we can excuse ourselves through other duty and work.

Is the church community seen as a good neighbour to those in need in our own area?

Illustration

There is a story about Martin, a cobbler. He looked forward to the coming of the Lord and felt he would soon come to visit his shop. He busied himself getting ready, but he was often interrupted. He saw a child getting into trouble in the market place, so he went out to help him. Then he saw a poor woman who was in need of better shoes. He called her into the shop and saw to her needs. After this there was an old man who looked frozen. He invited the man in and gave him a warm drink. Martin would have liked to have prepared more for the coming of the Lord but he ran out of time. Martin reached out to all who came his way. That night Martin had a dream in which he saw the Lord. The Lord told him how he had visited him when the child needed help, when the woman needed shoes and when the old man wanted some warmth. In caring for his neighbour, Martin met the Lord.

Intercessions

Blessed are you, Lord our God.
You come to us in our need.
You bind up our wounds and restore us to life.
May we be good neighbours
to all who are in need or distress
and so share in your saving love.
Blessed are you, Father, Son and Holy Spirit.

Lord God,
as you have called us to work with you,
show us the ways of your salvation.
May your Church care for the weak and defenceless,
for the needy and the poor.
Let us never avoid our responsibility and pass by
on the other side.
We pray for the work of the Samaritans
and for all relief organisations.

Silence

Show us your ways, O Lord,
and teach us your paths.

We pray for peace and justice in our world.
We ask your blessing upon all who have suffered
from the violence and robbery of others.
We remember those who have been driven off their land
or out of their homes
by the greed of multi-national companies
or of governments.
We pray for all displaced persons
and all who feel injured by others.

Silence

Show us your ways, O Lord,
and teach us your paths.

We give thanks for all who have cared for us
and who have given us support and comfort
in our needs.
We ask your blessing upon our loved ones
and our neighbours.
We pray for all who seek to build up
a spirit of community within our area.

Silence

Show us your ways, O Lord,
and teach us your paths.

We give thanks for all who work in the rescue services.
We ask your blessing
upon the ambulance and fire services.

We pray for social workers and carers,
for all doctors and nurses.
We remember those who quietly work
within their community
seeing to neighbours and meeting their needs.

Silence

Show us your ways, O Lord,
and teach us your paths.

We give thanks that you rescue us from death
and offer us your peace and your joy.
We remember friends and loved ones
who are departed from us
and ask that they might enjoy
a closer fellowship with you
in your kingdom of peace.

Silence

Merciful Father,
accept these prayers
for the sake of your Son,
our Saviour Jesus Christ.
Amen.

Memory verse

Take care of him; and when I come back, I will repay you whatever more you spend.
Luke 10:35

Suggested music

When I needed a neighbour
Help us help each other, Lord
Jesu, Jesu, fill us with your love

CANDLES

Aim

To show we are neighbours when we reach out to help one another.

Teaching

This is a story Jesus told about a good neighbour.

Once there was a man going on a very dangerous journey. He should not have gone alone but he thought he would be safe. Hiding behind some rocks were some robbers and when they saw the man was alone they attacked him. They beat the man, hurting him badly. They took all his possessions, even some of his clothes. They left the man lying at the side of the road. He would die unless someone found him soon.

A priest came along the road. That must be lucky. But the priest was worried about getting himself dirty and not being able to help in church services – so the priest walked past and left the man at the roadside.

Next there came a regular churchgoer. Surely he would be kind. He went close to the man but was frightened in case the robbers were still near. He left the man in the road. He did not know the man and did not want to be bothered.

Then came a Samaritan – a lot of the Jews did not like the Samaritans. This man had a donkey and was obviously going somewhere. He stopped and went over to where the man was and put oil and wine on his wounds to ease the pain and to stop them getting worse. The Samaritan then bandaged up the wounds to keep off flies and infection. After this he lifted the man on to his donkey and took him to a place to stay, an inn. All that evening he looked after the man. In the morning he wanted to go on his way. Before he left, he paid the innkeeper to look after the man until he was well again. The Samaritan promised that if the innkeeper needed more money to look after the man, he would give it to the innkeeper the next time he came.

Now, who do you think was the good neighbour? The one who really looked after the injured man? Jesus wants all of us to care for each other and show love and kindness to everyone we meet. Jesus wants us to do kind things like the Good Samaritan.

Activity

On the activity sheet is a picture of the Good Samaritan helping a man who had been beaten and hurt. Let the children act out various situations where *they* can help: a mother with some bags of shopping; a child has fallen down – let the children pretend to pick her up; an elderly person needs help to cross the road.

If there is time, the parable of the Good Samaritan can be acted out. Try not to let them be too keen to be the robbers!

Prayer

Lord Jesus, as you love everyone
help us to be loving and caring
to all who are in need.
Amen.

Song

As I look around me

LAMPS

Aim

To show that Jesus wants us to love others even when it costs us.

Teaching

A teacher of religion came to Jesus and asked him, 'What must I do to inherit eternal life?' Jesus asked him, 'What is written in the Law of God?' The man replied, 'You shall love the Lord your God with all your heart, with all your soul, with all your strength and with all your mind; and your neighbour as yourself.' It sounds easy: 'Love God and love your neighbour.' Most people know what to do but they do not do it. They do not love

God enough and they are not always kind to their neighbours. The man asked a question: 'Who is my neighbour?' Now, Jesus wanted him to know that anyone who needed help or who came into contact with the man was his neighbour – not just the people who lived nearby. Jesus told a story about travellers on a road. It is called the story of the Good Samaritan.

A man was going down from Jerusalem to Jericho, a downhill road nearly all the way: from Jerusalem, about 700 metres above sea level, it drops to Jericho, 400 metres below sea level. Jerusalem to Jericho is a rocky road with steep valleys and dangerous areas. Jerusalem to Jericho is where robbers and bandits hid and waited for those travelling without protection. Jerusalem to Jericho is not a road to travel alone.
Now read the story.

The man on his own was robbed, stripped and left half-dead. Soon he would be more than half-dead and he could do nothing to help himself.

How lucky that a priest came along. He would be a great help. But the priest avoided the man – he passed by on the other side. (At this point produce a 'question mark' and ask the children if they know why the priest did this. Let their suggestions be as wide-ranging as they like. Tell them how the priest thought it might make him unclean to touch the man. But all are excuses for here was a man in need. The priest was not a good neighbour.)

Then came a Levite – that is a good church-going person. Perhaps he sang in the choir. The man should be lucky this time. The Levite went over and had a look at the man but then passed by on the other side. (Produce the 'question mark' and ask why. Again let the children suggest as many excuses as they like. Maybe the Levite was frightened that the robbers might return or maybe he did not want to put himself out. The Levite was not a good neighbour.)

Then came a Samaritan. (The teacher to whom Jesus was telling the story did not like Samaritans.) It seemed he often travelled that way with his donkey. He went over to where the man was, feeling really sorry for him. He took some of his wine and put it on the wounds to stop infection. Then he took some of his oil and poured it on the wounds to ease the pain. He put the man on his donkey – and that meant the Samaritan would have to walk. Then he brought the injured man to an inn and there he took care of him. He spent the whole night looking after him and getting him food. The next day he said to the innkeeper, 'Here is two days' pay. Take care of the man and when I come back I will pay you whatever more you have spent.'

Now who do you think was a good neighbour? This is what Jesus asked the teacher but the teacher avoided saying, 'The Samaritan'; he only said, 'The one who showed him mercy.' Jesus said to the teacher, 'Go and do like he did.'

If there is time, talk about how we can be good neighbours and how we can care for the needy and those who cannot help themselves.

Activity

Act out the story of the Good Samaritan. Get the priest and the Levite to say why they did not help. Have a chorus of young people who quietly say, 'Excuses, excuses, excuses.' Let the Samaritan show generosity to the full.

Look at appeals from various charities and point out that all the people concerned are our neighbours.

Prayer

Lord Jesus, you love everyone
and are concerned when anyone suffers.
Help us to care for all who are in need or in trouble.
Amen.

Song

Jesus went out of his way

TORCHES

Aim

To show that serving God and following Jesus is not a soft option.

Teaching

Begin by exploring who we think are our neighbours. Does it include neighbouring countries? Does it include all peoples? Look at Luke 10:25-29. The lawyer was a teacher of the Jewish law. He knew the requirements of love. He most likely had them written down in a little leather box that was strapped to him always. The lawyer seems to be seeking to limit his responsibilities. In response to 'Who is my neighbour?' Jesus tells a story. Have someone read Luke 10:30-35. Now let us turn it into a drama.

Activity

As this story is told, have people mime the movement of the man, the robbers, the priest, the Levite, the Samaritan and the Innkeeper. You could even have two covered with a coat to be the donkey.

Narrator	There was a man on a downhill road.
Chorus	A downhill road.
Narrator	A rocky road, a dangerous road.
Chorus	A rocky road, a dangerous road.
Narrator	A road with robbers and brigands.
Chorus	A road with robbers and brigands.
Narrator	The robbers caught him. They mugged him and robbed him, leaving him half-dead.
Chorus	Half-dead. Half-dead.
Narrator	By good fortune a priest came along the road. He preached love and care.
Chorus	Love and care. Love and care.
Narrator	But he was afraid of getting himself dirty and passed by on the other side.
Chorus	On the other side. On the other side.
Narrator	Then came a Levite, who knew the law of love; a good man, a churchman.
Chorus	A good man, a churchman. A good man, a churchman
Narrator	He came and looked at the man. Not a pretty sight. He did not think there was much he could do and he passed by on the other side.
Chorus	On the other side. On the other side.
Narrator	The next one was a Samaritan. Not good news, for the Jews do not like Samaritans. But the Samaritan got off his donkey and came where the man was.
Chorus	Came where he was. Came where he was.
Narrator	He looked at the wounds and poured wine on them to stop infection and oil to ease the pain. Then he put the man on the donkey, so the Samaritan had to walk beside him. He took him to an inn. He cared for him.
Chorus	He cared for him. He cared for him.
Narrator	The next day he paid the innkeeper to look after the man. He promised he would give the innkeeper more when he returned. He was a caring man. Who was the neighbour to the injured man?
Chorus	Neighbour to the injured man. Neighbour to the injured man.
Narrator	Sadly, the Lawyer could not say, 'Samaritan'; he said, 'He that showed mercy'. Jesus said to him, 'Go and do likewise.'
Chorus	Go and do likewise. Go and do likewise.

Prayer

Lord Jesus,
as you love all and care for all,
may we share in your healing and caring ministry.
Make us aware of those in need
and how we can help.
Amen.

Song

Brother, sister, let me serve you

Proper 11

Aim

To show the need for stillness and to be receptive to our God.

Preparation

Make a recording of various voices. Have well-known voices including your own voice and those of other members of the congregation, or sounds from within the community where you live, like a town-hall clock or church bells.

Opening activity

Play the sounds and see who can recognise them.

Opening prayer

O Lord God,
you have given us many wonderful gifts.
Help us to know you are always with us
and make us attentive to your voice.
We pray that we may hear your call
and do your will.
Amen.

Opening song

Be still and know that I am God

Readings

Amos 8:1-12 or Genesis 18:1-10a
Psalm 52 or Psalm 15
Colossians 1:15-28
Luke 10:38-42

Thought for the day

Only Luke tells this story of Martha and Mary. Other stories tell us they had a brother called Lazarus and that they lived in Bethany near to the Mount of Olives and on the ascent to Jerusalem (John 11 and 12:1-8; Matthew 26:6-13; Mark 14:3-9). Luke does not mention Bethany. Martha invites Jesus to her home. This fact and her busyness in the house suggest that Martha is looking after the house and its occupants. Perhaps their parents were already dead and, as was the custom, the oldest daughter took on the responsibility for domestic affairs.

This was a place Jesus was really at home. It was a good base when he was visiting Jerusalem for festivals. Here he was obviously fed and most likely given accommodation. This is the house we hear of most near Jerusalem. Martha is busy. Well, she would be – she has a guest to look after. Mary sits at the feet of Jesus as a pupil would for a Rabbi. Mary is giving Jesus her attention and listening to him. Martha really could do with a hand. 'Lord, do you not care that my sister has left me to do all the work by myself? Tell her, then, to help me.'

But Jesus does not command Mary to get up. He speaks kindly to Martha. 'Martha, Martha, you are worried and distracted by many things; there is need only for one thing. Mary has chosen the better part that will not be taken away from her.' You cannot help but feel at this stage that Jesus is lucky that Martha does not wallop him with a cooking pan! We must look deep into this event, for Jesus did need feeding.

Martha was distracted and anxious and no doubt she had good cause. Very often the lady of the house has to work hard when there is company while others sit having a drink and being waited on. Sometimes we need share out our tasks better, and sometimes we need to realise that our guests are there to spend time with us and not just to be fed.

Many of our troubles and anxieties occur because we do not spend time in quiet with Jesus. Many churches are hyperactive, doing all sorts of activities but spending little time in prayer. God is our priority. If we make God our priority, then he will send us out. God does not want things from us; he wants our love and us. The same could be said of many who come to us as friends. We miss healing relationships if we are too anxious or busy.

> O what peace we often forfeit,
> O what needless pain we bear,
> All because we do not carry
> Everything to God in prayer.

Listen to St Paul: 'Do not worry about anything, but in everything by prayer and supplication with thanksgiving let your requests be made known to God. And the peace of God, which surpasses all understanding, will guard your hearts and your minds in Christ Jesus' (Philippians 4:6, 7).

It is because our sympathies are with Martha that we need to learn more from Mary.

Question time

Do we understand the need for a listening ministry in the church?

Is our church very active but lacking in stillness?

Illustration

The greatest danger of television is that it encourages us to switch off from one another. This is true of iPods and personal CD players. They all help to shut us off and enclose us in a world of our own. But we do not need any of these to be inattentive. A child comes in with an important message but the father is filling in his tax forms and the mother is busy preparing the dinner. 'But . . .' says the child and is still not given attention. The parents have not listened and the child is left feeling alone. The generation gap is often created because we do not listen to each other. The child goes out and wonders who will look at the washing machine that is overflowing!

Intercessions

Blessed are you, Lord our God.
You have given us the power of communication:
eyes to see, ears to hear and lips to speak.
Teach us to be attentive to your word
and to all who come to us each day.
Blessed are you, Father, Son and Holy Spirit.

We give thanks for the stillness of the church
and that you speak to us through the silence.
We pray for all who wait upon your word
and seek to do your will.
We pray for all pastors and counsellors
and all who are called to listen to the needs of others.
We pray for religious communities
and for all who wait upon you in silence.

Silence

Holy and Mighty One,
hear us and help us.

Guide all our leaders
in the ways of justice and of peace.
Keep our ears open to the cry of the poor
and the oppressed
and all who call for freedom.
We pray for the work of Christian Aid
and all who seek to feed the hungry.

Silence

Holy and Mighty One,
hear us and help us.

Lord, teach us to be sensitive to each other
in our homes and with our friends.
May we give time and attention where it is needed.
We ask your blessing of peace upon our homes
and all who are dear to us.

Silence

Holy and Mighty One,
hear us and help us.

We pray today for all who are anxious and over-worked,
all who are world-weary or deeply troubled.
We remember especially
any who feel the lack of love or attention,
those who feel neglected or unwanted.
We ask your blessing upon all who are ill
and those who have been taken into care.

Silence

Holy and Mighty One,
hear us and help us.

Lord, we give thanks
that you attend to our needs
and care for us through to eternity.
We ask you to bless our friends and loved ones
who are departed from this life
and now rejoice in the fullness of your kingdom.

Silence

Merciful Father,
**accept these prayers
for the sake of your Son,
our Saviour Jesus Christ.
Amen.**

Memory verse

Be still and know that I am God.
Psalm 46:10

Suggested music

Be still, my soul
Hark, my soul, it is the Lord.
What a friend we have in Jesus

CANDLES

Aim

To show that Jesus wants us to spend some time with him.

Teaching

Jesus and his disciples were invited to stay with some friends. Martha invited him and her sister Mary was very pleased because she thought it would be nice to listen to Jesus and to talk to him. Let us say the names of the two sisters: Martha and Mary. It seems Martha was the oldest and was responsible for looking after the house and anyone who came to it.

Because there were so many to feed Martha was very busy. I am sure your mother is busy when you have company. What sort of things must be done for your visitors? Getting the table ready, preparing a meal, cooking and, in Martha's time, keeping the fire burning to cook the dinner. There was a lot to do and Martha could have done with some help. Are you able to help at home when you have visitors?

Martha was getting tired and a bit cross because Mary was not helping her. Mary was sitting with Jesus and listening to him. Mary was giving all her attention to Jesus. Suddenly Martha came to Jesus and said, 'Lord, do you not care that my sister has left me to do all the work by myself? Tell her to help me.'

Jesus does not make people do things. Jesus would like us to do some things, like be his friend, but he would not make us. Jesus could see Martha was upset and spoke gently to her. He said, 'Martha, Martha, you are worried about many things.' Jesus would have liked her to spend more time with him but she was so busy doing all sorts of jobs.

Jesus was pleased that Mary sat at his feet and listened to him. He came to see his friends more than for food and he wanted to spend time with them. Jesus was also very pleased with Martha for looking after him and his disciples.

Jesus would like us to spend some time with him each day. He would like us to tell him what we are doing and how he can help. What do you call speaking to Jesus? Yes, it is called praying. We need to give Jesus some attention and say our prayers each day.

Activity

Play 'I spy'. This should encourage the children to give attention to each other and to the objects in the room.

Prayer

Lord Jesus, you love us and come to us.
Help us to know you are with us
and to say our prayers every day.
Amen.

Song

Father, we adore you

Activity

Play 'Chinese whispers' and show how important it is to listen carefully and give someone our attention.

There are ideas on the activity sheet for giving God some attention each day.

Prayer

God, you love us
and want us to spend time with you.
In the stillness you offer us your peace,
your power and your presence.
Help us to be still and quiet before you.
Amen.

Song

Seek ye first the kingdom of God

LAMPS

Aim

To encourage them to make an effort to talk with Jesus each day.

Teaching

Can you remember the names of the friends Jesus had in Bethany? There were two sisters and a brother. The brother was called Lazarus and his sisters were Martha and Mary. Martha invited Jesus to their house. When he came with his disciples it meant that it would be a busy time preparing a meal for them. I am sure they all wanted to eat.

Martha was in charge so she was very busy. While she was working hard, Mary just sat listening to Jesus and talking to him. She gave her whole attention to Jesus and did not notice how busy Martha was, preparing the meal.

Martha got more and more annoyed because Mary could have made her work easier. Martha came and said to Jesus, 'Make Mary come and help me.' Jesus does not make people do things – he only helps them when they want to do things. He had also come to see his friends and he would rather have had time with them than a big meal. Jesus did understand Martha and her worries but he told her that Mary had chosen to do something special – that is, spend time with him and give some attention.

Picture a house where both the mother and father are always busy. They make sure their child has lots of food, all the toys and presents he wants, but they do not spend any time with him. The child needs their attention but instead they give him things. What do you think the child would like most of all?

In the same way, God wants us to give him some of our time, our attention and our love. How can we best do this? We need to pray every day. Like promising to meet a friend, it is good to make a fixed time and a fixed place to speak to Jesus or we might forget.

TORCHES

Aim

To show we must not only be active but also still and quiet before our God.

Teaching

Today's story is hard because we do not know all the facts. We know Martha invited Jesus to their house. We know that this added to the workload of the house and Martha got very anxious and worried about getting a meal ready for Jesus and his disciples. Martha was busy indeed. It would seem she is the older sister and in charge of the household. Perhaps her parents were dead and she looked after Mary and their brother Lazarus.

We also know that while Martha was busy, Mary sat at the feet of Jesus, listening to him. Martha was sweating over the oven and Mary was relaxing in the presence of Jesus.

No wonder Martha sounded a little annoyed. She wondered if Jesus cared and asked him to make Mary come and help her. Jesus responds by saying, 'Martha, Martha, you are worried and distracted by many things.' Jesus does not order Mary to help Martha – Jesus does not force us to do things even though he would like us to do them. Now at this point Mary and Jesus are lucky that Martha does not box their ears!

It would seem the point of this story is that Jesus came for friendship more than food, for attention more than a plate of something. He wanted someone to listen to him. Mary had done just that. Too often people would rather offer God things than give themselves to him. Too often we say we have no time for prayer or to be still before God because we are too busy. It is a matter of choice, and our choice shows whether God is important in our life or just comes second, or even last.

Often when we say we are too busy for prayer we mean that God does not have a priority.

(I am sure Jesus and the disciples were grateful for Martha and the way she looked after them.)

Activity

A little play

Mother	John, come and help with the washing up.
John	I am too busy doing my homework.
Mother	John, your room needs tidying.
John	I am busy sorting out some stuff for school.
Father	John, can you help me in the garden?
John	I have an essay to write before tonight.
Father	I think that is Susan coming up the path.
John	Great! I am going out with her – we will be back in a couple of hours.

Discuss how John excused himself but found time to do what he wanted to do. How often do we say we are too busy for prayer or for church? Does this reflect on our love for God and the attention we are willing to give him?

There is an opportunity to plan a fixed place and a fixed time for prayer on the worksheet.

(Give out a copy of next week's teaching which is to be used at the beginning of next week's service.)

Prayer

Lord Jesus, we come to you in prayer
so that we may show our love
and our desire to be with you.
Help us to know your power and your peace
in our lives.
Amen.

Song

In the morning early

Proper 12

Sunday between 24 and 30 July inclusive

Aim

To explore the Lord's Prayer.

Preparation

Print or copy the Lord's Prayer to be used in the activity – let everyone take a copy home.

Opening activity and prayer

The Lord's Prayer in an extended version presented by the 'Torches' group.

Opening song

Thy kingdom come, O God

Readings

Hosea 1:2-10 or Genesis 18:20-32
Psalm 85 or Psalm 138
Colossians 2:6-15 (16-19)
Luke 11:1-13

Thought for the day

The Lord's Prayer belongs to the Jewish tradition of talking with God. This prayer is based on confidence in God, openness to God and the belief that not only will God provide but will also bring in his kingdom. These are all exciting themes and become part and parcel of the life of the person who prays the Lord's Prayer with their heart and mind.

The start of the prayer is surprising in its intimacy. The Aramaic word 'Abba' is the word behind 'Father' and it means 'Daddy'. We need to see that we are made by God and belong to God. We need to know he created us out of his love and for his love. God wants a living relationship with us. It is good to spend a part of each day knowing God has made you and God loves you.

To speak to God is to recognise his presence and so come before him in awe: 'Hallowed be your name.' May we make God's name holy in our lives by recognising his love and his kingly rule. God's kingdom will come in us if we seek to do his will. If we want to be part of the kingdom, we have to live by its rules. We are called to hallow God's name in the world.

In asking for our daily bread, it is easy to forget that millions are still starving in our world. We all need feeding and we need more than food. This request is for nourishment upon which our whole being depends: that is, nourishment for our mind and spirit as well as our bodies.

It is thought that Luke 11:4 changes Matthew's 'debts' (Matthew 6:12) to 'sins.' Both are about being released from our past and set free in the kingdom of God. We are expected to forgive as we are forgiven. We must think very carefully about this when we pray the Lord's Prayer.

The 'time of trial' is thought to be the troubles at the end of the world. We all have to face the end of our world at some time, and we need to ask God that we are well prepared. To know God and his love, to be aware of his power and his presence, to rejoice in his kingdom and the promise of eternal life totally transforms all we have to face.

Question time

Do we have a living relationship of love with our God?

Can we say the Lord's Prayer more carefully by taking a single phrase at a time and extending it to show what it means?

Illustration

When we turn to God in prayer we acknowledge his presence: that God is with us always and that he listens to us. You are actually in the presence, in God. We are in God in the same way as fish live in water and we in air. Listen to these words by the poet Francis Thompson from the poem 'No Strange Land':

> Does the fish soar to find the ocean,
> The eagle plunge to find the air –
> That we ask of the stars in motion
> If they have rumour of thee there?

We cannot search for God but we can open ourselves to his presence, and a good way of doing this is by speaking to him quietly each day.

Use the Lord's Prayer and pause between each phrase to be aware of the fullness and wonder of the words and of your God.

Intercessions

Blessed are you, God and Father of us all.
You created us out of your love
and redeemed us by your love.
We rejoice that you sustain us with your love
and that you never leave us.
We seek to know your presence
and to give our love to you.
Blessed are you, God, for ever.

As we rejoice in your love for all people,
may your Church strive for justice and freedom for all.
We remember all who are persecuted for their faith
and all who are oppressed by tyranny.
We ask your blessing upon all who witness
to the power of prayer and knowing you.
We pray for religious communities
and for all who preach the word
and administer the sacraments.

Silence

Father, your kingdom come in us
as it is in heaven.

As we pray for our daily needs,
we remember all who suffer
from poverty, hunger and homelessness.
We remember those who are deeply in debt
and all who are struggling to cope with life.
We ask your blessing upon all who are not sure
where their next meal will come from.
We pray for the harvests of the world
and for fair trade.

Silence

Father, your kingdom come in us
as it is in heaven.

We give thanks for all who have cared for us
and supplied our needs.
We ask your blessing
upon our homes and our loved ones.
We pray for all who are responsible
for upholding high standards and integrity
within our communities
and we ask that we may be an example to others.

Silence

Father, your kingdom come in us
as it is in heaven.

We give thanks for your forgiveness
and we pray for all who are burdened
with guilt and remorse
and who are striving to live a new life.
We remember all who are ill at home or in hospital.
We ask your blessing upon them
and upon those who care for them.

Silence

Father, your kingdom come in us
as it is in heaven.

We trust in your never-failing love
and commend to you
our friends and loved ones departed.
May they rejoice in the fullness of your kingdom,
in the joy and peace of life eternal.

Silence

Merciful Father,
**accept these prayers
for the sake of your Son,
our Saviour Jesus Christ.
Amen.**

Memory verse

As you have received Christ Jesus the Lord, continue to
live your lives in him.
Colossians 2:6

Suggested music

Our Father God in heaven.
Lord, teach us how to pray aright
Our Father (Caribbean Lord's Prayer)

CANDLES

Aim

To show that God likes us to talk to him and to ask for
things.

Teaching

There was once a man who had a friend who lived near
him. One night the man had a visitor who had come a
long way and was hungry. But the man had no food in
the house. It was now very late but the man said, 'Do
not worry. I will go to my friend and borrow some
bread.' Off he went and knocked at his friend's door.
From the inside of the house a voice said, 'What do you
want? The door is locked and we are all in bed.'

'I would like to borrow some bread.' But from inside
the voice said, 'I'm tired. Go way and do not bother me.'

Perhaps the man inside the house was not sure who
was outside and thought it might be robbers. He was
not going to get up. But his friend started to call his
name. 'Jacob, it's me, your friend Isaac. Please come
out.' Isaac kept shouting, 'Jacob, come out and help me.'
After a little while Jacob knew he could not ignore his
friend; he knew he would have to get up because if he
did not his friend would keep calling. Jacob got up and
gave his friend what he needed. Isaac was pleased and
said thank you. Then he went off to feed his visitor.

Jesus told this story when he was teaching people to
pray. He wanted us to see that just as our friends would
help us if we asked them and just as our parents would
give us what we need, God does the same. Our parents
would give us things if they knew we needed them.
Sometimes we need to ask them so that they know what
we need. (Give examples.)

God loves each of us and wants us to have the things
we really need. He likes us to ask for them and to talk to
him. God wants us to seek his love and his help. Jesus
really cares for us and likes us to talk to him each day.

Activity

Have the children act out the story of the man seeking
bread from a friend. There is an opportunity on the
activity sheet to make an opening and closing door with
'Jacob' behind it.

Prayer

Our Father in heaven,
we know that you love us.
We ask you to help us
and give us what we really need today.
Amen.

Song

Father God, I know you love me so

LAMPS

Aim

To understand the need to pray; to look at the Lord's Prayer.

Teaching

If you have something important to do and you are not sure how to do it, who would you go to? It is good to have people like our parents, friends and teachers who can help us and guide us. (Find out the things that the group seek advice and help on.)

When Jesus had something important to do he shared the ideas with his friends, but he also went to a lonely place, like the desert or a mountain or to a garden. A lonely place, but he was not really alone because he knew the Father God was with him. He spoke often to the Father God. These times with the Father God gave Jesus new power and courage; they gave him peace and knowledge of what to do. The disciples saw how praying helped Jesus and asked him to teach them.

Jesus taught the disciples a prayer. What is it called? Yes it is the Lord's Prayer. Do you all know it without having to read it? Let us look at it together.

'Our Father in heaven.' Although God is in heaven he is also near to each of us. Prayer is not a long-distance call; it is speaking to God who is always with us. When we pray, this means heaven is also close to us. God is our Father because he made us – and like any good father he loves us as his children.

'Hallowed be your name' means we will not only show respect when we speak about God but that we will respect all of his creation.

We say 'your kingdom come' because we want God's peace and love to be known in the whole world. It means we will obey God and do his will because he is our King.

We ask God for the things we need each day – not the things we want but what we really need. (Get them to talk about this.)

We ask God to forgive us anything wrong we have done, saying sorry and promising to try and not do it again. We share in God's forgiveness by forgiving others.

We ask God to keep us out of danger and trouble and to be our strength when we are tempted. (Ask the group to talk about this.)

Activity

Cut up photographs of people and animals from magazines into three or four pieces and hide them around the room before the lesson starts. Then ask the children to find them, telling them what is hidden. They should each have only one or two pieces and cooperate to bring them together.

Prayer

Father, you are always with us.
Help us to do what you would like us to do
and forgive us when we do wrong.
Keep us safe and under your protection.
Amen.

Song

Father God, you love me

TORCHES

Aim

To encourage a deeper understanding of the Lord's Prayer.

Teaching

Use the following to get the young people to understand the Lord's Prayer better and for them to use within the service. Let each section be said by someone different and all say the last section together. Have the congregation say, 'Alleluia. Amen' after the 'Alleluia' in each section. Instead of discussing the sections, seek for them to be extended in prayer.

Our Father, you love all that you have made. You love every person – even me. And you are with each of us now. (*Pause*) Alleluia.

In heaven – you are in heaven yet with each of us – so heaven and earth are one in you. We share in heaven (*Pause*) Alleluia.

Hallowed be your name. Let us come with awe and respect before all of your creation and all people and know you are within all. (*Pause*) Alleluia.

Your kingdom come, in us now today and every day. Let us know your peace and your joy. (*Pause*) Alleluia.

Your will be done on earth as in heaven. Let us serve you and do your will in all things so your kingdom will be revealed on earth. (*Pause*) Alleluia.

Give us today our daily bread. Lord, you know our needs before we ask and you care for us. Help us to trust in you. (*Pause*) Alleluia.

Forgive us our sins, even though they are many. Help us to start again. (*Pause*) Alleluia.

As we forgive those who sin against us. Wow! That is tough but I know you want us to share in your forgiveness. (*Pause*) Alleluia.

Save us from the time of trial and deliver us from evil. Lord, you are our protector and strength. Let us put our hope and trust in you. (*Pause*) Alleluia.

For the kingdom, the power and the glory are yours now and for ever. (*Pause*) Alleluia.

Activity

Lead the extended Lord's Prayer in church.

Prayer

Use the Lord's Prayer as in the lesson.

Song

Seek ye first the kingdom of God

Proper 13

Sunday between 31 July and 6 August inclusive

Aim

To look at the relationships we have with our possessions.

Preparation

Have appeals from missionary societies and relief agencies concerning hunger, poverty and fair trade. You may like to add a poster with a cut-out of a wealthy foundation or wealthy person and someone begging for alms and add the words, 'He who has bread is responsible for him who has none.'

Opening activity

Use five voices.

Voice 1 I do not give at all to anything.

Voice 2 So said the Dead Seas and died of what it kept.

Voice 3 I ignore the poor and they go away.

Voice 2 Yes, they go away – and die.

Voice 4 I give of my small change.

Voice 2 Then you can only expect a small change in the world.

Voice 5 I give as much as I can. I wish I could give more.

Voice 2 With your time, your talent and your giving, you are helping to change the world.

Opening prayer

Good and gracious God,
you have given to us out of your great bounty.
In our times of plenty
help us to share and to give to others
as you have freely given to us.
Amen.

Opening song

Be thou my vision

Readings

Hosea 11:1-11
or Ecclesiastes 1:2, 12-14; 2:18-23
Psalm 107:1-9, 43 or Psalm 49:1-12
Colossians 3:1-11
Luke 12:13-21

Thought for the day

The story that Jesus tells today arises out of a sad situation, a family row after the death of parents. It is amazing how many people have fallen out over a piece of furniture or an ornament. The father has obviously died and there is no clear indication of who should have what: each wanting to own, to possess and to say, 'That is mine'. At least one of them was being greedy. As people today resort to law, so the rowing parties come to Jesus as they would to a rabbi. Jesus refuses to tell them what they should do – they need to live by grace and graciously rather than under the law. Jesus warns the crowd, 'Take care, be on your guard against all kinds of greed; for one's life does not consist in the abundance of possessions.' Then he tells a story in three acts.

Act one is a bumper harvest. The land produced abundantly. The barns are full and bursting at the seams. Carpenters are at work building bigger and better barns. Lucky rich man – he deserves this reward for hard work. God must love him. Most would admire him and some would envy him.

Act two and the farmer is in his den totting up his books: Haven't I done well! I can take it easy now. I have enough for many years. I can eat, drink and be merry. I can relax and look after myself. Lucky rich man – most people would not mind swapping places with him. Go and enjoy yourself, you deserve it.

Act three. If you do not like unhappy endings, you had better walk out now. If you do not want a challenge, do not watch this act. The rich man has died – poor rich man. He has left behind his farm, his barns, his leisure time. All that he possessed and counted upon has gone, poor rich man. He stands in the presence of God who says, 'You fool!' In no way was he prepared for this. He was rich to human eyes but poor in the eyes of God – poor rich man. He had cared about possessions but not about other people or God. He was rich in things but poor in the important relationships – poor rich man.

Notice in this story how in three verses the word 'I' appears six times. This was someone who was full of himself. God does not measure by what we have as much as by what we share. Riches are measured by what we can give away; the rest are possessions, and many are possessed by their possessions. Riches are to be shared with the community and in this way the poor and the marginalised are cared for. As an old proverb says, 'He who has bread is responsible for him who has none.'

Question time

How can we avoid being possessed by possessions in a consumer society?

Have we considered how much we need and what we can actually give away?

Illustration

When John Wesley was at Oxford he lived by a rule that he set himself: 'Save what you can and give away what you can.' At first Wesley had an income of £30 a year. He then lived off £28 and gave £2 away each year. When his income rose to £60 a year he lived on £28 and gave away £32. As his income rose to £60 and then to £120 a year, he still lived on £28 and gave the rest away.

The Accountant General for Household Plate (a sort of tax collector) asked for a return from Wesley supposing he should have a good deal to show. Wesley replied, 'I have two silver teaspoons at London and two at Bristol. This is all the plate which I have at present; and will not buy any more, while so many people around me want bread.'

Intercessions

Blessed are you, Lord God of all creation,
for all things come from you.
You give us life.
You give us love.
You give us a world of plenty,
that we may learn to share with our neighbour
and give generously to each other
as you give to us.
Blessed are you, Father, Son and Holy Spirit.

Lord, as you have called us to serve you,
make us worthy of our calling.
Teach us to be generous and caring
to all who are in need,
knowing that in giving we are enriched.
May your Church be a good steward of its gifts
and reach out to where it can use its talents.
We pray for all who give of themselves generously
in mission or in pastoral care,
all who work for little financial reward
in the service of others.

Silence

Giver of all,
teach us to share.

We ask your blessing upon all who work
for fair trade and justice in our world.
Let us all realise that life cannot be bought or sold
or measured by financial worth alone.
We pray for all who are used almost as slave labour
and for those who do not get a fair day's wage
for their work.
We remember those who live in slum dwellings
or in refugee camps
and all who will hunger today.

Silence

Giver of all,
teach us to share.

We give thanks for all that you have given us,
for your blessing upon our homes and families.
We give thanks for all who have taught us
and been our benefactors.
We remember homes that suffer through greed
and those who, though they have many possessions,
are poor in spirit.

Silence

Giver of all,
teach us to share.

We ask your blessing upon the weary and the war-torn,
upon the weak and those whose powers are waning.
We pray for all who are ill
and especially for those who are near to death,
asking you to bless them and their loved ones
with your presence and your peace.

Silence

Giver of all,
teach us to share.

We give thanks
for all who, though poor in the eyes of the world,
are precious in your sight.
We rejoice in the fellowship of all your saints
and we remember friends and loved ones
who are departed from us.
May we all share in your love and in your kingdom.

Silence

Merciful Father,
**accept these prayers
for the sake of your Son,
our Saviour Jesus Christ.
Amen.**

Memory verse

Be on your guard against all sorts of greed; for one's life does not consist in the abundance of possessions.
Luke 12:15

Suggested music

When I survey the wondrous cross
When God made the garden of creation
Brother, sister, let me serve you

CANDLES

Aim

To show God gives us gifts to share.

Teaching

Read the hymn 'Who made the twinkling stars' (Kidsource 385) and get the children to repeat the last line.

When God made the world he made the sun, the moon and the stars, and all gave their light to the world.

Then God made the streams, the rivers and the seas, so that they could give life to all sorts of creatures.

Next God made the land, the hills and valleys, the mountains and the flat land, so it could be a place for things to grow in and live in.

God made the flower, the fruit, the tree, the green grass and all that grows on the earth.

Now he made the fish in the sea, the birds in the air and all the animals. (Maybe you have a favourite animal and would like to say 'Thank you' to God for it.)

Once all this was done God made the first people and from them more and more people. God gave us – you and me – life. He gave us the world to live in. He gave us his love. God likes to give and he likes people who give. He wants us to learn to share with each other and to share with the creatures. He did not give all the world to me or to (mention names of some of the children). The whole world belongs to God but he wants us to share it with him and to share it with each other. Mr Greedy and people who cannot share make God sad.

We should say 'Thank you' to God each day for all the good things he has given us. Let us now say 'Thank you, God'.

Then we should see what God wants us to look after and to share with each other. (This is not an easy concept for small children. Explore the idea of how the farmer, the miller and the baker and the shop all have to share in work if we are to have bread.)

Activity

Have a team race where everyone has to put a balloon between their legs, carry two bags and another balloon. Tell them how hard it is to move if you have too many things. Then have a team race where they each only carry one thing.

Prayer

Thank you, God, for the world
and for making us.
May we learn to be kind
and to share with each other.
Amen.

Song

Gives! Gives! Gives!

LAMPS

Aim

To show the need to care and share.

Teaching

Once there was a rich man who had a big house and a big farm. He had big barns and built bigger ones to put his big harvest in. He was very well-off and looked after himself very well. He really was a rich man.

At home he counted up all the things he had and he had a lot. So much money that he didn't need to work hard. He would have big meals and lots to drink, he would have a big long holiday and enjoy himself. He was a rich man and people thought him a big man because they measured him by all the things he had and he had a lot.

Then suddenly the big man died. What do you think he took with him to heaven? Nothing. He left it all behind. In heaven he came to be measured by the angels and he heard one of them say, 'Poor little man.' He could hardly believe his ears – he was a rich man, a big man. 'Poor little man,' the angel said again. 'Such a tiny little man with nothing to commend him.' He asked the angels why they thought like this. They asked him where his farm and his money was now. He had to say he had left them behind. He was no longer rich. 'But

you would be rich if you had shared with others. You are small and poor because you kept things to yourself. You are small and poor because you only thought of yourself. You are small and poor because you did not give things away, because you were greedy. We do not measure by possessions but by your relationship with other people and with God. You are poor because you did not have time to talk to God. You are small because your spirit has not been fed and so it did not grow. So it is with those who store up treasure for themselves but are not rich towards God. Poor little man.'

Activity

Play 'My sister went to London and bought . . .' This is a circle game where the first person says, 'My sister went to London and bought a . . .' Then they name something and mime it. The next person has to repeat what the first person said, and add something else, miming both things. So it continues until someone cannot remember the sequence. Then the person next to them starts it off again. It can be hard to hold a lot in your head!

Prayer

Lord, you are generous to us
in all that you give us.
Help us to be generous to others
and to share with the poor and needy.
Amen.

Song

Bring in the harvest

TORCHES

Aim

To show our need to share this world's resources.

Teaching

Have someone read the story of the rich farmer. Ask the group to count how many times the farmer uses the word 'I' in such a short story.

As it ends, say, 'Poor rich man.' Ask the group why he is poor. What did he leave behind when he went to heaven? What did he take with him?

He had only himself. He was poor because he did not see beyond himself. He did not see beyond this world. He had neglected his prayers and the worship of God so that he could make money. He was poor in spirit.

The Blackfoot Indians of America used to have a Blanket Ceremony each year. Blankets represented wealth. They saved all the year round to buy blankets and when the ceremony came they gave them away. The person who was able to give away the most blankets was counted the richest. The richest person is not the one who has the most but the one who is able to give away the most.

Activity

Have cuttings of advertisements from magazines and see who can recognise the most. Point out that often advertisements play on our greed rather than our need.

There is an opportunity to look at the parable in more depth on the activity sheet and also to look at some statements concerning possessions.

Prayer

Lord God, you have created a world
where there is enough for everyone's needs
but not for everyone's greed.
Help us not to hoard or squander your creation
but to share with each other.
Amen.

Song

For the measure of the treasure

Proper 14

Sunday between 7 and 13 August inclusive

Aim

To encourage people to trust in God and to invite him into their daily life.

Preparation

Have a poster or an enlarged postcard of William Holman Hunt's painting 'Light of the World'. Beneath it have these words: 'Listen! I am standing at the door, knocking' (Revelation 3:20).

Opening activity

Jesus	Knock, knock.
Voice	Who is there?
Jesus	It is the Lord.
Voice	Come in.
Jesus	The door is locked.
Voice	I'll open it later – I am busy.
Jesus	Knock, knock.
Voice	I cannot be listening to that – I'll turn up the stereo.
Jesus	Knock, knock.
Voice	Ignore it and he might go away. Anyhow, I keep the door locked because I am scared.
Jesus	*(very quietly)* Knock, knock.

Opening prayer

Come, Lord Jesus,
enter into our homes and our lives.
Drive away from us all worry and anxiety
and let us know you are near.
Let us share in your kingdom,
in your peace and in your love.
Amen.

Opening song

Thy kingdom come, O God

Readings

Isaiah 1:1, 10-20 or Genesis 15:1-6
Psalm 50:1-8, 22, 23 or Psalm 33:12-22
Hebrews 11:1-3, 8-16
Luke 12:32-40

Thought for the day

The times that Jesus lived in were troubled times. There were wars and rumours of wars, people suffered from famine, from acts of violence or from illness. In fact, in many ways the times were like our own. We are still being troubled: by global warming, wars, acts of violence and by illness. Many people are anxious and fearful about the future.

Today's Gospel begins with Jesus saying, just as God said to Abraham at the beginning of today's Old Testament reading (Genesis 15:1), 'Do not be afraid.' Someone counted that the Scriptures have the words 'Do not be afraid' scattered throughout them 365 times: that is one for each day of the year. God does not want us to be overcome by fear or anxiety, even in troubled times. Here are some wonderful words spoken by God through the prophet Isaiah (43:1b-3a): 'Do not fear, for I have redeemed you; I have called you by name, you are mine. When you pass through the waters, I will be with you; and through the rivers, they shall not overwhelm you: when you walk through fire you shall not be burned, and the flame shall not consume you. For I am the Lord your God, the Holy One of Israel, your Saviour.'

We need to know that even in times of trouble God is with us, and God cares for us. It is God's pleasure to give us the kingdom. He gives us the kingdom not through our own efforts and merit but freely through his own grace and goodness. Our lasting treasure is to be part of God's kingdom.

We need to be alert to the fact that God is with us, God cares for us and God seeks entry into our lives. God will not force himself upon us. He stands outside our lives waiting to be let in. We must open the door and invite him to come in. In the book of Revelation (3:20), Jesus says: 'Listen! I am standing at the door, knocking.' You need to spend time each day inviting God into your life. In this way you will not only discover God is with you, you will know his peace and his love. You will know that nothing can separate you from the love of God in Christ Jesus. (See Romans 8:39.)

Question time

Do you spend time each day welcoming God into your life?

Do you recognise that without God fear overcomes most people at some time?

Illustration

Look at Holman Hunt's painting 'Light of the World'. Here Christ is at a door knocking. The lack of a handle on the outside of the door shows it can only be opened from within. The weeds around the door show that it has not been opened for a long time. The apples lying on the ground remind us of the fall from grace in the Garden of Eden. Through sin, people and God become separate. Jesus comes to unite us again with God if we will let him into our lives.

Intercessions

Blessed are you, Lord our God,
for you have called us to know you and to love you.
You, Lord, are our strength and our shield,
our protector and our joy.
Blessed are you, Father, Son and Holy Spirit.

Lord, in your power
may your Church be a place of peace for the anxious
and a stronghold for all who are troubled.

We ask your blessing
upon all who are involved in pastoral work
and in caring for others.
We pray for the Church's ministry
to the outcasts and marginalised people of society.

Silence

Powerful God,
protect us and give us your peace.

We pray for our world
where there are always wars and rumours of wars.
Lord, grant us peace.
Show us the peace we should give
and the peace we need to forego.
We pray for all who are struggling
against acts of violence,
against poverty and against hunger.
We ask your blessing
upon all who work for relief agencies
and upon the work of the emergency and rescue services.

Silence

Powerful God,
protect us and give us your peace.

We give thanks for the peace and security of our homes.
We ask your blessing upon our families and friends.
We pray for homes where there is neglect or abuse.
We remember all who are afraid
and unable to speak out
about their troubles.

Silence

Powerful God,
protect us and give us your peace.

We rejoice in your abiding presence
and pray for all who feel lonely or anxious at this time.
We remember all who are fearful of the future
and those who are terminally ill.
We pray for those who await a doctor's diagnosis
or who are preparing to go into hospital.
We ask your blessing upon all who suffer
and upon those who care for them.

Silence

Powerful God,
protect us and give us your peace.

Lord, all our hope is in you
for you are the giver of life and life eternal.
Bless our loved ones who are departed from us.
May they share with your saints
in the glory of your kingdom.

Silence

Merciful Father,
**accept these prayers
for the sake of your Son,
our Saviour Jesus Christ.
Amen.**

Memory verse

Do not be afraid, little flock, for it is your Father's good
pleasure to give you the kingdom.
Luke 12:32

Suggested music

Do not be afraid
Thou didst leave thy throne
O God, our help in ages past

CANDLES

Aim

To show that God cares for us and is with us.

Teaching

(The activity takes place at the beginning of the sesssion.)

Who found Mr Wolf scary? If it had been a real wolf
with big teeth, it would have been very scary. (Explore
what makes the children afraid and what helps them to
be brave and strong.)

One little girl lived on a farm and had a long walk to
school. In the winter it was sometimes dark when she
left school. The lane she walked down had dark corners
and big black trees. She was not scared to walk down
the lane for a few different reasons. Can you guess what
they were? She had a torch to give her light. If it was dark,
her mother or her father always came to meet her. If the
weather was very bad, her mother or father would come
in the car so that they would be sheltered from the storm.
The little girl was not afraid because of who was with her.

When Moses was in the desert, God promised to look
after him and his people. God went with Moses and
protected him from the heat and was with him to give
light when it was dark. When the people were hungry,
God provided them with food. God looked after them
all the time they were in the desert and this helped
Moses to be brave and strong.

God has promised to be always with us. He wants us
to know he loves us and protects us. He says, 'I am with
you, do not be afraid.' We cannot see God but we can
speak to him each day. What do you call speaking to
God? Yes, praying. We can say our prayers each day
and know that God is with us and that he says to us,
'Do not be afraid, for I am with you always.'

Activity

At the beginning of the session: play 'What time is it,
Mr Wolf?' Let the wolf be as scary as possible.

Prayer

God, help us to know
that you are always with us;
you love us and protect us.
Keep us and those we love safe
and in your peace.
Amen.

Song

God is love: his the care (verse 1 and chorus)

LAMPS

Aim

To encourage them to invite Jesus into their daily life.

Teaching

Invitations can be exciting. You may be invited to go to a party or to a football match. You may be invited to join a team or to take part in a concert. What sort of invitations have you had? Some events have a little notice attached to them that says, 'By invitation only'. What do you think that means? Sometimes at concerts or plays once it starts you cannot get in. If the doors of a building are locked, it means no one can get in unless they have a key or someone opens from the inside. (See if the children can give examples.)

A famous painter called Holman Hunt once painted Jesus knocking on a door. (If possible, get the children to look for a while at this picture.) Jesus has a light in his hand because he is sometimes called the Light of the World. Jesus brings light to those who are in the dark and afraid. Jesus is knocking at the door but he cannot get in. If you look at the door closely, you will see why. (Let them discover there is no doorknob or handle.) The door can only be opened from the inside. Now the door has not been opened for a long time – how do you know that? Notice the briars and weeds around the door. We do not know how long Jesus has been knocking but he waits to be let in. Jesus will not force his way in. He will not kick the door down or call on powers to break it down. Jesus will only come in if invited.

The painting is about anyone's life. Jesus wants to come to us. He wants to be our friend. He would like to share his life with us and for us to share with him. But he will not come uninvited. Jesus waits until we ask him to share in what we are doing. Jesus waits to help us and be our friend, but he will only do that if invited. Do you invite Jesus into your life and your home? It is good to say each day, 'Come, Lord Jesus' and to quietly enjoy the fact that Jesus is with you.

Activity

Play 'Jacob and Rachel'. Blindfolds are needed for two people who become Jacob and Rachel. Once blindfolded, Jacob must shout, 'Rachel', and Rachel must reply, 'Jacob.' By his constant calling and Rachel's replying, Jacob should be able to find Rachel. It can be decided from the start if Rachel wants Jacob to find her or if she wants to keep on the move and avoid him. The rest can enjoy the fun before having a turn.

Prayer

O come to my heart, Lord Jesus,
there is room in my heart for you.
Amen.

Song

Seek ye first the kingdom of God

TORCHES

Aim

To show we have to be alert for the coming of Jesus and to invite him into our homes and lives.

Teaching

Have the following four paragraphs read out by someone acting as policeman.

> Julie was complaining about the loss of her mobile. She had a habit of leaving it on the seat beside her on the bus. When asked when it disappeared her reply was, 'Never noticed'.

> Jim had gone into the house to get a book. He left his keys in the car. When he returned the car was gone. When asked if he had seen anyone in the street he replied, 'Never noticed'.

> Helen nipped out to the shops and left the flat door open. Later that day she discovered her laptop was missing. When asked when it had gone she could only say, 'Never noticed'.

> A neighbourhood watch has been created in the area. People are watchful and alert and crime has dropped considerably. It pays to be on the lookout.

Jesus describes his coming like that of a thief in the night. He comes quietly, without a lot of sound. He comes unnoticed by many people. Jesus asks us to be ready for his coming just like those waiting for their master to come home. For we may not notice but Jesus comes to each of us.

The door of an eastern house was barred from the inside. No one could get in at night unless the person inside let him or her in. Jesus is pictured coming and knocking. Now this is where Jesus is different from the thief. The thief breaks in to steal. Jesus stands outside and knocks. The thief comes uninvited. Jesus waits to be asked in. Jesus does not force himself into our lives but waits for us to invite him. He comes to us constantly each day and yet we can ignore him if we choose.

As Christians we need to give some time each day to prayer and to actually invite Jesus into our lives and homes. The danger is we are often not alert to his coming and so ignore him. Let us promise to give some attention to Jesus each day.

Activity

Play 'Thief'. Everyone sits in a circle. One person is blindfolded and sits in the centre. There is a bunch of keys in front of the blindfolded person. One from the group is chosen as thief. She sneaks up and steals the keys and goes back to her place. The blindfold is taken off. Everyone sits with their hands behind their back and tries to look guilty. The thief must occasionally rattle the keys. The person in the middle tries to guess who has the keys. He can have three guesses. If correct, the person with the keys goes into the centre. If he is wrong, he stays in the middle after getting the keys and begins again.

Prayer

Come, my Lord, my light, my way.
Come into my life today and each day.
Come to me and be my friend.
Stay with me through each day's end.
Amen.

Song

The God of Abraham praise

Proper 15

Sunday between 14 and 20 August inclusive

Aim

To show we need to be active in our faith and that we need to practise.

Preparation

Have photographs of athletes and, if possible, details of their training schedules. You can show musicians and a note saying how they practise every day. Have a PE outfit near the altar or pulpit.

Opening activity

Have two children race down the church. Let the younger one be able to outrun the older one. Give the older one two heavy and awkward bags to run with. Ask the older one why they were so slow. Encourage them to express the frustration at being handicapped by these heavy bags.

Opening prayer

Lord God, open our eyes to your presence
and our hearts to your love.
In the journey of life
let us never lose sight of Jesus
and his saving power,
that in our daily routine
we may know he is always there.
Amen.

Opening song

God of grace and God of glory

Readings

Isaiah 5:1-7 or Jeremiah 23:23-29
Psalm 80:1, 2, 8-19 or Psalm 82
Hebrews 11:29–12:2
Luke 12:49-56

Thought for the day

Picture a large crowd of people in some great amphitheatre or football stadium. Every seat is taken so that the crowd can watch what is going on. Look closely and you will see the saints, men and women who have given their lives in the service of God. There are holy people who dedicated themselves to prayer. There are martyrs who died for the faith, crowds of men and women who proclaimed the gospel and witnessed to the power of God. All are watching the arena and the race that is taking place.

It is an important race, for much of what they lived and died for is at stake. The one sitting at the end of the track is the King. He also watches, for his kingdom is in some ways dependent on these runners. If the runners do not give themselves and dedicate themselves to the race, then the kingdom could be lost to the earth. The spectators know that if the runners do not win, much of what they have laboured for will have been in vain. This is a terribly important race.

Now look at the runners. You should recognise them for you are among them. It is we who are in the arena: we are fighting to win. It is a battle for our eternal soul, and more: it is the only way the kingdom can be established on earth. The saints depend on us for their work not to be lost. We are called to witness and to proclaim the gospel. Christ and the saints rely on you: 'They would not, apart from us, be made perfect.'

We need to realise that the battle for the world and to win it for God goes on, and it is now our turn. The good advice from Hebrews is to 'look to Jesus' who has already won the battle. In him, though we lose round after round, victory is assured as he has triumphed over evil.

Question time

Are we aware that the forwarding of our faith is dependent on each of us and our witness?

Do you see that you have a part to play in the mission and outreach of the Church?

Illustration

There were two brothers. Both were runners. One was very good and won most races when he was small. He always used to beat his brother. Because he could run well, he decided he did not need to train. It was more fun playing computer games and going out with his friends. He thought practising was a waste of time. The other brother knew that he had to improve his style. He practised often. He practised sprinting and long-distance running. He did exercises to increase his breathing powers and his physical ability. He was seen on the track most nights. His brother said he was wasting his time. By the time they were in their teens, the brother who had been the best now lagged far behind. He was paying the price for not practising and keeping his eyes on what he could do. His brother was now winning competitions and all sorts of prizes. If asked how he became a better runner, he said, 'By a lot of practice and by being willing to dedicate myself to the job.'

Intercessions

Blessed are you, Lord our God,
for you have called us to share
in the inheritance of your saints in light.
You give us strength and support for our journey.
Let us look to you
who are the Lord and Creator of all.
Blessed are you, Father, Son and Holy Spirit.

O Lord our God, among the many distractions
and temptations of the world

keep our eyes and our hearts fixed on you.
As you have called us,
make us worthy of our calling,
that we may be the people you want us to be.
We pray for all who are seeking
to share in the outreach of your love
and in the proclaiming of the gospel.
We pray today for those who publish Bibles
and make them available in different languages.

Silence

Holy and Strong One,
help us to keep our eyes fixed on you.

We remember today
all who are involved in commerce and trade.
May they seek justice and fairness in all their dealings.
We ask your blessing
upon all involved in the leisure industry.
We pray for all who are training as athletes
or who are dedicating themselves
to some form of daily routine and discipline.

Silence

Holy and Strong One,
help us to keep our eyes fixed on you.

We give thanks for our homes and loved ones
and for all who have shared their vision of life with us.
We pray for families and individuals
who seem to have lost their way
and who feel life has no meaning or purpose.

Silence

Holy and Strong One,
help us to keep our eyes fixed on you.

We remember before you
all who are exhausted or world-weary.
We pray for those who have lost sight
of where they belong or where they are going.
We pray for all lonely and marginalised people.
We ask your blessing
upon all who are ill and suffering at this time.

Silence

Holy and Strong One,
help us to keep our eyes fixed on you.

Lord, we look to you for life and life eternal.
We pray for our friends and loved ones departed
and ask that they may share with your saints
in glory everlasting.

Silence

Merciful Father,
**accept these prayers
for the sake of your Son,
our Saviour Jesus Christ.
Amen.**

Memory verse

Let us run with perseverance the race that is set before us, looking to Jesus, the pioneer and perfecter of our faith.
Hebrews 12:2

Suggested music

Fight the good fight
Be thou my vision
Rejoice in God's saints

CANDLES

Aim

To know that God loves us and wants us to love him.

Teaching

In the beginning God decided to make a beautiful world out of his love. He made light, he made the sun, the moon and the stars and he loved them.

God made water. He made rain, streams, rivers, seas and he loved them.

God made the dry land, hills and valleys, mountains and flat ground and he loved them.

God made all the things that grow on the earth. He made the trees, the grass, the fruit and corn and he loved them. (Encourage the children to name one thing that God made and that he loved. For example, 'God made flowers and he loved them.')

God then made all sorts of animals. He made things that fly in the air. What do you call them? Yes they are birds. Can you tell me the name of a bird? God made them and God loves them all.

God made all the things that live in the waters and the sea. Can you tell me the names of any of them? God made them and God loves them all.

Then God made the creatures that live on the land and he loved them all. Can you tell me the name of your favourite animal? God made it and God loves it.

Now God wanted to make something special that he could love and that would love him. Who knows what that is? It is people. God made people. God made them out of his love and wanted them to love him. God loves everybody on the earth and he wants everybody to love him. (Have each of the children stand up and say their Christian name and that God loves them. For example: 'I am Jane and God loves me.' Once all the children have done this, get them to say, 'We love you, God.')

Activity

Play 'Musical statues'. At each stop tell the children the animal they have to be when the music starts again. Once the music stops, anyone who moves is out. Remind the children that God loves all the animals and all of us too.

Prayer

Thank you, God,
for making me
and loving me.
Help me to love you always.
Amen.

Song

There are hundreds of sparrows

Prayer

God, I thank you for your love
and that you are always with me.
Jesus, help me to know you are always with me
and that I can talk to you about all I am doing.
I know you want to keep me safe
and in your peace.
Amen.

Song

When a knight won his spurs

LAMPS

Aim

To show we have to be regular in our prayers and in remembering that Jesus is with us.

Teaching

Start the session with the activity.

Talk together of how much harder a race is when you have to carry a heavy load. Racers seek to wear light clothing and not to carry much body weight. To keep fit and to be good in the race, it is necessary to train. Lots of runners train every day. In the same way, people who play the piano or another musical instrument practise regularly. (See if any of the children go to music classes and talk about their training.) Anyone who trains or practises has to give up other things.

If we are to be good at our prayers, we need to practise in the same way. We have to set aside some time each day to talk with God. If we do not have a special time each day, it is likely we will forget our prayers. We will do other things and they will prevent us from saying our prayers. So we have to learn to have a bit of time every day when we speak to God. We have to remind ourselves every day that Jesus is with us and that he loves us. This sounds very easy but I know it is quite hard, so we must discipline ourselves like people who are training for a race. (Ask the children when they say their prayers and how often. It may be good to suggest that they have a fixed place and time for prayers. With small children their bedroom and at bedtime is often good.)

Let us all promise that we will say our prayers every day and remember that Jesus is with us.

Activity

Have a team race where the runner has to lift two heavy carrier bags and run with them. (You can always put a few old books in the bag.) Once they have run the course they hand over to the next one to run in the same way.

TORCHES

Aim

To look to Jesus and his power.

Teaching

When you first learn to drive a car you are tempted to look down at the pedals and at the gears. The instructor will say, 'Keep your eyes on the road.' Looking down hinders your progress and can make your driving dangerous. The writer of the letter to the Hebrews gives much the same advice to learners of Christianity (get someone to find it in the Bible and then read Hebrews 12:1, 2): look outwards; look to Jesus; do not be downcast.

In many sports when you learn to play the advice given is 'keep your eyes on the ball'. To ignore this advice and to let your attention stray can mean that you fail to achieve what you had hoped to.

When people first learn to dance with a partner there is a great temptation to look down at their feet – as if they don't trust them. As long as you look down your posture is bowed and your movements hindered. You need to look up and towards where you are going. (Get someone else to read Hebrews 12:1, 2.)

It is much the same when people learn rock climbing. Good advice is look where you are going. Look up, not down.

As a runner in a race does not watch his feet but has his eyes fixed on the finishing line, so we are asked to look to Jesus.

The writer sees life as a race where all the holy men and women of the past are looking on. We are running the race. They are now dependent on us. Two thousand years of Christianity is now dependent on us. We must not lose sight of Jesus in our daily living and in what we are doing. We should seek to bring others to see him and to know he is our goal. In athletics new records are being made as people extend themselves more and more. This comes only with discipline and dedication. We are called to keep our sights on Jesus and we will need to show discipline and dedication in doing it.

Activity

Play a game of blow football. You can use straws and a table tennis ball for this. Point out that if there were no goals to aim at, there could be no scoring.

Prayer

Thanks be to you, O Lord Jesus Christ,
for all the benefits which you have won for us;
for all the pains and insults you have borne for us.

O merciful Redeemer, Friend and Brother,
may I know you more clearly,
love you more dearly,
and follow you more nearly,
day by day.

Richard of Chichester (1197–1253)

Song

Lord of all power, I give you my will

Proper 16

Sunday between 21 and 27 August inclusive

Aim

To show that coming to Jesus gives us a glorious freedom.

Preparation

At the back of the church have a display about the prison service and the work of prison chaplains. You may be able to get a prison visitor or chaplain to speak to the congregation.

Opening activity

Have one person come in bent over and walking with a stick. Let her hobble down the aisle and suddenly stand up straight saying:

Amazing grace, how sweet the sound
that saved a wretch like me.
I once was lost but now am found,
(she casts her stick away)
was bound but now I am free.
(she skips back to her seat)

A second person strides down the aisle and comes to the front. He is followed by two children with a bandage. As soon as he starts to talk, the children wrap him in the bandage from knees up to his shoulders. The man says:

Well, I'll be bound.
You are not to come for healing on the Sabbath.
You are not to work on the Sabbath.
Rules are more important than people.
Break the rules and we will kick you out.
Well, I'll be bound.

(He hobbles back to his seat where a kind neighbour will unloose him.)

Opening prayer

O Lord our God, in your love
you loose us from our sins
and from all that would hinder us
in leading a full life.
Help us to rejoice in the glorious freedom
of the children of God.
Amen.

Opening song

Praise, my soul, the King of heaven

Readings

Jeremiah 1:4-10 or Isaiah 58:9b-14
Psalm 71:1-6 or Psalm 103:1-8
Hebrews 12:18-29
Luke 13:10-17

Thought for the day

I would like you to look at two people today and compare them. One is a woman who is terribly bent and the other is a man who is very unbending.

The woman has a curvature of the spine. It sounds like some crippling form of arthritis. We are told she has suffered this way for 18 years – definitely a chronic illness. Every movement is difficult and she needs a stick to walk with. It would be so easy for her to fall over. Yet she still made the effort and came to the synagogue on the Sabbath. Her suffering made her look in towards herself. This is often the danger of illness: it makes us inward-looking.

The man was the leader of the synagogue, an upright citizen, a man of good standing and rather unbending. He did not suffer fools gladly and he was quick to point out when people did wrong. He made sure that people kept the rules of their faith and did not stray. He was a law-abiding citizen and we need such as him – except that he was so unbending.

Jesus was in the synagogue where the man was the leader. Jesus was teaching in the synagogue on the Sabbath. Sadly this is the last time we hear of Jesus in the synagogue on the Sabbath. No doubt the leader was listening to Jesus and trying to take in what he said. Then the woman arrived. Jesus saw her struggling and as she came near he invited her to come closer. Jesus said, 'Woman, you are set free from your ailment.' Then Jesus laid his hands upon her back and she was able to stand up straight. She was able to look upwards and outwards. Jesus had given her a new vision of life. Jesus had freed her from being in a locked position. The woman was thrilled and immediately began praising God; the God in whom she trusted.

You would think everyone else would be thrilled. The leader of the synagogue was not pleased; in fact, he was indignant. He was annoyed because Jesus had healed the woman on the Sabbath. It was a day of rest when no one should work and Jesus had done work by healing this woman. The man could not bend: the law is the law. He kept saying to the crowd, 'There are six days on which work ought to be done; come on those days and be cured, and not on the Sabbath day.' He looked like a free man but he had become bound with a narrow outlook on what God requires. He was caught up in law rather than love. Such an attitude often binds people fast.

In life it is easy to become bound by rules and regulations or to hide behind them. People get stuck in routines, in watching television, in sport, in front of the computer – and all out of habit. We often think we have no time and it is because we have bound ourselves to certain patterns. It is easy to trap ourselves and lose the freedom that God wants us to have. Let Jesus touch your life. Come to him for he invites you. Come close and spend time with him. Break your routine and make space in your life for God – let him set you free.

Question time

Are we too unbending in our attitudes? Is our church?

How can our lives express the glorious freedom of the children of God?

Illustration

Robert was in prison for repeatedly breaking the law. He was a violent person. Taking drugs fuelled his violence. He was an addict – and that made him a prisoner as much as being in jail. He was not a likeable character and had few friends. Whilst in jail he went regularly to a rehabilitation unit to cure him of his dependence on drugs. Slowly he was freed from the habit. Whilst this was going on he had a regular visit from the prison chaplain. At first Robert rejected him and refused to listen but then he accepted a Bible. One day when he was reading St Luke the tears began to flow. When the chaplain came later Robert showed him the story of the crippled woman and said, 'Jesus has done the same for me. He has set me free.'

Intercessions

Blessed are you, Lord our God,
for you sent your Son
to set us free from sin and death.
You offer us the glorious liberty of the children of God.
Help us to reveal your love and your freedom
in the way we live and deal with each other.
Blessed are you Father, Son and Holy Spirit.

We give thanks for all who have found newness of life
and the power to start again in Christ Jesus.
We ask that our church may be welcoming
and friendly to newcomers
and invite them to share in our fellowship.
We pray for the work of prison and hospital chaplains.
We ask your blessing
upon all that are seeking to be faithful to your word,
especially any who are being persecuted
for their faith.

Silence

Lord, forgive our sins
and heal our infirmities.

We give thanks for all works of renewal and restoration.
We pray for reconciliation units
and for all who seek to bring peace
to families, communities or to the world.
We pray for those who work
in the rehabilitation of drug abusers or prisoners.
We ask your blessing
upon all who work for freedom and justice
in our world.

Silence

Lord, forgive our sins
and heal our infirmities.

We give thanks for the community to which we belong
and for all who maintain its well-being.
We pray for local councils
and organisations that help to enhance our world.
We ask your blessing upon our families and friends.

Silence

Lord, forgive our sins
and heal our infirmities.

We pray for all who have lost their freedom
through tyranny or war.
We remember all political prisoners
and all who are in refugee camps.
We pray for all who are prisoners
due to vice or drugs.
We ask your blessing upon all who suffer
from a physical or mental handicap.
We pray for all who are housebound or in hospital.

Silence

Lord, forgive our sins
and heal our infirmities.

We rejoice in the fellowship of all your saints.
We commend ourselves
and our loved ones departed
to your love
and look forward to the freedom
of your eternal kingdom.

Silence

Merciful Father,
accept these prayers
for the sake of your Son,
our Saviour Jesus Christ.
Amen.

Memory verse

He forgives all your sin and heals all your infirmities; he redeems your life from the grave and crowns you with mercy and loving kindness.
Psalm 103:3, 4

Suggested music

Be still and know that I am God
Lord, today your voice is calling
Bless the Lord, my soul (Taizé)

CANDLES

Aim

To tell the story of the woman with the bent back.

Teaching

Begin by asking the children about remembering to say their prayers and see who has kept last week's promise. Encourage any who have not succeeded to try to do better.

Once Jesus was in the synagogue (explain how this is the church of the Jews) and it was the Sabbath day. The Sabbath is the main day for Jews to go to church. Do you know which day it is? The day we go is a Sunday because that is the day Jesus rose again. The Sabbath is a Saturday, which is the last day of the week. They had the Sabbath as their holy day because in the story of

God making the world, he took six days to make the world and rested on day number seven. Let us count on our fingers from Sunday to Saturday. The Sabbath is Saturday and it is meant to be a day of rest. On that day people were not meant to work, or to cook or to go on a journey. Everyone was to have a rest day.

Jesus was in the synagogue on the Sabbath day when a woman came in. She came very slowly because she could not stand up straight. She was bent and had to walk with the help of sticks. She had suffered from this trouble for a long time, 18 years. (Let us count to 18.) She could not hurry and could not stand up straight. Jesus called out to her, 'Woman, you are healed.' From that moment she was able to stand up straight. Her bent back was made well again. She was very happy.

But there was one man who was not happy. He was the leader of the synagogue and he was annoyed. He said that Jesus had worked on the Sabbath. And he started to tell people not to come for healing on the Sabbath – they could come on any of the other days.

Everyone else seemed very happy with what Jesus had done.

Activity

Get the children to act out the story. This could be repeated two or three times so that most could have a part. Have as actors Jesus, the crippled woman and the leader of the synagogue. The rest can be a delighted crowd who cheer when the crippled woman stands up straight. Use the play as a means for the children to grasp the events of the story.

Prayer

Lord Jesus, thank you
for healing the woman with the bent back.
We know that you care
for all who are ill or in trouble.
Amen.

Song

Jesus' hands were kind hands

LAMPS

Aim

To understand the story of the healing of the woman who was crippled.

Teaching

Start the lesson with the activity.

What made running difficult? If your back was bent like that, how hard would it be to do things? What things could you not do if your back was bent like that? The word we use for people with troubles like this is 'handicapped'. They suffer from a handicap – that is, something that prevents them from living life to the full. Sometimes a handicap can make a person feel like a prisoner.

Discover if the group understand what the words 'synagogue' and 'Sabbath' mean. Explain that on the Sabbath no one was supposed to work – this would include the cooking of meals.

One Sabbath, Jesus was teaching in the synagogue. As he did this, a woman who could not stand up straight came in. Her back was bent and she had to walk with sticks. The poor woman had been like this for 18 years. In some ways she had got used to it but it stopped her doing many things. Jesus noticed her struggling to come forward. Jesus called out to her, 'Woman, you are set free from your illness.' Then he went over to her and put his hands on her back. She straightened up and was able to walk like anyone else. She was really very happy and started to give thanks to God for her healing.

Others who were there were also pleased that she had been freed from this trouble. But there was one man who was not pleased. He was the leader of the synagogue. He was angry that Jesus had broken the Sabbath rules. Jesus had done some work on the Sabbath. (Discuss what work this was.)

Jesus was sad that the man could not see that it was good to heal the woman. He tried to explain to him that when creatures need caring for, we do it. Should we not in the same way show care for any who suffer? (Have the young people talk about this.)

Activity

Have a team race where each runner has to put their hands on their knees and keep them there during the time they are running. Anyone who fails to do this must start again. Explain this will be a slow race because if they go too fast they will fall over.

Prayer

God, we give you thanks for your love
and for your healing power.
Help us to care for any who are struggling
or suffering.
We ask this in the name of Jesus.
Amen.

Song

Oh! Oh! Oh! How good is the Lord

TORCHES

Aim

To see how Jesus comes to set us free from being bound.

Teaching

Begin by discussing how the Sabbath is a day of rest. Explain that it was to remind the Jews of how God created the world in six days and rested on the seventh. So they kept the seventh day as day of worship and rest. (Have someone read Deuteronomy 5:12-15.) The Sabbath celebrated the day of rest and God-given freedom. For many it was very important because it was a day when they were not forced to work – slaves and animals were given a rest day each week. Such a day was of great benefit to many and needed protecting.

One Sabbath, Jesus was teaching in the synagogue. While he was there he saw a woman approaching very slowly. She had a bent back and could not stand up straight. She had suffered from this handicap for 18 years. In all that time her movements had been restricted and there were many things she was not able to do. Yet she struggled to get to her place of worship. Jesus saw her and called to her, saying, 'Woman, you are set free from your ailment.' He then went to her and placed his hands on her back. He probably took her by the hands and helped her to stand upright. The woman was cured of her trouble, set free from her handicap. She was delighted and began to praise God for this wonderful healing.

Others were delighted for her. But the leader of the synagogue was not pleased. Jesus had done work on the Sabbath by healing this woman. He could have done it on another day. He started to say to the people, 'There are six days in which work ought to be done; come on those days and be cured, and not on the Sabbath day.'

Jesus spoke out against this and said the people who were objecting were hypocrites. Jesus asked if they unloosed their ox or donkey and led them to water on the Sabbath, knowing that they were doing so. 'Then should not this daughter of Abraham, whom Satan has bound for 18 long years, be set free from this bondage on the Sabbath day?'

Activity
Discuss how Jesus was able to free the bound and bent woman but unable to set free the law-bound upright man. Get three people to act this story out. End with two more binding the leader of the synagogue.

Prayer
Lord Jesus, you have come to set us free
from the captivity of sin and death.
Keeping rules alone cannot save us –
and in rule-keeping we all fail.
Set us free to worship you
and to enjoy life to the full.
Amen.

Song
Amazing grace

Proper 17

Sunday between 28 August and 3 September inclusive

Aim

To think about how God sends his messengers to us and comes himself in others.

Preparation

Have a few cuttings from magazines of beggars, refugees, outcasts and rejected people. Display them in the entrance and then get a few people to walk around the church with some of these as someone reads the following poem from the Hebrides.

Opening activity

I saw a stranger yestere'en.
I put food in the eating place,
Drink in the drinking place,
Music in the listening place,
And in the sacred name of the Triune
He blessed myself and my house,
My cattle and my dear ones,
And the lark said in her song,
'Often, often, often
Goes the Christ in a stranger's guise.'

Opening prayer

Holy God, you come to us in others;
you send your angels in the form of others
to tell us of you and your love.
Make us sensitive to the other who comes to us,
that in them we may welcome you.
Amen.

Opening song

Ye holy angels bright

Readings

Jeremiah 2:4-13 or Ecclesiasticus 10:12-18
Psalm 81:1, 10-16 or Psalm 112
Hebrews 13:1-8, 15, 16
Luke 14:1, 7-14

Thought for the day

Hospitality was a very important issue in the Holy Land. When Abraham gave hospitality to the three visitors, he was not only visited by men but also, through them, by angels and by God (see Genesis 18:1-16).

The sun was at its height and, as is the custom of the desert wanderer, Abraham rested in the shade of the tent door. As he looked out over a land of shimmering heat, three shapes came towards him out of nowhere. As they got closer, Abraham saw that it was three men. He offered them hospitality and provided them with good food. They were ordinary men who were dusty and hungry – but they had a message for him. They were messengers of God – angels. In this visit Abraham and Sarah his wife encountered God and angels.

It is with this story in mind that the writer to the Hebrews (13:2) said, 'Do not neglect to show hospitality to strangers, for by doing that some have entertained angels without knowing it.' What a marvellous disguise: God comes to us through other people. God sends his angels to us through the people we meet.

Throughout his ministry Jesus was dependent on the hospitality of many people and you often hear of him sharing a meal. On this occasion he was in the house of a leading Pharisee and he noticed how guests were trying to find the best seats where they would be seen. These people were full of themselves. They invited each other to parties because they would be invited back. There was little room for a stranger and certainly no room for the poor and the outcasts. Yet if God comes to us in the other person, they would miss out on meeting God by their own exclusiveness and narrowness. God often comes in the most unexpected way and person. Do not neglect to show hospitality to strangers, for by doing that some have entertained angels without knowing it.

Who knows when God seeks to come closer to us? Who can tell which messenger of God is sent to bring us peace, joy or love, or to open our eyes to his presence? Often God seeks to change our life through an encounter with another. It is only when we are sensitive to others that we can be truly open to the great Other who is God. God sends his messengers regularly to us. Remember the word 'angel' means messenger. By being insensitive to others we often fail to hear the angel of God.

Question time

In a world where we often turn our backs on others, is it surprising we do not understand they can be angels of God?

Is there an experience in your life when you can say, 'Yes, that was an angel of God'?

Illustration

Sadhu Sundar Singh was the first Christian Sadhu. He suffered great persecution in his missionary travels in Tibet. Often the sadhu declared that he was rescued by angels. The following tells of such an occasion.

The sadhu was arrested for entering Tibet and preaching Christianity. The Lama condemned him to death. The sadhu was thrown into a deep dry well. The well was covered and locked. The key was kept around the Lama's waist. The remains of others who had met a similar fate were in the well. The sadhu could not see this because there was no light. For two days and nights he was without food and water. On the third day, when he was exhausted, a wonderful thing happened. He heard the key turn in the lock and the cover was removed. A rope was lowered. It had a loop in the end for the sadhu to put his foot in. He was then gently lifted to the surface. He helped his rescuer to put the cover back on the well. When the sadhu turned to thank him, he was gone. It was only some time later, when the sadhu resumed his preaching, that the Lama discovered what had happened. Yet the key was still fastened at his waist.

I am sure it was a caring human being that rescued the sadhu. Just as I am sure and agree with Sadhu Sundar Singh that it was an angel of God that set him free.

Intercessions

Blessed are you, Lord our God,
for you come to us in love and with blessings.
You are to be met in our encounters
with friends and with strangers
as you are in all and about all.
Blessed are you, Father, Son and Holy Spirit.

We give thanks
that you have called us to know you
and ask that we may always serve you faithfully.
Bless all who are called to preach the word
and administer the sacraments.
We pray for all who are training for ministry
and all who are seeking to understand
and proclaim your word.

Silence

Lord God Almighty,
hear us and help us.

We pray for peace in our world
and ask your blessing upon all who are seeking
to end hostilities.
We remember all who work
for the reconciliation of relationships
in nations and in individuals.
We pray for the United Nations
and all peacekeeping forces.

Silence

Lord God Almighty,
hear us and help us.

We give thanks
for all who have shared their lives with us.
We pray for our homes and our loved ones.
We remember all who spend their lives
in caring for others
and we ask your blessing
upon all who work as hoteliers
and who offer accommodation to others.
We pray for the work of Shelter.

Silence

Lord God Almighty,
hear us and help us.

We give thanks for all who work in the healing ministry
and we pray for doctors and nurses.
We ask your blessing
upon ambulance workers and upon carers.
We remember before you
friends and loved ones who are ill.
We pray especially for those
who are no longer able to look after themselves.

Silence

Lord God Almighty,
hear us and help us.

We give thanks for the gift of eternal life
and ask that your blessing be upon our friends
and loved ones who are departed from us.
May we come to share with them,
in the fellowship of all your saints,
in your glory that is for ever.

Silence

Merciful Father,
**accept these prayers
for the sake of your Son,
our Saviour Jesus Christ.
Amen.**

Memory verse

Do not neglect to show hospitality to strangers, for by doing that some have entertained angels without knowing it.
Hebrews 13:2

Suggested music

Brother, sister, let me serve you
A new commandment
Angel-voices ever singing

CANDLES

Aim

To show how a messenger of God, an angel, visited Cuthbert.

Teaching

Once there was a boy who enjoyed being outside but suddenly he found playing difficult. He was called Cuthbert (let us say his name together).

Cuthbert was only 8 years old when he could no longer go out to play because his knee was so swollen and painful. He loved playing games and running but he could not even walk properly because of his knee. He was often carried out of the house and sat against a wall in the sunlight. As he sat outside he wished someone would come and make him well again.

One day while he was sitting alone he saw a stranger coming towards him. He was riding a beautiful horse and he was dressed in white. When the stranger came near, Cuthbert said he was sorry that he could not stand to welcome him because his leg was so painful and swollen. The stranger got off his horse and looked at Cuthbert's knee. Then he said, 'When you go inside get those who are looking after you to put some wheat flour in a bag and then boil it in milk. Then, while it is still hot, spread this on your knee. If you do this, soon your knee will be strong and healthy again.'

Then the stranger got back on his horse and rode off. Cuthbert watched as he disappeared in the distance. After the stranger had gone, Cuthbert had someone put the hot wheat flour on his knee. Soon his knee got better and he was able to go out again. Cuthbert then decided he was visited not just by a man but also by an angel of God. From that day Cuthbert always believed that God had sent a messenger to tell him how to get better.

The word the Bible sometimes uses for messenger is 'angel'. Once it could mean any messenger. So if your mummy sent you to give a message to someone in the garden or another room and you did it, she could call you an angel because angel means messenger.

Later only God's messengers were called angels. Cuthbert was sure God wanted him to get better and that God had sent an angel on horseback to make him well.

Activity

Play 'Traffic lights'. Get the children to understand that 'Red' means stop and 'Green' means go. At 'Red' they must stop and not move at all. At 'Green' they run around. When you say, 'Amber', they have to continue what they are doing. If they are running at 'Amber', they must keep moving; if they have stopped, they must not move.

At the end of the game you can say how Cuthbert was stopped moving around by an illness until God sent an angel to help him to move again.

Prayer

God, we thank you for doctors and nurses
and all who help to make people well again.
Amen.

Song

Wide, wide as the ocean

LAMPS

Aim

To get the children to think about Cuthbert and a visit by an angel.

Teaching

Cuthbert was a monk and spent a lot of his time in prayer. For while he lived at Ripon in Yorkshire and there he was given the job of looking after guests who came to the monastery. Often people came begging for food or for help. Cuthbert spent a lot of time looking after other people.

Early one December morning Cuthbert went into the guesthouse and there was a young man sitting waiting for him. The man looked as if he had been on a long journey and now he was seeking food and shelter. The poor man looked frozen. Cuthbert removed the man's ragged footwear and began to rub his feet to bring warmth back into them. Cuthbert then persuaded the

man to wait until the bread was cooked for that day: he promised it would not be long. Cuthbert then went to say his morning prayers.

When he returned he saw the man and said, 'The bread should be ready now. I will go and get you a nice warm loaf.' Cuthbert was only away a short while but when he returned the man had gone. Cuthbert hurried to the door, but there were no footprints to be seen in the snow. Cuthbert looked around the other side of the building and there was one set of tracks but they were his own. Cuthbert came back to the guest room and was aware of a beautiful smell. Looking around he saw three lovely pure white loaves. Was this a gift from his visitor? He had been ready to feed the stranger but ended up with a gift of food himself. Cuthbert thought of some words from the Bible in the Letter to the Hebrews (get a child to find the words and read them): 'Do not neglect to show hospitality to strangers, for by doing that some have entertained angels without knowing it' (Hebrews 13:2). Cuthbert would always remember this strange visitor and how he had suddenly disappeared, and he would always tell people that an angel had visited him.

Activity

Have everyone sit in a circle. Tell them they are unable to move unless the visitor touches them. The one chosen as the visitor wanders around the outside of the circle and then touches someone. They must jump up and run around the circle in one direction and the visitor in the other direction. The aim is to fill the gap in the circle. The one left becomes the visitor.

Prayer

Lord God, help us to care for the hungry
and the lonely of our world.
Through our church
may we look after them as much as we can.
Amen.

Song

God is love: his the care

TORCHES

Aim

To see how we are called to share in the generosity and hospitality of God.

Teaching

Jesus has been invited to the house of a leader of the Pharisees to have a meal on the Sabbath. It sounds as if he was not particularly welcome and as if they were maybe setting a trap for him (see Luke 14:1-6).

Jesus notices how the guests sought out places of honour. No doubt there were a good few there who thought that they were important. Jesus warns them about having inflated ideas of themselves. It would seem it was the sort of group that invited each other in turns – a 'You ask me and I will ask you back' situation. It is amazing how people seem to want a reward for what they do. Many may have been asked to keep up good relationships and to curry favour. People do not change much.

Jesus suggests something that must have sounded as odd to them as it still does to us. 'When you give a luncheon or a dinner, do not invite your friends or your brothers or your relatives or rich neighbours, in case they invite you in return, and you would be repaid. But when you give a banquet, invite the poor, the crippled, the lame and the blind' (14:12, 13).

Let us discuss what this means. Jesus is talking about generosity, about giving without rewards. He is talking about attitudes towards others and our motives for giving.

Some are invited out of a sense of duty – in the same way we pay our taxes. We do it because we feel we have to. There is no love or generosity in this. Remember the Pharisee did invite Jesus.

Some give because it is a good investment – even a bribe. They give to get in return. People are invited who will give a large present or do something in return. In the same way some think they can build up a good credit account with God, they do things because they think they earn a reward. God gives freely to all who turn to him.

Others show their superiority by giving – 'Well, I am richer than you; I can throw a more splendid party. I am rich, you are poor: you depend on me.' Too much missionary giving seem to have this attitude.

We should give because we appreciate what we have and know we are meant to share. Think of the old saying, 'He who has bread is responsible for him who has none.' God gives because he loves (John 3:16). And God loves a cheerful giver (1 Corinthians 9:7).

Activity

Make a circle and exclude a person. They have to try and find an opening but the group closes its ranks and turns its back. Often the opposite side of the circle will show an opening until the person runs around and finds the ranks closed. Then welcome the person. Let all face round in a circle and let the excluded person now enter and be welcomed by going round the circle shaking hands with everyone.

Prayer

Lord God, as you give freely to us,
teach us to be free in our giving.
We pray that the resources of the world
may not be hoarded or squandered
but used for the benefit of all.
Amen.

Song

When I needed a neighbour

Proper 18

Aim

To know we are in the hands of God and that he can restore and renew us.

Preparation

Show pictures of broken-down places, communities and people. Have the text written large: 'Just like clay in the potter's hand, so are you in my hand.' If possible, show a potter working with some clay.

Opening activity

Reader 1 We live in a throwaway society. Everything is counted as disposable.

Reader 2 We have throwaway bottles and throwaway nappies. It is good to throw some things away!

Reader 3 But we need to learn to treasure things. There are things worth repairing and restoring.

Reader 4 Relationships with each other – and with God – belong to this group. God does not dispose of us but renews and restores us. Put yourself in the hand of God.

Opening prayer

Into your hand we commend ourselves, O God,
for you have redeemed us, O God of truth.
At all times we trust in you, God Almighty,
because we know that you love us
and have the power to renew us.
Amen.

Opening song

One more step along the world I go

Readings

Jeremiah 18:1-11 or Deuteronomy 30:15-20
Psalm 139:1-6, 13-18 or Psalm 1
Philemon 1-21
Luke 14:25-33

Thought for the day

Jeremiah saw that there was trouble ahead for Israel. The Babylonian Empire was rising and Judah was caught between Babylon and Egypt. The old securities were being broken down and there was danger that even Jerusalem could face a breakdown. As he watched a potter at work, he realised that in the hands of God such breaking down of the nation could lead to its renewal.

Enter the potter's shop with Jeremiah. Have a look around. In one corner is a large pile of unused clay. It looks like useless lumps, dirty and not very attractive. But we know that in the hands of the potter it can be transformed to something of worth and beauty.

Look at the lovely things that the potter has made from the clay. If he can do that with clay, think what the Creator could do with you – even if you feel like an unattractive, useless lump!

Look at the potter: he seems to be in difficulty with a lump of clay. It is not going as it ought to go. For a while the clay seemed all right but then it got a wobble. The potter seeks to form it but it still has a wobble. The potter stops the wheel. What will he do? He could throw the clay away and get another piece. Instead, he takes it in his hands and gently shapes it, or, if necessary, he breaks it down so that it can be rebuilt. A piece may be broken down two or three times but the potter is patient, and as long as the clay remains malleable, he will make something of it.

It is easy to see how we are like the clay. How many men and women have been counted worthless or have felt like a useless lump until they have put themselves in the hands of God? God says to us, 'Just like clay in the potter's hand, so are you in my hand' (Jeremiah 18:6).

We need to see that breakdowns are not always bad – they can be warnings that we are going in the wrong direction. Nervous breakdowns, business breakdowns, health breakdowns can change in the hands of God. In his hands a breakdown can become a breakthrough into a better life and a stronger life. All things are possible with God if we do not become too set in our ways.

We fear death as the ultimate breakdown. You can see it in a new way. The potter is taking you in his hands, planning to give you a new and more glorious shape and purpose. Remember God's words: 'Just like clay in the potter's hand, so are you in my hand.'

Question time

Do we regularly commit ourselves into the hand of God?

Can you see that some so-called breakdowns are an opportunity for, if not a call to, a breakthrough?

Illustration

In the saleroom there was a violin. It looked battered and neglected. One or two people picked it up and pulled the bow across it but the sound did not seem good. The auctioneer wondered why it was in the sale. He thought it should have been scrapped. It looked a sorry sight. Most people never even noticed it. It would probably sell for a few pence.

Just before the sale an elderly gentleman came in. As the seats were filling up he went over to the violin and retuned it. Then he started to play. The music was wonderful. The capabilities of the instrument were amazing. In the master's hand, the poor-looking instrument was transformed.

When the violin was put up for auction the bidding was brisk. People realised it was a precious instrument and that it had great potential. It is amazing how things can be changed in the hands of the master.

Intercessions

Blessed are you, Lord our God,
for you have created us and redeemed us;
you are ever ready to refresh and restore us.
By you we are renewed
and given the power to start again.
Blessed are you, Father, Son and Holy Spirit,
One God for ever and ever.

We come as a Church broken by divisions and factions
and seek your healing.
Sometimes we have broken faith
with you and with each other.
We pray for all who strive to bring unity to the Church.
We ask your blessing upon churches
that are struggling to survive
or are faced with violent opposition.

Silence

Lord, we come to you:
only you can make us whole.

We ask that we may be used as instruments of peace.
We ask your blessing
upon all who seek to heal the troubles
between nations and peoples.
We pray for all agencies of reconciliation
and ask your blessing
upon the work of the United Nations.

Silence

Lord, we come to you:
only you can make us whole.

We give thanks for our homes and our loved ones.
We ask you to bless and protect them always.
We pray for families that are suffering
from broken relationships.
We pray for all those with broken hopes
and broken dreams.

Silence

Lord, we come to you:
only you can make us whole.

We give thanks that you are our strength and salvation.
We remember all who are broken by illness.
We pray for those struggling with a nervous breakdown
and all who feel their lives are on the edge of collapse.
We ask your blessing upon all
who are no longer able to care for themselves.

Silence

Lord, we come to you:
only you can make us whole.

Lord, you make all things new
and you are the giver of life and life eternal.
We ask you to bless our loved ones departed from us,
that they may rejoice in the fullness of life.
We commend them and ourselves to your unfailing love.

Silence

Merciful Father,
**accept these prayers
for the sake of your Son,
our Saviour Jesus Christ.
Amen.**

Memory verse

Just like clay in the potter's hand, so are you in my hand.
Jeremiah 18:6

Suggested music

Take me, Lord, use my life
Spirit of the living God (Iverson)
Have faith in God, my heart

CANDLES

Aim

To show that in the hands of God all can be made new.

Teaching

Start with the activity.

Who knows what a potter does? He makes things with clay.

Once there was a man of God called Jeremiah. (Let us say his name together.) Jeremiah was sad because his country and its big city Jerusalem were in danger from war. Men would come and seek to break down the walls of the city and take people away as prisoners. Jeremiah was very sad because he felt things were breaking down. God said to him, 'Go to the potter's house and watch him.'

When Jeremiah went to see the potter, he was busy with some clay on a wheel. (If possible, show a picture of a potter at his wheel. If you cannot do this, it may take some explaining.) The potter was trying to make something beautiful. He had the clay in his hands as it turned and it was going very well. Then suddenly it began to wobble. (Let us all stand up and wobble.) If it kept wobbling, it would fall to bits. The potter tried to put it right but it was getting worse. So he stopped the wheel and took the clay off it. He broke it down again into a lump. Do you think he threw it away? No, he took it in his hands and reshaped it, just like we did with the playdough. After kneading the clay with his hands the potter put it back on the wheel. Now he made a beautiful pot from the clay.

Jeremiah now knew why God asked him to go to the potter's. Just as the potter can take a piece of clay and make it into something beautiful, so God can take us and make us into something beautiful. God cares for us and keeps us in his powerful hands. God does not want us to be useless but to be beautiful for him. God made us and God can help us to be what he wants us to be. Listen to what God said to Jeremiah: 'Just like clay in the potter's hand, so are you in my hand.'

Activity

With playdough or plasticine ask the children to make various things. Start off with something simple like s snake. Ask them to make a flower and a giraffe. Finally ask them to make something they really like. While they are doing this, go round and ask them what they are making. They might like to come out and show their handiwork.

Prayer

God, you made the whole world and us.
Help us to care for all the things you have made because we know you care for us.
Amen.

Song

There are hundreds of sparrows

LAMPS

Aim

To show that we are in God's hand and in his renewing love.

Teaching

Jeremiah lived at a time when his country was in danger of being broken down by a mighty army. It looked as if the country could come to an end. But Jeremiah believed that God cared for his people and wondered how it could be so. Jeremiah was feeling rather sad. Then he heard God saying to him, 'Go to the potter's house and watch him.'

Jeremiah wondered what he would see. What do you think he would see in a potter's workshop? He would see all sorts of useful and beautiful pots, pots for drinking and pots for storing, big pots and little pots. He would see a pile of clay ready to be used. He would see the wheel that the potter put clay on to turn it.

Jeremiah watched the potter put a piece of clay on the wheel and then pedal with his foot for the wheel to turn. In the potter's careful hands the clay began to take an interesting shape. Then suddenly it began to wobble. It looked as if it would fly off the wheel. A crack appeared in the clay. The potter stopped the wheel and broke down what he was making. Jeremiah watched and wondered if he would throw the clay away. But the potter took the clay and gently kneaded it in his hands. He put a little water on it. Then he put it back on the wheel and started to turn. This time it was making a good shape and soon it would be a beautiful pot. The potter had broken the clay down so that he could reuse it. Jeremiah then realised that this was why God had sent him to the potter. He heard God telling him, 'Just like clay in the potter's hand, so are you in my hand.'

Jeremiah began to understand that God cared for him and for his people. Even when things are breaking down it is not the end because we are in the hands of God. God can take us and remake us. Even when things are breaking down God can rebuild them and renew them. Whatever happens, we are still in the hands of God and God still loves us. When Jeremiah left the potter he felt happy because he had learnt that God cares for his people and is able to make them into something wonderful. Say after me: '"Just like clay in the potter's hand, so are you in my hand," says God.'

Activity

Give the group some playdough and ask them to take it in their hands and to make whatever they want to. Ask them to make their favourite animal. Then ask them to make their favourite person. Tell them God loves each of them: he loves every one. Get them to say, '"Just like clay in the potter's hand, so are you in my hand," says God.'

Prayer

God, you are strong and loving.
We are always in your hands.
You hold on to us even when we are in trouble and you still love us.
You help us to begin again and to do new things.
Thank you, God.
Amen.

Song

God, you can use me

TORCHES

Aim

To show that following Jesus is not an easy option but a costly one.

Teaching

Imagine you have been chosen by an explorer to go on an adventurous journey. If you want to go, it will mean leaving home. He wants you to raise some of the money that is needed for the adventure, so it is quite costly. Then he warns you of the dangers of the wild animals and the steep mountains. If you are willing to face this, then you can come. It is not easy, it is not cheap, but it is a great adventure.

Jesus had crowds following him but not all of them were disciples or would follow him for long. Jesus was on his way to Jerusalem. He was on his way to the cross and yet many in the crowd thought he was on his way to be king of an earthly empire.

Jesus turned to the crowd and said some hard things because he knew what lay ahead. (Read Luke 14:25-27.) They are not words to make him popular. They are about commitment. If we are truly to give ourselves to Jesus, he wants us to love him with our greatest love: to love him more than life itself. He does not want us to hate our loved ones but he wants us to be able to leave them and follow him. The disciples are a good example of this. If we cannot leave our home and our possessions, we will find it hard to commit ourselves to Jesus.

Commitment is costly and it takes planning. Jesus gives two examples. (Read Luke 14:28-33.) The man was probably building a tower in the vineyard. But he ran out of resources to finish it because he had not counted the cost. Maybe Jesus thought of the Temple at Jerusalem which Herod the Great had started to build in 19 BC. Most of the work was done in ten years but it took until AD 64 until it was finished. By AD 70, just six years after its completion, it was left in ruins.

Many of Jesus' followers had the idea of chasing out the Roman army: they had a mind to do battle. They had no idea how powerful the Roman army was; they did not know how large the Empire was. Jesus was advising them to learn to live in peace – costly though this is.

We have to decide to become real disciples of Jesus and not just followers. We have to be willing to face the costs. If we are unwilling, it shows we do not love Jesus or see him as God.

Activity

Have the group look at how they commit themselves to Jesus. Let them look at their churchgoing, prayer, Bible reading, their relationship with the world and with individuals. See if they could make a few simple rules to keep.

Prayer

Dearest Lord, teach me to be generous;
teach me to serve you as you deserve;
to give and not to count the cost,
to fight and not to heed the wounds,
to toil and not to seek for rest,
to labour and not to seek a reward,
save that of knowing that I do your will.

Ignatius Loyola (1491–1556)

Song

Take my life, and let it be

Proper 19

Sunday between 11 and 17 September inclusive

Aim

To show how God delights in all who turn to him.

Preparation

Make some sheep to hide. Either draw a sheep and photocopy it 12 times or make them out of wool. Then hide them around the church. Make some relatively easy to find and others a little harder.

You could use chocolate money instead of sheep.

Opening activity

Invite the children to hunt for the lost sheep or coins. When they discover any, they have to shout, 'I have found one', and everyone then cheers and claps.

Opening prayer

Lord God, you love us with an everlasting love
and you search for us
when we have forgotten you
or when we have strayed from your way.
Lord, we come:
we turn to you,
that we may share in your joy and in your love.
Amen.

Opening song

The King of love my shepherd is

Readings

Jeremiah 4:1-12, 22-28 or Exodus 32:7-14
Psalm 14 or Psalm 51:1-11
1 Timothy 1:12-17
Luke 15:1-10

Thought for the day

The Pharisees believed that they could keep themselves and their religion pure by being exclusive and keeping out anyone they thought of as a sinner. Tax collectors were among the wrong sort of people because they worked for the Romans and had regular contact with Gentiles.

The Pharisees complained that Jesus welcomed sinners and ate with them. No doubt they included Matthew the tax collector and Mary Magdalene among the sinners. The Pharisees were lucky not to need repentance! There is nothing as off-putting as the self-righteous to those thinking of becoming believers.

Jesus does not suggest that there is no need for repentance. He wants people to see that law-keeping by itself is not enough. Negative goodness, where we say what we do not do, is not enough. What do we *do* to fulfil God's ways and reflect his love in our lives?

In Luke 15 Jesus tells three stories in a row about returning to God and the delight it gives. In each story there is a party. God, the Father, delights in those who return. But in the last story the sad thing is he cannot get the self-righteous son to come in and join them.

The sheep gets lost through its own foolishness. How often we err and stray like lost sheep. The sheep followed its appetite, looking for new food and for fresh pastures. It never noticed it had entered a danger zone and could perish. The shepherd missed it and sought it out. He sought to bring it back. When he found it he was delighted. Because it was exhausted he carried it. When he got home he threw a party to express his joy. The party could have cost more than the sheep but the sheep was more valuable to him than money.

The coin got lost through no fault of its own. It was a victim of circumstance. That which fastened it to others had broken loose. It just dropped off without a sound. But the woman missed it because it was of great sentimental value to her. She loved it and it was an expression of her love. She would search for it until she could find it. When she found it she was delighted. What a joy! She threw a party and invited friends to share in her joy. The party might have cost more than the face value of the coin, but the coin could not be measured by its face value because it was precious to her.

Jesus says that every time a sinner repents there is delight and joy in heaven. Every time someone turns to God the angels rejoice. We need to know that God seeks us and waits for us to turn to him. God delights in our love and offers us his love and life eternal. He will not force any of this on us but he will seek us and our love for ever. He could replace us but does not because we are precious in his eyes.

Question time

Do you take time to turn to God each day?

God's love is not exclusive but we can exclude ourselves. How can we make sure we abide in him and he in us?

Illustration

A letter from God

When you awoke, I was there, waiting upon you. I wanted to share in your love.

At breakfast you listened to the radio and rushed your breakfast. You had no time to speak to me. I waited but you did not turn to me.

Though you travelled by rail you spent your time on your laptop and reading the news. You did not once give me a thought. And I waited for you to turn to me.

During your work there were lots of small gaps. There was more time at lunch. But you did other things and had no time for me. Yet I waited for you to turn to me.

At the end of the day you watched the television and played a game. For a while you dozed before you had your last drink of the day. And I waited for you to turn to me.

Now, I thought, you will have time – just before you go to sleep. Instead, you read until you were tired. You worried about tomorrow and at last fell asleep.

I will surround you with my love this night. I will wait for you tomorrow and if you do not remember I will be there the day after. I will wait until you turn to me.

All my love, God.

Intercessions

Blessed are you, Lord God,
for you have called us out of darkness
into your glorious light.
You seek out and save all who are lost
and willing to turn to you.
You are our God and Saviour.
Blessed are you, Father, Son and Holy Spirit.

Lord, we thank you for those
who made us welcome within the Church.
May we always be open to all who are seeking you
and turning away from their sin.
We ask your blessing upon all who are pastors
and who care for your people.
We pray for all who are involved
in the ministry of reconciliation and of healing.

Silence

Lord, we turn to you:
hear us and help us.

We pray for all who have been led astray
and are caught up in crime or vice.
We ask your blessing upon all who are addicted to drugs.
We remember all who do not know of you
or love you.
We ask you to guide and strengthen
all who work for the good of others
and all who seek to bring peace to our world.

Silence

Lord, we turn to you:
hear us and help us.

We give thanks
for those who have taught us the Good News
and for all who have shared their faith with us.
Lord, help us to turn to you each day
and to be faithful to you.
We ask your blessing upon all who are suffering
from broken relationships and broken homes.
We pray for our families and our friends.

Silence

Lord, we turn to you:
hear us and help us.

God, we remember all who feel lost
and whose life seems to have no purpose.
We remember all who feel they have failed in life
and all who despair at this time.
May they know your love and your saving power.
We pray for all who are ill at home or in hospital
and those who are caring for them.

Silence

Lord, we turn to you:
hear us and help us.

We rejoice that you care for each of us
and you delight in our coming to you.
We ask your blessing upon all our loved ones
who are departed this life.
May they delight in you and in your love.
We commend ourselves and all of creation
to your loving care.

Silence

Merciful Father,
**accept these prayers
for the sake of your Son,
our Saviour Jesus Christ.
Amen.**

Memory verse

There is joy in the presence of the angels of God over one sinner who repents.
Luke 15:10

Suggested music

Hark, my soul, it is the Lord
Souls of men! Why will ye scatter?
The Lord's my shepherd

CANDLES

Aim

To show that God loves us and seeks us out.

Teaching

Have you ever been lost? It is awful when you get lost and do not know where to go. Who found you when you were lost? Mummy and Daddy would get very upset if they thought you were lost and they would not give up looking until they had found you. When they found you they would hug you and be very happy. (Send two children out of the room and let a third hide. The two have to find the hidden one and then give them a big hug.)

Jesus told the story about a lost sheep. The shepherd had a hundred sheep. That is a lot of sheep but he knew each one of them and loved them. One day he noticed that one of the sheep was lost. He knew that it had wandered off and it could get itself into trouble. When it got dark, it would be alone and it might fall down a cliff. When the sun was burning hot in the daytime, it might not be able to find shelter or water and it could die. Even a wild animal – a wolf or a lion – could come and catch it and eat it. The sheep could easily die. So the shepherd went out to look for it. He looked in the dark places and in the dangerous places, he searched the dry places and the hot places, and for a long time he could not find it. The shepherd was sorry that it had wandered so far away and he was worried in case it got into trouble. At last he heard its call. It was in a very dark place but the shepherd went down into the dark and he lifted the sheep up. He put it on his shoulders and carried it safely home.

When he got home he called to his friends and neighbours, 'Come and rejoice with me.' They came running and asked what had made him so happy. 'I had lost a sheep and I searched for it and now I have found it. I am so happy.'

'That is wonderful,' said his friends, 'for it would have been awful if it had been lost and was harmed.' Everyone was so happy together because the sheep had been found.

When Jesus had finished telling the story, he said some of us were like the lost sheep. We had wandered away from God. We did not speak to him or let him know we loved him. All the time God loves us. God loves us so much that he looks for us every day and wants us to come to him. Jesus said that all of heaven is glad when we turn to God and give him our love.

Activity

Show a sheep cut-out from paper, like those used in the opening activity. Tell them they are all to close their eyes and turn away while you hide the sheep. Now they have to guess where it is. The one who guesses or the one who finds it after a search is allowed to hide it for the others to find. Every time the sheep is found, encourage them all to cheer and clap their hands.

Prayer

God, we are happy
because we know that you love us
and do not want us to be lost.
You want us to come
and give our love to you every day.
God, we love you.
Amen.

Song

Loving Shepherd of thy sheep

LAMPS

Aim

To understand that God seeks for us and delights in our coming to him.

Teaching

Let me tell you about the inside of an eastern house. It is very dark inside. The light comes in through one tiny circular window and there are many shadows. There are no floorboards or carpets; the floor is just the earth and it is covered with dry grass or straw. There is hardly any furniture. If you dropped something small on the floor, it would be very hard to find.

When she was preparing for marriage a woman who lived in the Holy Land saved as much as she could. She saved silver or gold coins and made something like a necklace out of them. All the coins were threaded together. Then they were worn on her head. (Show a band with ten coins on it and show how it was worn on

the head.) The richer the woman was, the more coins her headdress had on it. The lady in our story was probably not very rich because she had only ten silver coins. Each coin was worth a full day's pay but she probably had to save a long time to get to ten. When she was married the woman took them off at night and wore them again in the morning. She often looked at them and loved each coin for it was a sign of her marriage – just like a wedding ring is. Each coin was linked to the next by a silver chain.

One morning when she picked up the headdress to put it on she noticed that one silver coin was missing. She had lost one somewhere. She had to think hard. She was sure she had it when she came in the evening. The coin must have worked loose from the rest and slipped off the silver chain. She would have to look for it. But it would not be easy because it must be somewhere in the straw. She searched for a long time but could not find it. She looked in every corner. She decided to sweep the straw out of the house and look at it every time she brushed some more out. She had to do it carefully and it took her ages. She was very sad because she thought she might have lost it for ever. Then suddenly she saw it glinting among the straw. She picked it up and kissed it. Then she called to her neighbours, 'Come and celebrate with me for I have found the coin that I had lost.' Her neighbours came and they were all happy that the coin was found.

Jesus said some of us are rather like the coin. We get separated from the God who loves us and we forget that he is always with us. But God searches for us and wants us to turn to him in our prayers. Let us not be like a lost coin but turn to God each day.

Activity

Follow the instructions on the activity sheet to make an eastern headdress.

Prayer

Lord God, we know that you love us
and like us to talk to you.
We will remember you each day
and turn to you in our prayers.
Amen.

Song

I have a friend

TORCHES

Aim

To show that though we forget God, God seeks us to turn again to him: God is a God revealed through love rather than law.

Teaching

The God of much of the Old Testament is seen as a God of the Law. If you break the law you are in trouble with

God. Sometimes the 'righteous' actually prayed that all those that broke the law should be destroyed. The attitude of the Pharisees was often like this. Their God was a severe God.

Jesus also believed that we are to keep God's laws. We are not to go against the will of God. But God is a loving God, a forgiving God. God may not like our sin or our law-breaking but he does not cease to love us and waits for us to turn to him. When we stray, God seeks to bring us back to him. Jesus showed the love of God in the way he dealt with those who were counted as sinners and outcasts.

St Luke, chapter 15, is sometimes called the 'Lost and Found' or the 'Gospel in miniature'. Each story seeks to illustrate how God cares for the lost. The lost sheep (Luke 15:4-7) just wandered away without thought, like so many people who just stray away without meaning to.

The lost coin (Luke 15:8-10) became unattached, no longer joined to the rest. It was not through any fault of its own. Maybe it slowly worked loose and sadly no one noticed.

In each case the owner sought for it until he or she found it. Then they threw a party. Jesus tells us there is as much joy in heaven over a sinner that repents; there is much joy when God finds a lost person.

The prodigal son in Luke 15:11-32 deliberately left home. It was an act of his own free will. He chose to go elsewhere and party and live a 'free' life. One day he realised where he was truly loved and who cared for him, and he decided to turn around and return to his father. All the time the Father had waited patiently for this day. He would not force his son but he longed for his return. Then there was a party to celebrate the return of the lost. It was a pity the 'righteous' son was not able to join in the joy.

Activity

Look at the words from the poem. 'Hound of Heaven' by Francis Thompson:

> I fled Him, down the nights and down the days;
> I fled Him, down the arches of the years;
> I fled Him, down the labyrinthine ways
> Of my own mind; and in the mist of tears
> I hid from Him, and under running laughter.
> Up vistaed hopes I sped;
> And shot, precipitated,
> Adown Titanic glooms of chasmèd fears,
> From those strong Feet that followed, followed after.
> But with unhurrying chase,
> And unperturbèd pace,
> Deliberate speed, majestic instancy,
> They beat – and a Voice beat
> More instant than the Feet –
> 'All things betray thee, who betrayest Me.'

Prayer

Lord God, you forgive us
when we stray away from you
and you seek us with love.
Lord, we turn to you
and give our love to you this day.
Amen.

Song

Amazing grace

Proper 20

Sunday between 18 and 24 September inclusive

Aim

To see where our priorities lie and how we give our time to God.

Preparation

At the entrance have suggestions for making money, and offers from banks, building societies, credit cards and loan companies. Give the opening speakers Monopoly money to throw around.

Opening activity

Let each speaker throw a handful of Monopoly money as they speak.

Reader 1   Money, money, money.
Reader 2   We spend our lives getting it and spending it.
Reader 3   Gaining it and losing it.
Reader 1   Saving it and borrowing it.
Reader 2   Exchanging it for goods and exchanging goods for it.
Reader 3   People have died trying to keep it.

(*Let the three readers start picking it all up*)

Readers 1-3 Money, money, money.
Reader 4   Yet no one can take it with them. It is a small thing in comparison with life and life eternal.

Opening prayer

Lord God, you entrust this world to our care;
you give us stewardship over all your creation.
Help us to use the resources of the world
to the benefit of all
and to your praise and glory.
Amen.

Opening song

Guide me, O thou great Redeemer

Readings

Jeremiah 8:18–9:1 or Amos 8:4-7
Psalm 79:1-9 or Psalm 113
1 Timothy 2:1-7
Luke 16:1-13

Thought for the day

Today's story is a strange one in that it is about a rogue. To understand it, we need to know a little of the background. On one level it is obviously about possessions and our use of them, but beneath that there is something deeper.

Money often shows what we are like: mean or generous, shrewd or silly, to be trusted or not to be trusted. What we have gathered around us reveals the sort of person we are.

The Jews were forbidden to lend money at interest. They often got around this by lending in kind. Two common commodities for lending were wheat and oil. They were also ways of paying rent to the owner of the land. It could be that the steward had been lending his master's materials in kind and at extortionate rates. What he deducted from the bill was the interest, which had a lower rate on wheat than on oil. It would appear the interest rate on wheat was 25 per cent and on oil the rate was an extortionate rate of 50 per cent. If he reduced the bill, his master would not lose anything and his debtors would be delighted.

No doubt the unjust steward was trying to buy friendship in these actions. One way or another the steward had cooked the books and used for his own gain what was not really his. Yet he had assured for himself some sort of future. Not a silly man but a shrewd dealer.

Jesus sees us as stewards of God's world. We are not the owners. It is not ours to possess: we cannot keep it for ever. It is ours to use for the benefit of others and for the praise and glory of God. Yet, like the steward in the story, we tend to use most things to our own ends. We invest more time and energy in gaining and keeping than we ever do in thought about our spiritual life and our future. Most of us have chosen to serve the world and its ways first and God only second. If you doubt this, look at how much time you invest in work, in sport, in recreation and how much time you actually spend in prayer. It is amazing how many Christians never mature in their faith. They learn all sorts of complex things in life but remain unskilled and weak in their relationship with God.

The steward is called to account. We will all be called to account. Those who are found faithful and trustworthy in small things will be trusted to be responsible for greater things. If we have misdirected our worship to things of the earth and neglected the things of the spirit, we will have to account for this.

Question time

How do we act as stewards and not owners of the world? Do we know we need account to our God?

Do we take our spiritual growth and well-being seriously enough to invest time and energy in them?

Illustration

Richard became a junior in the sales department of a large firm when he left school. It was soon discovered he had a flair for sales. In time he became chief salesman, and at that stage he negotiated a percentage of each sale for himself. He was becoming well-off. He had a wonderful home, two expensive cars and a good deal of shares in the business. He was made head of the sales department and then a member of the board. All was wonderful and he was rich indeed. Yet something told him all was not right. One night, returning from a sales conference, he was involved in a serious accident and nearly lost his life. Whilst unconscious he said he was aware of some being in white saying, 'Pity he has not done so well in the things that matter. This man is still a child in spiritual things.' When he recovered he went back to work for a while. His 'visitation' bothered him. He started going to church with his wife and realised he had a lot to learn and that he was poor in spirit. But he gave himself to this as he did to his work. After a year he offered himself to train for the ministry. He was ordained and after two curacies, moved to Africa with his wife and family where they worked for a relief agency. When asked about his wealth, most of which he had given away, he would reply, 'I was never as rich as I am now.'

Intercessions

Blessed are you, Lord our God,
for you have given us a wonderful world to live in.
You have given us life and all that we need
and much to enjoy.
We give you thanks and praise
for the beauty and wonder of creation,
for all things come from you.
Blessed are you, Father, Son and Holy Spirit.

We give thanks for all who serve you faithfully
in their daily work,
for all who seek to reveal your glory.
We pray for all involved in leading worship
and in preaching the word.
We ask your blessing upon all
who are seeking to care for your creation
by working for the relief of others
or for the conservation of nature.
May we all show respect for what you have given us.

Silence

O God, our Saviour,
help us, for the glory of your name.

We ask your blessing upon Elizabeth our Queen,
upon all rulers and leaders.
We pray for our government
and all the governments of the world.
We remember the work of the United Nations.
May all who are in positions of power
use their office to the benefit of others
and the good of all.
We ask that the world may accept
the peace that you offer us,
that all may live in harmony and none be oppressed.

Silence

O God, our Saviour,
help us, for the glory of your name.

We rejoice in the love and protection we have received
through our homes and our loved ones.
We ask your blessing
upon all who are struggling with their relationships
or who suffer from poverty or violence.
We pray for families who have been separated
by illness or circumstance.

Silence

O God, our Saviour,
help us, for the glory of your name.

We give thanks for all who do medical research
and all who work for the health and well-being
of our world.
We ask your blessing upon the World Health Organisation.
We remember before you
all who are in pain or distress,
all who are ill at home or in hospital,
all who suffer from neglect or from loneliness.

Silence

O God, our Saviour,
help us, for the glory of your name.

We give thanks for the gift of life
and the promise of life eternal.
We rejoice in the fellowship of all your saints
and in the faithful departed.
We commend them and ourselves
to your unfailing love.

Silence

Merciful Father,
**accept these prayers
for the sake of your Son,
our Saviour Jesus Christ.
Amen.**

Memory verse

You cannot serve God and wealth.
Luke 16:13

Suggested music

Inspired by love and anger
Lord, we come to ask your healing
Stand up, stand up for Jesus
Lord, thy word abideth

CANDLES

Aim

To show that God wants us to love what he has given us and to care for it.

Teaching

Have you got a favourite toy? Tell me what it is. (Let the children spend some time talking about the things they love.) How would you feel if someone came along and threw it about or broke it? What if someone threw it away? I am sure you would go and seek for it and bring it back and hug it. Do you remember last week's story about the lost sheep? What did the shepherd do when he discovered it was lost? And when he brought it home he was so happy he had a party to celebrate. I am sure you would not like to lose anything you love.

Jesus told us that God loves each of us. He loves everyone – including you and me. Because God loves us he wants us to love each other and to care for each other. God does not like anyone to be hungry or poor. He wants those who have a lot to share with those who are in need. (Show some pictures of people helping each other.)

God did not just make *us*; he made the whole world and everything in it. Name one of your favourite animals. God loves all these animals because he made them. He wants us to look after the animals and the flowers and the trees. Name other things that you think God wants you to look after.

God likes us to care for the things he has made and to say 'Thank you' for all the wonderful things he has given us. Let us all say, 'Thank you, God, for . . .' (Get each child to say this in turn and add the name of something they love.)

Activity

Play 'Musical statues'. Ask the children to be a certain animal and to run around. When the music stops, they have to be absolutely still. In the stillness say, 'Thank you, God, for . . .', adding the name of the animal. Now tell them to be another animal. If you make it an elimination game, get the children who are out to join you in the 'Thank you'.

Prayer

Thank you, God, thank you.
You have given us a wonderful world
and lots of beautiful creatures.
Thank you for our homes and all our loved ones.
Thank you, God, thank you.
Amen.

Song

And God said the sun should shine

are not here just for our own benefit. We have to give account to the owner. It is God's world and he has trusted us with it. But he will want to know if we have looked after it and what is in it properly. He does not want us to waste or spoil his world. God trusts us, but can we be trusted? Do we spend any time giving our love and our care to God who gives us all?

Talk about how we can care for what God has given to us.

Activity

Play 'Who is in charge?' One person is sent out of the room, then someone else is put in charge of the group. The group has to do whatever the person in charge does. The person who comes back has to guess who is in charge. If the actions are quick enough, it is often hard to see who is in charge.

Prayer

Lord God, we thank you for the world
and all that is in it.
Teach us to care for it
and for all your creatures.
Let us not be responsible for the hurt
or spoiling of anything,
but let us help to make your world
a good place to live in.
Amen.

Song

When God made the garden of ceation

LAMPS

Aim

To explore the story of the unjust steward and the idea of trust.

Teaching

Today's story is about someone who was trusted to look after some farms and the people on them. He was expected to collect what the owner was due from each farm. But he cheated. He betrayed his master's trust. He charged more than he should have and was not giving the owner the proper share.

The owner realised something was wrong. He would check over the farms and see what he should have received. He told the steward – the person he trusted – that he was coming. Panic, panic! The steward knew he would be found out. So he went around trying to make things better so that his future might be safer. When the owner came, he found things had been sorted out and he was pleased that the steward had worked hard to get it sorted.

Jesus wants us to know we are all like the steward. God has given us a world to look after and care for. We

TORCHES

Aim

To look at the unjust manager and our own managing of the world.

Teaching

There was a rich man who had a manager. The rich man trusted him and gave him a good deal of land to look after. But the manager began to waste what he was given. In doing this he was cheating his boss. There was no doubt that one day he would be found out. Someone told the boss that the manager was wasting his goods.

The manager was called before the owner and asked what was going on. He had to give an account of his managing. He did not feel like having to work hard. He did not want to become a beggar. So he decided to go around the farms and put things right. He had been taking too much from the farmers, and if he put it right, they would be friendly towards him. He realised it would be better to have some friends that to try and have more money. So he changed how much each of them owed. The one that owed 100 containers of oil, he said, he need only give 50. The one that owed 100 containers of wheat, he said, need only pay 80. When he came, the owner praised the manager for making a wise move.

Jesus expressed his concern about people who were more concerned with making money than making friends; people who were too occupied in doing all sorts of things and not coming to God.

God has entrusted us with the care of his world. Whatever we have, we have received through him. God wants us to look after what he has given us and not to hoard it or squander it. Too many people are possessed by their possessions. Too many people think that the world is theirs and they are to keep as much as they can. Many of the world's resources are used by a tiny proportion of the population. One day – if not every day – God wants us to account for what we are doing. He wants us in all of this to give our love to him.

Get the group to discuss openly the issues raised by today's Gospel.

Activity
There is an opportunity on the activity sheet to continue to look at our stewardship and our need to give account to God.

Prayer
God, you are the Creator of all things.
You give us life and this world to live in.
Help us to use all to your glory
and to the benefit of your creation.
Let us not hoard or squander
but use what you have given us with love and care.
Amen.

Song
Oh, Lord, send us out

Proper 21

Aim

To encourage a greater sensitivity towards each other and to the poor.

Preparation

Obtain posters from relief agencies and organisations such as Shelter and The Children's Society.

Highlight the needs of the poor by displaying these around the church as well as in the entrance.

If possible, have a Fair Trade stall before or after church.

Opening activity

Have some of the posters around the readers.

Reader 1   We who are poor, do we not have eyes, mouths, stomachs, senses, passions?

Reader 2   If you deprive us of food, do we not starve?

Reader 3   If you injure us, do we not bleed?

Reader 1   We catch the same diseases as you. We need healing like you.

Reader 2   We need to be able to laugh and enjoy ourselves.

Reader 3   But if you ignore us, we will go away. We will curl up and die.

Reader 4   And the Christ says: As much as you did it or failed to do it to these, you did it to me.

Opening prayer

O God, you have given us the riches of your world.
You are a generous giver.
Help us to reflect your love and grace
in our dealings with all people
and with your creation,
and at all times to be sensitive to the needs of others.

Opening song

O God of Bethel, by whose hand

Readings

Jeremiah 32:1-3a, 6-15 or Amos 6:1a, 4-7
Psalm 91:1-6, 14-16 or Psalm 146
1 Timothy 6:6-19
Luke 16:19-31

Thought for the day

Today's parable arose from Jesus noticing those who loved money. Money is not evil but to give it our love is to misdirect our vision and our passion. It can turn our love away from God and from others. Today's parable is about insensitivity.

There are three scenes. *Scene 1* shows a rich man. He is clothed in purple and fine linen (same as the High Priest). His clothing probably costs about three years' pay of a labourer. The rich man is looking after himself. He dines sumptuously: he is a gourmet and loves exotic dishes. Jesus never tells us his name, though he is often called 'Dives', which is Latin for 'rich'. At his gate is a poor man covered in sores and he is hungry. He hoped for crumbs from the rich man's table. The rich man never seemed to notice him – well, there are a lot of poor people. Today this scene could be a family tucking into a good dinner whilst watching the starving of Africa or India on the television. (Does it not at least put you off your food?)

In *Scene 2* the poor man has died – well, he would, wouldn't he! Now he is with Abraham in heaven.

The rich man dies and is buried – he took nothing with him. The rich man was in Hades and was in torment. He looked up and saw Abraham and Lazarus far away. He issued a request and an order. He asked for mercy and that Lazarus should come with water and cool him. So he *had* noticed Lazarus; he even knew his name. The rich man is told it is not possible.

Scene 3 is like scene 2. The rich man thinks of his five brothers and asks that Lazarus be sent to warn them of what could happen to them. Abraham replies that they have Moses and the prophets and that they should listen to them.

The rich man suggests that if someone – Lazarus – goes to them from the dead, they would repent.

Abraham replies, 'If they do not listen to Moses and the prophets, neither will they be convinced even if someone rises from the dead.' And so the curtain closes.

There was no suggestion that the rich man was a wicked man or that he did not keep the outward observances of the church. But we do know he was insensitive to the needs of Lazarus. Jesus says: 'Truly I tell you, just as you did not do it to one of the least of these, you did not do it to me' (Matthew 25:45).

Question time

Are we sure that we are sensitive to the people around us and to the call of the poor?

How can we as a church witness to our concern for the needy of the neighbourhood or the world?

Illustration

I know a planet where there is a certain red-faced man. He has never smelled a flower; he has never looked at a star. He has never loved anyone. He never does anything in his life but add up figures. And all day long he says over and over, just like you, 'I am busy with matters of consequence,' and that makes him swell with pride. But he is not a man; he is a mushroom!

A what?

A mushroom.

(From *The Little Prince* by Antoine de Saint-Exupéry.)

His insensitivity made the man less than human.

Intercessions

Blessed are you, Lord our God,
for you have created us
and supplied all we need.
You have created a world
where there is enough for everyone's need
but not for everyone's greed.
Teach us to live graciously
as you are gracious to us.
Blessed are you, Father, Son and Holy Spirit.

God, we ask your blessing
upon your Church throughout the world,
that it may witness to your love and your saving power.
We remember especially
where the Church is reaching out
to the extremely poor and the outcasts of society.
We ask you to guide
all who stand against injustice and oppression.
May your Church work for the liberation
of all who are used as slave labour
or who are in refugee camps.

Silence

God, we trust in you:
hear us and help us.

We give thanks for all you have given us, O Lord.
We remember before you all who are suffering
through famine, war or poverty.
We pray for all who live in shanty towns
or in impoverished dwellings.
We bring before you
all who do not have proper medical care or education.

Silence

God, we trust in you:
hear us and help us.

As we give thanks for the comfort of our homes,
we remember all who have been made homeless.
We ask your blessing upon all who are orphaned
and have no one to care for them.
We ask your blessing upon all children
who have been taken into care.

Silence

God, we trust in you:
hear us and help us.

We give thanks for our health service
and for all who attend to our well-being.
We pray for those throughout our world
who are suffering from AIDS
or from other illnesses for which there is no cure.
We remember especially
families who have lost their income
through the adults of the house being ill.
We ask your blessing on friends and loved ones
who are suffering at this time.

Silence

God, we trust in you:
hear us and help us.

We give thanks for the faithful departed
and pray for our loved ones
who have entered into the fullness of life eternal.

We rejoice in the fellowship of all your saints
and pray that we may share with them
in your heavenly kingdom.

Silence

Merciful Father,
**accept these prayers
for the sake of your Son,
our Saviour Jesus Christ.
Amen.**

Memory verse

There is great gain in godliness combined with contentment; for we brought nothing into this world, so that we can take nothing out of it.
1 Timothy 6:6, 7

Suggested music

When I needed a neighbour
Bind us together, Lord
Be thou my vision

CANDLES

Aim

To be sensitive to the needs of others.

Teaching

Start with the activity and then talk about what makes someone rich and what makes others poor. Do they think the rich can help the poor?

This is the story of a very rich man and a very poor man. We do not know the name of the rich man but the poor man was called Lazarus (let us say his name together).

The rich man wore very expensive clothes. They cost more money than ordinary people had. He wore the colour purple because that was the most expensive. (Can you see any purple in the room?) The rich man had great big meals that cost lots of money and he ate lots every day. His house was large and beautiful and it had a big gate to stop anyone going too close to it.

At the gate sat a very poor man called . . .? Lazarus had only rags for clothes. Often he had no food at all except the scraps other people threw away. He was very hungry. Because he did not get enough food, his body had lots of sores on it. And the dogs came and licked his sores.

Every day the rich man came out of his gate but he never noticed Lazarus. He never helped him. He never gave him any food. In the end Lazarus died and went to heaven and was looked after by Abraham. Now Lazarus was happy and well looked after.

The rich man died. Guess how many of his treasures he took with him. None! He did not go to heaven but was stuck in a dark and hot place. A long way off he could see Lazarus and Abraham, and he shouted to Abraham. 'Abraham, send Lazarus to help me. Send Lazarus to bring me some water.' So he knew Lazarus and yet had never helped him. Abraham told him that Lazarus was not allowed to come to him. The rich man had had all the wonderful things in his lifetime and had not shared them. Now he would know what it was like. The rich man wished he had taken more notice of Lazarus when they were both alive on earth.

Activity

Cut out from magazines photographs of rich people. Have obvious ones and those that are not so obvious, such as people with a house or children at school.

Cut out photographs of the poor, the hungry and the homeless. Relief agency magazines have plenty of photographs.

Try and have enough photos for everyone to be able to pick a rich one and a poor one. Ask them to do this and then to say why a person is poor or rich. See who can notice the difference.

Prayer

God, you have given us lots of lovely things.
Teach us to share with those who have none.
Help us to be kind and generous with others.
Amen.

Song

God loves you

LAMPS

Aim

To understand the story of the rich man and Lazarus.

Teaching

All over the world there are people who are starving and have no one to help them. Sometimes people have to queue all day for a small bowl of rice to feed their family. Sometimes children search rubbish heaps and refuse bins for food. Often very rich people who have more than they need are near to these people, but they do nothing to help them; in fact, they have got so used to them that they do not even notice them.

Jesus told a story about a rich man and a poor man. The rich man wore the most expensive clothes. He ate the finest of foods and he ate lots every day. He lived in a big house that had a gateway to it. At his gate there was a poor man who sat there every day. This man was starving and his body was covered in sores. The dogs came and licked his sores. Often the rich man would pass that way but he never noticed Lazarus. He never gave him any food. He never gave him any help.

Lazarus died and went to heaven. The rich man also died but he did not go to heaven. He was in a place of shadows and it was very hot. He could see Lazarus a long way away with Abraham. The rich man shouted to Abraham for help and asked that Lazarus might be sent with water. So he did know about Lazarus but he had

done nothing to help him. He was told Lazarus could not come because there was a barrier between the two places and people could not cross from one place to another. Then he asked that Lazarus might be sent to warn his brothers what happens if you are greedy and do not notice the needs of others. Abraham replied that his brothers already knew this from their Scriptures, from the Law and the Prophets. (You might like to explain this further and give an instance of 'loving God and our neighbour'). He said if they did not listen to the Scriptures, they would not listen if someone went to them from the dead.

Jesus told this as a story to teach those who loved money more than people that they were wrong in ignoring people.

Activity

If possible, provide magazines for the children to find examples of rich and poor people. Guide them to show that nearly all the people in this country, including them, would be counted as rich. Have them read and act out the parable.

Prayer

God, there are lots of hungry and poor people
in our world.
Show us how to help them
and not to be greedy with what we have.
Let us learn to share and to care
as you care for us.
Amen.

Song

There are hundreds of sparrows

TORCHES

Aim

To show that we have to be sensitive to the needs of others.

Teaching

Do you know that the love of money can make people go blind and deaf? In the desire to have more money, people cease to see how they can help the troubled and they can no longer hear the cries of the poor. To protect their wealth they become insensitive to the suffering of others. In the making of wealth they can even cause the suffering of others. Cheap products in one country can mean poor wages in another country.

Jesus tells the story of the rich man and Lazarus. The rich man has the finest clothing that would cost more than most earned in three years. Purple was an expensive dye and so implied wealth. He ate sumptuously every day. He was obviously a gourmet. He enjoyed his wealth.

At his gate is Lazarus, dressed in rags, covered in sores, dying of hunger. The rich man does not move Lazarus. He does not notice Lazarus. He does not hear

Lazarus as he cries for food. He does not see need. He does not feel for the poor man. The rich man is insensitive.

Are you sensitive to the needs of the world? Do you realise that cheap goods are usually made by cheap labour? Some people work 12 hours a day for money that will hardly provide food for their families. Others are used like slaves to produce cheaper goods.

Large areas of the world do not have running water or proper sanitation. In many countries children live alone on the streets and feed off rubbish heaps.

In one place 60,000 patients a year visit a tin-roofed mud-built shack for treatment. Most of the rooms are only seven feet long by less than three feet wide, and yet here 60,000 patients receive treatment and more are turned away without help.

Are we aware that we are asked to love our neighbour as ourselves?

St Teresa of Avila said, 'We cannot know whether we love God, although there may be strong reasons for thinking so, but there can be no doubt whether we love our neighbour or not. Be sure that as in proportion you advance in brotherly love, you increase your love of God.'

Activity

Look at information about Fair Trade and about the needs of the world. The group may like to try and make an updated version of the parable of the rich man and Lazarus.

Prayer

Lord, make us channels of your love.
Where there is poverty, let us share of our riches.
Where there is sadness, let us bring joy.
Where there is despair, let us bring hope.
Where people have no food, let us share ours.
Where people are oppressed, let us proclaim liberty.
Amen.

Song

Brother, sister, let me serve you

Proper 22

Sunday between 2 and 8 October inclusive

Aim

To seek to deepen our relationship with God.

Preparation

Have pictures of relationships of love. Include lambs with their mothers and infants being hugged. Show also a few lonely people and beggars. Have a poster saying, 'We all need to know we are loved.'

Opening activity

A little scene of two people interviewing a joyful and confident person.

Reader 1 How do you do what you manage to do?
Reader 3 All you need is love.
Reader 2 Why are you not afraid of the dark?
Reader 3 All you need is love.
Reader 1 What gives you the peace and the joy that you have?
Reader 3 All you need is love.
Reader 2 How do you have such a trust in the future, whatever happens?
Reader 3 All you need is love.
Reader 1 I do not understand how you can have such confidence.
Reader 3 Confidence means faith. All you need is a loving relationship with God.

Opening prayer

O God, you love us with an everlasting love.
Nothing in all of creation
can separate us from your love.
Even when we forget you,
you do not forget or cease to love us.
In you is our hope and our strength,
through Jesus Christ our Lord.
Amen.

Opening song

New every morning is the love

Readings

Lamentations 1:1-6 or Habakkuk 1:1-4; 2:1-4
Lamentations 3:19-26 or Psalm 137 or Psalm 37:1-9
2 Timothy 1:1-14
Luke 17:5-10

Thought for the day

The disciples have decided that their faith is weak and ask the Lord, 'increase our faith'. Jesus realises that it is not a great faith they need but faith in a great God. We need to distinguish between faith and belief. When it comes to belief, we are told that even the devil believes with fear and trembling. Belief is to do with how our minds work and how we see the world. Many people believe in God but are weak in their faith. Faith is about a loving relationship with God, with a great and powerful God. Faith is not just to know with our mind but also to experience in our lives and in our heart. Faith is allowing God to work in us and through us; it is to experience his love for us. For this to happen we have to build up a relationship with God. Say with the writer of Lamentations, 'The steadfast love of the Lord never ceases, his mercies never come to an end; they are new every morning; great is your faithfulness' (Lamentations 3:22, 23).

You might like to express it in the words of the hymns 'New every morning is the love' or 'Great is thy faithfulness'. Both of these hymns express the abiding presence and love of God towards us.

It is interesting to note that a baby lamb or any small creature thrives better by being looked after by its mother than by humans. The relationship is as important as the food it needs. Many modern psychologists would say that a living relationship – love – is the power that enables people to thrive and to live to the full. A baby can go through hell if it feels it has been left on its own. Teenagers often get into trouble when they have been given everything they wanted but not love. When relationships break down it affects our whole way of living. This is as true about our relationship with God as our relationship with each other. Jesus suggests that faith, that relationship with God, is the most powerful thing in the world.

That which seems impossible by ourselves becomes possible with faith; faith can move mountains. Much that is not possible on our own becomes possible by our relationship with God. We have no power of ourselves to help ourselves.

We have to be clear about this relationship. We cannot put God into our debt. It is God who has made the world and us. We owe all to him. Our creation, salvation and preservation all are gifts from God. When we say we do something for God it is only our duty and our joy.

Were the whole realm of nature mine,
that were an offering far too small.
Love so amazing, so divine,
demands my soul, my life, my all.

It may be possible to meet the needs of the law but love knows that we can do more than the law asks. Our service to God is not to appease him or to repay a debt, though we are greatly indebted to him, but to give our love to him who gives his love to us. To say we are 'worthless' before him means we cannot demand but only ask of his love. And to live by that relationship is to live by faith.

Question time

Can you distinguish between belief and faith?

Do you and your church have a vital relationship with our living and loving God?

Illustration

George Matheson looked forward to a good life. He was studying for the ministry. He was preparing to marry the one he loved. Then he began to go blind. His world began to go into darkness. He lost many of his friends, and his loved one decided she could not cope with a blind man and left him. His world was shaken but not his relationship with God. George Matheson wrote the hymn 'O Love that will not let me go'. The second verse is 'O Light that follow'st all my way' and the third 'O joy that seekest me through pain'. George had faith in a great God. The final verse 'O Cross that liftest up my head' affirms not only his steadfast relationship but God's relationship with him. Now *that* is faith.

Intercessions

Blessed are you, Lord our God,
for you have created us out of your love
and for your love.
You have revealed your love in Jesus Christ
and by the sending of the Spirit.
Lord, as you love us,
we give our love to you.
Blessed are you, Father, Son and Holy Spirit.

Lord God our Father,
as we ask your blessing upon us,
may we and your whole Church
reveal your love to the world.
May people look upon us
and know we are Christians
by our love for you and for all people.
We ask you to guide all who are our pastors;
we pray for all bishops and clergy.
Give wisdom to all who seek to bring others
to a deeper faith in you.

Silence

Father, we trust in you:
hear us and help us.

We give thanks for all who give their lives
in the service of others.
We remember all leaders of people,
members of governments and all rulers.
We pray that they may keep
the interest and love of others in their hearts.
We ask your blessing upon all
who seek to bring peace and healing to our world.

Silence

Father, we trust in you:
hear us and help us.

We give thanks for all who have loved us
and given us confidence.
We ask your blessing upon our homes
and all who are dear to us.
We pray for the community in which we live.
We remember especially
any who may be in need of help or guidance
at this time.

Silence

Father, we trust in you:
hear us and help us.

We give thanks for all who work
for the healing and well-being of the world.
We pray for all who are suffering
from broken relationships and loneliness.
We ask your blessing upon any
who feel unloved and unwanted.
We remember before you all who are ill
and their loved ones as they share in their suffering.

Silence

Father, we trust in you:
hear us and help us.

We give thanks for your everlasting love
and for the gift of eternal life.
We ask your blessing upon our loved ones
who are departed from us.
May we all know we are one in you
and in your love.
We rejoice in the fellowship of all your saints
and commend this world and ourselves
to your unfailing love.

Silence

Merciful Father,
**accept these prayers
for the sake of your Son,
our Saviour Jesus Christ.
Amen.**

Memory verse

The steadfast love of the Lord never ceases, his mercies never come to an end; they are new every morning; great is your faithfulness.
Lamentations 3:22, 23

Suggested music

Great is thy faithfulness
Have faith in God, my heart
O Love that will not let me go

CANDLES

Aim

To show God is always with us and loves us.

Teaching

When you were very small and afraid of the dark, or did not like to be alone, who came to help? Mother, father, sister, brother, they would stay with you and perhaps hug you. God was also there and God loves us. (Get the children to talk about this and the next two paragraphs. Draw out the fact that people love them and care for them.)

When we hurt ourselves and we were crying, who usually came to help us? They would look at what we had done and help to make it better. God was also there and wanting to help us.

When we got lost or when we had been naughty, who still cared for us, looked for us and hugged us? Your family should always love you and help you to grow and be happy. God also loves us and would like us to love him.

Do you remember the story of the lost sheep? (If possible, get the children to tell it.) It is a story Jesus told to remind us that God cares for each of us and seeks us if we are lost or in trouble.

Let us take turns to say that God loves us and that we love God. (Get the children to stand up in turn and say: 'God loves . . . and . . .loves God.' This may be slow to start but the children soon like to get into the rhythm of it.)

Activity

Play 'Stuck in the mud'. Whenever a person is tagged, they have to stand in one spot with legs apart and hands outstretched and keep shouting, 'Help'. A player who has not been tagged can crawl between their legs and set them free. If the one who is 'it' is finding it hard to catch everyone, have two 'its' so that it is easier to catch more people.

Prayer

God, you love us and are always with us.
You are ready to help us
and make us strong.
God, we give our love to you.
Amen.

Song

Father God, I know you love me so

LAMPS

Aim

To know that God is with us and seeks to care for us.

Teaching

God seeks to be our friend and our helper. When we are lost, God seeks us. Can you remember the story about the lost coin? Who can tell the story, including what Jesus said about joy in heaven?

It is very easy to forget God and not to say our prayers. For this reason it is necessary to know some easy prayers that remind us of God. This prayer we are going to learn today is called 'The Prayer of Seven Directions'. This is a prayer that has been used by people for hundreds of years. It is easy to remember and it tells us God is all around us.

(*Point forwards*) Direction one is 'God before us'; the next one is its opposite: 'God behind us.' The third direction is 'God on our right' (*hold your right arm out-stretched*) and the fourth – what do you think that is? – (*hold out your left arm*) 'God on our left.' Then the fifth (*point upwards*) is 'God above us' and the next one (*point downwards*) is 'God beneath us'. How many have we

said? Six directions. Let us say them together, pointing in the directions as we say them:

God before us; God behind us.
God on our right; God on our left.
God beneath us; God above us.

That is six directions and they remind us that God is all around us. Who can guess the last direction? God is all around us and within us. That means God is always with us. We are never left alone and we are always loved.

Our last line reminds us that God is around us and within us. (Get each one to point to themselves.) Now let us put it all together.

Activity

God before us
 (*point forwards*);
God behind us
 (*point behind you*).
God on our right
 (*stretch our your right hand*);
God on our left
 (*stretch our your left hand*).
God beneath us
 (*point downwards*);
God above us
 (*point upwards*);
God around us
 (*stretch your right hand out and turn, making a circle*);
God within us
 (*end up by pointing at yourself*).

Repeat this and tell the children to show their parents when they get home how to pray the Prayer of Seven Directions.

Prayer

God, you are all around us.
You keep us in your love
and you protect us from evil.
Help us to remember that you never leave us
and you are always happy to hear our prayers.
Amen.

Song

Trust and obey (chorus from 'When we walk with the Lord')

TORCHES

Aim

To know that God cares for us and protects us.

Teaching

When the fishermen from the Hebridean Islands go out to sea, they are working in one of the most dangerous parts of the world (show on a map). There are strong currents and mighty waves; there is even a whirlpool.

They know that they risk death each time they go out. This is a prayer they used to pray (give out copies, so that they can be the crew):

Sea Prayer

Helmsman	Blest be the boat.
Crew	God the Father, bless her.
Helmsman	Blest be the boat.
Crew	God the Son, bless her.
Helmsman	Blest be the boat.
Crew	God the Spirit, bless her.
All	God the Father,
	God the Son,
	God the Spirit,
	bless the boat.
Helmsman	What can befall you
	and God the Father with you?
Crew	No harm can befall us.
Helmsman	What can befall you
	and God the Son with you?
Crew	No harm can befall us.
Helmsman	What can befall you
	and God the Spirit with you?
Crew	No harm can befall us.
All	God the Father,
	God the Son,
	God the Spirit,
	with us eternally.

This prayer reminded them that God is always present and cares. In the worst of storms God did not leave them. Even if a boat and crew were lost they knew that God would not let them perish but give them eternal life. The awareness of God and his love gave their lives a confidence and a meaning. We need to be able to turn to God as easily as they did.

Activity

Create a similar prayer for school or for travelling today. This is a good prayer for the commencement of any endeavour by a group as it affirms faith in God and in his love.

Prayer

God ever with us,
God before us; God behind us.
God on our right and on our left.
God beneath us; God above us.
God this day within and about us.

Song

Do not be afraid

Proper 23

Sunday between 9 and 15 October inclusive

Aim

To encourage an attitude of gratitude and to make people aware of the needs of lepers.

Preparation

Contact the Leprosy Mission, Goldhay Way, Orton Goldhay, Peterborough PE2 5GZ. Obtain posters for the entrance, pew leaflets and prayer guides. You might like to encourage a donation or a collection to help the Leprosy Mission.

Opening activity

Have ten children scattered around the church. Let them have bandages over their arms or head. Each should have a notice hung on them saying, 'Please do not touch' or 'Keep your distance'. If anyone comes too close, let them shout, 'Unclean!' At the beginning of the service let all be told to take their bandages off and go and show themselves to the priest. When he pronounces they are clean, all except one run back to their seats. One comes to the centre of the church and declares:

Lord, I give you thanks for your love.
Lord, I give you thanks for your healing.
Lord, I give you thanks for you are my Saviour.
Alleluia.

Opening prayer

Praise and thanks to you, Lord God,
for you forgive our sins and heal our infirmities.
You renew us and restore us.
For our life and for your love
we give you thanks and praise.
Amen.

Opening song

Give thanks with a grateful heart

Readings

Jeremiah 29:1, 4-7 or 2 Kings 5:1-3, 7-15
Psalm 66:1-12 or Psalm 111
2 Timothy 2:8-15
Luke 17:11-19

Thought for the day

Leprosy was one of the most feared diseases. If you caught leprosy, you were asked to leave your home, your community and to live out in a desert place. You may never see your loved ones again. Leprosy was like having a death sentence. It was believed that leprosy was infectious and, as a safety measure, lepers were asked to keep their distance and to live 'outside the camp' (Leviticus 13:45, 46).

Jesus was in a remote area between Galilee and Samaria. Here in this barren land lived a group of lepers brought together by their illness. Even here the lepers had heard of Jesus and his power. As required, they kept their distance. They call out, saying, 'Jesus, Master, have mercy on us.' Jesus simply tells them to go and show themselves to the priest and as they go, they are healed. Only one returns to Jesus. They all did what he asked but one returns praising God with a loud voice and prostrating himself at the feet of Jesus. Leprosy often affects the vocal cords, so the loud voice was a sign he was cured. That he could come so close to Jesus was also a sign of his cure.

It is worth noticing again that all the lepers did what they were asked. But in this life keeping the rules is not enough. There are some very severe rule-keepers. The Samaritan does more than keep the rules; he comes before Jesus in love and in gratitude. He appreciates what Jesus has done for him. He praises God for his well-being. Such thanksgiving is always a sign of joy. It is very hard to be sad and grateful at the same time. Today many people demand their rights by law but it gives them no joy. Thanksgiving and appreciation are what fill us with joy, and that is a sign of a greater healing than just the body.

We should promise this day that we will not take our friends, our life, our God for granted.

Question time

Do you give thanks each day for all that you have? (See Ephesians 5:20; Philippians 4:6.)

Are you in danger of taking for granted the people who have loved you and cared for you? How can you show your thanks?

Illustration

Richard was diagnosed as having a serious cancer. He had a brain tumour and if nothing was done, he would die. He was a rich and powerful man and also a man of prayer. The first thing his illness did was make him appreciate all that he had and what was precious to him. Amid the fear of what lay ahead a new joy had entered his life and his home. Each time he went for treatment he committed himself not only to the hospital team but also to the love of God. He was sure, whatever the outcome, he would not be separated from God and his care. Richard was fortunate and he was cured and given a good few years to live. He never ceased to show his appreciation for life and all that was around him. He gave thanks to God each day for all he was able to do. On top of this he gave a proportion of his income each week to Cancer Research in thanksgiving for what had been done for him.

Intercessions

Blessed are you, Lord our God.
All that is within us blesses your holy name
for you forgive all our sins
and heal all our infirmities;

you save our life from destruction
and provide us with many good things.
Blessed are you, Father, Son and Holy Spirit
now and for ever.

We give thanks for your Church throughout the world
and ask that it might share in your healing
and bringing of peace.
We remember before you all priests and pastors,
spiritual healers and those who are chaplains
and carers of the terminally ill.
We pray for the Leprosy Mission
and its work throughout the world.

Silence

Lord, we give you thanks:
hear us and have mercy upon us.

We give thanks for all
who maintain good government and care of the nations.
We ask your blessing upon all leaders,
rulers and politicians.
We remember the work of the World Health Organisation
and all who work to relieve
the needs and suffering of others.
We pray for our own community
and ask that we may appreciate
all who work to keep it in good order.

Silence

Lord, we give you thanks:
hear us and have mercy upon us.

We give thanks for our homes and our loved ones,
for all who have helped us and taught us in life.
We ask your blessing upon our families,
our friends and all our relationships.
We pray for those who are separated from their loved ones
through illness or circumstance.

Silence

Lord, we give you thanks:
hear us and have mercy upon us.

We give thanks for our life and our health.
We remember before you
all who are suffering alone with no one to help.
We pray for those who are in isolation wards
and all who are unable
to join in the full life of the community.
We remember also those whom we know
who are in hospital at this time.
We ask your blessing
upon all who work in healing and in caring for the ill.

Silence

Lord, we give you thanks:
hear us and have mercy upon us.

We give thanks that nothing can separate us
from the love of God in Christ Jesus.
We remember our loved ones
who are departed from us
and ask that they may enjoy the fullness of life eternal.
We rejoice in the fellowship of all your saints
and commend the world and ourselves
to your unfailing love.

Silence

Merciful Father,
accept these prayers
for the sake of your Son,
our Saviour Jesus Christ.
Amen.

Memory verse

Praise the Lord! I will give thanks to the Lord with my whole heart.
Psalm 111:1

Suggested music

Now thank we all our God
Praise, my soul, the King of heaven
What a friend we have in Jesus

CANDLES

Aim

To show how it is important to say 'thank you' to God.

Teaching

Who can count to ten? Let us count together. Today I want to tell you a story about ten men. All of them had to leave home because they were ill. They had to stay away from home because they had a skin disease. Have any of you been away from home and in hospital? It is sad when we cannot be at home but at least our family could come and see us. The ten men were not allowed any visitors. They were not allowed to see their children if they had any, and they were not allowed to go into any town. They had to live out in the wild country and there was no one to help them. They were ten sad men. If anyone came near to them, they had to cry out, 'Unclean!' and keep away from everyone. They had each other's company but they were ten sad men.

One day Jesus was in that part of the country, on his way to Jerusalem. When he came near the men, he could see they were sad and not very well and that they were not allowed to come close to him or his disciples. They kept their distance from Jesus but shouted to him, 'Jesus, Master, have mercy upon us.' They believed that Jesus could help them.

Jesus said to the ten sad men, 'Go and show yourselves to the priest.' He did not touch them but told them to go to the priest who would look at them like a doctor would to tell them if they had been made well. When they started off they still had spots and sores on their hands but they did what Jesus asked them. As they went towards where the priest lived, their skin got better – the sores and spots disappeared. When the priest looked at them carefully he told them they were well again and could go home to their families and friends. They were not ten sad men but ten glad men. They wanted to rush home as quickly as they could and off they went.

One of them thought of Jesus who had made him well again. Jesus had saved his life. He wanted to go to Jesus and say 'thank you'. Nine did not remember Jesus and to say 'thank you' but hurried off home. One came back. All the way he was shouting 'thank you' to God that he was well again. When he got to Jesus he bowed down before him and said, 'Thank you.'

Jesus asked, 'Were there not ten made clean? But the other nine – where are they?' Only one had remembered to give thanks to God. Jesus said to him 'Get up and go on your way; your faith has made you well.'

Show me on your hands how many make ten. Yes, that is all of your fingers. Now put nine down. How many are left? Only one, and only one man came back to say 'thank you'. Jesus made ten sad men glad and only one said 'thank you'. It is good to say 'thank you' whenever we have been given anything and to say 'thank you' to God for all that he has given to us. Let us say 'thank you' to God for our lives and for something we really like. We will take it in turns to say, 'Thank you, God, for . . .'

Activity

Choose one person to be the 'leper'. This person tries to touch others as they try to avoid him or her. Once touched, they also become lepers. The last one is to be Jesus and all who are lepers stand still until Jesus says, 'Your faith has made you well.' All respond by saying 'thank you'. This can be played two or three times.

Prayer

God, we thank you for your love
and that you have given us this world to live in.
We thank you for our lives and our homes.
We thank you for all that you have done for us
and for Jesus our Lord.
Amen.

Song

Thank you for the world so sweet

LAMPS

Aim

To look at the healing of the lepers and the need to say 'thank you'.

Teaching

When you have a birthday and get presents, or when you get Christmas presents, what should you remember to say or do? You should remember to say 'thank you' or to write a 'thank you' letter. This is a story about ten sad men and how only one returned to Jesus to say 'thank you'.

The men were sad because they were lepers. Does anyone know what this means? It means they had a skin disease and their body had sores or spots. Everyone was afraid of this disease because they believed that it could kill you. It was a painful disease and people did not want to catch it. So they said that anyone who had this disease had to leave their village or their town.

They could not live at home any more and no one except others with the disease could have any contact with them. Obviously it was very sad for anyone who had this disease and was made to leave their home and all their loved ones. (Ask the children for suggestions of what it would be like.)

The ten men who were together all had leprosy. They were not allowed to come close to anyone who was fit and well. They had to stand a long way away and shout, 'Unclean!' so that no one would come near. They also had to live out in the wild country where no one else lived.

Jesus was travelling across country on his way to Jerusalem when he saw the ten sad men. They had heard of Jesus and his power. They did not dare come close to him but shouted from a distance, 'Jesus, Master, have mercy on us!' (Let us shout those words: 'Jesus, Master, have mercy on us!') Jesus told them to go and show themselves to the priest. The priest acted like a doctor and was responsible for saying if a leper was well enough to return to his home. The ten sad men obeyed Jesus: they did as he asked. As they went, they noticed that their skin improved and looked well again. The priest said every one of the ten was made well. They were no longer sad but glad and anxious to get going. They wanted to go home, to see and to hug their loved ones. They were ten glad men as they rushed off.

One man realised how wonderful Jesus was and what a marvellous thing he had done for him. So he returned to where Jesus was, all the time giving thanks to God for his healing. When he came to Jesus, he bowed down and said a great big 'thank you'.

Jesus asked about the other nine but they had forgotten to say 'thank you'. It is amazing how often people forget to say 'thank you'. Jesus said to the man, 'Get up and go on your way. Your faith has made you well.'

Spend the rest of the session exploring what we should be saying 'thank you' for. Look at how so many people provide for us, what God has given to us, and what Jesus has done for us.

Activity

Play 'Clean and unclean'. This is a version of 'Stuck in the mud'. One person is chosen as the leper. He or she has to touch as many people as possible. All those touched have to stand still, arms outstretched and feet well apart. They have to shout, 'Unclean!' They can be rescued if someone not touched manages to crawl between their legs. If the single leper is making little progress, let there be two of them.

Prayer

God, we thank you for our life
and for our health.
We thank you for the world in which we live
and for all our loved ones.
Each day may we give you thanks and praise
for all that you have done for us.
Amen.

Song

Thank you, Lord, for this new day

TORCHES

Aim

To show how leprosy separates people from their loved ones, and how we should give thanks for what we have.

Teaching

Jesus was on his way to Jerusalem. He was with his disciples in the wild border country between Samaria and Galilee. As he came to a village, ten lepers approached him but kept their distance. Why? They had to do this. People feared leprosy and believed it could easily be caught from someone with the disease. As it was a disease that showed itself on the skin, it could be very disfiguring and this was also frightening for some people. Leprosy made you have to break from your loved ones, your home, your family, your work, your friends. It isolated you and you could only live with other lepers. You had to keep your distance from healthy people and shout, 'Unclean!' if they came too close. It was horrible to live without the contact of your loved ones.

Jesus heard the ten shouting from a distance, 'Jesus, Master, have mercy on us.' Jesus sent them to show themselves to the priest, who acted like a doctor in certifying whether the disease had left a person or not. As they went, they realised they were healed. The sad men had become glad men. They had done what Jesus asked and were made well. All had obeyed but one turned to Jesus to give thanks. Ten were healed but one came praising God and bowed before Jesus giving him thanks. Now he was able to make contact with Jesus. Jesus told him to rise – just as if it was from the dead – and said his faith had made him well.

Spend the rest of the session talking about the need for thanksgiving and about the power of Jesus to make people 'rise'.

Activity

Let the group look at literature from the Leprosy Mission and see if there is anything they can do to help.

They might like to explore the reality of Jesus rescuing us from death and giving us the power to rise.

There is an opportunity on the activity sheet to arrange a daily thanksgiving to God.

Prayer

Lord, you give us life and life eternal.
We give you thanks and praise.
In you is the power of healing
and you can make us rise.
We give you thanks and praise.
You give us this world and all that is in it.
We give you thanks and praise.
Amen.

Song

Oh! Oh! Oh! How good is the Lord

Proper 24

Sunday between 16 and 22 October inclusive

Aim

To show that we need to persevere in our prayers.

Preparation

Have prayer cards and various aids for prayer available in the entrance. Give everyone the chance to write an intercession that will be offered at the offertory.

Opening activity

A mini family sketch

Mother	Have you finished your homework?
Child 1	I was gonna.
Mother	Did you say your prayers today?
Child 2	I was gonna.
Mother	Have you practised your music?
Child 3	I was gonna.
Mother	Have you cut the lawn yet?
Father	I was gonna.
Mother	Did you wash behind your ears?
Child 4	I was gonna.
Commentator	And so it went on all their lives until they were gonners.

Opening prayer

Lord, you are always ready to hear us
and to help us.
Give us a sense of joy and love through our prayers,
that we may never forget you.
If we ever forget you, let us remember
you have never forgotten or left us.
Amen.

Opening song

Be still and know that I am God

Readings

Jeremiah 31:27-34 or Genesis 32:22-31
Psalm 119:97-104 or Psalm 121
2 Timothy 3:14–4:5
Luke 18:1-8

Thought for the day

In many homes there are objects that were bought with the intention of using them. These can range from an exercise bike to a piano, from a piece of knitting to a box of paints. They are there in case we may use them one day. Think of something you started but did not finish, like taking up a gym routine or practising the piano. Some people have done this with churchgoing or with their daily prayers. Francis Drake, that great sailor and explorer, once wrote, 'There must be a beginning of any great matter, but the continuing unto the end until it be thoroughly finished yields the true glory.'

Jesus was well aware that some people give up easily in their prayer life and that it is just too possible to lose heart (Luke 18:1). One of the great weaknesses of the Church is that many of its people are not really praying people. If we do not pray regularly, it is a sign that God is not among our priorities. Prayer is not always easy but we can even express this to God. It is important for our own health that we keep in contact with our God.

Jesus told the parable of a widow who sought justice. The judge was used to giving sentence in favour of the one who could impress him most. He feared neither God nor man. This sort of fear is about awe rather than dread. Maybe Jesus was hinting he was not a wise judge for, as the people knew, 'The fear of the Lord is the beginning of wisdom' (Proverbs 1:7). Many of the judges decided in favour of the one who could pay them the most. For this reason, they were known as 'robber judges'. Being a widow was usually a sign of being poor and defenceless. She had no resources, nothing to offer, so could not hope for justice. But she did have a weapon: she was persistent; she pestered the judge until he gave in. The widow was praised for chutzpah, her nerve, the fact that she did no lose heart or give up.

If the woman persisted with her plea to the judge, how much more should we persist in prayer to the God who wants us to live our lives to the full? It is easy to stop saying our daily prayers but without them we lose a vital link with God. Make sure that God is your priority and that you keep your prayer life alive. Sometimes prayer is difficult and we have to wrestle with it, as Jacob wrestled with God. Yet a relationship with the loving God is always rewarding.

Question time

Have you got a fixed time and place for your daily prayers?

Do you see that God is among the priorities of your day?

Illustration

St Teresa of Avila showed a great enthusiasm for life. In the front of her prayer book these words were written:

Let nothing disturb thee,
Nothing affright thee,
All things are passing,
God never changes.
Patient endurance
Attaineth to all things.
Who God possesses
In nothing is wanting.
God alone suffices.

These are deep words indeed and should be thought about with care. (Make copies available – as a bookmark – to all who would like to think about the words.)

Intercessions

Blessed are you, Lord our God.
You are always more ready to hear
than we are to pray,
and to grant more than we desire or deserve.
May we rejoice in your presence
and know your abiding love.
Blessed are you, Father, Son and Holy Spirit.

We give thanks for all who proclaim the gospel,
especially those who risk their lives
or their comfort for your sake.
We ask you to bless all who preach the word,
theology students
and those who take part in Bible study groups.
We pray for those who meet quietly together
to pray and to contemplate your presence
and your love.

Silence

Lord, hear us,
mercifully hear us.

We ask you to guide all who work
in the judicial system.
We pray for law courts, judges,
barristers, solicitors and juries.
We ask your blessing upon all
who seek to keep law and order.
We pray for the police
and for social workers and probation officers.
We remember all who suffer from injustice
and whose voices are not heard.

Silence

Lord, hear us,
mercifully hear us.

We give thanks for all
who have shared their wisdom and learning with us.
We ask your blessing upon all who teach
and who influence the lives of others.
We pray for Sunday schools and day schools.
We pray for all who are deprived of a good education.
We ask you to bless and protect our homes
and our loved ones.

Silence

Lord, hear us,
mercifully hear us.

We remember in your presence
the sorrows and needs of our world.
We pray for all who are oppressed
and those who have lost their liberty.
We ask your blessing upon all who are ill,
especially those who are unable to get proper attention.
We ask for your love and care
to be shown to all our loved ones
who are suffering in any way.

Silence

Lord, hear us,
mercifully hear us.

We give thanks that in your grace
you offer us eternal life.
We rejoice in the fellowship of all the saints
and we pray for our loved ones who are departed from us.
May we all share with you
in the fullness of your kingdom.

Silence

Merciful Father,
**accept these prayers
for the sake of your Son,
our Saviour Jesus Christ.
Amen.**

Memory verse

My help comes from the Lord, who made heaven and earth.
Psalm 121:2

Suggested music

I lift my eyes to the quiet hills
Lord, teach us how to pray aright
O Lord, hear my prayer (Taizé)

CANDLES

Aim

To encourage the children to say their prayers.

Teaching

Jesus knows that some people find it hard to remember to say their prayers. God is so wonderful and so loving that we should never forget him, yet people do because they think they are too busy or do not have the time. Who remembered to say their prayers this morning? God is always ready to hear us, so if we forget, we can start again. God likes us to talk to him each day.

Jesus told the people a story about a poor woman. She was a widow. Who knows what a widow is? Yes, she had no one that could help her and to bring her enough money to look after her home. Someone had done something she did not like and she wanted a judge to put it right. Who knows what a judge is? He makes decisions and tells people what they have to do to put things right. He gets paid for his work and rich people could pay him a lot. The poor woman did not have anything to give him. But she would not be put off. She kept coming back to the judge. She kept asking him. She pestered him until he listened. I know some children who pester their parents when they want something. The judge gave up because she would not stop coming. The woman won because she would not give up.

Jesus wanted us to know that if such a judge would listen to the woman, God would certainly listen to our prayers. But God cannot listen to our prayers if we do not pray them. God cannot answer our prayers if we do not speak to him. Let us make pictures of the things we will speak to God about each day. (Although there are suggestions on the activity sheet, it would be good for the children to make their own personal list.

Activity

On the worksheet there is an opportunity to draw something for each day of the week and for us to thank God for that thing.

Prayer

God, you are always ready to listen to us.
We can come to you and say 'thank you'
and we can ask you to help us each day.
We are glad that we can speak to you.
Amen.

Song

Two little eyes

LAMPS

Aim

To help the group to persist in their prayers.

Teaching

Jesus knew that some people find it hard to pray and soon give up. He told a story of a woman who did not give up. She was a widow and that meant she was very poor. Some people take advantage of the poor and take away even the little they have. The poor are often robbed of their land and their homes. This poor widow had suffered something like this and she went to the judge. Who knows what a judge is? A judge is a person who makes decisions about right and wrong and he is often paid for doing it. The woman was so poor there was not much she could offer to the judge, so he could not be bothered to listen. He felt he had more important things to do. But the woman kept coming to him and asking for help. The judge got tired of her pestering him: she was wearing him out with her words. He knew she would keep coming until he listened to her. So that he would be left in peace, he decided to listen to her and put right the trouble she complained about. The woman succeeded because she would not be put off.

Sometimes we are easily put off. We miss our keyboard lessons or our netball practice. We do not finish things we have started. Some people put off getting up on a Sunday for church, and others have stopped saying their prayers. But you are here so you are not easily put off. Do you say your prayers every day? God would like us to do that. If the judge listened to the woman, we can be sure God listens to our prayers. He likes to hear our prayers and for us to spend some time with him each day. Let us make a weekly list of prayers we can say to God and see if we can use it every day.

Activity

Create a prayer timetable for the week. Although there are suggestions on the activity sheet, get the children to suggest things themselves.

Prayer

God, we know that you love us
and wait for us to turn to you.
You are always ready to hear us and help us.
Let us remember you and your power every day.
Amen.

Song

I love to be with you

TORCHES

Aim

To encourage a healthy attitude to our prayers.

Teaching

'Isn't Church boring!' 'I have stopped saying my prayers because it is dull.' 'I do not go to church because I get nothing out of it.' How often do we hear words like these? Those who excuse themselves are excluding themselves. Surely to know that God is with us and cares for us can never be boring. To be told you can communicate with the greatest power there is cannot be anything other than exciting. Sometimes the way we do things and the way the church does things can seem boring. But God is never boring. It is more likely we *have* allowed ourselves to become dull and boring in our prayers. Jesus saw the danger of this and told a story for those who were in danger of giving up on their prayers and losing hope. He told a parable.

There was a poor widow. She had little if any resources and she was suffering from an injustice. There was a judge who made decisions and she went to him. The judge was usually paid well for what he did and often he would decide in the favour of those who paid him the most. He did not want to waste his time listening to this poor woman. She did not give up but persisted. She pestered the judge. (I know young people who pester their parents when they want something!) The judge would not have bothered but she kept coming and would not be put off. In the end the judge decided to listen to her so that he could get some peace.

Jesus suggests that if a woman persisted with a judge who refused to listen, we should persist in our speaking to God who is always ready to hear us. What did you come to church for today? What did you want to thank God for? What did you want to ask him? What were you brining to offer to him? If our prayers are to be lively, then we do have to make the effort. Every time we pray or come to church we should know what we are about to do.

Activity

There is an opportunity on the activity sheet to develop a pattern to help the young people to have a more interesting attitude to their prayers.

Prayer

Lord God, you are always ready to hear us
and to receive us when we come to you.
Give us a new liveliness in our prayers
and help us to know that coming to you
is coming to the source of our life
and to all that keeps the world in place.
Amen.

Song

Lord, have mercy on us, hear us as we pray

Proper 25

Sunday between 23 and 29 October inclusive

Aim

To make God the centre of our prayers and to rejoice in his grace and goodness.

Preparation

Have prayer cards and various aids for prayer available in the entrance. Give everyone the chance to write a prayer of praise to God for his grace and goodness.

Opening activity

A mini sketch

Obedient son Father! Look at me. I am good. I don't smoke, I don't drink, I am much better than my brother – he's a waster. I have totted up a big balance of being good. But if you let my brother come in, I cannot. I could not share a party with him.

Prodigal son Thank you for forgiving me. It was wonderful the way you ran to meet me. You must have been waiting for me to turn to you. I am not worthy of your love. You rejoice out of your grace and goodness. Thank you, Father. Pity my brother – he is unaware of your love for him.

Opening prayer

God, we come to you
trusting in your grace and goodness.
Though we are unworthy,
you are ready to forgive us and to accept us.
Your love for us is an everlasting love
and is revealed in Jesus Christ our Saviour.
For this we give you thanks and praise.
Amen.

Opening song

Just as I am, without one plea

Readings

Joel 2:23-32 or Ecclesiasticus 35:12-17
or Jeremiah 14:7-10, 19-22
Psalm 65 or Psalm 84:1-7
2 Timothy 4:6-8, 16-18
Luke 18:9-14

Thought for the day

This Gospel reading is the follow-on from last week and it is still about prayer. This week's story would be funny if it were not so serious. Too often there are still people with the attitude of the Pharisee. We must not stereotype all Pharisees as bad; as in all groups of people there are good and bad. The rabbis themselves listed all sorts of Pharisees. (1) There was the God-loving Pharisee, who lived by faith and was full of good works. There were many of these. (2) There was the Fearing Pharisee who was worried about the wrath of God and knew little of his love. (3) Then there were the Bleeding Pharisees. No Jewish rabbi was supposed to speak to a woman in the street, not even his wife or mother. The Bleeding Pharisees took it further by closing their eyes in the street so as not to see a woman. As a result they were always bumping into things and hurting themselves. (4) Then came the Hump-backed Pharisees who walked bent almost double in pretend humility – like Uriah Heep. (5) The Wait-a-while Pharisees always found an excuse for putting things off to another day. (6) The Shoulder Pharisees were those who wore their religion to be seen and to gain praise. (7) The last group were the Ever-reckoning Pharisees who added up their good deeds and struck up a sort of balance account with God – as if they could put him into debt.

Jesus told the story of the Pharisee and the tax collector to warn those who thought they were righteous and held others in contempt. Jews said their prayers three times every day at 9am, at noon and at 3pm. It was thought that it was better to pray in the Temple.

It would seem the Pharisee in the story was of the last two groups. Sadly we are told he prayed with himself. (Many translations have 'with himself' rather than 'by himself'.) We are able to see how self-centred he is: 'God, I thank you am not like other people . . . I fast . . . I give.' This man was the centre of his prayers, not God. He was the subject of the sentences and God the object. It was as if he was declaring God to be in his debt.

From the beginning of the story many would wonder about the tax collector being in the Temple praying. Who did he think he was? He had made himself unclean and unworthy by working for the Roman army. He is lucky no one kicked him out! This man did not dare look up to heaven (And rightly so, thought some of the hearers.) He could only beat his breast and say, 'God, be merciful to me, a sinner.' God in his grace and goodness is in control. God is the active party in the request. God is the subject of the sentence and the man sees himself as the object – the object, however, of God's love and mercy.

Jesus kept the punch line until the end: 'I tell you, this man went down to his home justified rather than the other, for all who exalt themselves will be humbled, but all who humble themselves will be exalted' (Luke 18:14).

Question time

Are we sure we are among the God-loving rather than those who seek to put God in their debt?

How can we make sure that it is God who is the centre of our prayers?

Illustration

The outside of the house looked well in the twilight. The whitewashed walls seemed to shine and even more so in the moonlight. Then during the night it snowed and we awoke to a bright morning. How shabby the outside of the house looked against the brightness of the snow and the sunlight – it certainly needed a coat of paint. How we are depends on what or whom we compare ourselves with. When we are placed before the grace and holiness of God, all that we can truly say is 'God, be merciful to me, a sinner.'

Intercessions

Blessed are you, Lord God,
for in your grace and goodness
you have called us into life and to your love.
Though we are unworthy,
you accept us and love us.
Blessed are you, Father, Son and Holy Spirit.

Father, you hear the prayers of the lowly
and accept the penitent sinner.
Help your Church to welcome
all who seek forgiveness and newness of life.
Let us show how we all share
in your grace and goodness.
We pray for those who hear the confession of others
and for all who counsel those
who are full of guilt and remorse.
May we all learn to trust in your love and acceptance.

Silence

Lord, hear us;
in your mercy hear us.

Father, we give thanks for your creation
and ask your blessing upon all who are working
to conserve and protect the earth.
We pray for the peoples of the earth
who have been moved out of their homes and land
through the greed and power of others.
Father, forgive us
when we are insensitive to those who suffer
as a result of our desire for cheap products.
May we do all we can
to bring justice and fair trade to peoples and nations.
We pray for all who are oppressed at this time.

Silence

Lord, hear us;
in your mercy hear us.

We give thanks for our families and loved ones.
We remember how they have cared for us
even when we seemed to have failed their love.
We ask you to bless all who are suffering
from broken relationships and unforgiving hearts.
We remember all who are full of anger or resentment
and lack your love and peace.

Silence

Lord, hear us;
in your mercy hear us.

Father, we know that you love and care for us.
May we show that same love to others.
We ask your blessing
upon all who are outcasts or refugees,
all who have been made homeless
and have nowhere to go.
We remember all who are ill at home or in hospital
and ask that they may have courage and hope
in their troubles.

Silence

Lord, hear us;
in your mercy hear us.

Father, you offer us the gift of eternal life
even though we are unworthy of you.
You welcome us into your kingdom.
We pray for our friends and loved ones
who have departed from us.
As they shared their lives on earth with us,
may they now share with you
in the fullness of eternal life.

Silence

Merciful Father,
accept these prayers
for the sake of your Son,
our Saviour Jesus Christ.
Amen.

Memory verse

God, be merciful to me, a sinner.
Luke 18:13

Suggested music

Lord Jesus, think on me
Rock of ages
Amazing grace

CANDLES

Aim
To show that God loves us.

Teaching
Think of a little sparrow. It flies into church because someone left the door open. Now it believes that because it can fly, it can get out; it just has to go higher. But it cannot. Then it flies at a window and nearly knocks itself out. It keeps flying round and round and cannot get out. It will not be able to get out by itself. Does it matter if it dies? It needs help. If it stays like this it will die. What could we do? If there are windows, we could open them, or we can open the door wide. Once it sees the light or feels the air it will find its way out. It could not open the door by its own efforts; it had to depend on us. We would do this because we care.

Let us sing the first verse of 'There are hundreds of sparrows'.

God likes that we cared for the sparrow. God wants to care for us and show that he loves us. God loves us from the beginning but some people think they have to make God love them. Jesus told a story about a very proud man and another more humble man.

When the proud man said his prayers he wanted to tell God how wonderful he had been. He spoke like this:

God I am good. I am not naughty.
I say my prayers. I go to church.
I give money to the church.
I keep all its rules.
God, look at me because I am good.
I am not like that man. He is not good.

God wanted to tell this proud man that he loved him. But the proud man was so busy talking about himself that he did not hear God telling him of his love.

The other man did not think he was all that good. Maybe he even heard the proud man say so. He spoke to God and knew that God loved him. God had always loved him because God loves everyone. He prayed quietly and said, 'God, be merciful to me, a sinner.' He knew he was not wonderful but he also knew that God loved him. When he left the church he was happy and he could have easily said, 'God loves everyone and God loves me.'

Let us now sing the last verse of 'There are hundreds of sparrows'.

Activity

There is an opportunity to make a 'thank you' to God for his love.

Prayer

God, help me to know that you love everyone,
even me.
Because you love me always
let me learn to give my love to you each day.
Amen.

Song

There are hundreds of sparrows

LAMPS

Aim

To show how God loves us and wants us to speak to him and to know he loves us.

Teaching

Who knows the rhyme of Little Jack Horner? Let us say it together:

Little Jack Horner sat in a corner
eating his pudding and pie.
He put in his thumb and pulled out a plum
and said, 'What a good boy am I!

I want to tell you a story about a man who thought he was good, just like Little Jack Horner. He thought he was very important. He lived at the time of Jesus and he was someone who went to church and said his prayers. Like Jack Horner he stood by himself and in his prayers was saying how good he was: 'God, look at me, I'm good. I do not do bad things. I do not forget my prayers.

I give to the church. I am not like that horrible tax collector. I am good!'

The important Pharisee
stood in a corner talking to God on high.
He lifted his hands and said with a loud cry,
'Look at me, how important and good am I!'

God wanted to speak to him and tell him he loved him. But the Pharisee was too busy speaking to God about himself to listen. When he went away he did not know that God wanted to tell him he loved him. He was too busy thinking about himself to let God give his love.

In the same church there was a tax collector. It was thought that nobody loved tax collectors. They took money from people when they came in or out of the city and gave it to the government. Some people even said that tax collectors should not be allowed in church. The Pharisees thought that the tax collector was horrible. The tax collector stood a long way off and did not dare look up to heaven. His prayer to God was 'God, be merciful to me, a sinner.' He asked God to love him and he waited quietly. In the quiet he learned that God loved him because God loves everyone. If we will only let him – because he loves you and me. Let us be quiet for a moment and in the quiet know that God loves us. Then we can tell God how we love him.

Activity

There is an opportunity to make a 'thank you' to God for his love.

Prayer

God, you love us always.
Even when we have done things that make you sad
you still love us and always love us.
Thank you, God.
Amen.

Song

Father God, I know you love me so

TORCHES

Aim

To show we approach God through his love and not our own goodness.

Teaching

Can you remember the story of the prodigal son? There is no doubt the father loved both the sons but one of them found it hard to accept that unconditional love. Sometimes it is very sad when righteousness can be so stern. Self-righteousness can easily make us exclude ourselves from the love God wants to give to us.

Today's story was meant to be funny in the absurd way the Pharisee acts – yet it cannot be funny to those who still act this way. We all know people who think they are the centre of the world and everything should revolve around them.

One way to describe the Pharisee, which is not kind, is to say he is 'a self-made man worshipping his own creator' (think about this).

Can you remember the story of the man who built bigger barns? He was always saying 'I'. (Have someone read Luke 12:16-20.)

Today's story also has a person who is always saying 'I'. He thinks he is better than others, though he picks the obvious sins and forgets about pride. He thinks himself above a tax collector. He feels that he is good: 'I pray. I fast. I give to the church.' He sounds like little Jack Horner saying, 'What a good boy am I.' There is a feeling that he is doing God a good turn: he is putting God in his debt. God must owe him for all that he has done. The righteous son in the story of the prodigal son had the same attitude. Such righteous people are usually stern and forbidding.

The tax collector was counted as an awful person, one of the lowest of the low. He was working for the enemy who occupied the country, the Romans. Many said he should be banned not only from the Temple but from the synagogue also. That a tax collector even prayed may have come as a surprise to some. Those who listened to this story would be delighted with the tax collector's prayer – they knew he was unworthy. But the punch line of the story shocked them. God was also delighted with the tax collector's prayer. The tax collector asked for forgiveness and it was given.

We need to learn that we can only approach God through his love and his grace and not in our 'righteousness'. To be righteous in the proper way is to live in a right relationship with God.

Activity

Play a game of 'True or false'. Each person in turn has to make a statement about themselves and the rest have to guess whether it is true or false. There is an opportunity on the activity sheet to look at true or false things about the Pharisee and the tax collector.

Prayer

Lord, though we are not worthy
or good enough to come before you,
you love us and accept us with love.
As you give yourself in love to us
help us to respond
by giving ourselves in love to you.
Amen.

Song

Lord, have mercy on us, hear our humble plea

All Saints' Day

1 November
or Sunday between 30 October and 5 November inclusive

Aim

To rejoice in the communion of saints.

Preparation

Prepare a quiz as suggested below. Provide candles for all who would like to light a candle in thanksgiving for the life of a holy person. This is a good day to have a procession with children carrying banners or paintings of saints. If you have stained-glass windows with saints in them, you could stop at each and give thanks for that saint.

Opening activity

Quiz

- Who is the patron saint of our church?
- Which saint was the mother of Jesus?
- Which saint was the husband of Mary?
- Who was the saint who doubted the resurrection?
- Who was the saint who saw Jesus on the road to Damascus?
- Who is the patron saint of Ireland?
- Who is the patron saint of ecologists?
- Who is the patron saint of music?

Opening prayer

Lord God, you bring us
to share in the communion of saints
and to join in their worship and praise.
As you have called us, Lord,
make us worthy of our calling,
that with them we may rejoice
in the fullness of your eternal kingdom.
Amen.

Opening song

For all the saints

Readings

Daniel 7:1-3, 15-18
Psalm 149
Ephesians 1:11-23
Luke 6:20-31

Thought for the day

At this time of the year, from All Saints' Day (1 November) until the Sunday before Advent when we celebrate Christ the King, we are asked to rejoice that we are part of God's kingdom, and not only us but the whole Church in heaven and on earth. We are part of the communion of saints. We are in communion with the Church Triumphant in heaven because we are all in the heart of God. We are called to be saints – that is, to belong to God, to witness to him and to help to bring in his kingdom.

When Paul writes the Letter to the Ephesians he addressed it 'to the saints in Ephesus'. In the same way he addressed his letter to the Corinthians as those 'called to be saints' (1 Corinthians 1:2). In the same way Paul would have addressed us as the saints in (*Name*). It should make you think if you are addressed as the saints who are faithful in Christ Jesus. Do you see yourselves as dedicated people, for that is what you are?

Paul now lists some of the hallmarks of the Church – to show if it is the genuine article and not some dull copy.

'You are sealed with the Spirit.' Paul knew that when anything important was sent off it was sealed to show whom it belonged to and that it should arrive intact. In baptism you were sealed with the Spirit, called to be holy, a people dedicated to God. Paul calls this sealing with the Spirit a 'pledge', and by this he means a deposit laid down, a first instalment, with the guarantee of much more to come. We have a far greater inheritance offered to us.

'I have heard of your faith in the Lord Jesus and your love towards all the saints,' says Paul (Ephesians 1:15). Another hallmark of our calling is love, love towards God and towards each other. Love cannot be healthy if we fail to love God or each other.

Paul prays that we might have wisdom, the gift that is more than just knowledge, as it involves discernment and is a gift of God. We have to be a thinking and a sensitive people.

Paul prays that we may come to know God; that we may see with our hearts as well as our heads; that we may know what is the hope, and the inheritance to which we are called. Paul asks that we may experience the power of God, and that we may know the resurrection of Christ.

He continues to ask that we may know that Christ rules over all and is all-powerful.

Then he reminds us that we are the body of Christ, that Christ works in us and through us. We are to work with him and for him.

These are enough hallmarks for anyone to think about. When you go home, quietly read today's Epistle – Ephesians 1:11-23 – each day this week.

Question time

You are called a saint. How can you live up to your calling?

What do you see as the hallmarks of your church that show it to be living up to its calling?

Illustration

A man presented himself to the minister leading the service once it was over. 'I would like to become a Christian.' The minister enquired what had brought him to this decision. Was it a sermon, a book or some event in his life? The man was a little embarrassed at this point and said how he read little and hardly ever attended church. 'It's my boss at work – he is a real tough chap and we are a hard bunch of men – it's the way he deals with us. I wanted to know what made him so sensitive and caring, what made him strive to be honest and fair to all. He told me it was because he was a Christian. If that is what a Christian is like, that is what I want to be.'

The best advertisement for God and for our faith is the way we live and witness to what we believe.

Intercessions

Blessed are you, Lord our God,
for in you and your love
we share with the saints in glory.
For all the saints who have gone before us
and revealed your love,
for those in weakness who have revealed your power,
for those who challenge us by their deeds,
we give you thanks and praise.
Blessed are you, Father, Son and Holy Spirit.

We give thanks
for all who have built up your Church
through their holiness, their witness
and their faith in you.
We give thanks for those who have inspired us
and challenged our way of life.
Lord, grant us the power
to be the people you want us to be
and to do what you want us to do.
Bless all who minister to us
and teach us your holy word.
We pray for all who are being prepared
for baptism, confirmation, marriage or ordination.

Silence

Lord, make us to be numbered with your saints
in that glory which is everlasting.

As we give thanks for our faith
and the world around us,
we remember all who are being persecuted for their faith.
We ask your blessing upon all who are risking their lives
to maintain peace and order in our world.
We ask you to bless and guide
all who stand up for the freedom and well-being
of the poor and the oppressed.

Silence

Lord, make us to be numbered with your saints
in that glory which is everlasting.

We give thanks
for all who have revealed your love to us
through their own love.
We ask your blessing upon our homes and our loved ones.
We remember all who are quietly sacrificing
their lives and their freedom
in the care they are giving to others.
We ask you to bless all who are caring for the ill
and those who are handicapped or infirm.

Silence

Lord, make us to be numbered with your saints
in that glory which is everlasting.

We give thanks for all who have risked pain or death
to forward your kingdom.

We ask your blessing
upon all who are struggling at this time,
all who are oppressed or who are in danger.
We pray for all who are ill at home or in hospital.
We remember all who are suffering
because of their faith:
the scorned, the persecuted and the ignored.

Silence

Lord, make us to be numbered with your saints
in that glory which is everlasting.

We rejoice in the communion of saints,
that we are one in you and your love.
We remember those whose service on earth is done
and now rejoice with you in glory.
We ask your blessing
upon all who have been an inspiration to us
and have enriched our lives by their love
but are now departed from us.

Silence

Merciful Father,
**accept these prayers
for the sake of your Son,
our Saviour Jesus Christ.
Amen.**

Memory verse

The holy ones of the Most High shall receive the kingdom and possess the kingdom for ever – for ever and ever.
Daniel 7:18

Suggested music

Rejoice in God's saints
Captains of the saintly band
Ye watchers and ye holy ones

CANDLES

Aim

To show how Aidan wanted people to know of the love and generosity of God.

Teaching

Aidan lived a long time ago, before there were any cars or buses or aeroplanes. Let us say his name together: Aidan. How do you think Aidan would travel around? He lived near the sea so he could go by boat. But many places were not near the sea so he had to travel by riding a horse. Aidan preferred to walk. He said that when you are on a horse you look down on people. He would rather meet people on their own level. It was slower than travelling by horse but he was not in a hurry and it was easier to talk to other people this way. Aidan used to ask people if they believed in Jesus. If they did, he said, 'Let us pray together and say thank you to Jesus.' If they did not believe, he asked them, 'Why not?' He would spend some time teaching people about Jesus. People knew Aidan was very generous. If he was given money, he gave it away to the poor and was always ready to help where he could.

One day he was far from the island where he lived. He was over 100 miles away from his home. He was visiting a king called Oswin. The king was also a Christian and was very kind and generous. He was worried that Aidan had a long way to walk and that it would take him many days. So he gave Aidan a gift to help him. What do you think he gave Aidan so that he could travel quicker? Yes, he gave Aidan a horse. It was one of king Oswin's best horses. He also gave Aidan a good saddle and reins for the horse. There were some expensive metals on the saddle and reins. Aidan would rather have walked but he thanked the king for his kindness.

When Aidan rode out he travelled quite quickly. It was a good and fast horse. He had not travelled very far when he met a very poor man begging. The man wanted something to get food with. Aidan had no money as he had already given it away. What do you think he did? He gave the beggar the king's horse with its expensive saddle and reins. He just gave it away. The beggar could not believe it. No one had ever been so generous to him. He knew he could sell the horse for a lot of money – he felt Aidan had made him rich. Aidan told him how God loved him.

Now Aidan had to walk again but he did not mind. He believed it was right to be generous and to give to the poor. People said that Aidan was a saint, a holy man of God. Aidan not only told people about God's love and kindness but also showed it the way he lived.

Aidan did say sorry to the king but also told him that giving to a poor person was more important than keeping a horse. The king knew that Aidan was a saint, a holy man of God.

Activity

Let the children act out this story with Aidan meeting and speaking to people, the king giving him a horse and Aidan giving it away. There is an opportunity to colour a drawing on the activity sheet.

Prayer

God, we thank you for St Aidan
and that he was kind to the poor.
May we be kind and generous to others
and show them your love.
Amen.

Song

Come on and shine

LAMPS

Aim

To show that saints trusted in God and his power.

Teaching

Who knows what a saint is? It is a man or woman who has given their life to God and trusted in him. They are not people who have never done wrong but they are people who try and do what God wants them to do. Some saints have died for God; others have spent their lives or part of their lives showing how good God is. Some saints went to other countries to tell people about God. Can you tell me the names of any saints?

I want to tell you about a saint who lived in Ireland over 1400 years ago. He is called Columba, which means 'dove'. Sometimes they called him Columcille, which means 'dove of the Church'. Columba helped to build many churches and to tell a lot of people about Jesus. He was a poet, a writer, a scholar and a storyteller.

After building many churches in Ireland he set sail with some other monks for a little island called Iona on the west coast of what we now call Scotland (show on a map). On Iona he built a monastery and from there many men went out to teach about Jesus. Columba also went out across Scotland. On one journey he was aiming to go to the palace of a king at Inverness. This meant he and his monks would be passing Loch Ness (show it on a map). It was a very large stretch of water. When he reached the loch he saw the people burying a man who had been killed by a monster from the loch. It had seized him and bitten him and so he died.

Columba asked one of his monks to swim across to the other side of the loch. As the monk swam, the monster appeared and was ready to catch him and eat him. Everyone except Columba was terrified. Columba believed that God would save the monk. He could not do it himself but God could. Columba called on God and made the sign of the cross. Then he told the monster to stop and to go no further and not to touch the monk. The monster was near the monk but it turned immediately and was gone. Everyone was amazed and gave thanks to God for saving the monk and for the power of the prayers of St Columba.

Columba prayed to God, trusted in God and worked for God. Columba fought against evil whenever he could and tried always to do what God wanted him to do. Columba is remembered as a saint.

Activity

Play 'In the river'. Everyone stands in a circle. The monster stands in the middle. When he calls out, 'In the river', everone has to jump in the river. When he shouts, 'On the bank', they have to jump backwards on to the bank. If the monster shouts, 'On the river' or 'In the bank', no one must move not even wobble. If they go wrong, they are counted as eaten by the monster and are out. The last person is the most obedient and the winner.

Prayer

God, you have called us to love you
and to work for you.
Help us to be like the saints,
to do what you want us to do
and, like Columba, tell others about your love.
Amen.

Song

When a knight won his spurs

TORCHES

Aim

To look at some of the qualities that make a saint.

Teaching

Who can tell me the name of a saint? Which saint is our church named after? Can you tell me the names of the saints who are shown in the stained glass of our church?

Thinking of stained glass, when a child was asked what a saint is she replied, 'Someone who lets light in.' Actually this is a good description because saints help to show us what God is like by the way they live their lives.

The saints were not perfect; like any other human being, they made mistakes and sometimes did wrong things. Sometime saints lived quite wild lives when they were young and only became saintly later. To be a saint means to belong to God. As we all belong to God we can be called saints or at least 'called to be saints'. God wants all of us to be his saints – and for us that is not easy!

Let us make a list of some of the things we would expect of a saint. (Get the group to suggest various qualities.)

- Have a living relationship with God
- Pray often each day
- Trust in God's strength not our own
- Witness to God and his saving power
- Care for God's world and all of creation
- Show God's love in our lives
- Show God's love in the way we deal with others
- Face death for the love of God
- Seek to do the will of God

Mother Teresa of Calcutta made it all sound simple when she said all that is required is to 'do something beautiful for God'. She meant, of course, that we should do this as often as possible.

The writer to the Hebrews suggests that all the saints of the past and their work now depend on us. He suggests that the main ingredient of being a saint is a living relationship with God (faith). Have someone read Hebrews 11:32-39 quite slowly. Then get the group to talk about the following: 'So that they would not, without us, be made perfect' (Hebrews 11:40b).

Activity

There is an opportunity on the activity sheet to design a stained-glass window either to depict a favourite saint or some of the qualities of saints.

Prayer

Lord God, as you have called us,
give us the strength to live up to our calling,
that we may become the people you want us to be
and to do what you want us to do.
Amen.

Song

Oh when the saints go marching in

Fourth Sunday before Advent

Sunday between 30 October and 5 November inclusive
For use if the Feast of All Saints was celebrated on 1 November and alternative propers are needed

Aim

To know that Jesus comes to where we are and seeks to help us to rise with him.

Preparation

Have a picture of the Good Shepherd on display in church (a child's drawing with the title will do very well). Surround this picture with cuttings from magazines of outcasts, prisoners, drug users and similar.

Opening activity

Mini sketch

(*Someone comes in and looks under the pews*)

Voice 1 What are you looking for?
Voice 2 My bracelet – I have lost it.
Voice 1 It's not worth the bother.
Voice 2 It is to me. It is precious to me. It was given to me as a token of love. I will seek for it until I find it.
Voice 3 Who does that remind you of? Yes, Jesus. He comes to seek and save the lost. Like a Good Shepherd he knows us each by our names and loves us.
Voice 1 What – even tax collectors?
Voice 2 Yes, even tax collectors!

Opening prayer

Lord God, we give thanks
for your love that will not let us go.
Even when we ignore you, you still love us.
We may forget you, but you never forget us.
You seek us until the day we turn to you
and then you hold us in your love.
We give thanks that you have sought us
in Jesus Christ the Good Shepherd.
Amen.

Opening song

Dear Lord and Father of mankind

Readings

Isaiah 1:10-18
Psalm 32:1-8
2 Thessalonians 1:1-12
Luke 19:1-10

Thought for the day

Jericho is at a strategic crossing of the river Jordan. It is an oasis in the desert, a place of palm forests and balsam trees. The smell from the balsam and the gardens of roses travels for miles. It has a perpetual supply of fresh water from a spring. There has been a city on this site for 10,000 years! It is one of the oldest cities in the world and it was a wealthy place with a great income. One of its strange features is that it is 400 metres below sea level – the lowest city in the world, and it lived up to this by its decadence. It was here that Jesus healed blind Bartimaeus and he set the story of the Good Samaritan on the road from here to Jerusalem. It was here that Zacchaeus lived and worked as a tax collector. It was a very lucrative job in a rich city and he was the chief tax collector, in charge of the others and making more money than the others. He was a big name in Jericho, with a big income and a big house. In the world of commerce Zacchaeus was a big man. But he was little in the eyes of the faithful, he was small in stature, a traitor to his country; he was not popular and he was held in low esteem. Someone described him as the lowest man in the lowest town in the world – and you could hardly get lower than that.

Zacchaeus had heard that Jesus was in town and he wanted to see him. Zacchaeus heard that Jesus was a friend of tax collectors and sinners, and Zacchaeus certainly needed a friend. He had to see Jesus. But Zacchaeus was so small and hated the crowd squeezing him out. Why should he be allowed to see Jesus?

Zacchaeus, not to be put off, goes on ahead and climbs a tree. He peers through the leaves and wonders if he will be noticed. Jesus misses nothing. Jesus looks up and says to him, 'Zacchaeus, hurry and come down; for I must stay at your house today.' The crowd grumble: Why does he mix with sinners? Why does Jesus stoop so low? Why does he mingle with the dregs?

One day some would realise that Jesus descended into the depths to lift us up. He came to the lowest to raise them to the heights. Jesus came to sinners exactly where they are: not where they ought to be or want to be but where they are. So he came to Zacchaeus and he called him by his name! Jesus reached out to the lonely, money-grabbing, no-hoper Zacchaeus.

In turn, Zacchaeus becomes a changed man. He offers to give half of all his possessions to the poor, and if he has defrauded any, to give them back four times as much. Zacchaeus wanted to show he was a changed man.

Jesus reminds us this is the reason for his coming: 'to seek out and to save the lost'. Have we allowed Jesus to enter into the depths of our lives to make friends with us? Jesus descends to lift us up. As the Good Shepherd, he calls us by name and seeks for the lost until he finds them.

Question time

Do we realise there is no one beyond the call of Jesus unless they choose to be?

Are we willing to let Jesus into the depths of our lives to change us?

Illustration

John was put in prison for the third time. He had a good mind but he used it for crime. He was a robber and occasionally given to violence. Even his family had given up on him. He rarely had any visitors other than the official prison visitors. One day he asked the man who had been coming to see him regularly why he bothered. The man explained he believed that everyone was important and could change, even John. He also told him that he was a Christian and so believed everyone was precious in the eyes of God. This really made John think: a God that actually knew him and loved him, that he need not be condemned for ever. John began to read the Gospels and the story of Jesus. He said he had never felt such a love or known forgiveness up to that time. John became a changed man. When he was released from prison he got work with an aid agency through the help of his prison visitor. He became a trusted and hard worker and in time held a position of great trust. He never hesitated to explain how he had plumbed the depths and how Jesus had reached down to him.

Intercessions

Blessed are you, Lord our God,
for you love us with an everlasting love.
You sent your Son
to descend into the depths of our lives,
that he may raise us up to the fullness of life eternal.
In you and in the power of your Spirit
we can be changed
and have the power to live to your glory.
Blessed are you, Father, Son and Holy Spirit.

We give thanks that you seek and desire to save
all who are lost or in the depths.
We ask you to guide and bless
all who are new to the faith,
the newly converted, the baptised
and the confirmed.
Bless, O Lord, all who are seekers
and those who are longing for a change in their lives.
We remember all who are growing in the faith
and those who have discovered
a living relationship with you.

Silence

Lord, you seek and save the lost:
hear us as we call upon you.

We ask your guidance
upon all who are involved in commerce
and in high finance,
upon tax collectors, workers in the stock market
and bankers.
We remember all who are involved
with the International Monetary Fund.
We ask your blessing
upon countries that are deeply in debt
and upon the poor of the world.
We pray for all who are spiritually or materially bankrupt.

Silence

Lord, you seek and save the lost:
hear us as we call upon you.

We give thanks to you for our homes
and all that you have given us.
May we learn to share with those around us
and to be aware of the needs of others.

We remember all who have lost their homes
or their employment this week
and we pray for children taken into care.

Silence

Lord, you seek and save the lost:
hear us as we call upon you.

We remember all who have lost their way
and become involved in drugs or violence,
all who are suffering
through the decadence of society.
We ask your blessing
upon all who are ill at home or in hospital
and all who are fearful for their future.

Silence

Lord, you seek and save the lost:
hear us as we call upon you.

We give thanks that Jesus came down
to seek us and to lift us up into your kingdom,
for the forgiveness of sins
and the opportunity to amend our lives.
We rejoice in the fellowship of all the redeemed.
We ask you to bless our loved ones
who are departed from us
and are now in your nearer presence and love.

Silence

Merciful Father,
**accept these prayers
for the sake of your Son,
our Saviour Jesus Christ.
Amen.**

Memory verse

For the Son of Man came to seek out and to save the lost.
Luke 19:10

Suggested music

All that I am
The Spirit lives to set us free
At the name of Jesus

CANDLES

Aim

To show that Jesus cares for us all and loves us.

Teaching

Have you ever gone somewhere and not been able to see what is going on because you are still small? It is harder to see over hedges or fences when you are small. In a crowd if you are not at the front, it is very hard to see what is going on, unless you are lifted up. (Encourage the children to talk about this and who helped them to see.)

I want to tell you about a little man called Zacchaeus. Let us all say his name together: Zacchaeus. He lived in a big city called Jericho. He collected money from everyone who came into or went out of the city, some for himself and some for the government. Zacchaeus was very rich. He had a big house with lots of beautiful things. He had lots of money and could buy whatever he wanted. But he was not happy. He did not have many friends and he knew that most people did not like him.

Zacchaeus heard that Jesus was coming to Jericho and he was excited. He heard that Jesus often cared for people whom others did not like. Maybe he would care for him. Zacchaeus went out into the street to see Jesus. Because the people did not like him they kept him to the back and he could not see. The people made sure he was where he could not see. Zacchaeus would not be put off. He hurried down the street and climbed a tree. Some of the people laughed at him when they saw him.

When Jesus came past he did not laugh. He stopped and said, 'Zacchaeus, hurry and come down, for I must come to your house today.' Zacchaeus was surprised that Jesus knew him and spoke to him. But he hurried down and showed Jesus where he lived. He was so happy that Jesus cared for him that he promised to give half of everything he had to the poor people. He would give from the other half of his money to any who thought he had cheated them. This made Jesus happy.

Jesus had come to show Zacchaeus that God loved him and that he wanted Zacchaeus to be kind and loving to others. Zacchaeus would never forget the day that Jesus came to stay at his house.

Activity

There is an opportunity on the activity sheet to put Zacchaeus in a tree and to bring him down to meet Jesus.

The children could act out this story.

The song could be sung in two parts of four lines each.

Prayer

Jesus, we know that you love everyone
and that you love us.
Help us today to love you
and to be kind and generous to others.
Amen.

Song

Zacchaeus was a very little man

LAMPS

Aim

To show that Jesus loves us and that he seeks and saves the lost.

Teaching

Zacchaeus live in a big city called Jericho. He was an important man because he was in charge of the tax collectors who worked for the government. He got people to pay for coming in or going out of the city if they were carrying anything worth money. He taxed their food and their donkeys, he taxed the people who made perfume and who sold roses. This meant he had a lot of money and he kept a lot for himself. Zacchaeus was rich. But he was not happy because nobody liked him. People hated him. Now Zacchaeus was only a small man, so they made sure that when something happened they got in front of him so that he could not see. If they could, they squeezed and punched Zacchaeus.

Now Zacchaeus heard that Jesus was in town and he knew that Jesus showed his love to all, even to tax collectors. He wanted to see Jesus and for Jesus to see him. To make it possible Zacchaeus went ahead of the crowd and climbed a tree. He thought that from here he would get a good view of Jesus. He did get a wonderful view and Jesus noticed him. In fact, Jesus called him by name. 'Zacchaeus,' he said, 'hurry down for I want to stay with you.' Zacchaeus could hardly believe it. Jesus knew him and said he would stay with him. Some people complained but Jesus said he had come to seek and save the lost – just like a good shepherd.

Zacchaeus took Jesus to his house. It was wonderful for Zacchaeus to know that Jesus did not hate him. Because Jesus cared for him, Zacchaeus decided to show he also cared for others. He promised to give half of everything he had to the poor. If he had cheated anyone, he promised to give them back four times as much. People saw that Zacchaeus had changed and was now a nicer man and many began to like him.

Jesus reminded everyone that he came to earth for people like Zacchaeus. He came to seek and to save the lost.

Activity

On the activity sheet there is an opportunity to make various characters in this story and then to re-enact it with the children.

Prayer

Lord Jesus, you are the Good Shepherd.
You seek out the troubled and the lost
to bring them safely home.
Teach us always to be generous
and to care for others as you care for us.
Amen.

Song

Nobody liked Zacchaeus.

TORCHES

Aim

To show how Jesus seeks out those who are in need.

Teaching

Zacchaeus was a big man in the city of Jericho. He had a big staff of workers because he was the chief tax collector. He had an important position. He had a big house and lots of lovely things. He had quite a big appetite and plenty of rich food.

The rich people of Jerusalem liked to spend the winter in Jericho because it had a wonderful warm climate. One king had a winter palace there. People came to the market and bought and sold, and every time they did this Zacchaeus made big money. He thought big.

But he was a little man: not very tall, and hated by most of the people. They saw him as a traitor to their country because he worked for the Roman government. They believed that he took lots of tax for himself and not just for the government. Zacchaeus was wealthy but not happy. He knew they called him a horrible little man. He had hardly any friends. When he heard that Jesus was in town he wanted to see him. He understood that Jesus was a friend even of tax collectors. Zacchaeus knew the crowd would squeeze him out and buffet him. Some would spit at him or punch him if they could. Yet he wanted to see Jesus and would not be put off. He got ahead of the crowd and climbed a tree and waited. At last he could see Jesus coming.

Jesus stopped right under the tree and called him by name: 'Zacchaeus, hurry and come down, for I must stay at your house today.' Here we see the Good Shepherd at work, seeking out and saving the lost. People complained of the company Jesus kept and did not like him staying with Zacchaeus. But this meeting changed the life of the tax collector. He knew that someone cared for him and now he could care for others. Zacchaeus promised to give away half of all his possessions. With the other half he would refund any one who felt he had cheated them. Not only would he pay them back but give them four times as much. Jesus had changed Zacchaeus and soon he would no longer be hated but accepted by many people.

Jesus said of Zacchaeus, 'Today salvation has come to this house, because he too is a son of Abraham. For the Son of Man came to seek and save the lost' (Luke 19:9, 10). (If there is time, get the group to talk about these words and their meaning.)

Activity

Send someone outside the room. Now make a circle and keep them on the outside of it. They have to try to break into the circle but the others do their best to prevent them. (No rough stuff!)

Then a leader, who was chosen while the person was out, breaks the circle and lets them in. The outsider has to discover the welcoming person.

Prayer

Lord Jesus, in your care for us
you seek us when we forget you.
You keep a grip on us
even when we lose grip of you.
You look for us until we turn to you.
We thank you for your saving power
and your love.
Amen.

Song

Rich man Zac

Third Sunday before Advent

Sunday between 6 and 12 November inclusive

Aim

To rejoice in the resurrection and newness of life.

Preparation

Have pictures of transformation from caterpillar to butterfly, from grub to dragonfly, from egg to chick. Have in big letters, 'We believe in the resurrection'.

Opening activity

Ask people to quietly give thanks to God for life and for life eternal. During their thanksgiving play a recording of 'I know that my Redeemer liveth' from Handel's *Messiah*.

Opening prayer

Lord God, we thank you for Jesus your Son
and for his death and resurrection.
Help us at all times to know your love
and to trust in the gift of the resurrection
to eternal life.
Amen.

Opening song

God of life, God of love

Readings

Job 19:23-27a
Psalm 17:1-9
2 Thessalonians 2:1-5, 13-17
Luke 20:27-38

Thought for the day

Jesus met with a group that denied the hope of resurrection. They are the Sadducees. The Sadducees were mainly the wealthy Jews who were friendly with the Romans. They were collaborators with the occupying forces – as rich groups often are because they have more to lose in any rebellion. They were conservative and fundamentalist by nature. In dealing with the Scriptures they looked almost exclusively at the five Books of Moses and only allowed a minimalist interpretation of the Scriptures. Because the resurrection is not in the early texts they refused to accept it. They were strong on tradition but not on relating new experience to it. (There are still people like this within the Church.) The Chief Priest and the High Priest were chosen from the Sadducees: they were the ruling class.

In their meeting with Jesus we see them offering a nonsense question as they did not believe in the resurrection. According to their law (See Deuteronomy 25:5ff), if a man's married brother dies childless, then he must marry the widow and so provide children for his brother. In many ways this was to protect the woman from poverty and loneliness. The Sadducees took it to a ridiculous length by suggesting that seven brothers married this woman and then died in turn and asked whose wife she would be in the resurrection.

Jesus saw this question for what it was: a trap that came out of minds that were not willing to accept change and newness. They were not like the poor; the Sadducees didn't have to worry about justice and fairness – they had the lion's share. Their life was rich enough not to worry about the future. Their thinking was limited to this world and a God that they contained within their own image. The God of Jesus is a God greater than us all, who is able to do whatever he wills. The world beyond what we know is beyond our limited minds and imagining, but it does exist: it is new and different, in the way an egg is different from a hen, a seed from a plant or a caterpillar from a butterfly. If we believe in a loving and Almighty God who is a God of justice, it brings us to think about the possibility of the resurrection. Jesus came partly that we might know that there is a resurrection.

Question time

Do you believe in the resurrection, and how would you illustrate it?

Have you learnt to bring experience to bear on the Scriptures and the Scriptures to bear on your experience?

Illustration

High up on the moors there was a group of men setting the old heather on fire. The plants had become gnarled and twisted with age: they had come to the end of their usefulness. No longer did they provide food for the sheep or the birds. So the heather was burned and you could see large flames rising. Later there would be no signs of heather, only blackened ground were it had been. These men knew what they were doing. They made sure it was a controlled burning. Under the surface, hidden from sight, were living roots. The heather would rise again: having lost its gnarled and twisted quality, it would be fresh and nourishing to the creatures.

And so it is with the resurrection of the dead.

Intercessions

Blessed are you, Lord our God,
for you give us life and life eternal.
You have given us the power to grow and to change.
You have given us the freedom to ignore or turn to you.
In your love you seek us
and want us to have the fullness of life.
Blessed are you, Father, Son and Holy Spirit.

God, we thank you for the Holy Scriptures,
for those who have preached the word
and brought the Good News to our land.

May we not be narrow-minded in our views
or fail to bring the Scriptures to bear on our experience.
We ask you to guide all who are intolerant
towards the faith of others,
that they may be more loving.
We seek your blessing
upon our own clergy and ministers.
We pray for all who are struggling with their faith.

Silence

Lord, hear our cry:
listen to our prayer.

We give thanks for all we have received
and we ask that we might be generous in our sharing.
We ask your blessing upon all who are working
for justice and fair dealing.
We remember all who suffer from oppression
or from poverty.
Lord, give strength to all who are working
for the freedom of others
and for peace in our world.

Silence

Lord, hear our cry:
listen to our prayer.

We give thanks for the wonder of life,
for growth and for change.
We pray to you for our parents
and for those who have helped us to grow and learn.
We ask your blessing upon all who care for families
who are in trouble or in difficulty.
We pray for social services and probation workers.

Silence

Lord, hear our cry:
listen to our prayer.

We give thanks for the renewing powers of the body.
We ask your blessing upon all
who are involved in healing and in the care of the ill.
We ask you to protect and strengthen
our loved ones who are suffering at this time
and we remember before you all suffering peoples.

Silence

Lord, hear our cry:
listen to our prayer.

We give thanks
for the power of the resurrection of our Lord.
Through him may we come to rejoice in eternal life.
We ask your blessing upon our loved ones
and all the faithful departed.
May they share in the joys of your kingdom.

Silence

Merciful Father,
**accept these prayers
for the sake of your Son,
our Saviour Jesus Christ.
Amen.**

Memory verse

I know that my Redeemer lives.
Job 19:25

Suggested music

Now the green blade riseth
I know that my Redeemer lives
My God, how wonderful you are

CANDLES

Aim

To learn about the God of surprises and the resurrection.

Teaching

God made a world full of surprises. I like surprises, do you? Well, I have brought a bag and in it is a surprise – and later I might let you see it. If I told you it was a nice surprise, would you believe me? Some people would not believe Jesus and they were called Sadducees. Let us say it together: Sadducees. Jesus wanted them to know that God loves us and invites us to live with him in heaven – but they would not believe it because they had not seen it. We believe in Jesus and that we can live in heaven.

If you had never seen a seed, you would never believe what it could become. (Show an acorn or a chestnut.) Who knows what this could become? Wrapped up in this tiny thing is a tree – God likes giving us surprises.

Now show another seed. (You could use a sunflower seed from birdseed, or a cabbage seed. Whichever seed you show, have a photograph or a seed packet.) What do you think this seed will become? If I sowed a cabbage and got a flower, I would have a surprise! But each seed grows its own plant.

Show an egg and a chocolate egg. Look at these. Now from one of them a surprise could come if a hen sat on it. What would you get? Yes, out of this egg you would get a chick. God made a world full of surprises.

Show a picture of a caterpillar and see how many can guess what it would become. A butterfly. Once there was a strange worm that lived in the bottom of a pond among the mud. It was not beautiful and had never been out of the pond. One day it crawled up a leaf and became wrapped in something like a box. Everyone thought it had died. But after a while the box split open and wings appeared. The crawling creature had changed and had become a beautiful dragonfly. Our God is a God who likes surprises and gives many creatures new and beautiful bodies – and he can do the same with us.

Now for my surprise. I have some seeds in here. I wonder if anyone would like to eat some. (Produce from your bag grapes or raisins. You could also have peanuts but be careful about allergies.)

Activity

You may like to plant some cress seeds. If you do, they need to be carefully tended until they grow. Show pictures of caterpillars, lambs, kittens and babies, and ask the children to say what each will grow into.

Prayer

God, we thank you that we can grow and change.
You have given us strong bodies
and you make us new.
We love you because you give us life.
Amen.

Song

Alleluia (x 8) . . . Jesus is Lord . . . And I love him . . . Christ is risen

(Sing these four verses.)

Activity

Have a time of seed recognition. See who can guess the most seeds. Have one or two that are a little difficult. Using the drawings on the activity sheet, get them to make the caterpillar card with the 'surprise' inside.

Prayer

God, we thank you
that you have many hidden surprises in life
and in our own lives.
We trust in you
and we believe that you will keep us safe
for ever.
 Amen.

Song

A butterfly, an Easter egg

(Sing verse 1 and chorus)

LAMPS

Aim

To show that our God gives newness of life and sometimes it is beyond the recognition of the old.

Teaching

Show various seeds and encourage the children to capture a sense of wonder that in a small seed can be wrapped up the plans for a tree or for a flower and each seed has its own plan. Look at the life cycle of a frog or a dragonfly, then a butterfly. Explore the idea that each of these creatures have already had more than one body. Give thanks to God for the wonder and the mystery of creation. Look at an egg and talk about how it could become a tiny chick and then a full-grown bird. Sometimes it is hard to guess the next stage in life. But even when we do not know how it happens, it still happens. God is a wonderful God and full of surprises. In some creatures like the caterpillar or the grub of the dragonfly, they appear to have died if you do not know about it. In the case of an egg, unless you have experienced it, it is hard to believe what it can become. Our God is a powerful God and full of surprises.

When the disciples saw Jesus die on the cross and then be buried in the tomb, they thought it was the end. But God is powerful and full of surprises. What happened after three days? Yes, Jesus rose again from the dead. What do we call that wonderful day when Jesus rose again?

Some people find it hard to believe in the resurrection. We believe because we know Jesus has risen. We know our God loves us and is able to give us life for ever.

TORCHES

Aim

To show how God gives each of us our own body and forever renews it.

Teaching

You will need photographs of the same person since they were born until they were elderly. The Queen is a good subject for this – if brave enough, you could be another! You should have at least five or six stages in a life. Begin by showing a picture of a baby and see if they can guess who it is. Continue by showing them each of the pictures in turn.

God is wonderful to us. He gives us many changing bodies in our lifetime. If we always had our baby body, life would be difficult. It would be funny if I had a body like this baby and was trying to teach you. If you look at photographs, you can see that about every seven to ten years we have a new body! At the moment you have not had as many new bodies as your parents or your teacher.

In the same way, God gives new bodies to all sorts of creatures as they grow. Show a caterpillar, a baby bird, a tiny puppy. Also show an acorn and a chestnut. God gives each of them new and different bodies. If God can do that with things all through their life, he can do it again after they die. As Christians, we say we believe in the resurrection of the body. It is not only a theory about life because we believe that Jesus rose again. What do you call the day when Jesus rose again? (You might like to review their understanding of the resurrection stories.)

Now the Sadducees argued with Jesus about the resurrection. (Get someone to read Luke 20:27-38). They argued only from the oldest books of the Bible and did not let new learning or experience touch them. They refused to believe in the resurrection. Jesus wanted them to know the power of God and that God could make all things new.

Activity

Have photographs of famous people, or people they know, as children and see if they can guess who they are.

Prayer

Lord Jesus,
we thank you that you rose from the dead.
May we know the joy of life and life eternal
and always give thanks to the Father
for our wonderful lives.
Amen.

Song

Alleluia, alleluia, give thanks to the risen Lord

Second Sunday before Advent

Sunday between 13 and 19 November inclusive

Aim

To show that, though troubles will come, our God is with us.

Preparation

Cut out headlines about wars, famines, disasters and predictions of the future. Place these in the entrance to the church. Have with them the following texts:

> Remember I am with you always.
> *Matthew 28:20*

> For God so loved the world that he gave his only Son, so that everyone who believes in him may not perish but may have eternal life.
> *John 3:16*

Opening activity

Ask everyone to sit quietly and affirm the presence of God and the power of God. After a minute play 'When you walk through a storm (You'll never walk alone)'. Have someone read 'Footprints' (included in the teaching for Lamps).

Opening prayer

Lord God, you are always there.
You are with us in the sunshine and the storm.
You are always there,
in the light and in the dark.
You are with us in times of trouble
and in times of joy.
Help us to know you
and to put our trust in you always.
Amen.

Opening song

Christ, whose glory fills the skies

Readings

Malachi 4:1-2a
Psalm 98
2 Thessalonians 3:6-13
Luke 21:5-19

Thought for the day

Jesus was never one to promise us good times always. He was well aware of the troubles that beset our fallen world. There were some admiring the Temple and its beauty. This is not surprising. The Temple rebuilding had began 20 years before Jesus was born and it was becoming more and more splendid. The cloisters and the columns were made of pure white marble. There was a vine made of gold and each cluster was as tall as a man. Josephus, in his book *The War of the Jews*, writes of the Temple that its front 'was covered all over with plates of gold' . . . and at the first rising of the sun, reflected back a fiery splendour, and made those who forced themselves to look upon it to turn their eyes away, just as they would have done at the sun's own rays. But to strangers, when they were at a distance, the Temple appeared like a mountain covered with snow, for as those parts of it that were not gilt, they were exceeding white' (Book 5, section 5). No wonder it was admired. However, there is always a danger of worshipping the symbols of worship and not the true subject.

Jesus could sense the troubles ahead. In their attempt to make him a king, they would be showing the signs of political unrest. Jesus saw a disaster in the making with a head-on clash with the Romans. The temple was not finished until AD 64; by AD 66 strife had really begun and by AD 70 Jerusalem had fallen, the city and the Temple destroyed. Over a million Jews died in this conflict and a further 97,000 were taken away captive.

Jesus knew there would be wars and rumours of wars, earthquakes, famines and plagues – and the media still seem to glory in this sort of news! Christians will not escape; they will suffer persecution and imprisonments. But, says Jesus, 'do not be terrified' (21:9), use this as a time of witness (21:13). Jesus himself will be with us through all the troubles. He will give us the words we need and the wisdom to cope (21:15). Though we may be hated and killed, we will not perish (21:18): through Jesus we are not perishable goods. For us death is not fatal! Now that *is* Good News. We are not alone, our God is with us at all times – even in the dark days – and he gives us the power to endure through the gift of eternal life.

Question time

Do you ever feel God-forsaken? Remember, feelings can be liars!

How can you affirm in troubles that your God is with you?

Illustration

Life was often bleak for the people who lived in the Hebrides. Sometimes the future did not seem to hold any promise and when the mists came down it did not help. Here is an affirmation prayer that faces the reality of the cheerless day but also a much deeper reality of the love of God and our future in him.

> Though the dawn breaks cheerless on this isle today,
> my spirit walks in a path of light.
> For I know my greatness.
> Thou hast built me a throne within thy heart.
> I dwell safely within the circle of thy care.
> I cannot for a moment fall out of thine everlasting arms.
> I am on my way to thy glory.

Alistair Maclean, Hebridean Altars

Intercessions

Blessed are you, Lord our God.
You never leave us or forsake us.
You are a present help in our troubles.
You are our strength and our salvation.
In you, O Lord, we trust.
Blessed are you, Father, Son and Holy Spirit.

We give thanks
for all who have shared their faith with us
and all who have witnessed to you
in times of trouble.
We ask your blessing
upon all who are struggling with their faith at this time,
all who are caught up with doubt
or who are giving way to despair.
May the light and love of Christ bring them new hope.
We remember before you
all who are being persecuted for their faith.
We pray for churches that are suffering
from war, violence or vandalism.
We pray for all who have lost their place of worship.

Silence

Lord, you are our strength
and our salvation.

Lord, guide and strengthen the leaders of the world.
Give wisdom to all who rule
and who are in government.
We pray for all who are involved with famine relief
or who seek to bring peace among nations.
We remember all who have been made homeless
or driven off their own land.

Silence

Lord, you are our strength
and our salvation.

We give thanks for the shelter and security
of our homes.
We remember homes where it is hard to be a Christian
and where faith in you is discouraged.
We pray for children who are not given any sense of faith
or confidence in the future.
We ask your blessing upon our families
and all our loved ones.

Silence

Lord, you are our strength
and our salvation.

We remember all lonely and uncared-for people;
may they know your love and your presence.
We ask your blessing upon all who are ill
and those who fear the future.
We pray for those who are in care
and for all who cannot cope on their own.

Silence

Lord, you are our strength
and our salvation.

We give thanks to all who have witnessed
to your love even to death.
We pray for all who have died
for their faith in you
and we remember the holy martyrs.

We ask your blessing
upon our loved ones departed from us.
May we share with them
in the joys of your eternal kingdom.

Silence

Merciful Father,
accept these prayers
for the sake of your Son,
our Saviour Jesus Christ.
Amen.

Memory verse

Surely God is my salvation; I will trust, and will not be afraid, for the Lord God is my strength and my might; he has become my salvation.
Isaiah 12:2

Suggested music

Christ be near at either hand
Guide me, O thou great Redeemer
Do not be afraid

CANDLES

Aim

To let he children know that God is always with them.

Teaching

Once there was a little boy who was afraid of the dark. So every night his mother or father stayed with him until he was asleep. If he cried during the night, they came to him. In this way they showed how they loved him and did not want him to be afraid. When he got a little older they left a light on in his room and told him they were just in the next room. Even though he could not see them, they were there. The light was to remind him that they were there. If he wanted them, he just had to call and they would come. Soon he was not afraid of the dark because he knew his parents loved him and would come to him.

When he grew up he saw terrible things happen to the world; he saw war and people ill. He knew what it was to be hungry, and sometimes he felt as if he was on his own. But he remembered the words of his parents: 'Even when you do not see us, we are there and you just need to call.' Well, his parents were now far away and he could not call on them but he knew from the Bible that Jesus had said, 'I am with you always.' Whenever he was troubled, and also when he was happy, he spoke to Jesus. In fact, he spoke to Jesus each day. He loved to talk to Jesus and to know that Jesus loved him and cared for him. What do you call it when you talk to Jesus or to God our Father? Yes, it is called prayer and we should learn to say our prayers every day. Jesus likes to hear from us because he is with us and he loves us. Let us say together, 'Jesus is with me and loves me.'

233

Activity

Play 'What time is it, Mr Wolf?' The children follow the wolf around and ask him the time. The wolf can say any time he or she likes. When he answers, 'Dinner time', everyone must run as fast as they can to the safety of the teacher. The person the wolf catches is the next Wolf.

Prayer

Be near me, Lord Jesus,
I ask thee to stay
close by me for ever,
and love me, I pray.
Bless all the dear children
in thy tender care
and fit us for heaven
to live with thee there.

Song

Jesus' love is very wonderful

(With these actions: stretch as high as you can when you sing 'so high'; go down low when you sing 'so low'; stretch out your arms when you sing 'so wide'; clap your hands when you sing 'oh wonderful love'.)

LAMPS

Aim

To tell the story of 'Footprints'.

Teaching

When you were small and got too tired to walk, what happened to you? Yes, your mother or your father carried you. If you hurt yourself and you found it hard to walk, they would do the same. If you were afraid of the dark, they would stay with you. Then if something dangerous was happening, they would pick you up. In the same way, God cares for us and wants to help us at all times. There is a well-known story about a man who dreamed about God's love and care.

One night a man had a dream. He dreamed he was walking across a beach with the Lord. Across the sky flashed scenes from his life. For each scene he noticed two sets of footprints in the sand: one belonging to him, and the other to the Lord.

When the last scene of his life flashed before him, he looked back at the footprints in the sand. He noticed many times along the path of his life there was only one set of footprints. He noticed it was at the very lowest and saddest times in his life.

This really bothered him and he questioned the Lord about it. 'Lord, you said that once I decided to follow you, you'd walk with me all the way. But I have noticed that during the most troublesome times in my life there is only one set of footprints. I don't understand why, when I needed you most you would leave me.'

The Lord replied, 'My son, my precious child, I love you and I would never leave you. During your times of trial and suffering, when you see only one set of footprints, it was then that I carried you.'

Yes, even grown-up people, when they are in trouble, need to know that God is with them and will carry them if they are tired or in danger. Let us remember our God is always with us and ready to help us.

Activity

Draw around your feet to make sets of footprints. Write on one 'God is with me', and on the other 'God loves me'. Get the children to walk around the room and say with one step, 'God is with me', and with the next, 'God loves me'. Tell them not to hurry in doing this.

Prayer

Lord God, you are always with us,
even when times are bad.
You never stop loving us
and you are always ready to help us.
At all times let us remember you and your love.
Amen.

Song

We are marching in the light of God

(Let them march in a group around the room as they sing.)

TORCHES

Aim

To look at the cheerless day and the presence and power of God.

Teaching

Jesus never promised that everything would be all right or easy. He warned his disciples about the troubles that lay ahead. He told them how the Temple in Jerusalem would be destroyed and how they would be persecuted and maybe even put to death. Jesus warned of wars, of famines and of plagues. But he also promised to be with us always. Even in the worst times he would be there.

Julian of Norwich lived in a time of war and plague. She reminded people that God was always with them. She said, 'He did not say, "You will not be tempted; you shall not be travailed; you shall not be afflicted." But he did say, "You shall not be overcome."' Julian could say this because she knew that God cares for each of us and never leaves us.

The Outer Hebrides is a place of great beauty but it is also a place where life has been hard for many of its people. They were often people of a strong faith in God but it did not prevent them from having to face troubles, hardship and even death. It is no use pretending these things do not happen in our world because they do. But we need also to remind ourselves that God is with us, God loves us and we cannot fall from his protection and care. No matter how dark the day, we carry a light within us. Let us look at the prayer from the Outer

Hebrides and then we will say it slowly together. This is a prayer of contrasts, for the day is cheerless and there is no apparent joy in it. It is easy to imagine the mists have come down and with them the cold. But the person who prays sees beyond the mist; he is able to walk in the light of the Lord. He knows his greatness because he is loved by God. It is wonderful when you experience that. Seek to know that you are in the heart of God – and nothing in this world can separate you from the love of God. Because of his care we will not perish but have everlasting life. Not for one moment can we fall out of his protection and love. If you know this, you will walk with confidence and know hope when others find none.

Activity

Provide an obstacle course and blindfold someone. Let them set off on their own but keep an eye on them. Then let someone guide them. Have as many as possible experience going it alone and then being guided. Talk about the difference it makes if we can trust in someone.

Prayer

Though the dawn breaks cheerless on this isle today,
my spirit walks in a path of light.
For I know my greatness.
Thou hast built me a throne within thy heart.
I dwell safely within the circle of thy care.
I cannot for a moment fall out of thine everlasting arms.
I am on my way to thy glory.

Alistair Maclean, Hebridean Altars

Song

The Spirit lives to set us free

Christt the King

Sunday between 20 and 26 November inclusive

Aim

To know that Christ is our King and wants us to share in his kingdom.

Preparation

At the entrance have a large cross with a crown of thorns upon it, and beside this a golden crown. Alternatively, you may like to have a cross with 'Christ the King' upon it. Below the cross have the words, 'The head that once was crowned with thorns is crowned with glory now.'

Opening activity

Have a large wooden cross laid on the floor and a large candle near it. Give everyone a tea-light to light (the smaller children may need help). Let everyone sing 'Jesus, remember me when you come into your kingdom' (Taizé) as the candles are placed on the cross or around it. Begin the singing very quietly, increase its volume, then end with it sung almost as a whisper.

This is a good day to sing the Benedictus or the Te Deum.

Opening prayer

You, Christ, are the King of Glory,
the eternal Son of the Father.
May we welcome you into our lives
and seek to do your will.
Then, Lord, let your kingdom come in us now
as it is in heaven.
Amen.

Opening song

The King is among us

Readings

Jeremiah 23:1-6
Canticle Luke 1:68-79 or Psalm 46
Colossians 1:11-20
Luke 23:33-43

Thought for the day

At the end of the Church year we look at the end of Jesus' life as a travelling teacher. The Crucifixion is horrible and we think about it near the time when we are preparing for Christmas so that we may avoid a slushy sentimental faith. Our faith is rugged and hard and makes demands. We have an odd sort of King because he died for us. Most kings would expect us to be willing to die for them and to protect them. Jesus our King died for us: he died that we might have life eternal. In his final battle Jesus conquers death itself through his obedience to the Father. Evil powers seek to prevent Jesus doing God's will and to sway him from his purpose, but Jesus is faithful to the end. Most sufferers would call down curses on their tormentors. Jesus prays from the agony of the cross, 'Father, forgive them; for they do not know what they are doing.'

Nearly all Jews wore five different garments – an outer-cloak, an inner tunic, girdle, sandals and a covering for the head. As four soldiers led him to the crucifixion, they each had one article of clothing as their perk. Then they gambled for the outer-robe, as it was the more precious of the garments.

The leaders mocked Jesus, saying, 'He saved others, let him save himself.' They did not recognise that Jesus' purpose was to save others, including them. He did not come to save or to look after himself; he came for us and for our salvation.

They continued their mocking with the word 'If' – 'if he is the Messiah of God, his chosen one.' This is a little word but very destructive. The devil used it at the beginning of Jesus' ministry, using almost the same words to go with it (Luke 4:3, 9). Often the way to defeat a person is to create doubt in their mind about their purpose. Jesus never wavered and he knew that it was for this he came. He came to do the will of the Father. The soldiers also mocked him, saying, 'If you are the King of the Jews, save yourself!' They did not understand that Jesus did not come to use force but love. He did not come to conquer but to win by love. We can accept him as our King or, if we choose to, we can turn our backs on him. The inscription over him read, 'This is the King of the Jews'. The sad comment by the chief priests to Pilate is 'We have no king but the emperor' (John 19:15). Too often we are all caught worshipping worldly power and might.

One of the criminals crucified with Jesus also taunted him but the other rebuked his fellow criminal, saying, 'Do you not fear God, since you are under the same sentence?' I wonder how often we realise Jesus shares our pains and our sorrows. Whenever there is distress, suffering or injustice, he is there alongside the sufferers. This criminal says, 'Jesus, remember me when you come into your kingdom.' You can view this as a recognition of faith, however small – or even a sign of penitence. Whatever, when a person turns to Jesus, Jesus willingly accepts him. Let us turn to Jesus and know that we can walk with him in his garden. In the quiet hear him say to you, 'Today you will be with me in Paradise.'

Question time

To become children of the King is simple: it is to do his will. Do you help to bring in his kingdom in this way?

Can you say how the rule of Jesus is different from that of an earthly ruler?

Illustration

In science fiction films there is often a scene when the earth or a space ship is hurtling towards disaster. No human could possible save it. Obviously they try everything they can but they just get more exhausted. Some lose hope altogether. Then a mysterious being enters the story, someone or something from beyond our world. He or she has powers beyond our wildest dreams and can change destruction and disaster into peace, calm and order. The world is restored: the being is thanked and then gone from sight.

This is a salvation story and, although fiction, understands something of our need for salvation. It knows we have no power ourselves to help ourselves. It tells of the love from a being far greater and more powerful than we are and of our salvation. There is such a story in the Gospels and it is not fiction. It is the greatest love story and rescue story of all time and yet we do not always make it our own.

Intercessions

Blessed are you, Lord our God,
for you love us with an everlasting love
and sent your Son to be our Saviour.
He came and died that we might live.
Now he is the King of kings and Lord of lords.
May we do your will and share in your kingdom.
Blessed are you, Father, Son and Holy Spirit.

Father, we give you thanks
that in Christ Jesus you have redeemed the world.
He died that we might live.
He reigns with you
and seeks us to be part of his kingdom.
We pray for all who are seeking to serve you
in their daily lives.
We remember especially
any who are being persecuted for their faith.
Lord, give us the courage to speak for you
and to witness to your love.

Silence

Lord, your kingdom come
in us as in heaven.

We ask your blessing upon all leaders of people,
all governments and rulers.
We long for the time when the kingdoms of earth
will become the kingdom of Christ our Lord.
We ask you to guide and strengthen
all who work for peace and justice.
Inspire all who seek to enrich your world
through art, music or through their daily lives.

Silence

Lord, your kingdom come
in us as in heaven.

Lord Jesus, come as our King and rule in our lives.
May we seek to serve you in our homes
and in our daily work.
May we strive for your kingdom in all our dealings.
We ask your blessing upon all who are dear to us;
through their love may we learn to love you more.

Silence

Lord, your kingdom come
in us as in heaven.

We remember all who have lost faith in you
or in their neighbours.
We pray for all who walk in darkness,

for the discouraged and the despairing.
May they come to know your love and saving power.
We ask your blessing upon all who are suffering
and all who are distressed at this time.
We pray especially for friends who are ill.

Silence

Lord, your kingdom come
in us as in heaven.

We give thanks for the victory of our Lord
over hatred, darkness and death,
and that he has opened the kingdom
to all who turn to him.
We pray for your blessing
upon our loved ones departed from us.
May they rejoice in the fullness and glory
of your kingdom.

Silence

Merciful Father,
accept these prayers
for the sake of your Son,
our Saviour Jesus Christ.
Amen.

Memory verse

He has raised up for us a mighty Saviour, born of the house of his servant David.
Luke 1:69

Suggested music

O worship the King
Hail the coming Prince of Peace (*Celtic Hymn Book*)
God is love: his the care

CANDLES

Aim

To review the life of Jesus and show he is a different sort of king.

Teaching

Who can tell me which animal is called the king of the jungle? Yes, it is the lion. Why do you think it is the lion? It is because the lion is strong and powerful, the lion is fierce and can be frightening. Let us all growl like a lion.

Now who knows the name of our queen? Where does she live? Is she rich or poor? What does she wear on her head on special occasions?

Kings and queens are powerful people and make others do what they are told.

Jesus is a very different sort of king. He was not born in a palace. Can anyone tell me the sort of place Jesus was born in? He was born in a stable because there was no room in the inn. Do you know the town where Jesus was born? Yes, it was Bethlehem.

Jesus did not live in an expensive house; he lived with his mother Mary and Joseph in a small town. Do you know its name? Yes, it was Nazareth. What sort of work did Joseph do? He was a carpenter. That meant he worked with wood and made things like tables, and mended things like carts for the donkey to pull. Jesus would often help Joseph in his work with wood. Jesus grew up in an ordinary home just like you or me.

When Jesus grew up and left home he asked some men to help him. Do you know how many? Yes there were 12 and they were called disciples. With Jesus they went around the country, telling people about God and helping to make ill people well again. Jesus was often more like a servant than a king. He once washed the feet of his disciples when they were tired.

Some people wanted to make Jesus a king and for him to lead them into battle – but Jesus did not want to do this. He did not want to make people do things. He wanted people to do things because they loved God. Jesus would not use force or his power to make people obey him. He is the King of Love. We are to learn to love him and to love God his Father.

Even though he was kind and loving, evil people decided to kill him. How did Jesus die? Yes, on a cross. They put a crown on his head but it was not of silver or gold. Does anyone know what it was? It was a crown of thorns and it hurt Jesus when it was pushed on his head. After Jesus died he was buried in a cave, but on the third day something wonderful happened. What was it? Yes, Jesus was alive again. Jesus had won a battle against evil and against death and he had just used his love to do it. Now Jesus is alive for ever.

Jesus is our King and he wants us to be his friends. Jesus wants us to follow him and do what God wants us to do. He wants us to love him and to love God his Father. We are very lucky because we are children of the King. Let us say together, 'We are children of the King.'

Activity

Play 'Sleeping lions'. Everyone pretends they are lions in the jungle. They are very sleepy. One person counts slowly to ten, watching while the others sleep. Anyone who moves, twitches or speaks is out and must look for other twitching lions. The last person in is the king of the jungle.

Prayer

Jesus, you are our King and our God.
Help us to love you as you love us.
We know that you protect us.
You are always with us.
Hurrah, for you are our King.
Amen.

Song

Who's the King of the jungle?

LAMPS

Aim

To contrast the kingship of Jesus with that of an earthly power.

Teaching

Why do you think that the lion is the king of the jungle? It is because of his power and his fierceness.

Let us look at some of the things that make a powerful king. Write on a board the suggestions of the group. For example:

- Palace
- Crown of gold
- Rich
- Makes people do things
- Lots of servants
- Army – can use force
- Everyone must keep the rules of the king

Now let us see how Jesus sees his kingship. The wise men expected to find him in the royal palace, so they went to Herod in Jerusalem. This was a mistake. Where was Jesus born? In a stable – in Bethlehem.

Do you think he lived in a rich house? Where did he live and what was the work of Joseph? When he grew up and called together his men, he did not have a mighty army. How many men did he have? Only 12 ordinary men and they were not soldiers.

He did not go around the country giving orders. He worked like a servant, he healed the sick, looked after the troubled – he even washed the disciples' feet. He was a Servant as much as a King.

When he rode into Jerusalem he did not use a war-horse but a donkey. He did not come to start a war but to bring peace. Sometimes he is called the Prince of Peace.

Even though he went about caring for people and serving others, the authorities put him to death on the cross. They did not give him a golden crown but another sort of crown. What sort? A crown of thorns. Jesus was powerful enough to destroy all his enemies. He could have called on the power of God. But he did not want to force people to follow him. They had to accept him of their own choice. So some chose to reject him and kill him.

Yet he obeyed his Father and showed his love. On the third day he rose from the dead. He had won a victory over darkness and death, over hatred and evil by obeying the Father. He rose to be the King of heaven. We can share in his kingdom – if we choose to do his will, to live by his love and to care for others as he did.

Jesus still will not force us to turn to him. If we want him as our King, we have to choose to do so. When we do, we have to try and be the people we know he wants us to be. Let us quietly promise to be servants of the Servant King.

Activity

Have three or four cardboard crowns painted gold, or use gold card. Divide the group into teams with a crown for each team. The crown starts at the back of the line and is placed on each head in turn. When it reaches the front, that person runs to the back and the process starts again. When the original person gets to the front again and the crown is placed on his or her head, it is removed and placed on the ground and the whole team bows towards it. The team to do this first is the winner.

Prayer

Jesus, my King and my God,
let me work for you,
let me tell of you,
let me love you,
let me obey you
and let me be part of your kingdom.

Song

The King of love my shepherd is

TORCHES

Aim

To discover what led to the death of Jesus.

Teaching

Jesus grew up, unknown, in a little town called Nazareth. Only when he was in his thirties did he begin to be noticed. He invited 12 men to follow him and then went around teaching about God and healing people. You would hardly feel that Jesus was a threat to the power of Rome or of the Jewish Church. Yet he did come to change a world that did not want to be changed. He wanted people to trust in God more than in systems or rules. He wanted people to express themselves in love rather than in power. He wanted people to have greater care for each other. Throughout his life he sought to serve, but at the same time he challenged the authorities.

The Church felt that Jesus was unwilling to keep the rigid rules of the Sabbath. He often spoke against the narrow-mindedness of some of the Church people. They also felt he was guilty of blasphemy against God because it was hinted that he is the Son of God. Riding into Jerusalem seems to be the last straw. Although Jesus rode a donkey to show he was not seeking to raise an army, this was used as a pretext to claim he was a threat to Rome. Pilate probably did not see Jesus as a threat. He could have had him hauled in at any time. But the Jews insisted that Jesus was claiming to be a king and the Messiah. He was likely to cause a rebellion. When Pilate later brought Jesus before the chief priests and said, 'Behold, your king', the rather telling reply was 'We have no king but the emperor.'

Do you accept Jesus as your King? He will not force himself upon you: force is not his way. He wants us to turn to him in love. If we want to be part of his kingdom, we know we will have to keep the rules of his kingdom. Do we seek a relationship with the risen and ascended Lord? Remember, the King is among us – the choice is yours whether you turn and serve him or reject him and ignore him.

Activity

Make red and white crosses out of card or cloth. Everyone should have two crosses. They are to wear or carry the red one until they have said their prayers and then they can exchange it for the white one.

Prayer

Jesus our Lord, our King and our God,
ruling in might and love,
all power on earth is given to you,
you are our King above;
help us to use the power you give,
humbly to order how men live.
Lord, we are called to follow you;
this we ask strength to do.

Patrick Appleford

Song

King of kings and Lord of lords

Acknowledgements

The Publishers wish to thank all those who have given their permission to reproduce the following copyright material.

Fifth Sunday of Lent

Torches

The text of 'Said Judas to Mary' by Sydney Carter, © 1964, Stainer and Bell Ltd.

Fifth Sunday of Easter

Candles

The words of 'Jesus is my friend' by Julia Plaut, © 1995, Thankyou Music.

Pentecost

Complete Resource Book/Torches

The words of the first verse of 'Spirit of the living God' by Daniel Iverson, © 1935, renewed 1963, Birdwing Music, EMI Church Music Publishers/Adm. by Kevin Mayhew Ltd.

Proper 8

Complete Resource Book

The following extract by Dietrich Bonhoeffer:

> Cheap grace is the deadly enemy of the Church . . . cheap grace is the preaching of forgiveness without requiring repentance, baptism without church discipline, communion without confession, absolution without contrition. Cheap grace is grace without discipleship, grace without the cross, grace without Jesus Christ, living and incarnate.

Proper 21

Complete Resource Book

The following extract from *The Little Prince* by Antoine de Saint-Exupéry:

> I know a planet where there is a certain red-faced man. He has never smelled a flower; he has never looked at a star. He has never loved anyone. He never does anything in his life but add up figures. And all day long he says over and over, just like you, 'I am busy with matters of consequence' and that makes him swell with pride. But he is not a man; he is a mushroom!
> A what?
> A mushroom.

Second Sunday before Advent

Torches

> Though the dawn break cheerless on this isle today,
> my spirit walks in a path of light.
> For I know my greatness.
> Thou hast built me a throne within thy heart.
> I dwell safely within the circle of thy care.
> I cannot for a moment fall out of thine everlasting arms.
> I am on my way to thy glory.

Hebridean Altars, Alistair Maclean, Hodder & Stoughton.

Christ the King

Torches

The following from a hymn by Patrick Appleford:

> Jesus our Lord, our King and our God,
> ruling in might and love,
> all power on earch is given to you,
> you are our king above;
> help us to use the power you give,
> humbly to order how men live.
> Lord, we are called to follow you;
> this we ask strength to do.

© 1962, Josef Weinberger Ltd.

Every effort has been made to trace the owners of copyright material and we hope that no copyright has been infringed. Pardon is sought and apology made if the contrary be the case, and a correction will be made in any reprint of this book.